"**S**arah Liborio lovingly recounts how a prince came and won her heart, honored her as his queen, and through their relationship and his tragic death, steeled her to handle the challenges and battles inherent with a thriving spiritual life. The fact that 'I am Second' was used by God to inject direction and calm in the midst of a crisis is humbling to all of us in the I am Second movement. We thank God for how the Lord used Hugo, how his influence continues today, and how his spirit is captured for eternity in the words of his wife."
John Humphrey
Director of Communications
I am Second

"**I**t is good read even for men, macho men, who do not like to sit and read."
Ron Bishop
Founder of SCORE International

"**S**arah is a courageous Christ-follower whose story shows God's power at work through love, loss, and everything in between. You'll find strength for your own story through hers!"
Ellen Vaughn
New York Times bestselling author and Christian speaker

"**T**he story of Hugo and Sarah Liborio has impacted many lives in a short amount of time. There are no incomplete lives in God's plan. All lives are lived to completeness, as we can see in Sarah's story. Their impact as a couple in their service, both internationally and domestically, defined this truth. I am blessed to have walked with and been ministered to by Hugo Liborio. This story is a testimony that all of us must live our lives with eternity in mind. Hugo lived that life, and his goal was very simple—'Make Christ Known To All.' We will never forget Hugo, and we are motivated to serve with all our hearts by his impact on our lives."
John Zeller
President of SCORE International

"**J**ack Wyrtzen said so many times, 'Only one life, 'twill soon be past, Only what's done for Christ will last.' Here you will read a wonderful story of how two young servants of Christ, Sarah and Hugo, carried out that very truth. I am sure you will be moved as you read this story of true love and service for Christ."

Dr. Joe Jordan
Executive Director, worldwide ministries, Word of Life
Founder, Word of Life Argentina (Palabra de Vida).

"**I** met Sarah on (where else?) a mission trip to the Dominican Republic where I first heard her story. I knew right away it was a story that had to be told because her story touches all that is beautiful and brave all at the same time. Read it with the same sense of adventure that I did."

Bill High
President, National Christian Foundation: Heartland

My Once Upon A Time

By Sarah Liborio

With Michelle Hoag

xulon PRESS

My Once Upon A Time
by Sarah Liborio with Michelle Hoag

Printed in the United States of America

ISBN 9781613791011

www.xulonpress.com

Heavenly Father,

Thank you for the power of the Cross to save me from my sins. Thank you for being so BIG that I can trust that you are all-powerful over all circumstances in my life. But, also thank you for being "small" enough that you care for the smallest detail of my life. Because of who YOU are I know the true love story . . . You in my life, the story of your love for me since before time began, will never end. "Being confident of this, that he who began a good work in you will carry it on to completion until the day of Christ Jesus." (Phil. 1:6)

To my wonderful children, Mattias and Layla, for being the constant reminder of the faithful love of a man and the unmerited blessing of God in my life.

Mattias,
I see the heart of your Daddy in you. Be faithful to what God wants to form in it.

Layla,
You will always be "beautiful" in your Daddy's eyes. May you grow up to be the princess that God wants you to be.

Acknowledgments

Thanks to . . .

Michelle Hoag for being a huge answer to prayer. You were the key to all of this. I'm so thankful God used you to help me realize this dream he gave to me. Thank you for your willingness to put your sweat and tears into this book with me. Thank you for pushing me much further as an "author" than I ever thought I could go. You are a true friend. "GO Rockies!" (Check out her awesome recaps at www.rockieswoman.com/. She's a true fan.)

Bill High for confirming in my heart what I believed God had asked me to write, and for giving me the contacts to accomplish the vision!

Alan Goforth for being available to me for advice, encouragement, and pointing me in the right direction.

My cousin, Erica Fulton, for taking a day off work to edit and help me make important decisions on how to make the book the best it can be.

My aunt, Carolyn Darst, for reading and editing sections of my book. She is a book lover, and her opinion means a lot to me.

My Ladies Bible Study Group at North Oak Community Church, who have prayed faithfully but also spent hours in initial editing to help me meet a deadline. They saved me about a week of work.

Mario Gutierrez for letting me sit for hours in the "anointed seat" at the Bravo Coffee Bar during the five months I was in intense writing mode.

Hugo's family and church in El Salvador, for believing in me, praying for me faithfully, and entrusting me to share part of the legacy of their son, brother, and friend. We will always be family.

My parents, David and Debbie Breeden, for going beyond the call of duty as grandparents while my mind, and energy were focused on writing. And for encouraging me to continue when I just couldn't go on one more chapter.

Everyone who has prayed for me, my children, and this book. Thank you for following me on Facebook and all the encouraging comments. They helped me to keep pushing on. May God answer our prayers that this work give all glory to Him and His unchangeable character.

Linn Ann Huntington for being the final piece of the puzzle that God brought into my life to complete the vision of this book. Your understanding of my life circumstances, your faith in Our Savior, your friendship, and your professionalism in editing were the perfect fit for the ending of a yearlong process.

My SCORE family. "If one part suffers, every part suffers with it; if one part is honored, every part rejoices with it." (I Cor. 12:26 NIV) Thank you, thank you, thank you for being willing to suffer with me. I fully realize how hard that first year was on all of us. I can only pray that we can now rejoice together as God honors each one of us in different ways. I love you all.

Edurne Nieves for translating my story into Spanish, the language of so many of the people in my life whom I love.

Table of Contents

About the Co-Author

Michelle Hoag originally hails from Colorado. She first met Sarah Liborio when they were staff counselors on Word of Life Island in Schroon Lake, New York, in 2002. She graduated from the University of Georgia with a degree in Middle School Education. She now attends Manhattanville College in Purchase, New York, where she is pursuing a Master of Arts in Writing. Her most current work can be found on her blog, Rockies Woman (rockieswoman.com), which is an excellent source of information about the Colorado Rockies.

Michelle's dream is to move home to Colorado after graduation and find a job teaching creative writing and literature to middle or high school students while maintaining her blog.

Foreword

Sarah Liborio has written a wonderful, compelling story of passion for her mission and her man. Normally, I would not read a love story. However, this is a book I could not dismiss. Once I began to read, I was captured!

In this book, you will laugh and cry. However, the great passion of the heart of a woman can be seen and FELT! As a man, I envisioned what Sarah experienced. However, I KNEW in my heart that I was asking for the impossible. I would never fully understand the devastation of dreams for a long life of companionship and shared ministry. Sarah had to experience this valley in the hands of Jesus, on the shoulders of a few friends, and with the support of family. She endured indeed!

I knew Hugo! I remember the first time I saw him in Argentina. Hard working, energetic, passionate with a personality that riveted the attention of those around him. I coveted the man for our ministry. Working at a MUFA PUFA, a Word of Life youth event, he seemed tireless, confident, and competent. His work ethic fascinated me. I knew I had to recruit Hugo for our ministry.

Although Hugo only worked a short time with SCORE, he left a lasting legacy. We will NEVER forget his BIG smile, his love for people, and his desire to bring people to Jesus Christ. He led praise and worship drawing complete attention to glorifying the Son of God. It is so inspiring to see an El Salvadorian bringing American teens to their knees to worship at the feet of Jesus. His heart for evangelism was exposed and envied.

Sarah's love for Hugo is only exceeded by her desire to serve Jesus. Every man has a need for love. She met that need for Hugo. She gave him affirmation, affection, and much attention. Together, they were a wonderful team!

When Hugo went HOME, Sarah went through a process that demonstrated her complete and total commitment to the divine plan for her life. The CALLING of God was without repentance. She RETURNED to the MISSION FIELD as a single parent of two small children. It is difficult for any of us to understand her struggles. However, we have nurtured Sarah and helped strengthen her for the long journey ahead. Her response has been phenomenal and inspiring.

Today, Sarah is walking on a journey to fulfill her calling to missions that she received from God as a young girl. We watch her walk with God, alone but NEVER alone. I know Hugo is proud of Sarah! Her unwavering and unconditional commitment to glorify God and make His plan her passion is heartwarming.

This is why even an old college basketball coach could not put down the book until I finished reading it. You will laugh, and you will cry. But when you finish reading this story, you will be blessed and different.

Enjoy!

Ron Bishop
Founder of SCORE International

Introduction

God used a man named Hugo to change my life dramatically at age 19 and then again at age 29. This book is a little bit about what happened before and after those two dates in my life, but it's mostly about the divine adventure that took place during those ten years.

This book is a lot about me. I wish I could tell more about Hugo, but I believe God led me to write about my own journey. I've prayed for this book to be eternal and proven as gold, as God works in others' lives so that they may see His faithfulness to me, a humble servant. I pray the Holy Spirit uses my honest testimony to help you see His faithfulness in your own story and to encourage you to look to Him as the true Author of your life.

I pray that you will look at the events of my story and see that it was only Christ shining through me. I want readers to see that His Word is living and active. But before anyone can be encouraged, I need to start at the beginning, which is really part of the end.

Not long before I started work on this book, I went through writer Beth Moore's study about Esther, *"It's Tough Being a Woman!"*[1] for the second time. Recent events had led me to believe that maybe I wouldn't have my happy ending after all, and this time the study carried a lot more meaning for me.

I found the teaching to be very practical as I traveled through my desert. Moore says, "You are never more vulnerable than when God has taken you out of a known place and has you in the wilderness place."

I knew that I was vulnerable, but I also knew that I wanted God to use my suffering to change others' lives. When I read, "One of the most important parts of fulfilling our destiny will be transparency," God began to prepare my heart to be transparent in this story, to show my strengths and weaknesses. I pray the Holy Spirit will use my life to encourage others in a closer walk with their Savior. To Him be all the glory, honor, and praise!

So, why did I think my "once upon a time" was over? Well, for the whole answer you will have to read the book. And don't cheat and skip to the back! Let me share a few other things from Moore's study that encouraged me to tell my story.

"There is something delicious about writing the first words of a story. Perhaps the anonymous writer picked by God to pen the words of Esther thought something similar to Rene Zellweger's opening line in the movie "Miss Potter."[2] At first glance, the genesis-words to Esther's story don't seem delicious at all. Not even noteworthy. This is what happened. So what? But although it seems perfectly natural to pen a narrative in this manner, it is actually rare. Biblical narratives commonly begin with 'it happened' but omit 'in the days of.' On the other hand, prophetic writings are often introduced as having occurred 'in the days of King . . .' The Book of Esther unfolds, however, with the two intertwining. The result, according to some scholars, is an opening more like the opening of a folktale, with the aura of 'Once upon a time, in the days of the great and glorious Ahasuerus, King of the Persian empire.'

"Esther resembles the opening of a folktale because it tells such a great and true story." (Moore, p. 11)

Esther's "once upon a time" was a fairy tale in the truest sense. I have always felt that meeting and falling in love with my husband was my great fairy tale. People always asked us about how we met, and we loved to tell them, because it was such a fun story. A boy from El Salvador, a girl from Kansas. How does that happen? It's a God thing! But Moore went on to say:

"Has a negative event . . . made you lose hope about something important to you? Do you have any natural reasons to think that whatever your 'once upon a time' might have been, it can never be now?

"Remember the first words of Esther, 'This is what happened during the time of Xerxes,' and their similarity to 'once upon a time, in the days of the great and glorious Ahasuerus?' Those Hebrew words *wayhi bime* occur five times in Scripture. Without exception, all 'introduce impending catastrophe or doom.'" (Moore, p.13)

This is the moment I wrote in the margin my fear that my fairy tale was over. But I turned the page, and thankfully she continued:

"Our first reaction may be the thought, 'Then who wants a great story? Forget once upon a time!' Stick with me here a moment, because this perspective could make you feel better instead of worse.

"Unless you've lived in a place I've never found, with all your heart's desires met and without a soul who annoys you, Job was pretty accurate when he said, 'Man [or woman] born of woman is of few days and full of trouble' (Job 14:1).

"There's no escaping it until we escape these mortal bodies. But here's the good news. I also learned that in all five occasions where those same Hebrew words were associated with impending catastrophe, 'the ending to each story is happy, but before the happy ending is realized, much grief occurs.'

"I think we know the part about 'much grief'. . . In fact, as Job said, every life is full of it. When we trust our lives to the hand and pen of an unseen but ever-present God, He will write our lives into His story, and every last one of them will turn out to be a great read with a grand ending – and not just in spite of those catastrophes, often because of them. Don't just wait and see. Live and see." (Moore, pp.13-14)

Thank you, Beth Moore, for this teaching and encouragement. It was because of this study and its impact on my life that God led me to title my story *My Once Upon a Time*.

Chapter One

The Princess: My Life Before True Love
1980-1999

Wyoming, New York, Kansas, Philippines, Mexico and Zimbabwe

My "once upon a time" started not when I was born, but when most fairy tales start—when love entered the scene. A short but powerful chapter was written when I was 11 years old. I had just been reading my Bible and, stirred by the words I read, I copied this paragraph into my small red notebook, making it a personal prayer of my young heart.

> VERY SPECIAL
> "So, Jesse sent and
> had his youngest son
> brought in. He was a
> fine boy, tanned and
> handsome. The Lord said
> to Samuel, "Go, appoint
> Him because he is
> THE ONE." (I Sam. 16:12)
> One of the servants said, "I
> have seen a son of Jesse of
> Bethlehem plays the harp. He is
> brave and courageous.
> He is a good speaker and
> handsome, and the Lord is
> with him." (I Sam. 16:18)

It wasn't grammatically correct; I put my own emphasis on certain key words that were important to me, and maybe I took the words out of context. But I had started to seek a knight in shining armor and this was my "checklist": brave, courageous, good speaker, handsome, and, most importantly, "the Lord is with him." This was the deepest prayer of my young heart for my future husband.

Skipping ahead six years, when I was 17, I wrote out another prayer for a mate:

"On His Plan For Your Mate"
(Author Unknown)

Everyone longs to give himself completely to someone – to have a deep, soul relationship with another, to be loved thoroughly and exclusively. But God to a Christian says, "No, not until you are satisfied and fulfilled and content with living loved by Me alone."

I love you, my child. And until you discover that only in Me is your satisfaction to be found, you will not be capable of the perfect human relationship that I have planned for you. You will never be united with another until you are united with Me – exclusive of anyone or anything else, exclusive of any other desires and longings.

Don't be anxious. Don't worry. Don't look around at the things others have gotten or that I've given them. Don't look at the things you think you want. You just keep looking off and away up to Me, or you'll miss what I want to show you.

And then when you're ready, I'll surprise you with a love far more wonderful than any would ever dream. You see, until you are ready, and until the one I have for you is ready, I am working even this very minute to have both of you ready at the same time.

And, dear one, I want you to have this most wonderful love. I want you to see, in the flesh, a picture of your relationship with Me, and to enjoy materially and concretely the everlasting union of beauty and perfection and love that I offer you with Myself. Know that I love you utterly. I am God Almighty. Believe and be satisfied.

I wrote in response, "I commit myself to this poem God has sent me. May I have an everlasting love with God. I believe and am satisfied."

Another poem I clung to and read often to encourage myself to wait for God's timing was Russell Kelfer's "Wait."[1]

"Wait"
By Russell Kelfer
Copyright 1980, Reprinted with Permission
Desperately, helplessly, longingly, I cried
Quietly, patiently, lovingly God replied
I pled and I wept for a clue to my fate,
And the Master so gently said, "Child you must wait."
"Wait? You say wait?" my indignant reply.
"Lord, I need answers, I need to know why!
Is your hand shortened? Or have You not heard?
By faith, I have asked, and am claiming Your Word.
My future and all to which I can relate
Hangs in the balance, and You tell me to WAIT?
I'm needing a 'yes,' a go-ahead sign,
Or even a 'no' to which I can resign.
And Lord, I've been asking, and this is my cry:
I'm weary of asking! I need a reply!"
Then quietly, softly, I learned of my fate.

As my Master replied once again, "You must wait."
So, I slumped in my chair, defeated and taut,
And grumbled to God, "So, I'm waiting . . . for what?"
He seemed, then, to kneel, and His eyes wept with mine,
And He tenderly said, "I could give you a sign.
I could raise the dead, and cause mountains to run,
All you seek I could give, and pleased you would be.
You would have what you want – but you wouldn't know ME.
You'd not know the depth of My love for each saint;
You'd not know the power that I give to the faint;
You'd not learn to see through the clouds of despair;
You'd not learn to trust just by knowing I'm there;
You'd not know the joy of resting in Me
When darkness and silence were all you could see.
You'd never experience that fullness of love
As the peace of My Spirit descends like a dove;
You'd know that I give and I save, for a start,
But you'd not know the depth of the beat of My heart.
The glow of My comfort late into the night,
The faith that I give when you walk without sight,
The depth that's beyond getting just what you asked
From an infinite God, who makes what you have LAST.
You'd never know, should your pain quickly flee,
What it means that My grace is sufficient for thee.
Yes, your dreams for your loved one overnight would come true
But, oh the loss! If I lost what I'm doing with you!
So, be silent, My child, and in time you will see
That the greatest of gifts is to get to know Me.
And though often may My answers seem terribly late,
My most precious answer of all is still, 'Wait.'"

God did answer the prayer that first appeared in my 11-year-old heart, but beyond that, He taught me what it meant to truly experience the depth of His love.

I was born in New Castle, Wyoming, in a home in which both my parents were Christians. My dad was my pastor for the first fifteen years of my life. We went to church, and I was taught about God. I loved everything about church. I wasn't just religious; I was keenly aware of my personal friendship with Jesus. I had talked to Jesus a lot, but one day I decided I needed to thank Jesus for taking my place on the cross and dying for my sins, and ask him to forgive me. I was 5 years old, and by then my family was living in Jamestown, New York.

There was a special kids' event coming up at church, and I decided that I would pray with an adult then. Not because I thought I needed an adult to pray, but because I wanted to remember this decision for the rest of my life.

I can still see it clearly in my mind. I was at the home of the Steinhausers, a couple who still live and minister in New York with the Union Rescue Mission. I know it was fall, because I remember leaves blowing around the porch at the house where I was.

In my memory, it was the Steinhausers' daughter who prayed with me. There was something different about her that I was drawn to. I remember her giving a presentation in church about her mission trip and showing slides, the old-fashioned kind that make a *krupuk* sound as they go around the circle.

I also remember hearing the famous song that all missionaries played for their churches during their presentations back in the 1980s, "People Need the Lord."[2] I remember feeling something burning inside me and thinking, "This song is so true. People do need the Lord."

Many people look back at a young conversion to Christ and claim, "I didn't really understand what I was doing or what salvation was." But I remember clearly that I wanted to receive Christ, because I already believed in Jesus and thought I was a Christian, and I wanted to be sure that I knew 100 percent so I would never doubt again. I knew that I was a sinner and needed Jesus to pay for my sins for me to go to heaven when I died.

I understood my salvation so much that I remember really wanting everyone I knew to go to heaven with me. Once, I had three of my friends sitting side by side in a hammock that was hung between the clothesline poles in the backyard. I remember telling them that Jesus loved them so much that, as John 3:16 says, "He gave his one and only son, that whoever believes in Him will not perish but have eternal life."

I told them that they needed to say this prayer with me so that they could be forgiven of their sins and go to heaven and be with Jesus when they died. I didn't get many conversions that I know of. Usually people just kind of blinked at me and sat there quietly. I think I heard crickets in the silence, but I was too passionate to notice. And I think my excitement made them curious, so that they wanted to be a part of whatever I was excited about, whether they were on board with it or not.

I remember that for a Bible club at church one week, I practiced so hard with a girl from my neighborhood that we learned 14 verses to say for the leader. Every week my family filled our yellow station wagon with neighbor kids and hauled them to church on Wednesday night. I loved inviting my friends and seeing them grow.

I can even pinpoint the time I started to understand the work of the Holy Spirit and the power that I had in Him to change. I was about 8 years old at this time. Our next-door neighbors were very rough people, and we could often hear the mother cursing at her four children. Incidentally, when I would be mad, especially at my mom, curse words would come into my head. I cursed out loud only once, to my brother, but mom heard it and her hand told the seat of my pants that I wouldn't make that mistake again. Still, the words surged on in my head every time I got mad or upset.

I hated how it made me feel, so I prayed to the Lord to help take away these bad words. I decided to flee to my room when I got mad. Instead of whispering curse words to the ceiling, I prayed for God to take them away. And slowly He did, until I got to the point where I could be mad without hearing any bad words in my head. I remember being so amazed that I could use God to help me change something I didn't like about myself. I wasn't mature enough then to realize that God loved me, but He wanted me to be more like Christ too. The same grace that had saved me would sanctify me the rest of my life, so that I could become holy as He is holy.

In 1990, when I was 9, my family moved to Hays, Kansas. I know the temperature of my spiritual walk at the time only by the paragraph copied from my Bible, which I quoted earlier. There are just a few entries in that journal, so I don't have much of a record of what was going on in my heart. However, I know that I read my Bible, prayed, loved Jesus, and tried to obey my parents.

My mom would always ask me, "Why are you so precious?"

And I would always respond, "Because I love Jesus!"

I soon began to grow exponentially in my faith. In 1992, as a sixth grader, I finally could participate in Teens for Christ, a local ministry that was open to any teen who did not have a youth group. Some churches in Kansas are too small to have a full-fledged youth group, so Teens for Christ was created to combine all the Christian youth in one area into a group.

Ken and Mary Ann Massey were my youth group leaders, and Ken soon took me and several other teens under his wing to disciple us in deeper ways than were possible in a weekly large group meeting. He taught us about leadership and gave us responsibilities in the larger group.

A girlfriend of mine, Julie, and I got our start as the "Devotional Duo." We picked a short story from our youth Bible to read to the group. Leading the songs with motions and even being the emcee for the night soon became my responsibilities as well. More importantly, Ken taught me about having a daily quiet time, prayer life, and witnessing to my friends. Two of my closest friends, Danielle and Kristy, became Christians one night at a special bowling event. I remember praying for them as I watched them go into a room with other youth leaders after the gospel message had been given. I was so excited for them!

I grew so much spiritually in junior high. Yes, I was an outcast in many ways. But it was through these struggles that I drew closer and closer to God. I was the only kid to show up for "See You at the Pole" my seventh grade year.

See You at the Pole is a prayer rally held every year on the fourth Wednesday in September when students meet at the school flag pole before school to lift up their friends, families, teachers, school, and nation to God.

But, instead of standing with many people holding hands in a unified circle, I was sitting at the bottom of the flag pole, my head down, praying and trying not to call much attention to myself.

"Hey, do you feel okay?" I looked up to see a girl who sat behind me in math class. "Yeah, I'm fine."

"Then what arc you doing there?"

"Today is a national day for prayer for schools. It's called 'See You at the Pole,' and Christians are supposed to circle around their flag pole today and pray for their school."

"Uh, okay, well…" She wasn't sure what to say. "I'll see you later." She walked off, and I resumed my prayer position.

A few minutes later, I heard, "Why are you sitting out here?" It was a boy from gym class, one of the few boys who actually talked to me.

"Just sitting. I'm going in soon," I replied. I realized that if I explained myself to every single person that walked by, I would get no praying done whatsoever. Not to mention the fact that I was feeling the pressure to take a stand by myself, which I had not anticipated. I had truly believed other people would be there.

I remember taking a deep breath, looking at the guide papers I had in my hand, and reading the first verse on the sheet. "If two or three are gathered in my name, I will be with them also." I did not understand the theology to that verse, being only one under the pole, but I prayed anyway.

I did my best to live my Christian life at school, even though I was made fun of, or worse, ignored. My basketball team was really good at doing that. As an adult, I am 6 feet tall, but even in junior high I was taller than most of the boys, which I decided was God's way of keeping me from distraction. But being tall, I was a natural for the basketball team. "You can't teach height," the coaches used to tell me.

I loved basketball, but I did not love being ignored by my teammates. They just did not talk to me that much, maybe because we didn't have much in common. I couldn't relate to gossip and bad language. I prayed about living in a place where people would listen to the gospel and actually thirst to know more. God blessed me by allowing my friend Kristy to be bumped from B team to A team. Now that she traveled with us for out of town games, I could sit with her and was no longer forced to sit in the front seat of the Suburban with the coach.

My Grandma Jackson had told my brother, Mark, and me that when we moved from New York to Kansas God would bless us with many strong Christian friends. God answered that prayer over and again for us. By eighth grade, God had blessed me with a tight group of Christian friends, all in my grade: Julie, Kristy, Danielle, and Joella. This helped me deal with some of the loneliness that came with taking a stand for my faith.

Mark, who was two years older than me, and I were also pretty good friends, especially at this time in our lives. We had the normal sibling rivalry, but for the most part we were close. One of my favorite memories is the Saturday Mark and I helped a friend with a carwash to help her raise money for a mission trip. We went home a little tan and a little sunburned. When we got home, Mom had us paint the eaves in the back of the house and around the front door.

After we finished our task, Mark suggested we lay out in our swimsuits to even out our tans. We changed and went out to the back patio. Suddenly we felt cold water pelting us. Dad and Mom were firing cold water on us! We jumped off our lawn chairs and fled around the side of the house with Dad and Mom in hot pursuit.

"Sarah! Get the hose!" I heard Mark yell. I immediately made a beeline for the end of the hose as Mark cranked on the water from the spigot. A massive water fight ensued that lasted at least an hour.

It was great to be on Mark's side. He had lots of good ideas, and it felt so cool to be in cahoots with my big brother. Later that night Mark came up with the plan to bomb Dad and Mom with sock rolls while they watched TV.

We waited for a commercial and then gathered everyone's socks out of their drawers. We rolled them and tucked in the ends to make them into balls. Then we put our ammunition into the laundry basket.

Dad and Mom were on the couch. We hid around the corner until we were ready, and then we yelled and started throwing our sock balls in a surprise attack. Dad jumped behind the couch and Mom screamed and held up a pillow to shield her face. Dad grabbed her arm and dragged her behind the couch with him.

They started picking up the socks we had thrown and firing back at us. We took cover behind the recliner. The war lasted a good twenty minutes and advanced to all rooms of the house! It was good family fun, and similar scenes were a part of my happy childhood.

One of the great things about starting high school was being in the same building as my brother. I'm sure Mark did not think it was cool to have his little sister around, but most of the time he would help me out.

When the time came, we even started to talk about going to the same college. We discussed going to our mom's alma mater, Tabor College, and playing sports on scholarship, tennis for Mark and basketball for me. Tabor is a small Christian school in Hillsboro, Kansas, near Wichita. My only girl cousin, Erica, was like a sister to me, and her parents met while they studied at Tabor. Erica also dreamed of playing basketball on scholarship.

But before any of this occurred, God revealed the next step in His plan for me. The summer between eighth and ninth grade, all my friends would be going to TFC or other summer camps, as always. I was sad not to join them, but I knew God had told me to go on a mission trip, and I had to see where He wanted to take me.

This particular journey proved to be a turning point in my life, an experience similar to the ones the Israelites had when God commanded them to build an altar commemorating His faithfulness to them.

The year before, at the end of the summer of 1994, I was 13 and so in love with God, involved in Teens for Christ, and glad I only had one year left as a junior high student. About that time my youth group leader's son, Caleb, returned from a mission trip with Teen Missions International to Russia. He started to tell me about his experiences and all the places where Teen Missions took missions trips.

He handed me a magazine that gave details about all the trips for next summer. I pored over every trip and soon felt God wanted me to pray about which trip I should go on. I had done some construction trips with my youth group, which I loved, but I had never been overseas.

I was interested in one trip called Micronesia Island Hopping. I don't remember why I liked it—maybe I was excited about visiting islands—but it was a work team. Right up my alley! I ran it by my parents, never thinking that they might disapprove. I knew God had called me to this trip, so why would they have any doubts about it?

But the first time I asked them, they said no.

Discussions raged on for months. Mom would point out, "You can't even go to church camp for two weeks without getting homesick and coming home at the end in tears. How in the world do you think you can manage a two-month trip without Dad and me?"

"I don't know. I don't have all the answers to your questions. All I can tell you is that I know that God wants me to do this."

"Honey, explain that to me. Honestly, I want to know what God is telling you."

"You and Dad have taught me that finding God's will involves three things: prayer, Bible reading, and circumstances. When I pray about this trip, my heart burns deeper with the desire to go. When I read my Bible, all the verses seem to point me in this direction. And everywhere I turn, someone is talking about missions. But yours and Dad's permission to do this trip is the greatest circumstance that must change in order for me to go."

"I see. Well, we can bring it up with Dad again tonight over tacos. Okay?"

"Okay."

That evening we talked about it at dinner as Mom promised, but after we ate I cornered my parents to make a decision.

"The trip is coming up soon, and I still have to apply and have time to raise my money to go. You guys have to decide. Please."

Dad thought for a moment, looked at Mom, and then said, "Sarah, you and I will stay home from church on Sunday and have a half day of prayer about this trip." I knew my dad was taking this decision seriously, because we never missed church.

Two days later, Dad and I spent time in prayer. God did not reveal to me any profound truths, but He did confirm what I already knew in my heart about going on a trip with Teen Missions. I knew Dad's conclusion that morning was key for me. We met together in the living room.

Dad asked, "So how was your prayer time? What did God tell you? Any thoughts you want to share?"

"Oh, no new light bulbs. But I do feel that this is God's calling on my life right now. I know it will be hard, but Christ will give me strength. I won't be alone." I stopped and then asked hopefully, "And you? Did God tell you anything?"

"Yes, let me read you a verse."

"Okay." I leaned in closely, curious to see what verse he would read.

"Children, obey your parents in the Lord, for this is right." I thought he was gearing up to tell me that whatever his decision was, I needed to honor him. He continued, "Honor your father and mother – which is the first commandment with a promise – that it may go well with you and that you may enjoy long life on the earth." (Eph. 6:2-3.)

My heart started to fall. I was sure that I knew what the outcome of this discussion would be. He kept reading, "Fathers, do not exasperate your children; instead, bring them up in the training and instruction of the Lord." (Eph. 6:4.)

He finished reading and began to tell me what God had revealed to him through this verse. I only partly listened, thinking a negative answer would hurt less if I didn't really hear it. I just listened for the definitive "no", but it didn't come. What was he saying?

"So that is the verse that God used to show me that parents have a biblical responsibility to not exasperate their children. In my case, I see that if I say no to you this time for this missions trip, you may never ask me again, and I will have interfered with a passion that God put in you for a divine purpose."

My brain tried to pick out what he was really saying, "So I can go? Your decision is yes?"

"Yes! You can go on a mission trip this coming summer!"

"Yeah! Thank you so much, Dad! I love you so much, and thank you!" I hugged his neck and gave him a big kiss on the cheek.

I filled out an application and was accepted on the Micronesia Island Hopping team. As the summer neared, my trip changed. There were not enough kids for the Micronesian team, so they were sending us with an evangelism team to the Philippines and Guam.

At first I was really sad not to be on a work team, but God showed me that I had chosen a work team because that was familiar to me, and He really wanted to grow me into something new on an evangelism team.

So, shortly after eighth grade graduation, I went to the Philippines. It was extremely hard, and I cried a lot. After boot camp in Florida and a week in Guam, I found myself on a ship in Manila on my way to our main outreach on the west Island of Palawan. I was sitting along the railing of this huge ship, looking out at the city and the nastiest water I had ever seen in my life. It was a big port with lots of ships, so it was dirty from diesel, exhaust, and trash. I even saw a dead animal.

I was so horrified, but God directed my eyes to two little boys bathing and playing on the shore. I remember a voice that seemed audible, because it resonated so loud within my heart. God said to me, "Sarah, I know you miss your family and your home, but the work I have for you to do is more important than your missing them."

It was a turning point for me. I started to truly enjoy my trip instead of focusing on trying to not miss my parents. I really started to bond with the thirteen other, older team members, and God did great things in and through us.

Several weeks later we were back on the outskirts of Manila for debriefing. Debriefing helped prepare us to return to our culture. The last week of debriefing was fun and relaxing, but my emotions were shot after two months of intense ups and downs. I got to a point where I felt anxious, hyper, and angry about something I could not put my finger on.

I was experiencing mental, emotional, and spiritual shock from the life-altering time I had had during my mission trip. When I was in the field ministering, I didn't have much time to think about everything that was going on around me. At debriefing, I finally had time to think and process, and it was overwhelming. This is one of the reasons debriefing is required for all the summer teams.

I didn't recognize the symptoms, but my Filipino leader, Gilmer, noticed the difference in me and asked me what was wrong. I told him all that I was experiencing, and in his wisdom, as an older Christian, he told me, "God is trying to get your attention; He wants to talk to you. Go find a quiet place and just listen."

So off I went to a remote part of the compound to listen to God. I did some singing as well, and I came back to the group with a light heart. It turned out that God just wanted to fellowship with me and spend intimate time with me. He showed me how I had truly enjoyed my time on the mission field and felt so happy and alive as I shared the Bible with people in this country. He encouraged me and put a new peace in my heart. This peace was meant to prepare me for what would happen next.

That night, the main evening devotional was about hearing a call to full-time missions. The speaker challenged us by reading Phil. 3:7-8. He read the text boldly, "But what things were gain to me, these I have counted loss for Christ. Yet indeed I also count all things loss for the excellence of the knowledge of Christ Jesus my Lord, for whom I have suffered the loss of all things, and count them as rubbish, that I may gain Christ."

As the man spoke, I felt my heart burning within me. He also reminded us of the man in Matthew 13 who found the pearl of great price, sold everything he had, and bought it.

My mind began to wrap around the thought that it didn't matter what I did for Christ; it didn't matter if I laid down my life for mission work; life only counts when I give all to find Christ. Life is all about Him, and getting to know Him, and my work for him would not make Him love me more.

It was a wonderful check on my motives, but the speaker did not stop there. He added, "When we do find the pearl of great price, Jesus Christ, we will feel compelled to share his love with others. That is where the Great Commission comes into play. Matthew 28:19 says, 'Therefore go and make disciples of all nations.'"

As he continued to speak, the Holy Spirit was speaking to my heart. I could see how Paul saw Christ as the pearl of great price. The thought that Paul called everything else rubbish kept turning over and over into my mind.

The other pursuits I might have had in life paled in comparison to living the life of a missionary. If those other pursuits had been from God, they might have felt right in my heart, but as the man asked us to consider being overseas missionaries, I tested that idea in my heart, and it just felt right. I could feel the Holy Spirit burning a desire for missions into my soul. I trusted God would confirm this calling over the years until this passion became a reality, but I knew God had called me to be a full-time missionary.

I answered the call by coming up to the stage. A friend of mine was close behind me. As we both knelt, she put her hand on my shoulder. I took her hand and squeezed it. I knew the commitment I was making at this moment was one that I could not make with anyone else. God was calling me, and I had to take this step alone. I would never look back, never give up, never shrink down. This commitment, which I made in the light of my spiritual walk, I would never doubt in the darkness.

Because of my trip, I missed the first week of my freshman year of high school. I felt so behind. Everyone knew what was going on, but I was like a deer in the headlights. I was glad Mark was in my homeroom.

I remember leaving homeroom to find the library. I walked in a circle and ended up back where I started. I snuck back into the room and quietly asked Mark, "Where's the library?"

He took me out into the hallway. He pointed. The library was across the hallway from my homeroom. I was so embarrassed, but glad that only Mark knew my error.

My culture shock coming home was bad. My mom thought I had mono because I was so tired and listless. I remember missing my friends on the basketball team a lot while I was away, but I also felt God's call to mission so strongly, and waiting four years to do something about it seemed impossible.

Another big issue was living in a culture that did not seem to understand or care for the rest of the world. Even Christians just did what was trendy without batting an eye for the world that was dying and going to hell around them.

My worldview had been altered by my trip, and I would never be the same, nor did I want to be. It took some time for God to teach me how to live in the surroundings where He had placed me, while also holding onto the desire He had planted in my heart. I also had to learn not to judge people around me. God works in everyone in different ways and on different timetables, and I couldn't take credit for what He had done in my life.

A letter that my pastor's daughter, Rachel, wrote in my journal one morning at church shows that my passion for missions was still evident in me, even months after my return from the Philippines:

12/03/95

Sarah, Sarah, Sarah! What would I ever do without you! What do you think you will be doing in five or ten years? What do you think God will do with you? Will you be in some other country? That will be cool because then I would get mail from out of the country. I've always wanted mail like that! Right now Dad is preaching about Moses, when he didn't think he was qualified to do what God had told him to do. Just think, Sarah, you could do anything God wanted you to do because God will make you qualified!

That is so awesome because God will take you places and show you things you never thought you could go or see. I never understood why Moses gave excuses because if God told me to do something I couldn't do (on my own), I would be so excited because I would see God working through me to do something I could never do before. Whatever you do, Sarah, ten, fifteen, or twenty years from now, do it for the Lord.

Love, Rachel

Every summer after that first summer in the Philippines, I pursued another mission trip to refine the skills that I needed to make it my long-term vocation. I got involved with as many spiritual growth seminars and leadership training weekends as I could, for my own personal growth as a Christian, but also to gain what I needed to be a career missionary. In high school my summers were spent in Mexico, the Mississippi Delta, and Zimbabwe on a motorcycle mission trip.

God taught me so much about Himself on each adventure He took me on. When I went on my motorcycle trip to Zimbabwe, during the summer of 1998, one of my first letters home from boot camp read:

Dear Parents,

    Early boot camp is pretty hard. We moved a large mound of tires TWICE! Once so the lawn mower could mow underneath, and again to set up "city blocks." It is part of the motorcycle teaching course. Really hot work! We haven't even ridden yet! Today we got lots of free time. I did my laundry in Alligator Lake. We even got to swim in the really nice pool yesterday, instead of Alligator Lake, where we had to swim the last two days. There is an actual alligator in Bath Tub Lake, so no one can swim in there. They are trying to catch it and take it out. I saw an armadillo today. I snuck up on him and held really still. He just about walked over my boot!

Perhaps some girls experiencing these things would be in a panic, but I was in hog heaven and loving the dirt and challenge. This summer was very different than my first Teen Missions trip when I was 14.

I remember when my team first got to Zimbabwe. We had driven our motorcycles to a remote village that had no running water. We had enough water to cook and drink but would only be taking baby wipe baths for a week. We each had a one-person tent, and I had positioned mine under an old basketball goal. I felt a little closer to home that week. I called for my friend Shawna to come over to my "veranda," which was the strip of black tarp that stuck out from under my tent. This was a place where we had many heart-to-heart talks. I shared with Shawna my reservations about our ministry outing for the next day.

"Did you hear our leaders talking about the village we are going to find tomorrow?"

"No, what's up?"

"Well, they told a few of us on the team that this area we are going to has never heard the gospel. I mean, they have never heard the name of Jesus Christ before."

"Whoa, that is crazy. I can't imagine."

"I know. When I first heard about it last night, I felt unworthy to go. I thought that God should find someone really smart, really trained in sharing the gospel in case the village has any questions and needs someone who understands deep theology. But then this morning in my quiet time, God showed me I Cor. 2:1-5. Here, look at this verse."

I opened my Bible and moved my motorcycle helmet so I could lean closer to her. I pointed at the page and read, "When I came to you, brothers, I did not come with eloquence or superior wisdom as I proclaimed to you the testimony about God. For I resolved to know nothing while I was with you except Jesus Christ and Him crucified. I came to you in weakness and fear, and with much trembling. My message and my preaching were not with wise and persuasive words, but with a demonstration of the Spirit's power, so that your faith might not rest on men's wisdom, but on God's power."

I finished and looked up to her. She was waiting for me to explain why this was such a powerful verse to me. I explained, "You see, even the awesome apostle Paul chose to not speak with complicated words. He decided to only know Christ and Him crucified. I know that I know that.

"God wants my words to be simple so that His power can be shown. People will come to Christ because of the power of God, not because of fancy words. He has equipped us to do this, so we have to go boldly and be faithful to what God wants us to share."

Shawna nodded her head in agreement. "Let's spend some time praying that we will be bold and that God will prepare hearts to be open to the gospel and the work of the Holy Spirit."

Later that day, we showed "Jesus"[3] (also called The Jesus Film) on the side of a building. Then we shared the gospel with the whole village. "Jesus," a 1979 motion picture, depicts the life of Jesus Christ, according, primarily to the Gospel of Luke in the Bible.

Several of the leading men in the community accepted the Lord, which was unusual, but exciting, because they had great influence over the younger generations. To truly receive Christ, they had to admit that what they had been teaching was not the truth. Pride usually gets in the way of this type of public confession of faith. Praise the Lord for the work He did that night through our humble obedience to be there, and especially for the lives He saved from the pit of hell.

The teens at the secondary school we visited were so funny. I got to talk to a group of girls after our presentation. They asked, "Is it really true God is coming back?" "Who are Jesus' parents?" "What are heaven and hell like?" They asked so many good questions like these, and I was able to witness to them. Praise the Lord!

One girl asked, "Can I touch your hair?"

"Yes, you may," I said, and I also reached out to touch her hair. The whole group roared with laughter. All the girls touched my hair. They also played with my watch and asked lots of questions about the United States. They were so fun to talk to. When we left, they laughed at a few of us because we had a hard time getting our bikes started.

After another "Jesus" film presentation, a lady I had met in earlier days, Zamile, and her friends stepped forward to accept Christ. I was eager to talk to her and share

John 3:16. Shawna and I shared several verses from Romans with the four ladies. It was powerful to experience the eagerness they had.

As I read the passage, I would point to the words. Each woman held a corner of my Bible to pull it closer to them. I would read the verse and explain it, and their faces would burst with joy when they understood. I could physically see on their faces the Holy Spirit revealing truth to them. Then they would slowly read the passage again to fully understand. It was exciting to see them give their lives to Christ and be so eager to learn.

Africa was an amazing experience, and I started my senior year of high school even more ready to be done with high school and college and get on the mission field.

That sense of urgency was compounded during my senior year by a spring break experience that would eventually become a key part of my life: visiting the *Caribbean Mercy Ship*. My youth leader, Ken, took me and a few others to visit his son, Caleb, on the ship. Caleb was the one who first got me interested in trips with Teen Missions.

The ship was docked in Portland, Oregon, at that particular time. Mercy Ships is a partner organization of Youth With a Mission (YWAM). We flew into Seattle and rented a van to drive to Portland. We arrived at the dock, walked up the gangway, and were met by the ship's gangway watchman. Ken explained our arrangements to visit his son and daughter-in-law. The watchman pointed us toward the reception area. The receptionist made an announcement over the public address for Caleb or Sophie to come to reception.

Danielle asked Sophie where she was from.

"London, England," Sophie said and smiled.

"Yeah, that is what we thought," responded Danielle.

"We have about 15 countries represented on the ship right now. We have people from New Zealand, South Africa, Korea, Wales, Australia, El Salvador, Nicaragua, Guatemala, Honduras, Mexico, Dominican Republic, Puerto Rico, Ghana, Colombia, Canada, and obviously from here in the United States, too," Sophie told us.

"Wow! That is so amazing. How fun to learn about different cultures and languages."

Soon we found out how fun it was to sit down at the supper table with people from so many different countries and backgrounds. It was like one big heavenly family. The ship, surprisingly, had a homey feel to it. It was built as a Norwegian ferry, once called the *Polarys*. Inside the ship were lots of beautiful sea scenes carved into the wood.

We also learned more of the history of the ship. The *Caribbean Mercy* was acquired by Mercy Ships in 1994, contributing more than 20 percent of the Mercy Ships' total output for the three-ship fleet in terms of number of services, value, and beneficiaries, serving primarily in Central America and the Caribbean basin.

While in port, she housed an average crew of 120 volunteers from more than 20 nations. On our tour of the ship, we were told that the *Caribbean Mercy* offered an eye surgery unit, cargo capacity, and conference and seminar facilities used for a variety of programs. Her fuel and water tanks provided a cruising range of 12 days, or 3,600 miles.

I got totally lost during our tour, going up and down narrow, steep stairs on the outside decks and the circular stairs on the inside of each deck. I had to use the maps to navigate myself to the right deck, but eventually I learned my way around.

While we were there, I worked in the galley. I loved using the dumbwaiter to lift food to the pantry on the "A deck." The pantry workers would put the food out on the buffet for the crew to eat. We would keep the food hot in the ovens and then send up pans as they called for extras as food ran low.

I really loved the ship. After we left, I applied to the Texas office to go with the *Caribbean Mercy Ship* to Korea the summer after my senior year, but God had other plans, and I ended up in Mexico again.

I started to realize that it didn't really matter where I was. I loved missions! I loved the people, the challenge, going a week without a shower because there was only water for cooking, the dirt, the look of excitement when a person receives the saving power of Jesus.

It was exhilarating to work with a God that was out of the box and to do something different every day, knowing that He was leading and guiding me. I had experienced this at home, but on a much smaller scale. At any rate, I was hooked, and I was awed that God was calling me to do something full-time that I loved so much.

When I graduated from high school, I had already signed a letter of intent to play basketball at Tabor College, just as Mark, Erica and I had planned. Graduation was bittersweet.

I had just lost my Grandpa Jackson a few months before. I called him Grampa or Gramps. God touched my life in an incredible way the last hour of my grandpa's life; I doubt I will ever forget it.

I was lying in my bed when my mother called from Nebraska. She told Dad and me that Grampa was really struggling to breathe. She asked us to pray that God would take him, and that Grampa would relax and feel at ease to leave. I cried at these words, knowing that this was his time to leave for heaven. I decided to read my Bible for a while, not wanting to pray for Grampa to die.

I flipped around a while in the pages of my Bible, until finally my eyes landed on II Cor. 5:1-4: "For we know that if the earthly tent we live in is destroyed, we have a building from God, an eternal house in heaven, not built by human hands. Meanwhile we groan, longing to be clothed instead with our heavenly dwelling, because when we are clothed, we will not be found naked. For while we are in this tent, we groan and are burdened because we do not wish to be unclothed but to be clothed instead with our heavenly dwelling, so that what is mortal may be swallowed up by life."

I knew God had led me to that passage to comfort me. I wept and prayed that Grampa would be clothed with his heavenly robe and free of his earthly tent. I prayed with all my heart and believed that God was on His way. One hour later Grampa was at home in his heavenly dwelling. I wrote in my Bible next to the passage, "Grampa…Tent Free…January 8, 1999. I love you!"

Grandpa Jackson was special to me because I had spent so much time on his farm with him. I loved wearing a pair of his overalls and helping him do chores. I had spent a summer on the farm helping him put up hay.

One day we had gone horseback riding, and I couldn't believe how fast Grampa went. He was no spring chicken, but he was a tough old bird. The last thing we did together before we found out that he had lung cancer was plant morning glories on the side of the chicken barn. Though chickens no longer roosted there, I think the numerous farm cats enjoyed the flowers. Every time I see morning glories, I think of Grandpa Jackson. At that point in my life, losing him was the hardest thing I had ever gone through.

In honor of my Grampa, I used masking tape to write "For Gramps!" on my graduation hat. I drove home from graduation in my Grampa's farm truck. I hung my tassel on the rearview mirror, put my head on the steering wheel, and cried before I went inside to greet guests arriving for my graduation party.

Shortly after graduation, I left for my mission trip to Mexico with Teens for Christ. Ken and Mary Ann were the leaders. We heard from Caleb that the ship was in Korea and running into many problems, including a horrible voyage during which everyone became sick.

I then saw how God was protecting me from a bad missions experience that might ruin my vision of being a missionary, and instead was helping me continue to learn more Spanish. My high school classes had helped, but the practice I was getting was vital to actually learning the language.

At the end of the trip, I set my sights on college and started to prepare myself for this new experience. My basketball scholarship may not have been a big deal to some, but it was huge to me.

Getting a basketball scholarship was a dream come true. The dream was perfect because my cousin Erica would be playing her second year with Tabor and living across the hall from me. My brother was also in his junior year at Tabor on a tennis scholarship. We were finally living the dream.

One night, as I shot hoops in my parents' driveway, I contemplated how happy I was about this dream come true, as well as lots of other deep thoughts. I tried focusing my mind and turning everything over to God. It was a time to be still and listen to God. I listened, but I also poured my heart out to God, praying for His will in my life. I also told Him my desire to be loved by a man. What I remember more than anything was how the two subjects began to intertwine.

I shot a basket and prayed in my mind, "Lord, I will never marry a man who takes me away from your will in my life. I love You too much to settle on a love that takes me away from Your great purpose in my life." With that commitment ringing in my mind, I packed my boxes for college.

My first semester was great. The basketball was great. I didn't get to play varsity, but I did get to play second string. I just loved basketball and was so glad to be realizing my dream to play in college.

School, on the other hand, was not as fun. I just didn't get the point of taking all these classes when I knew I just wanted to be a missionary. I even took a Spanish class, which I actually did care about, but it was at a nearby school, and it was way too hard for my level. I ended up flunking the class. It's so ironic that the one and only class I ever flunked was Spanish.

I also went to church on Sunday mornings, but there was not much ministry for me to get involved in. I felt college was supposed to be all about me and what I wanted to do, but I was only interested in what God wanted me to do. When I considered getting a degree in education, I thought, "I've never liked school. Why would I want to become a teacher?"

During Christmas break, only one semester into my dream, God clearly gave me a choice. He told me, "Sarah, you can follow your dreams of a basketball scholarship at Tabor, or you can leave school, and I will give you a life that you could never imagine." The verse that He placed on my heart in that moment was Eph. 3:20, "Now to him who is able to do immeasurably more than all we ask or imagine, according to his power that is at work within us."

My parents were out of town at the time. They had won a trip to San Diego to watch Kansas State in a bowl game. While they were there, they stopped by the *Caribbean Mercy Ship*, which happened to be docked there. Caleb was still on the ship with his wife, Sophie. Also, my longtime friend Kristy had started serving on the ship as a receptionist. As my parents visited the ship, little did they know what God had in store for me back home.

I first talked to my brother Mark about what God was telling me. I remember we were loading the dishwasher in the kitchen together when I told him. I mentioned how conflicted I felt about giving up on basketball, one of my most treasured dreams.

He told me, "Sarah, you can't let basketball get in the way of what God has for you. Besides, I never really thought you'd live in the States for long anyway."

So when Mom and Dad got home, I talked to them about what I was praying about. They had the normal parental response—not too excited about me wanting to leave school. But they trusted me well enough to listen to my thoughts. It was hard because I didn't know what I would do when I left school. God had not revealed that part of the plan yet. He had just told me to leave and trust Him.

Tabor had a one-month semester in January, during which students took one intensive class. My agreement with my parents was that I would return to school for the month of January, pray about my decision during that month, and also seek counsel from the dean of women.

I did as they asked and returned to Tabor. I prayed, and God intensified the desire in my heart to follow His unimaginable plan for my life. All the verses in my Bible that I read repeated the same message to step out in faith. I was sure God wanted me to leave school.

The dean helped me process my decision and answered a lot of questions about my motives for leaving school. In the end she called my mom and told her, "You have to trust the God that is in her."

I started to tell my friends, professors, coach, and team that I would be leaving. They all had the same question, "What are you going to do?" It did not make sense to them for me to leave school when God had not shown the next step yet, but I knew God wanted me to go forward in faith and wait for Him to reveal it.

After the January semester, I left school. I went to my Grandma's farm in Nebraska to work for her. I knew that whatever God wanted me to do, I would need money, so working was the best option. Working for Grandma was a special treat. I had always loved the farm but had not had the opportunity to spend much time there since Grandpa had died my senior year of high school. I loved doing chores and redecorating Grandma's bedroom and kitchen.

About three weeks into living at Grandma's, I started to get impatient with God. I had prayed and asked for Him to do something or for the Holy Spirit to tell me some deep thought. Nothing.

I had read my Bible and tried to squeeze out an application for what I should do or where I should be going. Nothing.

I spent time walking and listening for God to speak to me. Down the long, dusty driveway; past the place Mark and I used to race our turtle, Speedy, in the ditch; down the gravel road to the small bridge where a duck used to sit on the water underneath. I'd kick a few pebbles into the pond and watch the rings get bigger and bigger.

Other times I would ride my mountain bike through the marsh and up to the cornfield on top of the hill. From there it felt like I could touch the sky. I'd watch the clouds pass. Sometimes I'd reach out my hand just to be sure that the heavens hadn't come down. The hues of yellow, red, and orange, mixed with the blue and purple, moved my soul.

In all this time, God did not speak. Oh, He loved on me. He told me how special I was. He reminded me He had a plan for my life, "plans to prosper *me* and not to harm *me*, plans to give *me* hope and a future." Jer. 29:11 (italics my own). I passed days of intimate closeness with God, and I tried not to be impatient for what was to come next.

On Valentine's Day, I went for one of my long walks, feeling especially restless. I wanted to get on with the next part of life that God had for me, and especially to find my one true love. Sarah means "princess" in Hebrew. Everyone knows a princess needs a prince.

In all my frustration, I told God, though only the cows were near enough to hear, "I quit school for You, but what do You want me to do? Please tell me! Be faithful to the words You gave me in Ephesians."

I went to bed and wrestled with God all night. "What, God? What would You have me do? I love You, and I want to serve You." I now realize that God loves our intimate time with Him more than He loves what we can do for Him, though the book of James explains how both are important in our spiritual lives. Whether God was ready to end our intimate time or not, He answered my prayer.

The next morning, I was on the floor of Grandma Jackson's farm kitchen, scrubbing off some ceiling paint I'd dripped on it. We had just finished redoing her bedroom and kitchen. The phone rang. Grandma answered and brought me the phone.

"Sarah, it's your dad."

Dad started the conversation as he always does. Even when I know it is him, he always says, "Hey, this is your dad."

"Yeah, Dad, I know. What's up?"

"Mercy Ships just called and they want you to be in El Salvador in one week. They'll just be getting there, and they need you to serve in the galley. What should I tell them?"

"Yes! Tell them yes! This is awesome! Whoa, I have so much to do to be ready to go in a week, but tell them yes!"

Family Picture David, Debbie, Mark and Sarah (1982)

Sarah serving on her first mission trip with Teen Missions in
the Philippines for two months (1995)

Sarah in motorcycle training gear at "The Lord's Boot Camp" of Teen Missions in Merritt Island,
Florida. After a two week boot camp Sarah will serve with Desert Angels III
for two months in Zimbabwe, Africa (1998)

Sarah working the dumb waiter in the galley while visiting
the Mercy Ship in Portland, Oregon (1999)

The group that visited the Mercy Ship in Portland, Oregon (1999), and my best friends through high school and now in life. L-R Sarah Breeden (Liborio), Steve Massaglia, Rachel Sprock (Privett), Julie Grahs, Ken Massey (Our faithful youth leader), Joella Fry (Wilson), and Danielle John (Massaglia; she married Steve!)

L-R Sarah's cousin, Erica Fast and Sarah playing basketball at Tabor College in 2000

Please visit my website, www.my-onceuponatime.com/, to see more pictures and videos from each chapter.

Chapter Two

The Prince: Hugo's Life Before True Love
1980-1999

El Salvador

Hugo was born in San Salvador, El Salvador. It was March 4, 1980, and El Salvador had recently begun a civil war. The Communist party, referred to as the guerillas, was on one side; the military was on the other side. Both sides were extremely vicious and committed horrible acts. At this time, the government had passed a law known as *Toque de Queda*, a curfew that made it illegal to be on the street from 8 p.m. to 5 a.m.

Hugo's mom, Irma, had been having severe labor pains since 2 a.m., and they were getting stronger. At the risk of being detained by the police, Hugo's dad took Irma in a taxi to the hospital before the morning curfew expired. The taxi weaved in and out of dead bodies as Irma watched, horrified.

The driver stopped several blocks from the hospital and said, "You'll have to walk from here. I could get in trouble for being out so early."

The hospital did not allow fathers to enter with their wives, plus Hugo's sisters needed to be taken care of, so Hugo's dad returned home in the taxi. Irma walked the rest of the way to the hospital alone. Thankfully, there were no more dead bodies, but the bodies she had seen had shocked her system to the point that her labor pains had stopped.

Once she was admitted into the hospital, the doctors induced labor again. Later, it became a family myth that Hugo scared easily because of the trauma his mother witnessed hours before his birth. All babies born in 1980 were called "war babies," because they were born the same year the war started.

Hugo was named after his father, Hugo. His full name was Hugo Amilcar Liborio Gomez. A Latino also preserves his mother's maiden name, listing it after his father's surname. Hugo's father's name differed only in this second last name, Hugo Amilcar Liborio Barahona.

When Hugo's parents took him home from the hospital, his two sisters were waiting anxiously for him at their apartment in the capital. Febe was three years older than Hugo, and Cesia (Se-see-uh) was three years older than Febe. When Hugo was 3, they moved to a quieter suburb called Santa Tecla. The neighborhood they lived in was called La Colina. *Colina* means hill, and there was a large hill a short ways off across the main street.

Their house shared a concrete wall with the neighbors on both sides. The area was cool and fresh in the earlier years, but grew hotter as more trees were cut and cement laid to build up the area. The main street that connected their neighborhood to the capital sloped and was quiet with traffic at this time. Hugo learned to ride his bike on this hill and tried a skateboard once. Once was enough, though, because it ended badly – specifically with lip skin on the sidewalk. He was left with a scar on his upper lip (girls love that, right?).

Hugo's dad worked in the government archives. He even helped design a computer program to convert hard copies of files to a digital format and organize them. Irma was a homemaker, but she added to the family's income by using her seamstress skills to sew projects for families in their church. She could sew anything. She was often asked to sew special wedding dresses and *quinceañera* dresses for Latinas' big fifteenth-birthday celebrations.

People in the church joked that Hugo was "born in the front row," because he was in church from birth. Hugo Sr. was a deacon in the church and led Sunday morning worship. He was gifted musically. He played organ and guitar along with just about any instrument he decided to pick up. He played by ear but also read music. He loved to pen his own hymns for the church, and also wrote words and music for a collection he put together. Irma was faithful with kids' and women's ministries.

Hugo was a normal boy, as likely to take apart a new robot toy to see how it worked as he was to throw a parakeet against the wall to see if it could fly, but he was also gifted in music. Hugo followed his father's interests and fell in love with music. He learned a lot about Jesus at church and heard all the Bible stories, but it was the music that drew him most. When he was 8 years old, his father told him, "Hugo, you come up on stage with me, and I will show you how to lead music."

"Wow! Great! I'd love to!" Hugo had watched his dad lead music many times before and had already figured out the basics, but he was eager to learn more.

As the intro started, Hugo Sr. started to move his arm in four-four time. Hugo followed, copying his father's movement exactly. It seemed easy enough, and it was exhilarating to be up front with his dad! Hugo was involved with the church's worship time from that Sunday forward.

Even though church was walking distance from their house, Hugo Sr.'s job was not, and soon the family could afford a car. Public transportation was readily available, but the luxury of a car made life a lot easier. The problem became where to store it at night. They did not have a garage. The parking lot two houses away was not a safe place to leave a vehicle overnight. A thief could easily hotwire it and be on the main road before anyone would know it was gone.

The only option was to park it in front of the house on the concrete walkway. But the walkway was wide enough for only one car. Everyone else on the alley parked their cars in front of their houses, too.

So everyone would park in the parking lot during the day, or along a side street, and then in the evening the "car dance" would begin. Hugo Sr. would park his car in first, in front of their house. Then everyone else on the street would park their cars in front of their houses in order. In the morning, if Hugo Sr. needed to go to work early and the other cars blocked him in, the option was to either honk the car horn until everyone came out to move their cars, or go knock on all the doors of people with cars.

Everyone would move into the street so Hugo Sr. could back out, and then they'd re-park in the alley. Such a rigmarole, but it was the only way to keep the cars safe.

The car was also related to a memory that Hugo had about the time he noticed his parents' marriage having problems. Once, Hugo Sr. took Hugo to worship practice at church, but when they got to church his dad told him to wait in the car. Hugo was upset, but knew his dad was serious, so he waited for almost two hours in the car while his dad was in the sanctuary practicing for Sunday worship. He did not understand, but later that night he heard his parents shouting at each other. They were fighting more and more all the time.

Before Hugo pulled the pillow over his head, he heard his mom ask, "Is she on the worship team?" Hugo knew it had something to do with why he was not allowed into worship practice that night. Maybe his dad did not want Hugo to see him with this lady, or get suspicious if he saw them flirting.

He was too young to understand all the aspects of what was going on, but he knew that he did not like his parents fighting all the time. They were supposed to love each other, right? Didn't the Bible teach that? Where was God? His parents seemed to love each other and God when they were at church, but why were they different at home? Cesia seemed to have fun doing things that were not really "Christian." Hugo thought maybe he should try something different, too.

He started to hang around with older kids when he was 10 years old. They were not a good influence on him, and soon he was trying to be like them. He liked getting their attention and tried to impress them by doing the things they did. Alcohol was not regulated at that time, and anyone could buy beer at any *tienda* (neighborhood family store), even underage kids. Hugo also started smoking cigarettes at age 12. Unfortunately, his parents were too involved in their own problems to see what was going on.

Around that time, a missionary came to Hugo's church and gave his testimony to all the kids and youth. The missionary told the kids about all the horrible things that he had done in his life: alcohol, smoking, drugs, women, stealing. He went on and on, giving explicit details of his past sinful life, including how he wound up in prison. At the end he said, "And then God miraculously saved my life from the pit, and He gave me an awesome testimony."

Hugo was impressed and thought, "He's a missionary, and he said that God gave him an awesome testimony. Well, I want an awesome testimony too! I should do a bunch of stupid stuff in my life and then God can use it all for good." He did not, however, consider the sadness, pain, and other unwanted consequences of leading a life of sin.

By high school, Hugo was very good at the double life he had developed. He was now helping the worship team at church. Many good members of the team came and went, but in his high school years the main worship group was comprised of Carlos, who directed the group; Hugo, who played guitar; Jose Carlos, who played the electric drum kit; Erick, who played bass guitar; and Alex, Roberto, Xiomara and Hugo's sister, Febe, who sang. The group was very talented and was even invited to play special events at other churches. Hugo's dad, by this time, was choosing not to attend church with the family, so Hugo took over some of the responsibilities of leading music on Sundays.

Hugo also was part of the youth group leadership. This was the Sunday face that Hugo put on for show. The rest of the week and at school he was a one-man rebellion show. His school was Christian, but once he stood up in class and argued heatedly with the teacher about religion. Hugo argued against the Bible. A girl from his church sat in front of him. Near the end of the argument, the girl looked back at Hugo with tears in her eyes and said, "But, Hugo you're a Christian. How can you say all of this?"

He teased her and other professing Christians at his school. He didn't care if anyone followed his rebellious ways or not. His closest friends, though, were his worship team buddies.

Hugo, Roberto, Alex, and Jose Carlos were closest in age and on the school's basketball team together, which caused a greater bond. Good or bad, they were in it together. Once another player fouled Jose Carlos intentionally, and Jose Carlos hit the concrete court hard. Hugo, Roberto, and Alex charged the other player, and soon both teams were in an all-out fist fight. Hugo hated fighting, but felt he had to have his friend's back.

As the fight was breaking up, Hugo looked around for Jose Carlos to see if he was okay. Hugo couldn't find him on the court, so he looked further out. Finally, he spotted Jose Carlos, casually getting a drink from the water fountain. The guy they were sticking up for had snuck out of the entire fight. But that was Jose Carlos, totally unpredictable.

Jose Carlos was also really funny, which brought Hugo's crazy side out even more strongly. Together they could get a group of friends laughing for hours. Hugo thrived on a crowd's attention. It was this inborn charisma that caused people to naturally follow him. Once, a teacher could not get the class's attention, so in exasperation she looked at Hugo sitting at the back of the classroom.

He rolled his eyes, but stood up and said, "Listen everyone, please be quiet, the teacher wants to get started." His whole class quickly took their seats. This was one of the times that he helped a teacher out, but that doesn't mean he never made a teacher cry!

At one point, Hugo had a cast on his leg from his ankle to his hip, because he had hurt his knee playing basketball. That day in class the teacher said, "Finish your work and then bring it up to my desk for me to grade."

Hugo was in a lot of pain, so he waited until the line was short at the teacher's desk before he used his cane and made his way painfully to the front, through a maze of students who were growing more and more rambunctious.

The moment he put his notebook on the teacher's desk she yelled, "Okay! You all are too loud! Everyone sit down and I will wait until you're all quiet before we continue!"

Hugo just stood there, because he thought she couldn't possibly be talking to him after he had hobbled up there so painfully.

But she continued to yell, "Hugo, please go and sit down!"

"But, I …"

"Go and sit!"

He moved slowly back to his desk in the back of the room. He turned to sit and immediately the teacher said calmly, "Okay, Hugo you can bring your notebook here."

Hugo lost his temper, yelling, "Here I am in a cast, in a lot of pain. I took my book up to you once and you sent me back. And then you waited until I got here to ask me to come back again. No way! What is wrong with you?"

The teacher was totally in shock. She didn't know what to say. She just sat down in her chair and put her head in her hands. No one in the class said anything. They could tell she was crying.

The girls motioned for Hugo to do something, but he was still mad, so he said, "Oh, great. Now you're crying? I'm the one in pain!"

It seemed like eternity before Hugo finally stood, took his notebook, and made his way to the front. He laid his notebook on her desk, tapped her lightly on the shoulder, and said, "It's okay. I forgive you." The teacher took his notebook, wiped her nose, and gave him a good grade.

The school administration had its own troubles with Hugo. The school had a rule about hair, which stated that a boy's hair could not cover his eyes. Hugo wore his hair long at this time, and it definitely covered his eyes. The director of the school would see him in the courtyard and say, "Hugo, cut your hair."

He'd go home and have it cut a tiny bit. He would get away with it for a while, but soon the director would see him again and say, "Hugo, cut your hair."

He'd get it cut a little bit, just enough to be let into school again. This went on for quite some time until Hugo got fed up with being bothered by the director. So he went to the barber, and this time he had him shave it off completely! The director never bothered him again, and this became Hugo's signature hairstyle. He loved a shaved head so much that he would always say, "I will be the happiest man in the world when I go bald!" He hated to spend time or money on anything related to his hair.

When he did get in trouble with the school administration, he'd always try to cut corners on the consequences. Once he got an in-school suspension, and the punishment was to copy the book of Psalms into a notebook. He would have to complete a certain section every day. It only took one day for him to figure out that if he did the work at home the night before, the next day at school he could mess around and do whatever he wanted. It was the best social week of school ever. He didn't exactly learn his lesson.

But as much as Hugo acted like a jerk, he could not change the fact that God had created him with a lot of character. When some other boys were making fun of a little girl who had beautiful blue eyes (uncommon for a Latina), but was a little on the chunky side, Hugo watched them from the side of the school's common area. When they crossed the basketball court, following the little girl and continuing to tease her, Hugo stood up and stepped between the boys and the blue-eyed girl. "Leave her alone," he said, glaring at the boys.

Nothing else was said. The guys went back to class. They weren't afraid that Hugo would hurt them; it was just that everyone liked Hugo and it was good to be friends with him. He turned and looked at the blue-eyed girl. She nodded to him and gave him a shy little smile. She was several grades younger than he, but he stood up for her, and she'd always respect him for that. Years later, that blue-eyed girl wasn't chunky anymore and the boys were fighting FOR her.

Hugo's mother Irma frequently tells another story that reveals Hugo's strength of character as a young man. Irma was always upset at Hugo because he would take things she gave him, find someone who needed them more, and give them away.

One time, she had worked hard to sew a couple of garments for a friend in the church. When the woman paid Irma, she used part of the money to buy Hugo a new lightweight jacket for the crisp mornings during the rainy season. It was a nice jacket. Not more than a week later, Hugo wore the coat to school, but when he got home he did not have it on. It was pouring down rain, and he was soaked through.

Irma figured he had just forgotten it at school. She asked him, "Hugo, where's your new coat?"

He looked down at the tile floor and mumbled something.

"What? I couldn't hear you."

He spoke up, "I was walking home from school and there was a drunk guy lying on the sidewalk. He looked really cold and it was raining. I took my coat off and laid it on him."

Irma was angry but proud, so she just nodded and said, "Okay." It was just like her son to take something he needed and pass it on to someone who had a greater need.

Hugo tried to keep most of his rebellious ways hidden from his mother, but she knew her son, and there wasn't much he was able to hide. She prayed for him daily, but he never came to her because he thought she wouldn't understand, and because she seemed to have her own problems with her marriage. No one in the family talked openly about what was going on.

Hugo did try to connect with his sisters as much as possible. Though he felt closer to Cesia because they had mutual tendencies toward rebellion, he loved to borrow a video game console and play with Febe for hours on end. They might stay in their pajamas and spend an entire Saturday trying to conquer Super Mario Brothers! She always appeared to be the more reserved one out of the three siblings, but in reality Febe is the funniest and craziest one.

Though Hugo tried to hide his rebellious actions from his mother and thought he was doing a good job, he knew that he was not hiding from his sisters. Cesia was now working, but she heard rumors from her friends and kept close tabs on what he was doing. Cesia had experienced the consequences of her own rebellion, and so she tried to reach out to her brother in a letter on his 16th birthday, which she gave to him along with a handsome shirt.

March 4, 1996
Hugo:
    I hope that this letter will be more than wishes and words, that every time you are tempted to do something wrong you may remember God above everything!!! God loves you and He has a purpose for your life. I was your age, and maybe I did everything you have done so far, or even more. But trust me, Hugo, I regret it now, and I thank God for allowing me to see the painful situation I was living.
    Don't wait to live and taste all the "good things" the world offers to change your relationship with God; do it now, later there will be too many wounds and consequences.
    Now I understand why our dad says that you are not given anything because you deserve it, but because you are loved.
    You have a big potential and intelligence; try to do something positive with it. Be smart and open your eyes. The world is not as you have been told (neither are the girls).
    I hope that you take good care of this shirt, so one day you may hang it in your home's closet after a good and Christian wife has washed and ironed it; that you, your wife and your children have so many blessings and prosperity from God that this is your cheapest shirt. Value the few things that you have because this is what we can give you. Study, because this is the way to be somebody in life and light in the world.

Have a happy birthday,
Cesia

Cesia was now working at an office, and a lawyer named Tito came from Argentina to visit. They interacted at the office and really hit it off. After several months, Tito asked Hugo Sr. for permission to marry Cesia. Hugo Sr. did not think it was a wise match and refused.

Tito was 20 years older than Cesia, divorced, and had two older kids. Since they could not get married, he offered to buy Cesia an apartment and come and visit her often. Cesia declined and said she would come to Argentina with him. Tito agreed, and soon Cesia moved to La Plata, Argentina.

It was then she found out the powerful position that Tito held in La Plata. Not only was he a federal judge, but his family name and lineage were also very prominent. His father was once the president of the local soccer club, Club de Gimnasia y Esgrima La Plata (otherwise known as *El Lobo* – The Wolf). In Argentina soccer is everything, so that link was an extremely powerful influence for Tito.

Tito was the kind of man that people either loved or hated. Most who knew him in a personal way loved him, and those who knew him as political or athletic opposition hated him. Tito also held the only position that he was allowed to as a federal judge, a university professor. He taught at Universidad Nacional de Lomas en La Plata.

Cesia gave Tito a new lease on life. They had fun together, traveled, and had many adventures. Cesia restored to Tito a part of himself that he had lost in his previous marriage and subsequent divorce: laughter. Cesia's classic move was to hide from Tito every morning while he was in the shower, then jump out at him and scare him. He'd jump and then say, "How is it that you manage to scare me every morning? I know that you are you going to jump out somewhere, but I'm always surprised anyway. You're crazy!"

Tito's friends and family loved Cesia and constantly told her, "Thank you, thank you for bringing the real Tito back to us."

After Cesia left, her family's house became lonely. Hugo had moved into the extra bedroom that had been added on top of the kitchen. He spent a lot of time alone up there. The only bad thing about living in the upper bedroom was that he had to use the bathroom that was outside on the patio. He hated to use it at night, because he could see the cockroaches scatter when he turned on the light. And if there was no electricity, he would never attempt the journey except in an emergency.

For some reason, whenever he brushed his teeth he imagined that a cockroach was in the faucet, and his gag reflex would engage when he'd be rinsing out his mouth. He already had a strong gag reflex, and the thought of a cockroach made it much worse.

His dog, Chato, kept him company most of the time, which was good because even Febe was out more and more with her boyfriend, Carlos. Carlos's family and the Liborios were good friends, and they had always done almost everything together. Miguel and Mercedes would bring Roger, Carlos, and Roberto on camping trips in their old beat-up truck, and Hugo Sr. and Irma would bring Cesia, Febe, and Hugo. The kids had all grown up together.

Carlos, like Hugo, did not walk with the Lord during his high school days. He loved cars, especially race cars, and was also involved in the lifestyle that accompanied late night races. But once Carlos started to look at Febe as more than a friend, he realized he'd have to get his spiritual life together to win her heart. He knew Febe would not be fooled by a fake religious act, and he began to genuinely seek God. It was for Febe, but also because he knew he was wrong and needed forgiveness for his sins.

Hugo's own dating record had been long and confusing, about twenty relationships by this point. At this time in El Salvador, you couldn't just ask a girl who was a friend to the movies. She had to be your girlfriend to go out on dates.

Hugo was never one to just sit at home, so he frequently asked a girl to be his girlfriend, just so he could be out and about doing something with someone. There were also pressures from his friends' parties, alcohol, and drugs. Most of his relationships with would last about a month, and then he would break it off. Nothing ever felt right. Somehow he knew that what he was doing was wrong, but his church never taught teens how to deal with real issues. They would just say, "Don't do it!"

As Hugo finished high school, he was not having much fun, and he was partying so much that most days he didn't remember what went on the night before. His life felt so empty. He felt something in his heart, but wasn't ready to acknowledge it yet. For his graduation, he chose to go party with friends instead of attend the ceremony. He was involved in the same activities as always, but he started to want something more. He wasn't sure what, so he kept an eye out for something different to spark his attention.

He never expected to find that spark at church, but there it was on the wall, a flyer saying that the church was going to host a missions seminar for six weeks. Traveling was something that Hugo had always been interested in, especially after Cesia had paid for him to come to Argentina as a graduation gift. He spent three months eating dulce de leche and smoking a pack a day, because practically everyone in Argentina smokes, but he also saw a lot of the country with Tito and Cesia. This experience, combined with his interest in the missions seminar, began to cause a stirring in his heart.

One night, the burning within him was so strong that he left the party he was attending. In the dark night he cried out, "God, either change my life or let me sin in peace!" He knew he had accepted Christ as a young boy and that the Holy Spirit was strongly convicting him of sin.

From the moment of that honest prayer by Hugo, God was faithful to bring change. The missions seminar was the beginning of the reconstruction of Hugo's life. He stopped hanging out with the worst of his friends and ended relationships that were bad for him. The greatest turning point came near the end of the seminar. Soon he'd be signing up for a practicum in a different country.

The missions director preached one night about giving up one's life and committing it for God to use on the mission field. Hugo felt that burning in his heart again, only this time it was not about sin. He knew that God wanted him to be a full-time missionary someday. He paused for a moment to be sure this was for real. His feet seemed to move almost before he had made up his mind. He walked forward and committed to be a career missionary on the foreign mission field.

The next week, the students in his class were given options for their outreach experience. Mexico and Peru were the main options, but the cost for these trips was more than what some of the students could afford, including Hugo.

A third option was found: the *Caribbean Mercy Ship*, which was in port in El Salvador. This option definitely appealed to Hugo, not only because he could afford it, but also because he had visited a ship called *Logos* once and loved it. *Logos* was a library ship that gave tours and taught people about the most important book, the Bible. The *Caribbean Mercy* was a medical ship, but Hugo and the others were told that they would work general crew jobs. Hugo wasn't sure what that meant, but he knew he was excited for this chance to do missions work.

The night before he was to travel, Hugo packed his bag for the five-hour drive to La Union, where the *Caribbean Mercy Ship* was docked. He and nine others would spend a week there serving as missionaries. Hugo thought and prayed as he packed his clothes. "Lord, please help me. I want to change, to serve you, but it is so hard. Please use this trip to change my life. Use my life to glorify Your name unto the nations." As he drifted off to sleep, he wondered if God would use the ship to drastically change his life. Anticipation to see God's will done almost kept him awake, but in the end sleep came.

Hugo with his mother, Irma Coralia

Hugo acquired his love for music from his father, Hugo Sr.

Febe, her husband Carlos, Cesia, Irma, and Hugo

Hugo's high school basketball team. He's the skinny guy with glasses in the middle back

Hugo and his beloved dog, Chato

Hugo, Irma, Cesia, Febe, Hugo Sr.

Please visit my website, www.my-onceuponatime.com/, to see more pictures and videos from each chapter.

Chapter Three

The Wrong One
2000

El Salvador

Two months before Hugo's Mercy Ship moment, I had mine. Apparently, Mercy Ships still had my application from a year before when I tried to go to Korea with them, and that is why they called to see if I would aid them during their outreach in El Salvador.

God had all the pieces in place, and within a week I was ready to fly to San Salvador, El Salvador. I was so excited to get to the ship and catch up with my friend Kristy, who was still working there. A driver picked me up at the airport, along with two others who would be joining the ship. During the five-hour van ride to La Union, El Salvador, I got to know the other two people quite well. One of them, Lori Beth, would end up being my closest friend during my time on the ship—and a forever friend as well.

La Union was where the ship would be docked during Mercy Ship's three-month medical outreach. I wrote in my journal as soon as I got there.

2/27/00

Wow! My first day on the ship! It was awesome! I love the people so much, and the environment is inviting. The captain helped lead the worship this morning at church; and this guy read this awesome story about grace! Kristy and I have been catching up a lot, and I love to see how she has grown up in Christ! I pray for the same change in my life. I feel God already tilling my heart for new growth! Kristy is teaching me so much! She has gone through many things these past months, and God is showing himself to her in so many ways. I want that light of Christ to flow out of me, too! I ache for that hand of God to touch me and change my passion towards Him alone. I hurt for the hard days to come, but gladly welcome them if it is what it takes to feel God in a new light, to feel that unfailing, unconditional love. And for me to learn to return that love in a real, radical way. I praise God for all He has done already, just getting me here. But, I also thank Him for the changes that are coming. I love God so much!

I could see Nicaragua, plus an island that is part of Honduras, plus El Salvador from my porthole. Three countries in one beautiful view!

Soon, one of the crew members gave me a two-hour tour and trained me to work in the galley. My job was to make all of the sandwiches for the crew who would be out during lunch the next day. Then I cleaned out the coolers and washed them down. I also cooked a little during the day and would be in charge of organizing the storage room below. I had to defrost foods the day before they were used and make sure the right supplies were brought up from storage.

I didn't have to start work until 1 p.m., but often I would be working until 11 p.m. finishing up the lunches. I'd write notes and draw smiley faces on the lids of the individual gelatin and pudding cups for the teams. I hoped this would encourage the team members, but mostly I wanted to spruce up the donated urine cups I was using.

Now, about that "Once Upon a Time…" Sadly, in real life a "once upon a time" often has a false start.

As I wrote this book, I prayed a lot about whether to include this part of my story, and I concluded two things. One, the grace of God can still be seen in the story, so it is worth including; and two, it may help someone else to be patient while God writes his or her love story.

So even though this next story is about a relationship, it was not true love, because it was not from God. I pray others may learn from my mistakes. Someone once told me, "Sometimes Satan sends his best first to tempt you away from waiting for God's best." I almost fell for Satan's trick and missed out on God's best for my life.

I met the guy I will call "Adam" the first day I got to the ship. Kristy and I were hanging out with the night watchman on the aft deck, and Adam came and joined us. He was a good-looking Latino man who also spoke English well. We talked and laughed and had a good time.

The next day, I was eating lunch with Kristy's friend Reuben, a nurse named Rose from New Mexico, and a Swedish lawyer. Joining us was a little national named Moses. He would come on the ship to hang out and talk to people. Moses was about 6 years old; he ate a lot of food for such a little guy. Mercy Ships had built a house for his family the previous year. Many of the crew knew him and his family, and his sister worked on the ship during the day.

After everyone left, I was sitting at the table alone, and Adam sat down across from me. He was nice to talk to, and I visited with him for quite some time. Adam told me that he had only one semester of credits left to graduate from college, but he had decided to pursue mission work instead. Completing his education was not as important as what he was doing now.

He asked me if I had a boyfriend. I didn't think that he liked me, but it was hard to tell because he was so nice. I think I enjoyed the attention, the good conversation, and the fact that he wanted to go into full-time missions. I liked that we could talk about mature subjects, but I didn't think he was not tall enough for me. I did think that he would become a great friend and that he could help me with my Spanish.

Later in the evening, I saw my new nurse friend, Rose, who told me about a lady who had had eye surgery just that day. Many years ago, a man came into this woman's home, killed her husband, and attacked her with a machete. She lost her hand in that attack. She had 15 kids at the time, and the youngest was 14 months old. The oldest daughter took care of her siblings while her mother was in the hospital. Four months later, the oldest girl was hit by a bus and killed. Still the woman rejoiced. She said, "God helps me not to be bitter." What an amazing woman!

The next morning, I went to the dockside unit to see the eye patches being removed. The woman who had lost her hand could now see again. She was so thrilled and smiled so much. She grabbed the nurse's face and exclaimed in Spanish, "Yes, I can see your pretty face!"

Later that day, I was in the kitchen trying to finish my sandwich-making a little early when Adam came in to get a bandage. He waited outside on the deck, and I brought him one. We saw Eric and some guys in the pool, so I asked him if he wanted to go swimming. We stayed there for a long time and talked. Another guy was there, too, and I was so relieved it was not just the two of us.

In the morning, I volunteered at the optical clinic. It was my day off, but I wanted to go and see what the clinic was like. Another girl, Jamie, and I prayed with one woman who wanted to accept Christ. We talked to her for a long time, and it was wonderful. We gave her a Bible.

When I came back, I immediately saw Adam in the dining room. I didn't want to sit down and start talking with him, so I left and changed out of the scrubs I wore in the optical clinic. When I came back, I brought my notebook. He saw me and pointed to a chair near him. We chatted, and I wrote a few things while he watched TV. Then he turned off the TV, and we talked. I told him everything I was learning in Spanish and showed him my notebook of words.

He added a few more and asked me, "How much do you want to learn Spanish?"

"I want it so, so much," I said.

So he took me under his wing. He was a good teacher and very patient. For two hours or more after supper each evening, he taught me Spanish. He made me speak only in Spanish and reviewed grammar with me. It was so much fun, and I learned so much. He gave me great confidence in myself.

We also began to talk about life. We were both in the same "I have no idea" place in our lives. He told me that he had quit school just before graduating because he wanted to show people that he would be successful in missions not because of a degree, but because God used him. He knew that diploma was for his own glory and not God's. We talked, walked, and played cards until midnight. I still didn't know what to think about all of this.

The next day, Adam and I rode in the back of a truck with some other people to San Miguel to shop. In the stores, and even in the bank, Adam taught me Spanish. He told me which people to listen to and learn from.

"What does the bank teller say when she wants the next person in line? What do the sales ladies ask you when you come in the store? Listening to the world around you is the best way to expand your language skills. Pay attention and learn."

Adam would also translate songs that we heard in stores. When we got back from San Miguel, I went with Kristy to see her discipleship school dedicate a mural they had painted in town. The mural was about spiritual blindness. Thirty people raised their hands to indicate they wanted to receive Christ at the dedication service. It was awesome!

After we got back, I looked all over for Adam, but could not find him. He had asked me to watch a movie with him, so I wanted to find him, but since I couldn't, I went to bed. At 12:45 a.m., the phone rang. It was Adam. My heart skipped a beat. We only talked for about a minute because he knew he had awakened me.

He said, "I just wanted to say `hi' and ask where you went."

I told him, "I went to the dedication with Kristy."

"Okay, I'll let you sleep. Good night."

"Night." We hung up, but sleep did not come to me for a while, because I was thinking and praying about Adam.

Church that Sunday was very good. I was not used to the passionate style of the worship service, but I felt God use it to speak to me.

After lunch, Adam and I were sitting on the deck when we were invited to go to an island. I was really excited to go. A Puerto Rican named Jarot would be driving the speedboat. My friend Lori Beth also would be going, as well as two other shipmates, Kristen and James.

The island had an infamous crocodile. The people we met there said it was gone, so we fearlessly swam in the water. The island had a cove to hang out in. The beach had soft, dark sand, and the waves, according to James, were "wicked." We even had the opportunity to water ski.

I felt as if I were in a movie. Several of us were stung by *"chichicastas,"* little jellyfish that leave painful red marks on our skin. That was no fun.

Adam and I continued to see each other and enjoyed our friendship. One night, after attending a Bible study with Kristy, I found Adam out on the dock with the ship's younger crowd. People were casually playing guitar, and some were singing.

Adam was there playing a game with a girl. I was not jealous, but he immediately asked me to play when I got there. I played a little, and then I decided to go near the railing by the water and be with God for a while. It was awesome to hear the waves and talk to God. I prayed and gave my relationship with Adam to God that night. I told Him, "Work it out if you want it to be, but I will not take over." I earnestly wanted God to be in control, so that I would know the relationship was from Him.

A couple of days later, as we sat on the dock, Adam confessed to me, "I like you a lot, and I love being with you all the time. Sometimes I get close to 'the line' with you, and I don't want to do that. I want to kiss you sometimes, but I know that is not appropriate."

He was so honest with me, and I told him, "We have to keep each other account-able so we will not step across the line. Because we do not understand how the other person thinks, we have to tell each other what is good or bad to do."

He agreed. By now, it was about 1 in the morning, and he told me to stand quickly and go toward the ship, because he was thinking about my lips. It took everything within me to stand and walk. As I moved toward the ship, I thought about all that had just taken place. I was dizzy at the thought of a boy liking me.

Despite our discussion about "the line," the very next night, while we sat on the dock, I rested my head on Adam's knees, and he kissed my neck. We did not stay that way for long, and he walked me back to the ship. After that, I read my Bible a lot to try to get closer to God. I learned a number of small things that eventually added up to big lessons.

I was trying not to get ahead of myself. I decided to ask Caleb and Sophie about the whole thing, just so that I could be accountable to someone. They counseled me, "Don't start a physical relationship. Be best friends and be open and honest. That way, whether it works out or not, you will still get a great friend out of it."

I felt really convicted to talk to Adam and tell him what I wanted, but I also didn't want to be the one to bring it up. I prayed that God would just take care of it, and that I would not have to be in control of this area. God answered my prayers. Adam and I found a place to talk that was free of distractions, and he brought up all the things I wanted to talk about.

He told me, "I really value our friendship. You are really special to me, because I have told you more about myself than anyone else in my life. I just want to get to know you and be best friends."

I was excited because that was my prayer from earlier in the day.

Then Adam said, "Let's pray before we talk anymore." He prayed in Spanish, because he said it was easier for him. He prayed for understanding for both of us, and that we would know God's will. Then we talked about the incident the night before, and how it should not have happened. He apologized to me.

I told him, "I will forgive you if you forgive me for tempting you and not saying no." We both agreed that we had started out the wrong foot, and that we would begin again from square one: God!

He said, "No matter what, we have to find God's will for our lives and not be influenced by the other person."

I agreed. I would be sad to lose Adam, but if God wanted me to do something that did not include Adam, then that was okay. I was learning to just give it to God and trust Him. I felt that God would tell Adam what to do with our relationship, and that I didn't have to worry. I only needed to share my love for Christ with him and encourage him. Nothing more. No fretting about whether he liked me or not. No thinking about the future. No action beyond being a friend. Adam needed to know God's will for his life, and I needed to know God's will for mine.

Friends on the ship invited me to go to Las Tunas for the day, stay overnight, and come back the next afternoon. I eagerly agreed, because I knew it would be fun, and I needed to get my mind off work. I quickly pulled stuff that the crew needed from the refrigerator and packed my backpack for the day.

The beach was refreshing. I spent the day collecting shells, lying on the sand getting sun, and sleeping in the shade in a hammock. Oh, the sacrificial life of a missionary!

The little place where we stayed was on the water, which flowed under the wood planks during high tide. I relaxed, listening to the waves and reading and writing. Adam didn't cross my mind as much as I thought he would. I simply focused on God and finding God's plan for my life. This meant taking Adam out of the equation and looking more deeply for God's will.

While traveling to Las Tunas on the bus, I looked at the people of El Salvador and witnessed how needy they were. I thought of my home, my parents, and my friends. I thought of my love for God and His love for me.

In all my thinking, I felt peace about full-time mission work. I no longer felt deeply connected with home and what that was. I longed only for heaven as my home. I no longer cared what people thought or about the struggles I would have, as long as I could serve God. I wanted to please God completely by my actions and words, and by my absolute trust and faith in him.

I felt courage to stand and fight, to go to the ends of the earth so that every last person could hear about God's love. With or without anyone else, I would serve God in missions work to the end of my days. I didn't know the how or when, but I trusted God to tell me in His perfect timing.

My friends and I slept in the hammocks overnight and woke up at about 5:30 in the morning. Three of us left to go back to the ship, leaving three others to return later. We walked to the bus stop and waited for about 45 minutes for the bus to come. No bus. Finally, a man came up to us, and from what I could make out in Spanish, he told us that the bus did not run that day. But that didn't make sense; the bus did not run on Sunday? Why not? I thought I'd misunderstood. We kept waiting. A bus went by with lots of people on it waving flags, but they did not stop for us. I was really confused. What could we do? There were no cell phones; we'd just have to figure out a plan to get back.

I sat down on a rock and asked God to get us home safely. I didn't want to go with just any person who came along; my Spanish was not good enough to find a reliable person. I asked God to send us someone whom we knew and who spoke English. Someone who knew what was going on and could get us home.

A while later, a red truck passed us and turned down another street, then stopped in front of a store. An older man told us that the bus was not coming and that we should ask the guy in the truck for a ride. Somehow, I knew it would be okay. Our other three friends showed up from the beach and arrived just in time to join us in our plan to get home. We walked down the street to the truck.

The driver came to the doorway of the store and one of my friends said, "Hey man, what are you doing here?"

I looked at the Latino guy, and then at my friend, and said, "You know this guy?"

"Yeah!" he said excitedly. "His name is Angel, and he translates for the ship sometimes."

I just about lost it! God had answered my prayer. I rode in the cab on the way back and told Angel about my prayer.

He told me in perfect English, "That is really awesome, because I usually do not go to town at this time. It's usually earlier!" Angel also told me that he had lived in the United States for high school and college, and that is why his English was so good. He was even more than what I had asked God for.

Angel also explained why the buses were not stopping for people on this day. "Today is an election day for the legislature in El Salvador. The buses only run to and from the voting booths. Each bus has a flag for the party it represents." I was so relieved that God had provided Angel to give us a ride back, because those buses never would have stopped for us.

I had been thinking about what the next step in my missionary training should be. If I wanted to work with Mercy Ships long-term, I needed to attend a Discipleship Training School (DTS). This also seemed like a good way to get more of the Bible teaching I craved.

To pray through this decision, I decided to fast on bread and water for the next three days. I would have just two pieces of bread per meal and lots of water. I wanted to eat bread, read and study the Bible so that I could get my spiritual and physical bread at the same time. I wanted to get as close as I could to God so that when He spoke, I would know His voice. Getting into His Word would be the best way.

During supper on one of my fasting days, I retreated to my room with two pieces of bread and an egg roll. I had decided that as long as I was with God, He wouldn't mind an egg roll. There in my room, I sang, prayed, and listened. I told God that if I was supposed to attend a DTS, He needed to tell me where I should go for it.

I also felt God telling me again not to press any issue with Adam, but rather to lie low and let Him work it out, especially since it was His will for my life that hung in the balance. I didn't want to upset Adam's or my own life with my eagerness to have a relationship. I knew I needed to let go and let God. He would work it out if it was meant to be, and if not, He had something greater in store for both of us. It was so reassuring to know God had it under control.

I ended my fast on Friday. On Sunday during Communion at church, I was so moved by the Holy Spirit that I stayed in my chair for ten minutes after the service was over. Something very basic, yet profound, had attached itself to my heart:

If Christ died to give me an amazing life and eternity with God, the least I could do was give Him my all, everything that was in me to serve Him, the rest of my life. Through the worst of times, He would provide the endurance that I needed. He died for me. Where would I be without that? I had to give my all back to him, no matter what it took. I knew it wouldn't be pretty. I might be hated, persecuted, penniless, homeless, friendless. I didn't care, as long as I could know God and His will. I would rejoice and count it all a blessing that I could suffer for Christ.

As I took my Communion that Sunday at church, I thought, "This is Your body, broken for me, and because You did that, I will serve You the rest of my life. This is Your blood that was shed for me, and because You did that, I will serve You the rest of my life, with my whole heart." I prayed that God would lead me and that I would clearly see His guidance, that He would use me in ways I never imagined, simply because I was available to Him.

At the end of those ten minutes, after sitting in my seat and dwelling on God and listening to Him, I came to a dramatic conclusion.

I'd always been afraid of promising God that I would be willing to die for Him. Sitting there thinking about how He died for me, I finally realized it wasn't my life anyway. I was Christ's to use as He pleased. He would know how best to use my life. If that meant dying so that one more person could come to Christ, then that was how I wanted God to use me. I knew I had no control over my own death anyway. If God wanted to use my death in that way, I would let Him, and I would be proud and honored.

I wanted God to fill every inch of my body, to have His Spirit flowing through me and out of me so that all could see Him in me. Tears filled my eyes along with an intense passion and desire to follow the Lord, but I felt so unworthy to be His servant.

Things with Adam continued to be exciting. Once, after I helped him with a project, he told me, "Thanks, you are a Proverbs 31 woman!"

What a compliment! Adam showered me with many compliments like this one. I thought he really liked me. On April 1 (April Fool's Day), I experienced my first real kiss. When it was over, we both realized that we could not do it again for a long time, and that we should concentrate on getting to know each other better.

The next day, however, it seemed like he did not even want to sit by me. I played the game too and ignored him all morning to show him I was mad. When I went upstairs for personal devotions time, he followed me. I told him I did not want to talk and I needed to cool down. I angrily flipped through the pages in my Bible and, frustrated, stopped in Acts 2.

The beginning reads, "I saw the Lord always before me. Because He is at my right hand, I will not be shaken." I loved this first part about not being shaken. I thought that verse was enough, but when I flipped to Psalms, I found the same verse.

David wrote it in Psalms, and then it was repeated in Acts. I was excited that I found both times that verse was written in the Bible. I knew I needed to keep God first, so that I would not be shaken.

Adam and I had several other talks about our friendship/relationship and other misunderstandings. I thought he was ignoring me and trying to make me jealous.

So I started avoiding him to see what he would do. It only got worse, and it hurt me so much.

I asked Jose Luis, the gangway guard who was a good friend, what I should do. He told me to be honest with Adam and talk to him right away. I knew that, but hearing it from a friend was reassuring.

I caught Adam on my way to a soccer game. It was the only moment he would give me, because he was avoiding me and hanging out with another girl who had recently come to the ship. We walked up to the boat deck and didn't even sit down.

I quickly got to the point. "Adam, what am I to you?"

He looked at me, knowing what I meant. "Sarah, you are just like any other girl on the ship to me."

"Okay. That's all I needed to hear."

"I'm sorry if I led you on to think that it was more than that."

It didn't make sense that his intentions and my interpretation could be so different all this time. But I understood his intentions now.

I left to catch a ride to the soccer game in Conchagua. I sat in the front so I could think. I was wounded, but surprisingly not as hurt as I thought I would be. Adam's honesty was a relief. I imagined I would be really hurt and upset, but I wasn't. Now we both knew we were just friends, and I wouldn't have to question my actions or his. It would be so much easier to actually be his friend. I learned so much from what happened. It would not happen again. I would not be so easy to convince if there was a next time.

Later Adam told me, "You have to guard your heart from me and other guys."

I thought, "Trust me, I will!"

Little did I know that it wouldn't be long before I would meet the real Prince Charming God had for me, Hugo Liborio.

Please visit my website, www.my-onceuponatime.com/, to see pictures and videos from each chapter.

Chapter Four

The Prince and Princess Meet
2000

El Salvador

If you asked Hugo how we met, he'd start with something like, "Well, I was walking up the gangway, and Sarah saw me, and she heard trumpets and saw doves and angels flying, and she fell in love with me that very moment!"

He'd always be looking at me to see if I were going to cut him off and set the record straight, or punch him playfully in the arm. He was always trying to convince people how I fell in love with him at first sight.

But he also loved to tell the long version of our love story to anyone who would sit long enough to listen. I was more of a pro at the quick, highlighted version of our meeting. The story picks up right as Hugo and the team from his missions seminar joined the *Mercy Ship* in La Union.

Sarah's Point of View – "The tall Latino"
A group of Latinos was touring the ship. I quickly scanned the group when they first arrived and noticed a tall guy. Since I am six feet tall, if a guy was not tall, I was not interested. I watched a movie with them that first night, but the tall guy was behind me and I did not get to check him out properly. The next day, I decided to take a second peek.

As I sat next to my friend Laura, the Salvadorians entered the living room. This time I really took a good look. He was so cute. I leaned over to Laura and whispered into her ear, "I am going to get to know that guy." I smiled to myself as he walked by, because he was wearing overalls with one strap unhooked. I thought he looked like a Latino New Kid on the Block.

That same night, Adam and I had our "break-up" conversation, and I went to Conchagua to play soccer. By the time we arrived for the game, I felt that I was completely over Adam. I did not forgive him until a month later when God convicted me of a bitter heart, but in that moment I instantly had no more feelings for him, which also confirmed in my heart that our relationship was not from God.

The first half of the soccer game was a blur, because I was still caught up in my own thoughts. I was excited to be done with the mess that Adam had caused in my life. Lori Beth and I were the founders and leaders of the ship's sports evangelism team at this time, but we decided to leave the game and go to our favorite *pupusaría* across the street from the court. A *pupusa* is a traditional Salvadoran food made of a thick corn tortilla.

The two most common *pupusas* are the *pupusa de queso* (cheese) and the more popular with mixed ingredients such as *queso*, *frijoles* (beans), and *chicharrón* (pulled pork, not to be confused with fried pork rind). *Pupusas* are typically served with *curtido* (lightly fermented cabbage slaw with red chilies and vinegar) and watery tomato salsa and are traditionally eaten by hand.

The restaurant was outside, so we could watch the players start the second half of the soccer game from where we were. Our friend Oscar had already shared the gospel, so our primary responsibilities were already taken care of.

Soon, the group I had spied earlier on the ship came our way. When we left the ship, I had not noticed if the tall guy had come, but now he was walking toward us in the group. They all sat with us because a few wanted to practice their English, and Lori Beth and I wanted to practice our Spanish. I talked with everyone as best I could with my developing Spanish.

At that point, I knew at least the common phrases by heart, but I was too embarrassed to talk to the tall guy. He seemed really popular in his group, and I was never one to catch the attention of popular guys, so I believed that if I did talk to him, he'd be stand-offish.

"What's your name?" Suddenly, I looked up and the tall guy was looking right at me. He was speaking to me in Spanish. No one else was in our conversation; he had broken from the group conversation to ask me a direct question. I swallowed my bite of pupusa.

"Sarah," I managed to say casually, even though my heart was beating so fast I was sure my voice would falter.

"Hola, Sarah. I'm Hugo. Nice to meet you," Hugo continued in Spanish. "How old are you?"

"Nineteen." I was too nervous to even reciprocate the question, but it didn't matter. I knew he had one last question. You see, at this age, Latino men almost always ask three important questions when they meet a woman. Hugo had already asked me the first two, and I was sweating it out for the third.

"Do you have a boyfriend?" Hugo asked, looking at me with a very beautiful but very direct gaze.

"No," I said, trying to stay as relaxed as possible. I turned back to the group conversation, ready for someone else to be in the hot seat.

Soon we went back to watch the end of the soccer game. Lori Beth had to leave, so I had no one to sit with. Hugo noticed I was sitting alone. He called, "Sarah," and then motioned to an empty area next to him.

"Oh, I'm fine, thank you," I said, waving him off. I very much wanted to go, but I wasn't willing to let my guard down again. Hugo knew he didn't have the English to beg properly, and I wouldn't understand his Spanish well enough, so he kept motioning with his hands. Finally, I shrugged my shoulders, stood up, and walked towards the space next to him.

A girl who had not seen what was going on approached quickly from behind Hugo and claimed the empty space right as I got there. He looked at me apologetically. I shrugged again and sat down in front of him. I felt silly and was mad at myself for being so girly.

I fumed through the final minutes of the game, and then made my way to the van as quickly as I could. By the time we entered the port, I had cooled off on the ride back and had decided that I needed to stick with this group, because I could learn a lot of Spanish from them.

Hugo disappeared once we got to the ship, but I stayed with the group and we started a game of Uno. I was having fun playing with them, and some of the team members who spoke English helped me follow the conversation.

Hugo came back with his friend Alex, and they joined in the game. They made it even more fun, because they were so animated pretending to take the game so seriously. Hugo laughed the loudest and most mischievously when any crucial card was laid during the game. It was hilarious, and all of us playing followed suit. We all laughed aloud with him at each twist in cards. We were being so loud that someone asked us to go play outside on the boat deck.

The group decided to just go for a walk down the dock. We made our way to the end of the dock, where we sat down to chat. One of the girls, Blanca, translated the main ideas for me.

Hugo was giving a backrub to one of the girls. She told me, "Sarah, you should have Hugo give you a backrub. He's really good at it."

I started to decline, partly because I had a rule about guys giving backrubs to girls, but mostly because I thought he, the popular guy, would not want to give me, a normal girl, that kind of attention.

But Hugo cut me off and said, "Yeah, here, move over this way … sit here." Everyone was already making room for me, and I really wanted a backrub, so I did not say anything more and moved to sit in front of him. He massaged my shoulders for a while as everyone else was visiting.

I heard Hugo's voice rise above everyone else's and announce, "Let's tell jokes. I'm going to go first." I moved next to Blanca so she could translate for me again.

"Once there was a son, and he asked his father for a gift. The father gave his son a little red marble.

"'What is the little red marble for, Dad?' asked the son.

"'I'll tell you when you're older,' the father replied."

This went on for fifteen minutes, as Blanca painstakingly translated the entire joke for me into English. Hugo kept stopping to look at me and ask, "You understand?" I would nod yes.

The son kept asking his dad the significance of the little red marble, and the dad would always tell him, "I'll tell you when you're older." For birthdays, Christmases, for graduation from high school and college, and even for his wedding, instead of a gift, the son wanted to know what the little red marble was for. The dad said each time, "I'll tell you when you're older."

Finally, the dad was on his death bed, and the son, fearing his dad would pass at any moment, begged his father, "Dad, please tell me what the little red marble means."

Hugo had been telling the longer version to this joke, and we were all desperate to get to the end. Hugo finally got to the punch line. His demeanor became serious, and he said, "The dad motioned for the son to move in closer. The dad leaned close to the son's ear. 'The little red marble ... it's for ... for ...'" Hugo paused dramatically. "And then he died. The end."

"Whhaattt?" we all said in unison, groaning. "That was the end of the joke?" Everyone was punching him, half playfully, half angrily. Hugo laughed, trying to deflect the punches, but failing because he was laughing so hard. I guess the joke was on all of us listeners.

Hugo's Point of View- "The tall Americana"

I was in the van on the way to La Union. It was about a five-hour drive from my neighborhood, La Colina. I was doing the practicum part of a mission school that I had just finished with some friends at my church. The church discovered there was a ship in El Salvador, called *Caribbean Mercy Ship*, where we could go and help for one week.

I was very excited because, ever since I saw *Logos* when I was younger, I had loved ships and always thought it would be cool to work on one. I was so excited to work on the deck department, as they told me I would be. I was fiddling with my favorite lighter in my pocket when I realized an unsettling fact. Since we had left, everyone had already called and checked in with their significant others.

"You all are crazy!" I said, pretty loudly, so they could all hear.

"What are you talking about?" My close friend, Alex, was the one who spoke, but the eyes looking at me all said the same thing.

I explained, "We have not even been on the van for two hours. We are going on a missions trip, and you all are distracted with your girlfriends or boyfriends."

Alex came back with the group's response, "You just say that because you don't have a girlfriend right now."

"Yeah, Hugo," said Blanca, "How come you don't have a girlfriend right now?"

I paused, not sure how much information to give to the group, but I went ahead and confessed, "I have been hurt a lot. I don't want to date anymore until I find a girl that is right for me."

A girl they called "Coca," who loved to gossip, spoke up, "What kind of girl are you looking for?"

"Well, first of all, she needs to love God more than anything. Second, I want someone who loves missions. But, I also want a girl who is my height or taller. That way I can play basketball with her and it will be a challenge!"

The van erupted into laughter. They all knew it was nearly impossible to find a tall girl in Central America. I was 6'2" and taller than everyone in my family and most people I knew. Salvadorians are not known for their height, but apparently I had a tall grandfather on my dad's side. I ignored their laughter, knowing God would provide the right woman when His timing was right. I slumped down in my seat, stuck my hand back in my pocket, and fingered my lighter again.

Once we made it to the dock in La Union, we boarded the ship, and they told us to go upstairs and eat right away. We stood in a long line waiting to get food off the buffet. While Alex and I chatted, he elbowed me in the ribs.

"What?" I looked at him, rubbing my side.

"Look," he said in a low voice. Alex and I had a secret way to look without be noticed. I gave a quick glance and, at the same time, heard Alex say, "She's tall."

I tried to look away, but my eyes were not obeying the secret glance rule. She was tall and beautiful. Her hair was so cool, the way it spiraled down her shoulders. She was behind the counter, so I figured she must work in the pantry or the galley. I tried to regain my composure and force my eyes to obey, because it was my turn in line and I was sure she would never talk to me if I didn't stop staring.

"Hola," I said.

"Hi," she said, smiling. I kept moving down the food line, but I was on auto-pilot, mindlessly dishing food onto my plate. It hit me like a ton of bricks: *She does not speak Spanish. I do not speak English.* This was going to be difficult.

The first night on the ship I was watching *Star Wars*, when suddenly I saw a big back in front of my eyes. I thought, "Who is that?"

I didn't see her again until we went to eat pupusas in Conatus. There she was, the tall girl with beautiful eyes and beautiful hair and an amazing smile like no other. I started asking, "Who's that girl? What's her name?"

And they told me her name: Sarah.

We went back to the ship, and I hurried to wake up Alex and tell him about this girl, called Sarah. But at the same time I thought, "No, she couldn't possibly know that I exist."

We tracked down our friends, and there was Sarah again. I was very happy, and I wanted to spend as much time with her as possible. We played Uno, which wasn't that much fun, but then we went for a walk to the wharf. I was very pleased because she was with us, too. But I was so nervous that I couldn't say a word, so I told a joke. I remember thinking, "I hope she liked it," and I believe she did, because she laughed.

That was our first meeting as Hugo remembered it. It's amazing how two people can have such different memories of the same situation.

My story continues the day after the little red marble joke. I had a day off and was in the dining room area spending my quiet time with God and poring over my Spanish books. Alex and Hugo had a morning break from the deck department. They both sat with me as they drank their water.

Hugo asked, "What are you studying there?"

Excited about the verse that I was reading in Jeremiah, I wanted to share it with them. "I'm reading in Jeremiah; let me read you the verse."

I picked up my Spanish Bible to look for the verse, only to realize it was a New Testament and did not include Jeremiah. I tried to explain the verse in Spanish to them on my own, but got really frustrated and gave up. I was really sad about it. Sooner than I wanted, Hugo got up, said something I didn't understand, and left. I tried to talk with Alex, but ended up just reading my Bible again.

Hugo came back to the table, and asked in Spanish, "Can I borrow your pen?"

"Sure," I said. I passed him my pen and kept reading. He sat in the chair in front of me and started writing something. He was wearing those overalls again with one of the straps hanging down. He was so cute.

I asked him, "Can I take your picture?"

"Sure," he said, smiling. He was so nice for a popular guy. I had observed that he smiled at and talked to almost anyone, and everyone else seemed to like him, too.

At that point I excused myself to go to the bathroom. When I got back, Hugo and Alex were gone. I sat down to my books and noticed my pen in the cover of a black Bible. I wondered if Hugo had left it. I thought that I would return the Bible to him later. I opened it to retrieve my pen and noticed my name at the top of the inside cover. Curious, I started to read:

Sarah:
> Espero que Dios te bendiga mucho y prospere tu ministerio y que nunca te canses de estar en sus caminos; te prometo q' orare mucho por tu vida, ministerio, etc. Cuida este lindo libro y espero q' te sirva para aprender español.
> "...no temas ni desmayes, porque Jehová tu Dios estará contigo en donde quiera que vayas."
-Josue1:9
Te Quiere,
Hugo

Sarah:
> I hope that God blesses you a lot and prospers your ministry and that you never tire to be in His ways; I promise you that I will pray a lot for your life, ministry, etc.
> Take care of this beautiful book and I hope that it serves you to be able to learn Spanish.
> ". . . Do not be terrified; do not be discouraged, for the LORD your God will be with you wherever you go."
-Joshua 1:9
In Friendship.
Hugo

I thought, "A guy who would think to give me a Bible must be really amazing." But the next gift he gave me seemed to say something a little different. It was Hugo's last night on the ship, and a large group of us were up on the boat deck dancing salsa and meringue. Hugo was enjoying teaching everyone the steps. Soon he pulled me aside to a deck chair and gave me a small package. I opened it and saw his lighter sitting there. What would I ever do with a lighter? I certainly didn't smoke.

But then Hugo explained, "When I give a gift, I like to give something that is really special to me. This is a limited edition Zippo lighter, and it is one of my favorite earthly possessions. I don't smoke anymore, but I still love to carry my lighter with me."

He took the lighter from me and showed me how he could open the lid simply by striking it against his jeans, and then with one more quick movement the flame was lit. Even though I detested everything about smoking, I had to admit that starting a lighter that way looked really cool.

I didn't let him know that, though. I just laughed and rolled my eyes, trying to keep the mood light. I did say sincerely, in the best Spanish I could manage, "Thank you. It is a beautiful gift. I know it was from your heart."

That week I used every Spanish word I had to get to know Hugo. Hugo knew no English. I had four years of Spanish in high school, and then there was the class I flunked at college. It wasn't much, so we also had to rely upon our friends to translate for us. It was so frustrating. The one person I wanted to talk to most, I couldn't.

The night before Hugo left, we pulled an all-nighter, watching movies in the TV lounge with two other couples. The next morning, when I hugged him goodbye, I could see tears rolling down his face despite his attempt to hide behind sunglasses. I wasn't sure why he was so upset. I was sad to see him leave, but I knew we'd keep in touch. I tend to be very optimistic in these kinds of situations.

A friend of mine from the ship, Rueben, traveled with the Latino group back to the capital. When he returned, he gave me a report. "Sarah, he cried for the first three hours of the trip. His friend, Alex, finally had to talk to him and tell him to snap out of it. I think he is really hung up on you. Here is a note he wrote to you on the way back."

Rueben handed me a folded-up scrap of an envelope. I unwrapped it, figuring it must have been the only paper that Hugo had been able to find to write to me. It said in Spanish:

Sarah.

> Hola: I hope that you are not as sad as I am. You know I didn't think that I had come to care and appreciate you so much, and well, goodbyes are super ugly. But, I am trusting in God that we will see each other again. So, behave "Caperusa!" And know that I am always thinking of you.

"Hasta la vista bebe"
P.S. Write ME!!
Love, Hugo

The next day, Hugo called. This phone call went more or less like all our phone calls would go for the next several months.

"Hola? Sarah?" he said.

"Si, Hola, Hugo. Como estas?"

"Bien, como estas tu?"

"Bien," I responded, while trying to formulate a question in Spanish in my mind at the same time. Nothing.

"Como esta tu trabajo?" he asked. I knew *trabajo* means work, so he must be asking how that's going.

"Bien, y tu?" Using the easy "and you" question helped me throw the same questions back to him.

"Bien. Puedo llamarte mañana?" he asked.

Oh great, I didn't get any of that. Spanish is even more difficult over the phone.

"Que?" (What?) I asked.

"Puedo llamarte mañana?" Did he say it even faster this time?

"Qué?" I asked again, trying to remember if mañana means tomorrow, morning, or tomorrow morning. Eventually, I figured he was asking if he could call me again, so I just said yes.

He slowed his tempo and said, "Voy a llamarte mañana."

"Bueno," I said, but I still wanted to show off the Spanish I did know, so I asked, "A que hora?"

"Como a las dos," he stated.

"A las doce?" I questioned as I pressed my ear to the receiver to hear the answer better.

"No, a las dos," he repeated.

"Okay," I said, my Spanish spent.

"Okay. Bye," Hugo said, using one of the two English words that he knew (the other being hello).

Needless to say, our phone conversations were quite comical. But, Hugo persisted and did call the next day, and every single day after that. He began to learn English and was highly motivated by wanting to speak to me more. My roommate, Erika, was from El Salvador too, but she spoke fluent English. When Hugo would call in the evenings, she would talk with him and tell me what he was saying, and then I would tell her what to say back. It might sound terribly unromantic, but in a way it was very sweet.

I had helped him set up an e-mail account when he was on the ship, so we also wrote e-mails back and forth. He did not have Internet at his house, so he'd either have to walk or take the bus to a nearby business that had a demo computer connected to the Internet. Or sometimes he would use his friend Xiomara's computer at work. Hugo was working as a messenger for a computer company, but Xiomara had a desk job and could check e-mails for him.

My friend Marcos e-mailed me about a Christian band, Petra, that was going to be in the capital of El Salvador. I told him I was interested in going with him and that if he would meet me, I would set it up for us to stay at Hugo's house, so that we didn't have to spend money on housing. He agreed, so I sent a note through Erika to Hugo in the capital.

Secretly, this concert was a way for me to get to the capital and see Hugo again. I really liked him, and I wanted an excuse to hang out with him more. Going to the concert with Marcos and staying at Hugo's house seemed to be the perfect plan. My thought process was that God would either convict me that I was going too far with Hugo or show me a way to continue developing the friendship. Maybe my logic wasn't exactly sound, but I was young and deeply infatuated.

I was able to make arrangements to go to Hugo's house. I would take the public bus with a guy from the ship as my "bodyguard," and he would escort me to Plaza Merliot, where Hugo would meet me. Hugo and I would spend time together, and then I would meet Marcos for the concert that evening. Oscar, a friend from the ship, would be in the capital at a soccer game the following night, so I would head back to the ship with him after another day with Hugo.

As complicated as this plan sounds, I knew I had to make it work. I wanted to go to the concert, but more than anything I wanted to get to know Hugo better.

The night before, my plan ran into a little hiccup. Marcos called and said that he would not be able to go to the concert with me. My "legitimate" reason for going to the capital was now blown.

I asked my female Latina friends if it was still acceptable for me to go to Hugo's house. This was one of my first experiences with Latino culture, which I knew to be conservative, and I did not want to be a stumbling block to anyone. My friends assured me that it would not be a problem if Hugo's mom or one of his sisters was there.

Elizabeth called Hugo for me and explained the situation and my concerns. He assured her that his mom and sister Febe would both be there. I got on the phone at the end of the call and told Hugo that I would come and asked if he would like to go to the concert with me. I could tell he was really excited.

My bodyguard traveled with me to the capital and helped me navigate the bus system to get to Plaza Merliot. My Salvadorian friends were wise to suggest that I not travel alone. El Salvador still suffered from the effects of its civil war, and gang violence was one of those. Plus, it was my first time alone in a foreign country. I was 19, tall, had curly hair, barely spoke Spanish, and basically stuck out like a sore thumb. I was an easy target.

I called Hugo's cell phone from a public phone, and he said, "I'm on my way."

I sat down on a ledge and started to wonder what I was doing. This was not like me. I didn't date anyone in high school or college, and then I met Adam and made a mess of things. Then, on the same day that Adam said, "You're just like every girl on the ship," I met Hugo. And now I was visiting this guy at his home in San Salvador, even though we didn't speak the same language and barely knew each other. I wondered if I was going insane.

But somehow, in my heart it made perfect sense. I had been asking other Christians who knew Hugo better what they thought of him and had gotten a good report. Maybe God was leading me to something amazing.

On the other hand, I hadn't been doing my quiet time regularly. I'd been distracted with the adventures of the ship and boys. I was frustrated with how girly I felt I was being. What if I was just in a rebellious, free-spirited phase?

My mind raced with all my motives and with how crazy it was going to sound to my parents: "Hey Mom and Dad, on my most recent day off I took a five-hour public bus ride to the capital, where I visited a Latino guy I barely know, who doesn't speak any English."

Yeah, that would go over well.

But as crazy as it sounded, I was at peace. I prayed, "God, I don't know why I am doing this crazy thing, but help me, protect me, and guide me."

Some time had passed since I sat down on the ledge. Out of the corner of my eye, I saw Hugo playfully slide up and bump into me. We hugged, and my heart nearly fell on the floor when I smelled the familiar scent of his cologne.

He was wearing a blue-checked button-down shirt with a jean jacket, sleeves rolled up to the middle of his forearms. I stared at him an extra second and thought, "Why does this guy like me? He is gorgeous and could have anyone. This is too good to be true. Lord, don't make me wake up from this dream."

We spent the rest of the day touring Hugo's hometown. He showed me where he worked as a messenger. He told me that sometimes he had to take money to the bank and that the manager would make him carry a gun, even though Hugo didn't really like to. He showed me his church, Iglesia Genezareth, and his old high school, Escuela Nazareth. The school happened to be having a sports day, and all the classes were competing against each other in different sports.

Hugo said, "Alex is playing today. Let's go watch."

I agreed, and we went into the school. The court that Hugo had grown up playing on was open-air with concrete flooring. I cringed to think how hard it must have been on his body to play every day on a concrete court.

Some of the freshmen were selling roses, and Hugo left me trying to talk with some of his friends on the sideline to sneak away and buy a rose for me. Of course, everyone asked if we were dating, and we said that we were just friends. We had not made it official yet, though we both knew that we liked each other.

Our situation was complicated. We barely spoke each other's languages and still knew very little about each other. We lived in different countries. And worst of all, my time on the ship would be over soon, and I would be heading home to Kansas.

It seemed like an impossible situation, so what would be the point of dating? We were just friends, totally smitten with each other, trying against all odds to get to know each other. We didn't know why we felt a desire to do that, but we prayed that what we felt in our hearts was God doing something special. Something only He could orchestrate. Something divine.

We talked as much as we could on the bus, but the music was blaring. Hugo said these buses were called Coasters. I thought maybe that was because the experience was like riding a roller coaster, but Hugo said that "Coaster" was the brand name of the bus!

Hugo explained, "The bus drivers fight. They drive really fast and try to pass buses that are further ahead, so they can be first to the next set of people. Then they have to keep going fast so the buses behind them don't catch up. It's insane."

Hugo yelled at the bus driver that we wanted off. The driver swerved over to the curb, and Hugo let me off first. He knew that the bus driver would take off as soon as possible, and he didn't want me to have to jump from a moving bus. The bus moved only slightly as Hugo's last foot left the bus step.

We walked up a busy road, and Hugo told me, "When I was little, I used to ride my bike by myself down this hill. There was no traffic then."

We went through a small parking area, down five steps, and then we were on a sidewalk that passed through a neighborhood of row houses. His home was the second on the right. He unlocked the front gate, and a dog started barking.

"That is Chato, my dog. Even when I am at the gate, he knows when I get home," Hugo said.

There was a slat window to my left for a front bedroom, and a bigger slat window on the right, which gave ventilation for the living room. As we entered through the metal door, I realized why air flow to the inside was so important – there was no air conditioning.

Later, I found out that Hugo had grown up with no hot water, but that recently the family had gotten a small hot-water heater that connected to the shower head. Anyone who wanted to take a shower had to turn on the water heater to get the water to come out hot.

The bathroom was directly across the living room from the front door, and to the left were two small bedrooms. The area to the right was the living room. A door next to the bathroom door led to the dining room, which doubled as Hugo's mom's sewing room. Beyond that was the kitchen. The washing machine was next to the sink. The "clothes dryer" was to the left of the kitchen, an open air patio area, which is common in Latino homes.

The patio also contained an all-important *pila,* a concrete reservoir that holds 50 gallons or more of water. It is imperative to have one because the electricity goes out frequently in El Salvador. No electricity means no water from the tap. The *pila* is then used for everything, from washing clothes and dishes, to flushing a toilet. Salvadorians knew the same trick I was taught in the Philippines – if you pour a gallon or two of water into the stool of a toilet, it will flush on its own.

After showing me the main part of the house, Hugo motioned to a set of concrete stairs on the side of the patio that doubled back to the top of the kitchen area. "My room is up there. You can see the roofs of all the houses in the neighborhood, as well as the volcano."

Hugo walked back through the kitchen and dining room and put my backpack next to the bed in the room where I'd be staying. I'd be sharing this room with his sister. Then I met his mom, Irma Coralia. Everyone at his church called her Coralia, but I could not pronounce that, so I called her Irma. Hugo Sr., his dad, was still at work. We'd be meeting Hugo Sr. (or Don Hugo, as he was often called, in a show of respect common in Latino culture) later at his archive office.

This whole conversation took a long time, as I had to rack my brain for the Spanish vocabulary to understand what Hugo was talking about, but Hugo's English had already improved, so we were making headway!

We walked to a neighbor's house to buy fresh dinner rolls for the evening meal. Irma served a classic Salvadorian meal that was also Hugo's favorite. It included blended brown beans, like refried beans but better. These were served with a soft, crumbly cheese and/or a thick sour cream called *crema*. Scrambled eggs were also served. Hugo made the eggs and added his secret ingredient, mustard. When he told me, I thought it would be so gross because I dislike mustard, but it actually brings out a wonderful flavor in the eggs.

Dinner eggs are sometimes served with sausages, tomato, and onion, but in general the typical Salvadorian dinner is beans, cheese, crema, bread, and fried bananas.

I noted that Hugo's family didn't really use the silverware; they mixed their cheese selections with their beans and used the bread to scoop it all up. Febe and Carlos ate with us, which was good because they had both studied English in San Salvador, so they helped translate for Hugo and me.

I also learned that Carlos was really into cars. When he was in high school, Carlos was just as unruly as Hugo was. Carlos was not racing cars anymore, but he was still an awesome driver who drooled over anything that had to do with cars.

Don Hugo came home for dinner. He was much shorter than Hugo, but other than that they looked a lot alike – much to Hugo's chagrin. He hated that people told him he looked like his dad. I later realized it had less to do with wishing he looked differently, and more to do with hoping he didn't turn out like his dad in character. Hugo had witnessed his dad make several huge mistakes in life, and he did not want to repeat those errors.

Hugo told me in a mix of Spanish and English that he was thankful for his dad because he'd learned several important life lessons from him, including a love for music. Slowly he explained to me in English, "My dad play almost any instrument. He play guitar, bass guitar, piano, organ, and accordion, but he can…agarrar? How do you say? Pick up?"

I smiled and nodded, confirming he had translated the word correctly.

He continued, "Yes, he can pick up almost any instrument and play it. He plays by *oído*, ear, but reads and writes music too. He has a whole book of songs he write."

"So, he must have taught you to play guitar, right?"

Hugo explained that he got his love for guitar from his dad, but that he learned to play from a chord chart he found in the back of a church hymnal. He didn't know how to read music, because it was so much easier for him to just copy what he heard others play.

Hugo also told me about how his dad taught him to lead worship by keeping tempo with his hand, and by bringing the congregation into the next section by singing out a couple of the words that were coming up next. Hugo and his dad would also listen to opera and Hugo would have to guess who the singer was. I started to realize that a big part of Hugo's love for music was connected to his dad.

One of the most amazing and moving things that Hugo shared had to do with how he hoped to be different from his father. He said, "I'm thankful God put my father in my life, because he taught me what not to do in a marriage and with my kids. I pray I will not repeat the mistakes he made. For that reason I do not want to be my dad. I forgive him, though. He is just a sinful human like the rest of us. I just am not going to let my family dictate how my own life is going to be. I choose to be different and, through the power of Jesus, break the chain of sin and selfishness."

Hugo and I watched a movie that night by ourselves. Irma and Don Hugo had already gone to bed, and Carlos and Febe were out until much later. It was raining pretty hard, so it was fun to snuggle up on the couch together to watch the movie.

We went to bed late, but at about 3 in the morning I was awakened by voices in my room. Febe was already in bed but Irma, Don Hugo, and Hugo were all coming in and out and talking in Spanish. I was too groggy to know what they were saying.

Hugo Sr. looked at me and said in broken English, "The water followed you from ship!"

He pointed to the floor. The room had flooded with water, and now Irma had a mop and was trying to dry the tile. I leaned over and picked up my backpack; it was soggy and dripping wet. Still under the covers, I started unpacking it immediately. Hugo had strung a rope through the living room and put hooks on it, which were used to hang wet clothes during the rainy season and for the occasional hammock. I passed my wet clothes to him, wringing them out on the floor as I went.

Once the clothes were rescued, I opened the front pocket of my backpack, where all my important stuff was kept. My new passport was soaked. I groaned, but what could I do?

Hugo came in dragging a blow dryer. This was the first time I had seen him in his glasses, because he usually wore his contacts during the day. He was exhausted from staying up late, too. But his parents had awakened him to serve as translator for us. It was that night that I learned the word *empapado*, which means soaking wet.

Apparently the drain in the patio had gotten clogged with Chato's fur, and the hard rain had entered the patio door into the kitchen, passed through the dining room, and then flowed through the living room. It ran into the room where I was sleeping because it was lower than the others near it. We finally got it mopped up and went back to bed.

The next day, Hugo and I walked around town, rode the bus, and chatted. We decided not to go to the concert and instead spend more time getting to know each other. I started to think that maybe God had allowed me to miss the concert just so I could have this time with Hugo.

That evening, Oscar was supposed to call after the soccer game. We were watching a movie and waiting for the call, but it never came. I called Oscar's cell phone.

He explained, "The game ended much later than we thought it would. Right now I'm on the other side of town, and the traffic is so bad that I won't have time to come to where you are. We're already on the road back to La Union."

"Oscar," I said, "how am I supposed to get back to the ship?"

"You'll just have to take the bus in the morning. Sorry, Sarita."

I hung up the phone and called my boss, Brian, on the ship. I had work in the galley to do the next day and was worried about what he would say. Brian was a hard worker and expected a lot from his team, but deep down he had a big heart. I was nervous as I waited for the ship's receptionist to page Brian to pick up my call. I imagined Brian hearing his name over the intercom.

"Brian, please dial 101. Brian, 101."

Brian picked up the call transfer on the galley phone.

"Brian, it's Sarah. I can't get back tonight. My ride left me in Santa Tecla. I can take a bus in the morning, but I'm not going to be able to get back in time for my shift."

"Well … okay. I'm not happy about this, but I can cover for you. You just had to organize the new foods the deck department pulled out of the cargo hold, right?"

"Yes, and organize the produce in the big fridge that Caleb is going to buy at the local market today."

"Okay, I'll do it. You know your day off is the next day, so if you want, you could just spend an extra two days there, and then come back."

"Thanks, Brian, you're the best!" I said, smiling.

I did spend another two days at Hugo's house, and then Carlos and Febe drove me back to the ship late at night. Hugo went with me, of course, and he held me tight the whole way, which was good because Carlos drove very fast. The roads weren't the best, but Carlos was a good driver, and I trusted him to navigate the tricky terrain in the dark.

As I laid my head on Hugo's chest, I could sense that he wanted to kiss me. He nudged my head with his head, so that I would turn my face to his.

I whispered, "Not yet." And he understood.

I was sure I was driving him crazy with my mixed signals, but I was still confused myself. Something about this relationship felt right, but I knew I needed to pray about everything more before I crossed the same boundary I had broken with Adam. I kept telling myself, "Guard your heart!"

Once we were on the ship, Hugo and I gave Carlos and Febe a quick tour. Hugo also talked to the human resources department to see if they had gotten his e-mail about his desire to join the ship.

Angie was still in the office and told him, "Yes, I got your e-mail. But, you have to learn more English before you can join the ship as personnel. It is a safety issue. If we were to have an emergency, everyone would need to work together and take directions. Maybe for our Guatemala outreach you will be ready. Keep studying hard."

I did not know he had applied to work on the ship, and I asked him about it on the way to the car.

He explained, "I am just getting my life together, and living my life according to what the Bible says. I've been a hypocrite for so long; I just need to get away from friends who pressure me into bad decisions. I know God called me to be a missionary during my mission school, and I want to start right away. But I guess I will go to college now, study English, and work until I can get on the ship. I want to be on the ship because I think it is so cool to meet people from so many countries and travel. It's exciting."

"Well, I'm happy for you. I have only one more month on the ship, but I think I am going to miss it a lot. It is so much fun and I've learned so much about myself and God. I pray God can bring me back someday. Maybe I will see you in Guatemala!"

"That would be buenísimo!"

We said goodbye as friends, not knowing the next night's conversation would take our relationship to a new level. Hugo called about bedtime when I was already in my bunk next to the porthole. My roommate, Erika, picked up the ringing phone. I had told Hugo which extension was close to my room, so he could find me in the evening after the reception desk had closed. Erika stretched the long cord from the hallway into our cabin for some privacy. She translated for us so we could have a deeper phone conversation than normal. After a fun discussion through Erika, Hugo said he wanted to talk to me directly. I was a little surprised, but I took the receiver from Erika anyway. Hugo's wonderful Latin voice melted me as he spoke in English.

"Hello, Sarita."

I regained my composure and said, "Hey, Hugo."

"I like you much. Would you be my girlfriend?"

This was not the conversation I was expecting, and I surprised myself by saying, "Yes! I like you a lot, too."

"Wow. Thank you. I'm very happy."

I was so shocked that I mindlessly handed the phone back to Erika, smiling like a fool. Hugo explained to Erika what he had done and she congratulated us both. Soon they hung up and Erika told me, "He said he would call again in the morning."

My heart was light as a feather as I put my head down to sleep.

The next morning, I woke up and prayed that I had not dreamed the phone call from the night before. I had never had a boyfriend before, and my heart felt strange and jittery. I had this smile that I could not wipe off my face. I quickly told my friend Lori Beth. She had recently been burned by a relationship with a shipmate, and soon she sent me a note that said:

Sarah Beara,
Fried Chicken,
    I wish you the best of luck as you move on in life. I wish you could stay here as long as I am but also know you're doing what's right. I reckon we will meet again on this earth.
    I want to give you two verses.
    Proverbs 4:23,:"Above all else, guard your heart for it is the wellspring of life."
    Song of Songs 2:7b: "Do not arouse or awaken love until it so desires."
    The Proverbs verse has been my relationship verse for years. I just found the Song of Songs one, but I think they go hand in hand. Keep your heart until you're ready to give it away. I love ya, chica, and I know you'll do great with everything. I look forward to seeing you in Victoria or Guate.

Take Care,
Lori Beth

I was grateful for the advice and vowed to be careful, as Hugo would be coming to the ship to visit me the coming weekend.

The night before he came I read the first ten chapters of a book, *Love, Sex, and Relationships*. I finished it the morning he arrived. Nervous for Hugo to come, I wanted to make sure I had everything in check before he came. I felt pulled in every direction at once.

One moment I wanted to keep him at arm's length and not even start this relationship, and then in the next second I wanted to tell him everything and hold him close. I felt very confused. One moment it seemed as if I could hear God telling me to break off the relationship. Then it seemed as if God were telling me to "wait."

Then I'd hear, "Just talk to Hugo about it." I prayed for God to give me courage and boldness to talk to Hugo and bring up all of this. The fact was, I didn't always feel like the relationship was "right." We started dating so quickly, and now I believed it was important that we backtrack and become friends.

Hugo arrived and gave me a CD by Danilo Montero. It was good worship music and helped me learn a lot about the Spanish language and culture. Right after Hugo got there, we spent the day visiting with friends on the ship. Later that night, we watched a movie in the TV lounge.

We shared a couch, and I leaned on him. Hugo rotated his body so that my head would slip off his shoulder to rest on the pillow on his lap. I looked up at him, and he kissed me for the first time. I smiled then and sat up to continue watching the movie. It was cute that he had maneuvered so carefully to be able to kiss me in such a romantic way. But it was awkward that we just kept watching TV as if it had never happened

The next day was beautiful and sunny. We took the public bus to a beach called Las Tunas with a few friends. I had been to this beach a couple times before with others from the ship.

We had found a great local place that served food and drinks and had hammocks under a thatched roof where guests could relax. This was important because twice a day during high tide the beach disappeared, and the hammocks were the only places to sit. The hammock area was up on stilts so that we could see the water through the bamboo floor.

Hugo and I walked along the beach together, hand-in-hand. I found a small sand dollar along the shore and was excited because I love collecting shells on the beach. Hugo thought my excitement was cute. He also shared stories about his life.

"Once, my family came to this beach for a picnic. My parents had just purchased me new glasses, but then a huge wave hit me, and my glasses were gone. I got in big trouble, but they bought me a new pair anyway. It was before I started using contacts."

"I have really good eyesight. It is 20/15, which is better than 20/20 vision," I told him.

"You have beautiful eyes," he said, looking deeply into them. I just smiled and shyly looked away. He hugged me and started another story.

"Another time, some friends and I went to a beach. Not this beach, but one like it. We were drinking and partying, and some of the guys were surfing. I was out in the water, but not too deep. Soon, one of my friends started yelling. He was caught in a current, with this crazy whirlpool in it. He was right there by me, and I reached for him, but I couldn't save him. He was sucked under, and we couldn't find him. People found his body on the beach about a mile away; the current had taken him along the shoreline."

He was quiet then, and we walked in silence. I realized that, coming from El Salvador, Hugo had lived a very different life from mine. He had developed a lot of street smarts. I thought about how valuable his skills could be working in missions in a Latino culture.

Later that night, we were back on the ship and enjoyed The Amazon Café. At the café, you could buy American comforts like my favorites, Dr. Pepper and peanut M&M's. Hugo had never had Dr. Pepper before, because it was not imported into El Salvador. He was hooked from the first sip. It was fun to see someone experience for the first time something that seemed so normal to me. It made life seem more interesting and adventurous because something that I view as a part of common life is really a new experience waiting to be discovered.

Hugo and I spent time talking with my friend Eric. Eric was from Mexico but spoke perfect English. I talked the most; Hugo was there, but he did not really understand our conversation. Eric filled in now and again, but, for the most part, Hugo was left out.

I started to think, "The one person I really want to talk to, I can't. This is messed up. What am I doing? As much as I like him, we need more time to get to know each other. The timing is not right. I'm leaving soon for the States, and then what? I should talk to Elizabeth."

At age 30, Elizabeth was much more experienced than me, and she understood Latinos because she was from the Dominican Republic. She had talked with Hugo several times and was one of the people who told me Hugo was a great guy.

I told Hugo that I needed to go to bed, but would see him in the morning. He would be leaving the next morning. I caught Elizabeth on her way to bed, and I explained to her my concerns about language, distance, and timing.

I told her I thought I should break up with Hugo until we could communicate better, plan when we would actually be able to see each other again, and look for God's timing for our relationship. I thought we were moving too fast. She told me to pray about it.

I went to bed and wrote Hugo a three-page letter in English. I knew I did not possess the Spanish words to voice what I was feeling. I would have someone translate it and send it in an e-mail.

It turned out that none of my friends had time to translate my letter. So, unfortunately, I broke up with Hugo in a revised one-paragraph e-mail that I was able to get the gangway watchman, Jose Luis, to translate. Essentially, I told Hugo that I wanted our relationship to go back to the friendship it had been before, and that I wanted to stay in close touch with him.

Little did I know that Hugo was writing his own letter to me:

> How are you? You know, tonight I got up and felt something distinct about where we were minutes before, and so I thought I needed to write you. Before anything, let me tell you that I like you a lot!!! And each moment I give thanks to God for your life and because He gave me the opportunity to come here to the ship.
>
> It is incredible how God already has everything planned, don't you think? You know I want to know so many things about you; but it is a little hard for me. If you haven't noticed already, I don't know a lot of English. But, even so, I want to "explain" myself a little, and I think that you can understand me. You see this Friday the 19th of May completes the first week that we have been dating. I don't know how you feel, but I hope good.
>
> You know I told you before that I have had various girlfriends (which is nothing fun) but with no one has passed things like what is passing with you. It is nothing bad. For example, I have never prayed for a relationship like this . . . never really with all my heart. But, anyways I felt something different tonight with you. Sometimes I am crazy and just wrong, but let me know what's up.
>
> Like I've told you before with other relationships, always I end up hurt and with a broken heart. You know this time I have a lot of fear so if something happens with you, tell me please. Before anything you are my friend, and I desire the best for your life and ministry. So, just remember in anything, just let me know.
>
> Whoever can say, "But this is impossible, they just met each other. How are this girl and this boy together, how?" You know, at first it was what I thought about and today, well, I still think that, but I believe that the best is to pray and leave everything to God. No more problems with my heart, best I leave it all to God.

I know you are talking with Elizabeth now. I think it is something bad, but I know that you are smart and God will direct you. Don't you worry about anything or anyone. Just that you feel good knowing that what you do pleases God and everything will be fine.

With Much Love,
Hugo

I still went back and forth with what God wanted me to do in this relationship. I really liked Hugo. Not just because he was extremely cute and treated me like a princess; there was something special about him. He had a beautiful heart that I could feel.

I did not need to know his language to understand his actions. He loved God and people with a unique passion. He served with such fervor. He was always having fun and had a huge, irresistible smile on his face. My mind thought it was impossible for us to be together, but my heart kept saying, "What if . . ." From all my praying and reading my Bible, as far as I could see, God's direction was still "wait and see, and just go slow."

I decided to take another trip to San Salvador to spend two days with Hugo. We needed to talk face-to-face, since our language skills were not very good on the phone, and this was not a conversation we wanted to share with our translator friends.

I took the bus that left at 4 a.m., and he picked me up at the bus station at 7 a.m. The whole morning was weird. We avoided the elephant in the room

Then we went to see Hugo's friend Xiomara. She knew more English and wanted to talk to me. Hugo had told her a lot about us. I tried to explain all the reasons I'd come up with for why Hugo and I would not work.

She said, "I understand your concerns. I don't know how God is going to work all that out. But let me tell you that when Hugo first met you, he called me the next day and told me about this girl that was so perfect, just what he had been praying for. Someone who loves God first, is tall, and has great hair. He was very excited about meeting you. He also stares at your picture on the computer screen.

"When he left to come home last week from the ship, he was miserable the whole day because you told him you were going to write an e-mail, and he was worried about what you would write. He cried when he read that you wanted to break up with him."

I thought a lot about what Xiomara had said. Later, when we were walking to the mall, I told Hugo, "You should come to Kansas. It's not fair that I get to meet all your friends and family and see your city, but you don't get to see mine."

He asked, "Why would you want me to come?" I knew that he was fishing for the answer to a bigger question. If I had broken up with him, then why would I want him to come to Kansas? I took the bait and dug into the conversation we had been avoiding.

"You mean, why did I break up with you?"

We stopped in the middle of the street. There was no traffic, and we just stood on a speed bump and talked.

He started quickly, as if he had been thinking this conversation through for a long time and wanted to get it out. "It was so sudden that I thought everything before was a lie, and now I don't know what to think."

I was much slower in my response. "I just need time. My life on the ship is so fast, and I like you a lot, so I do not want to make fast decisions and mess it all up. I want to do it right so it can last. The last night you were there, while we were talking to Eric, it just hit me that I wish. . . I wish I could talk to you like that, and it was just all wrong. Again, I just need time." I looked down, feeling sad that I had hurt him so deeply.

Hugo's hand touched my chin. He gently lifted it up so that I had to look at him. His eyes were compassionate. He spoke to me very softly. "Sarah, that is fine. Why did you not tell me sooner? It is okay if you need time. Take as much as you need. If you need a day, a week, a month, a year, whatever, it is fine. Take as much time as you need; I will wait for you."

My heart melted. I had never heard more romantic words in all my 19 years of life. My knight in shining armor had come. He asked me again why I hadn't told him any of this.

I told him, "Because it is so hard to communicate!"

"Okay, I understand. Let's just agree to forget what happened, all the bad stuff, and leave it in the past."

"Deal," I said, and we hugged for a long time, right in the middle of the street. It was strange, I realized that we had just had an in-depth conversation, and we both understood each other. I wasn't sure if we had spoken in Spanish or English, but somehow we had communicated in a way we previously had not been able to. The language barrier was something I had been so frustrated about, but God was making a way! I felt so close to Hugo now.

We did not hold hands or kiss the whole day. We went biking in the evening, and that was fun. When we got home, he wanted to make two trips and carry in both bikes. I got perturbed and walked away.

He said, "Okay, okay, you can help."

I shot right back with, "I am an American woman, and I can do it myself!" I knew that it was bad in his country for a woman not to let a man carry something for her. But I prided myself on being a strong, independent person. I had a feeling we would clash a lot in this area.

That night we watched a movie together, holding hands until we both fell asleep. I had to catch a bus at 4 the next morning, so we knew we had to get some sleep. As Hugo was about to walk into his room, I caught his hand. We squeezed hands and then drew close.

I looked at him and said, "I know we hope to see each other in Guatemala. If we do, that will be five months from now. And we might not see each other then, if you don't get accepted onto the ship, or if my parents don't agree to let me return. So who knows when we will ever be together again?"

We held each other in a hug forever. He whispered, "Be careful of all the boys in Kansas and on the ship!"

"Leaving you is really hard."

"I know," he agreed.

"Pray for us now?" I asked, and he prayed quietly in Spanish in my ear. We moved and touched foreheads. He kissed my nose and forehead. He tilted his head for a kiss. I told him, "No, por favor." He softly kissed my nose again.

"Thank you," I said. After we held each other a while longer, we moved to our own rooms.

I was so happy that I was able to say no. I wanted to kiss him so badly. But, I had to prove to myself that God was in control and so was I.

After my stupid kiss with Adam, I needed to know that I was able to say no to temptation, even when I felt it was not a sin. I could have kissed Hugo in good conscience. But now I knew it was possible to walk away, and no one had that power over me.

Before I returned to Kansas, I traveled to Guatemala with Adam, Marco, Keith, Laura, and several other friends from the ship for a wedding. We also spent some time touring the country, which was amazing. I loved Antigua, and Lake Atitlán was beautiful. There were three volcanoes on the south side of the lake. I read that the lake is considered one of the most beautiful lakes in the world.

I also got to see the little boy, Miguel, that my TFC group began supporting when I was in 7th grade. When I graduated from high school, I asked the youth group if I could continue supporting him on my own. They agreed, and I had been supporting him ever since. Never in my wildest dreams did I think I would ever get to visit my sponsored child.

But as amazing as my trip was, my thoughts constantly turned to Hugo. I did get to see him one last weekend before leaving. On the flight back to Kansas, I wrote in my journal.

6-4-00

I'm on a plane bound for Kansas City. This morning was hard, leaving Hugo. While saying goodbye I was fingering his necklace on his neck, like I sometimes do. He gave it to me and said, "Give this back to me when we see each other again." We both cried, but we agreed God knows the future.

These months are going to be so hard for both of us. Especially when we can't get to e-mail or anything. He made me this awesome card that tells me how much he loves me. It is so cute! This morning he was upset because he forgot to bring this other six-page letter that he wrote to me. I hope he sends it to me.

Hugo did send me that letter, and here is a part of it:

I got an e-mail from the ship. Angela told me: "Hugo, Bless you and all your efforts to learn English. You are doing a great job. Angie"

It´s good no?!

Oh my… now I´m very happy… :) … I am happy!!

Well…Sarah I love you so much. I need to see you! I need to see you and have news from you. I need to talk to you personally!!

And . . .

I love you, my beautiful angel!!

Every time I remember you and I say to myself: "I really love her." I love you!

I'd better not write longer or I will never send the letter! But remember that I love you, and that all the pages of my notebook won't be enough to express how I feel for you and how much I love you.

I also remember the song "Kiss Me" and I'd love to get a kiss from you!! Now! Why do I love you? First for your devotion to God and your love for missions, second . . . for you all! ☺ Your lips so sweet! The way you smell, your teeth, your eyes . . . the way you kiss, so sweet! . . . oh my . . .That's why I call you "MAMASITA RICA!" Your skin . . . your everything! Well baby, I'll mail this letter tomorrow. I hope it arrives soon!!

Kisses . . .

I LOVE YOU SO MUCH!!

I love you tons baby!!

My beautiful angel . . .

PS- Hugs and kisses . . .

Many kisses!!

Hugo!

I felt strange reading his long letter to me. He was so uninhibited in professing his love for me. On one hand, I was love struck and felt the same way. But on the other hand, I thought, "How can he love me so much when he barely knows anything about me?" My journal entry on the plane from El Salvador to Kansas continues:

This whole thing is so weird for me. I've never had this problem. Wanting to be with someone so badly and having to wait months. Wanting to talk to him and get to know him more. My heart aches for it. I find myself thinking of him a lot. Of course, it is so powerful to know that he loves me so much and that he will wait for me. I know I love him. I know I could marry him. But I'm so not ready for that now. I know that much! I did tell him that God has many things for me to do before whatever, but again he said he could wait.

I love that he is willing to wait for me. I love how he always holds my hand when we walk together. I love how he walks on the street side of the sidewalk. I love how he leads me into a room. I love how he tells me all the time that he loves me "much." I love playing basketball with him and having fun adventures. I love it when he proudly introduces me to his friends as his girlfriend. I love it when he sneaks in a kiss or a chance to hold me a little closer. I love it when it seems he has purposely set up a way for us to touch. Like when he opened my car door, rolled down the manual window, motioned for me to get in, shut the door, and then leaned through the open window to kiss me really good! It is like no one else matters except me.

I love how he loves to just look at my face and tell me how beautiful I am. I love it when I tell him, "You're crazy!" And he says back to me, "for you." I love sitting next to him in church and sharing a Bible, sitting so close he has to put his arm around me. I love to watch him play his guitar in church or to watch him worship God. I love holding hands and praying for our food. I love it when he is holding me or hugging me and I can hear him praying to God for me.

Love him? I know I do. But it is a love that has a long way to go. It is a love that has the capacity to become so much more. And I know he can love me more as we get to know each other and understand each other more. In one of his letters he told me that he thinks that I am his angel. He is so good with words . . . now that is ironic!

I did know that I loved Hugo, and I knew that I wanted to be around him all the time, but for the first time since we met we were going to be in different countries. And who knew if we'd ever be near each other again?

The Caribbean Mercy Ship

The second day after Hugo and Sarah met. Unbeknownst to Sarah when she took the picture, but Hugo was writing an inscription inside a Spanish Bible to give to her.

The week Hugo and Sarah met. Hugo and Sarah watch their first movie together on the ship in the TV lounge with friends.

Sarah visits Hugo in San Salvador (2000) and meets his youth group. (L-R)
Back: Vicky, Sarah, Elena y Arturo
Middle: Karen, Xiomara, Keren y Alex
Front: Carlos, Marvin, Jose Carlos, Eric, Febe

Please visit my website, www.my-onceuponatime.com/, to see pictures and videos from each chapter.

Chapter Five

Worlds Apart
Late 2000

El Salvador, California, Nicaragua, Panama Canal, Colombia, Guatemala

When I got off the plane in Kansas City, my mom took one look at my face and knew I did not want to be there. I gave both my parents a warm hug and said to them, "Remind me why I am coming home?"

My mom answered, "Because you had a plane ticket."

She was right. When we made the decision that I would leave Tabor, my parents hoped that I would eventually return. I had agreed to come back to Kansas after a short time on the ship and to at least discuss the possibility of finishing college.

But it became clear almost immediately that college was not for me. I was miserable at home, and all I wanted was to get back to the ship. My parents were understanding, and three months later I was off to San Diego to join the ship there.

It had just returned from a sail up to Victoria, Canada, and I had missed seeing the killer whales. I was happy to be with them in their new port in beautiful San Diego, which had a killer whale of its own at Sea World! I arrived a week after the ship did, so my friends, familiar with the area, already knew where the fun places were. A real pirate ship docked next to us, and we were allowed free tours. We also loved to walk to the mall and drink Jamba Juice smoothies. I had never had one before, and I really got addicted.

One of our favorite things to do was to take a tram to Tijuana, Mexico, and hang out for a while. It was so easy, and it was fun to say, "Been there, done that, got the T-shirt!"

Soon the fun in the sun was over; the ship needed to start its long sail to Guatemala. It would be about a 12-day sail total, including two stops. The longest we would be on open water would be about a week, as we sailed from California to Nicaragua. From there we would continue through the Panama Canal and on to

Colombia and Guatemala. We would remain in Guatemala for almost four months, until February.

The first day of our trip was unnerving. Even though I had spent a lot of time on the ship, this would be my first time sailing with it. After we left port, I stood on the deck a while, watching the land recede and the water get bluer and bluer. As I laid my head on the pillow that night, I knew that land was nowhere in sight. I told myself not to think about it, and to just go to sleep.

My cabin was in the aft part of the ship, so I could hear the propeller spinning loudly. After a while, the sound lulled me to sleep, but then it slowed and stopped, and I woke up. It occurred to me that maybe the propeller should not have stopped spinning while we were on the open ocean. I tried to forget about it and go back to sleep, but it was too quiet.

I threw on a sweatshirt and took the spiral staircase up to "A" deck to check out the situation. At the top of the stairs, I looked outside. The night was black, a black like I had never seen black in my life. I was drawn to it, because it was so unique.

I stepped onto the aft deck. The silence that surrounded me was deafening. It almost hurt to not hear anything. The ship rocked gently, so I knew we had to be in the water, although I could not see it. There were no stars, no moon, no people. I shuddered as I realized there was also no land. Even if I wanted to get off, there was nowhere to run. I started to get tense and feel a claustrophobic panic creep over me. I sprinted back to my cabin as fast as I could and jumped into my bunk. I squeezed my eyes shut, forcing my brain to think about something else. I was grateful when sleep came to me again.

I got used to the feeling of being trapped on the ship and not being able to see land. I just forced my mind to focus on other things and acted like it was perfectly normal to be floating in the middle of a giant body of water. I did not get seasick during this sail, even when we passed though the Gulf of Tehuantepec (Te·huan·te·pec), otherwise known as "Gulf of You-wanna-puke." We named it that because Captain John had told us that the gulf would be very turbulent due to winds coming off a mountain on shore. We would most likely see 20-foot waves, and we would be would be in the gulf for nearly 24 hours.

When Kristy's and my beauty products started to fall off the sink in the middle of the night, I knew we had reached the gulf. That was to be expected, so we ignored it and kept sleeping. Books, pictures, and decorations continued to fall, but then the bookshelf itself fell over!

"Ahh!" I yelled, frustrated. "What else can possibly fall? What a mess!" I looked around our tiny cabin. A cabin this small had to be kept in perfect order, and chaos would be our downfall. With all our things on the floor, there was nowhere to walk!

Kristy and I tried to get a few more winks before the morning, but soon we heard a new noise. Water! Water everywhere. I turned on the lights again. We looked to the only place where water could be coming from, the porthole. Sure enough, when the ship listed to the starboard side, our porthole went under the gulf's surface, causing water to seep into our room, down the wall, onto the bench, and then onto the floor.

We used our room phone to call the bridge to inform them. They said it was happening with many portholes, and it was nothing to be concerned about. They told us that someone would be coming soon to tighten the bolts. In the meantime, we prayed that our cabin wouldn't disappear underwater.

Kristy had to go to work in the reception office by then, but I tried to sleep again before breakfast. I knew that my stomach would feel a little calmer if I could lie down and let my body flow with the ship's movements.

Soon there was a knock on the door. Marco had come to tighten the bolts on the porthole. I yelled for him to come in. He was all business, because there were lots of people waiting for him to come and fix their leaking portholes. He saw all the stuff on our floor and waited for the ship to list to our starboard side. Then he used the momentum to jump completely over our stuff, landing with a *thunk* on the bench. He quickly worked with a few tools he had brought, and soon the water was sealed off. He turned, waited for the ship to list to port, and cleared the debris once again, landing in the hallway.

I was still under my covers in my bunk. Sometimes we were too much like family on this ship!

Deciding to test my sea legs in these waters, I slid out of bed—and promptly flew into the door when the ship listed. The floor was at a 70-degree slant! I spread my legs out wide to keep balanced, wondering what the waves must be like outside.

Balancing on one leg, I attempted to pull on a pair of shorts, which was nearly impossible. As the ship moved again, I flew into the bench under the porthole. I ended up having to hold onto the bed with one hand and pull my shorts on with the other hand.

Once I was dressed, I started up the spiral stairs. In every ship, when you go through most doorways, you have to step up over the elevated doorframe, duck down to fit under the top, or both. The doors that go to the outer decks only have an elevated doorframe. This is to prevent water getting into the ship when a wave crashes over the railing. There is a gutter system that drains the water back out into the ocean, but when the waves are big enough, the drain cannot keep the deck clear.

I reached the next deck and noticed that the elevated doorframe was doing nothing to keep the water out! The crew had rigged another board on top of the doorframe, but the water was still seeping in all over the floor and dripping down the steps. The good thing about a ship is that pretty much everything can get wet without damage! I just raised my eyebrows and kept going. I couldn't stop if I wanted to anyway, because the motion of the ship had me in a rhythm. Move fast to one side during a list, walk slowly when we were more or less on keel, then run fast again when we listed the other way. I was bouncing off each wall. I finally made it to the dining room.

The kitchen crew was cleaning up food off the floor, broken dishes, spilled juice. Apparently it had been a wild breakfast! The ship's dining room tables had a plastic surface on them to keep the plates from sliding, with a wooden ledge that could be raised and locked into place. These mechanisms were not enough to fight gravity today!

My friends in the pantry told me that the plates were bad but the chairs were worse. There was nothing to keep everyone's chairs from sliding all over the dining room floor. I was laughing at their stories while I poured myself a bowl of cereal. I let my bowl go for a second to get the milk out of the fridge. A big wave hit port-side; we listed far to the starboard. I remembered my cereal just in time to see it go flying across the pantry work table. I reached for it, but it was out of my reach.

"Watch out, Lori Beth!" I yelled.

The 20-gallon trash can next to me also took off in Lori Beth's direction. She was holding on to the table with one hand so she wouldn't fall, and with her other hand she caught my cereal. This meant she had no hands to stop the trash can that was barreling toward her. She turned her hip to the can; it hit her with a thump.

Lori Beth grunted, "Help!"

"I'm coming!" I exclaimed. Hand over hand, I used the work table to make my way to her. I pulled the can off her and she passed my cereal to me. "Sorry," I said. "I'm not used to this yet. My hands do things as they normally do, but I have to get used to a new normal!"

"No problem. Hey, we are going to play Twister later in the Amazon Café, do you want to play?" Lori Beth asked.

"Yeah, right! How is that going to work?" I asked.

"It's not supposed to be as bad later today, and the motion of the ship will make it really fun and different!" she said.

"Sure, I'll play!" I replied.

After breakfast, I went up to the bridge to watch the waves. There were white caps as far as the eye could see. It was incredible watching the bow of the ship dip low into the water and then crash into the next wave. The spray would splash up even to the windows on the bridge. It was about 20 feet higher than the cargo deck below, and 30 feet above the surface of the ocean. A permanent crane, used to move cargo, was parked on the deck, alongside a Frontier truck, an Xterra SUV, two vans, the water drilling machine, and a huge work truck. I feared we would lose one of them over the side! I watched them closely, but the deck department had done an excellent job securing them to the deck.

Marco, the guy who had tightened the portholes that morning, was just finishing his shift on the bridge. He was a deckhand who helped steer the ship. I was going to be changing from the pantry department to the deck department, so I was curious to learn more about what I would have to do. Marco showed me how the "deckies" took turns steering the ship or watching for smaller boats in the water that the radar did not pick up. I was really excited to become a deckie. There was so much to learn about being a real sailor!

Once through the Gulf of Tehuantepec, it was several days later before we were able to dock in Nicaragua. It was amazing to see land again, and even more spectacular to feel it! It took some time to reacquaint myself with land because sometimes my body would involuntarily move like it was still on the boat.

Even though we were in Nicaragua for only a few days, a group of street boys had a great impact upon me. They would hang around the port gate waiting for someone from our ship to come into town. Of course, they would beg us for money, but we knew we could not give it to them. They were glue addicts, and they didn't even try to hide it. They each carried a little container of glue, and periodically we would see one of them unscrew the lid to take a sniff.

It was so heartbreaking, knowing that there wasn't much we could do to help them in only two days. We just loved on them as much as possible. We would buy them ice cream or share food. More importantly we shared about the only hope they could have in their lives, Jesus Christ, and His perfect love for them. I left Nicaragua with their dirt-and-glue-streaked faces imprinted on my heart and mind.

Two days later, we approached the skyline of Panama City, near the mouth of the Panama Canal. I was surprised to see that Panama City looked very modern, almost like New York City. We anchored in the Gulf of Panama near the mouth of the canal. Ships surrounded us, and we had to wait our turn. We were allowed free passage through the canal because we were a mission organization. But that meant a longer wait, because paying customers got first priority in passing through the locks. When we did get our turn to pass through the locks, we were told it would take us all night – eight to ten hours. Passing through the canal would not be as easy and quick as I had assumed.

Oscar and I were posted on the lower aft deck. We didn't have to do anything except be available. A crew of Panamanians boarded the ship to take us through the southeast Miraflores and Pedro Miguel locks (due to the shape of the Isthmus of Panama, the Pacific end of the canal is actually the southeast end, and the Caribbean/Atlantic end is at the northwest).

I was surprised to see that the Panamanians were generally taller than other Central Americans I had known (Hugo was an exception also). I watched as the three men at my post expertly worked ropes and helped our ship pass through the locks. I was fascinated and thought to myself, "When I was in third grade learning about the Panama Canal, never in my wildest dreams did I think I would see it in person, let alone be on a ship sailing through it! God is so cool, and He is giving me the amazing, unbelievable life that He told me He would give me."

Once through the Pedro Miguel and Miraflores locks, we sailed slowly down to Gatún Lake, which was created by damming the Chagres River. We were at the highest elevation of the canal, 85 feet above sea level. I tried to stay awake all night as we passed through the lake. I was amazed by the view; the moon glimmered happily on the lake water. I finally headed to bed and woke early the next morning. We passed through the Gatún locks, which led us back down to sea level and into the Atlantic Ocean.

After entering the Atlantic, we hooked a right, and a day later we docked in Colombia. Colombia was not at all what I expected. I imagined a war zone or everyone smoking pot. Kind of how a lot of people think everyone in Alaska lives in an igloo, and everyone in Texas is a cowboy. In the city where we were docked, Cartagena, they told us we were safe from any guerilla attacks. Apparently the guerilla cells live in the mountains, and there were no mountains near the city of Cartagena.

The city was old and full of wonderful history. I especially loved the old city wall. One of Cartagena's nicknames is "The Walled City." I also visited a historic (16th- and 17th-century) fortress called San Felipe de Barajas.

Once crazy adventure I got to have in Colombia was a dirty one. The ship had arranged a tour for whoever wanted to go. About 30 of us loaded into a bus and went at high speed through the streets of Cartagenas. Soon we were in open country. After about 45 minutes, we turned off the main road and headed up an unsealed track. In a short while we crested a hill, where a strange vista came into view. At the foot of the track, about one mile ahead, was a large body of water, a freshwater lagoon of some sort. Directly in front of it was a mud volcano, which from that distance looked like a giant anthill.

As we drew closer, the volcano took on a surreal appearance, like something out of an Indiana Jones movie. It had a rickety wooden staircase leading to its summit, which was about 55 feet high. Its profile was incredibly creepy. Just below the summit we could see where planks had been placed over a rupture on one side of the cone. The fresher mud that had bubbled out was a darker color, and rivulets had formed, which looked like wax dripping from a candle. People had set up small restaurants and drink stands, called *kioskos*. After we bought tickets to enter the area, we changed into our swimsuits. Our intrepid group began the ascent to the summit, where we would "bathe" in the volcano!

Peering down into the crater of the cone was like looking into a cauldron of boiling gray goo. Every now and again, bubbles would surface slowly, because the mud was very viscous. So viscous, in fact, that when we descended the ladder on the inside edge of the crater, it was impossible to fully submerge ourselves unless someone pushed us under. The initial sensation was of floating in a thick, squishy, warm bath.

Every few minutes a bubble would slowly surface, then burst with an evil burping sound. There was no fathomable bottom to the crater, but it was impossible to drown because of the mud's viscosity. "Swimming" in the mud was tiring because of the resistance against our limbs. Since treading water was not necessary because we couldn't sink, most of us just lay on our backs and floated.

The attendant recommended that we cover our faces and hair with the goo, because it would be good for our skin. We had to be careful, though, not to get it in our ears and eyes. Soon everyone looked like members of some long-lost New Guinean tribe. In our masks, males and females were indistinguishable, and all races looked alike.

The attendant scraped off all the mud before we left the crater, so as not to deplete its reserve. We still had a lot in our hair and under our swimsuits. The guide asked us to follow him down to the lagoon, where young children were waiting to wash us. He gestured that we should remove our swimsuits once we were in the water. We could wash ourselves if we wanted to, but for most of us it added another hilarious episode to the day's events to be scrubbed down by a little scrawny Colombian! I have never heard so many people laughing while being scrubbed. The children may have been young, but they were experienced washers and had us clean in a jiffy.

On the bus ride home, our guide told us that the mud is produced by rotting vegetation that originates under the lagoon and is forced up through a fissure in the earth by volcanic heat miles underground. In 1999, a nearby volcano unexpectedly erupted and spewed forth a river of mud, which destroyed a village and killed one man. There are several mud volcanoes in the Cartagena area. The ones near Turbaco were first described by Alexander von Humboldt in 1801; they still exist, though they are more pools of mud than raised cones like the one at Totumo. I couldn't help but wish we had known more about the volcanoes before our strange bath!

We left Colombia knowing that our next stop would be more work and less play. The ship's big, four-month outreach in Santo Tomas, Guatemala, would begin. On the sail, Lori Beth and I spent time in prayer to gain focus for what God wanted us to accomplish during our time there.

We prayed for God to give us friends to minister to. We prayed and brainstormed about our sports outreach team. We planned to get official basketball uniforms for this outreach. We talked about how we should call our team the Marineros por Cristo (Sailors for Christ)!

Lori Beth and I spent almost every moment that we weren't working out on the basketball court making friends. Almost from the moment that we set out to start our sports ministry team, God blessed us with great people we could share our faith with. Patty, Carlos, Jeffrey, and Bruce were some of our first friends. Through them, we also met Piero, Helen, and Cesar.

Patty was a single mom with two kids who played basketball well. Carlos and Jeffrey were from Santo Tomas, but played on the Guatemalan national team in the capital, Guatemala City. Cesar was a taxi driver. Bruce was short and on the heavier side, but he was also a crazy coach for one of the local men's teams. Piero was a small, quick point guard who spoke great English, and his girlfriend Helen was an interpreter for the ship's medical staff.

I was still e-mailing with Hugo as much as I could. I was beginning to feel more and more disconnected from him. There was only so much we could learn about each other through e-mail with our limited written language ability. I was praying about what I should do, because I did like him, but I didn't see the point in keeping this up if we were never going to see each other again. He was supposed to meet the ship in Guatemala, and, because of this hope, I clung to our relationship.

Soon after we reached Guatemala, Hugo e-mailed me to say that he was not sure if he could come to the ship. Finances were a problem, and the people who had to approve his application were still not certain he had learned enough English. I e-mailed to tell him that I liked him, but our relationship as it was could never work. If this relationship was from God, then God would have to cross our paths again, so we could get to know each other more in person.

Essentially, I was breaking up with him. He didn't get the message. Oh, he got the e-mail all right, but he was too prideful to accept it. He was used to being the one who did the dumping. So he decided that breaking up over e-mail didn't count. He was still committed to me in his heart, even though all his friends said, "Forget it, man. That Americana has lost all thought of you!"

Hugo maintained his stand even when girls tried to break him. Some even asked him to go out on a date with them. He would just take my picture out of his wallet and tell the story of Sarah until they were scared off. He was not letting me go so easily. He was going to wait for a face-to-face break up.

I, on the other hand, felt as free as a bird. I loved my time in Guatemala. Lori Beth and I enjoyed getting out and exploring. One afternoon, Lori suggested that on Saturday we hike down a nearby river that was supposed to have beautiful waterfalls.

She was sure that particular river let out into the ocean right behind our ship. She figured that we wouldn't need a trail to follow, because we could just wade in the river and follow it all the way down. It made sense to her, so I blindly followed along. She was so confident that we didn't even ask anyone or check a map.

Saturday came, and we gathered a few other friends who did not have to work, Heather, Oscar, and Alex, and we had Jarot drop us off riverhead. Jarot mentioned that he would be taking the ship's speedboat across the bay at 5 p.m. to pick up some other crew at a local resort. We thought nothing of his comment and put it out of our minds.

In no time, we were surrounded by the lush green jungles that lined the banks of the rivers. The greenness was breathtaking, and our spirits marveled at the beauty of creation as we descended a waterfall.

When we reached the bottom, one of the guys froze in his tracks. A man carrying a rifle was approaching us. Lori and I both stopped short. We shot each other a sideways glance. I relied a lot on Lori's experience as a missionary kid, but she looked panicked, too. She told me later that trespassing was considered a serious offense in some parts of the world. The rifleman began shouting in Spanish. Thankfully, Alex had spotted him first, and he was able to assure the man that we were just passing through. The man gave us a funny look, told us never to come back, and then stepped to the side to let us pass.

We continued on. In many places there was no way to pass through the rain forest on the river bank, and we had to wade in the water. One section was really deep, and Alex stuck his wallet under his hat so that it would not get wet. When the terrain leveled off, we knew we were close to the ocean, but at that point we weren't enjoying the journey very much anymore. It was like a Vietnam movie, where the soldiers are marching though the stagnant, swampy rivers. They are waist-deep in the water with their hands raised above their heads. That was what we faced. No longer was it a trickling stream with beautiful waterfalls.

Lori Beth and I were still sure the ship would be waiting for us in the ocean. I was the first to come over the ridge. I stepped out of the mangroves, turned to my right to look for the ship, and burst out laughing. Lori was one step behind me, and she saw what I saw and started laughing too. By the time the other three caught up, we were no longer laughing, because the reality of our situation had set in.

The ship was nowhere in sight. It was 4 p.m., and we had about an hour and a half of daylight left. We know the ship was to our right, but there was no way to move in that direction, because all we could see was a sheer cliff. To go back the way we came would not only take hours, it would also leave us in the mountains five miles from the ship. Not to mention the possibility of another run-in with Mr. Rifle.

The only option was to go left and try to make it to the other side of the bay. That way, we would get to the resort before 5, when Jarot made the last speedboat run. We would have to swim along the shore until we could climb up to the road, and then run down the road until we got to the resort. No one knew exactly how far that would be.

None of us had dressed for the biathlon that this had become. We were all wearing long pants, T-shirts, and boots. Lori Beth and I were the only strong swimmers in the group. We would have to spend a lot of our energy helping the others.

It took us half an hour of swimming to get to a place where we could get out. When we were finally able to climb ashore, the terrain was like hard coral, which scratched our ankles. We were all completely exhausted.

There was no time to rest, though, because we only had a half hour left. We had no clue how far away the resort was on the road. After walking for about ten minutes, we sat down to drain the saltwater out of our shoes and clothes. That's when we heard the familiar hum of the speedboat's motor in the distance.

We threw on our shoes and clothes and started running as fast as we could down the road. At each bend in the road, I would sprint ahead, hoping to see the resort's sign, but then I would have to wait for my team to catch up. It was dangerous to lose sight of my friends.

After the third bend in the road, I spotted the entrance to the resort, Cayos del Diablo. I tried to explain to the guard what I needed. Alex and Oscar ran up and started to explain in better Spanish than I could.

They both talked frantically, because we knew Jarot would have everyone loaded up by now, all ready to head back to the ship. I think the guard was hesitant to let us in because we looked so bedraggled, and he was afraid we would scare away the guests. Finally, Alex demanded that the guard let me go in to stop our boat. He agreed, and I sprinted through the resort. I raced down to the beach just as the boat was taking off.

The motor surged as I splashed out into the water's edge, waving my arms furiously and yelling, "Jarot! Wait! Wait!"

The hum of the motor drowned out my voice, and everyone was turned toward the ship. They didn't see me! The guard must have finally decided to believe our story, because my comrades charged onto the beach behind me, also screaming. But it was too late.

Like whipped puppies, we walked back up the path to the front desk. We asked what we could do to get back. The front desk clerk could not have been less helpful. "No taxis, no rides, no phone, getting dark."

We were desperate! "What can we do to get back?" Alex pleaded in Spanish.

"You can pay $50 for a boat ride back to your ship," the clerk suggested.

We looked at each other. No one had brought money.

Alex reached up and felt his hat. His wallet was still there after everything we had been through. We all thought there was hope, but we were crushed again when he opened it to find only 10 bucks. He showed it to the clerk, who shook his head. I couldn't believe it. They were going to leave us stranded here.

"My business credit card!" Alex yelled.

"What?" I asked.

"I can use my business credit card to pay for the launch to get us back. My boss won't mind, and I will pay him back later," he said.

"Yeah!" We all jumped up and down with excitement. We were so full of adrenaline from everything we had been through.

Alex paid, and the clerk waved for another man to escort us to the launch. On the way back, we saw where we had been swimming and where we came out of the river. It was quite a feat of skill and divine help to have survived what we had.

When we pulled up to the ship, we called for someone to lower a ladder and open a door in the deck wall. Soon someone opened a space, and the boat driver settled the launch under the space as a ladder dropped down to us. I was the first one up, and was surprised to see that the ship's captain, John, had lowered us the ladder. He did not say anything, just casually helped each person off the ladder and onto the ship. I had no idea even where to begin to explain why we were pulling up to the ship in a launch, so I kept my mouth shut.

I think we all knew that Captain John's silence meant, "Don't let this become a regular occurrence." Captain John often led without words. We all respected him greatly, so we quietly exited the "C" deck to shower and tell our friends about the day's adventure.

Lori Beth's and my sports ministry continued going strong. We spent a lot of time at the basketball court and at Patty's house. She lived with her parents, since the father of her children had left a while ago. She slept in the same bed with her two kids, and her parents slept in the other room. There was one bathroom. They did most of their cooking, dishwashing, and laundry outside. We took Patty to a church that the ship was working with, and she seemed to like it. We kept praying for her and all of our friends to know the Lord.

The weekend after the river expedition, Lori Beth and I decided to go to Guatemala City to hang out with some of our friends there. We stayed at Pablo's house. He had been on the ship before, and his parents owned a coffee farm, so they were quite well off. Pablo was known as a ladies' man, although he knew the two of us well enough to know that we were wise to his charms and would not fall for his moves!

I had learned through e-mail that Hugo was going to be in Guatemala City the same weekend. He was helping his sister Febe and brother-in-law Carlos move into their Bible seminary, SETECA. I was frantically trying to connect with him, except I had no phone number I could use to reach him. Even though I had broken up with him, we still e-mailed off and on. I secretly still liked him a lot. I just knew it was not God's perfect timing yet.

As Pablo, Lori Beth, and I walked around a mall in Guatemala City, I felt so close to Hugo, yet so far away. How was it possible that we were in the same city and had no idea how to find each other?

Pablo took Lori Beth and me to a place where we could get our hair cut. Lori went first and then, when I was about done, the mirror in front of me started shaking. Then I started shaking. I looked at Lori Beth again, trying to use her missions experience to interpret what was happening.

She looked at me in the mirror and said calmly, "An earthquake." She said it like it was a normal event. Since she seemed so relaxed, I was able to keep from freaking out too much. I had never been in an earthquake before, and it seemed to last forever. It was not very strong, nothing fell from the walls, but everyone felt it.

We quickly finished, paid, and walked to Pablo's car, which was a little unnerving, because it was in the parking lot underneath the mall. We all thought about the possibility of another quake and being crushed under concrete, but we had to get the car. We listened to the radio and heard that the epicenter was in El Salvador. I immediately thought of Hugo. I knew he was safe in Guatemala, but where was the rest of his family?

The next day, Lori Beth and I bused the four hours back to Puerto Barrios and then took a taxi to the port in Santo Tomas. The ship was docked on a working port, so the walk from the front gate to the ship's gangway was a complicated maze of forklifts, containers, and 18-wheeled trucks. We scooted expertly though all the port traffic and made it to the ship. Our other friends instantly started telling us about the earthquake and how they had experienced it on the ship. The ship was already planning to send a team of medical staff and interpreters over to El Salvador.

I rushed to my room and tried to call Hugo's home phone. Nothing. I couldn't get through. I went to the lounge to e-mail him. Days passed and I got no response. I was really beginning to worry, and I felt helpless.

The ship had a team ready to drive over to El Salvador to help with medical care of the victims. One of the interpreters going with the team was my friend from Costa Rica, Katia. I gave Katia a piece of paper. I showed her what I'd written on it and said, "Katia, you have to look for my friend, Hugo Liborio. Here is his name and phone number. Please try to contact him. I am really worried about him. I have not heard anything from him yet, and I don't know if his family is okay."

She said, "Okay, no problem, I will see what I can do." I knew it was a long-shot in a country with six million people, but I felt I had to do something to find him.

I met with Lori Beth to discuss our outing for the weekend. The adventure we were planning was supposed to be safe. After the disasters with the river and the earthquake, Lori and I decided to plan a bit more carefully. There were some people on the ship from Indiana. It was a group of adults who were older than the average team we hosted, so we thought, "How much trouble could these people get into?"

The plan was to go with them to a village to show the Jesus film. It sounded easy, harmless, and it was a very missionary thing to do. We were excited to not have a life-threatening experience for once. We got on the bus with them and started to chat and make friends.

We weren't really paying attention to where the bus was taking us, but soon we stopped and the bus driver said, "This is it."

I looked around us and responded, "This is what? There is nothing here."

"This is the railroad."

"Okay, I see that. What does this have to do with showing the Jesus film?"

He seemed a little upset that I didn't know the plan, although the group obviously did. They were already unloading and acting like this was a normal stop. I was still confused. The bus driver pointed to two rail carts coming up the tracks toward us. "You have to take the carts to the village. There is no road to that village. Only railroad."

I nodded as if I understood, but this concept was totally foreign to me. I still wasn't sure what he was talking about.

I got out of the bus as the team was loading their film gear and generators onto two big wooden platforms. The platforms had no railings, just planks on each corner, which I soon learned were for pushing the carts.

We piled on, and even though I didn't quite feel safe atop the platform with nothing to hold onto, I still thought we would be fine because we were with responsible adults.

It began to get dark, which was good because we couldn't show the film outside during the day. A sense of adventure filled my heart.

I chatted with the woman next to me. She was about 70 years old, and this was her first mission trip. She said proudly, "It doesn't matter who you are, God can still use you."

I agreed with her and added, "And it is fun to learn new things on the mission field. I just took a first aid and CPR class yesterday on the ship. That's something I've always wanted to do."

The four men who had initially pushed the carts had gotten us up to speed, and now they jumped on next to us. We coasted freely on the tracks. Just as we entered a bridge, I noticed one of the men was looking intently down the tracks. I was wondering what he was looking at in the dark when he yelled, "TRAIN!"

The four pushers sprang into action and quickly brought the carts to a halt; we all jumped off and grabbed our stuff. My heart was pounding wildly because I did not know how close the train was to us. We still had to get back to the beginning of the bridge, because here in the middle there was nothing but air beside the rails. It was exactly like a movie I had seen once, and I was planning to do the same last-minute dive to safety the movie characters had done.

"Help!" I heard behind me, and I looked back. The woman I had just been visiting with was hip deep in the tracks. She did not realize we were on a bridge and that she could not step between the planks. Her right foot had slipped between the space and she had fallen hard. Now the space squeezed her tightly at her hip. Lori Beth was there trying desperately to lift her, but she was not strong enough.

My fresh first-aid skills jumped into action. I knew I had to help, but it had to be done right. I checked my surroundings first. I looked down the tracks toward the train. I saw the light and heard the whistle, both of which indicated that the train was far enough away. I stepped quickly back to them and looked directly at the woman, reassuring her, "We have plenty of time. Is anything broken?"

"No, I'm just stuck."

That was all I needed to hear. Adrenaline gave me greater strength, and I lifted her in one fluid motion. "Let's go!" I said.

The woman was limping badly as we quickly and carefully worked our way to the end of the bridge. The pushers had successfully lifted and removed the carts from the rails. We turned and pressed our backs against the jungle on the edge of the rail as I sighed with relief. Thirty seconds later, the train barreled past us, about three feet away from our noses. All of this had happened in the matter of minutes, even though it seemed like an eternity.

When we reached the village, it was pitch black, but the team quickly put up a white sheet and then started playing Veggie Tales in Spanish to attract a crowd.

I asked the villagers if anyone had ice. The woman who had fallen was already developing a nasty bruise, and it was starting to swell badly. A little boy ran down to a freezer and asked to have something cold. They gave him a couple of ice cubes, which he brought back to us, and my friend applied the cubes as best she could. It was too dark to see her bruises very well, so she pressed the ice where it hurt. The light of the movie, run by the generator we had brought, was the only light around.

Two hours later, the Jesus movie was over, and someone had preached the gospel through an interpreter. Several people were saved in that village and we prayed with them. It was a wonderful night, but I was dreading the cart ride back to the bus.

We loaded up again, and the little boys ran next to the carts as the pushers got us up to cruising speed. By the time the pushers boarded, the boys had been left behind. I was sitting in the very front of the cart and I could feel the wind in my hair. We seemed to be going faster on the way back. I figured we were on a downhill slant now. It crossed my mind that if we hit anything, I would go flying, and probably get run over by the cart. I was keeping my eyes peeled for a train. My eyes were watering from the wind, but I wanted to be sure we had enough time to clear the tracks if we encountered a train again.

At that moment, I saw a light. Oh great, I thought, here we go again. "Train!" I yelled loudly. I knew it was far away because the light was small. The pushers reacted and we halted quickly.

Everyone knew the drill and started to unload. Once it was quiet, we realized we did not hear the train as we had before. We all looked toward it. The light was still small, and there was no accompanying noise. We all froze, not sure what to do next.

Then we heard, "*Bruuummm….brrhummm…*" The light moved off the tracks, and a small motorcycle passed us on the left. We all burst out laughing! I blushed in the darkness, embarrassed that I had thought it was a train. I was a little trigger happy after my last experience with a real train!

That night, Lori Beth and I vowed to never leave the ship again. And we kept our vow, at least until the following weekend.

I wanted to e-mail Hugo my crazy story, but I still hadn't heard anything from him. Katia was coming home the next day, and I would be able to ask her if she had gotten in touch with him.

In the morning, Katia found me at breakfast. "Sarah, I have a note for you from Hugo. Come to my cabin at 10, and I will explain everything."

I was so stunned that I didn't even think to ask any questions. The way she said it told me that this story had too many details to share in the breakfast buffet line. My job that morning was to chip paint off the side of the ship, which was a constant chore because of the saltwater. I worked on it absentmindedly, not able to think of anything other than Hugo.

At break time, I raced to Katia's room. She was there. I started right in without any cordial greeting. "Katia, what do you mean you have a note from Hugo?"

"Let me tell the whole story, from the beginning," Katia said.

"Okay." I sat down in her doorway so I would not get her room dirty with paint chips.

Katia began to tell me about her experience in El Salvador. The Mercy Ship team ended up working with several different medical teams that were all connected to a local church. They gathered their resources and personnel to brainstorm a plan. The church where they were meeting volunteered several youth to work alongside of them for the week. The church was about eight blocks away from a mountain that had collapsed, killing 300 people. Many of the teens were from that neighborhood and wanted to help.

At first, Katia wasn't even thinking about trying to find Hugo. She was too busy to remember. There was a fun guy working with her all week, and on the last day he asked her, "Do you work with Mercy Ships?"

"Yes, why?" she asked.

He said, "Do you know a tall girl named Sarah Breeden?"

Katia's eyes widened. She pulled the paper I had given her out of her backpack. "Are you Hugo Liborio?"

"Yes." He was confused about why Katia was so excited, but she showed him the paper and told him about how I had asked her to find him

As Katia told me this story, I began to get more and more anxious to find out what Hugo had said to her. But she wasn't finished being amazed that she had found him in the first place. "Out of all the churches in El Salvador, of all the people helping the teams, the one person that you told me to go and find is the one person who was assigned to help me all week. That is impossible. I just can't believe it."

She calmed down and reached into her pocket. "He did not have much time to write you by the time I explained who I was. I left soon after that to come back to the ship, but here is the letter he wrote."

I took the piece of notebook paper she held out to me, unfolded it, and read in Spanish:

> Hey Fumada!!
>
> How are you?? I hope that you are good and that God is blessing your life a lot and your ministry.
>
> You know I worked with the team from the ship. I'm sorry you weren't here. But I hope to see you later.
>
> Please pray for my family and for my goals for this year, and I will be doing that for you too, ok?
>
> I hope that you are still on the ship when it goes to Honduras because YES I will be there, OK!!
>
> Take care of yourself and any questions ask Katia, ok!
>
> Well, a big kiss and blessings.
>
> Chau! Fumada!
>
> Hugo

I took the letter back to my room and read it again. It wasn't much, but I had a gut feeling that somehow this connection with Hugo was a God thing. It wasn't just a coincidence that Katia worked with Hugo, but what did it mean? What was God doing? I was thrilled just to be a part of whatever His plan was, and to see what would come next.

God was also working in the sports ministry. We had developed a good relationship with the local basketball teams and built closer connections with other people we had met on the basketball court. We were so close with our friends that instead of being depressed about spending Christmas in a tropical climate away from our families, we decided to fellowship with our friends in town. We went for a walk, not knowing where we would end up, praying that God would give us a divine appointment to minister to one of our friends.

Just then, Cesar drove up with Carlos, and they offered us a ride. We didn't know where he would take us, but we wanted to see how our prayers would be answered, so we got in. Cesar took us to a house close by. Lori and I were a little confused, until we saw Piero come out of the house.

Piero smiled to us at first, but he seemed really sad. The three boys were standing by the car, talking quietly. None of them seemed like themselves, and we felt something was up. We knew Piero was a Christian, so we decided to ask him what was going on.

"What's wrong, Piero? Why are you sad?" Lori asked.

"It's Helen." He started to tear up, and then opened the door to the one-room house and motioned for us to come inside. Lori and I looked at each other, confused, but then we noticed Helen lying on a bed right inside the door.

We entered and stood nearby as Piero leaned over and whispered something to Helen. Helen sat up, welcomed us, and tried to be her normal bubbly self, but we weren't fooled. Something was definitely wrong.

"Helen, what is going on?" I asked.

She started to cry, and Lori Beth sat on the bed with her. We waited for a while, and then Helen said quietly, "I lost the baby."

Lori Beth and I didn't say anything. I think we were both stunned. We knew Piero and Helen were Christians, but they weren't married, and she was admitting to sin. I didn't know what to say.

She continued on, "Piero and I wanted to start a family, but yesterday I was walking in town and I started bleeding a lot. Piero and Cesar took me to the hospital, but I kept bleeding and I lost the baby. It was so horrible." She was crying again.

Lori Beth spoke first. "I'm so sorry, Helen." There was nothing else to say. Nothing could ease the pain of losing her baby. We hugged her, held her, cried with her, and prayed with her.

After a while, we could see she needed to rest again. As we left, she said, "Thank you for coming. Piero has been very comforting to me, but it was special to have women to talk to. God knew exactly what I needed today."

We smiled and said, "You're welcome. It was God who brought us to you today."

We opened the door to find the guys still leaning on the blue taxi, talking quietly. When they saw us, Piero left to go back in the house, and Cesar and Carlos got back into the taxi. They didn't seem to know what to say. We were all silent as Cesar drove back to the port. He let Lori Beth and me off at the front gate.

Lori Beth and I chatted as we dodged the container trucks on the walk to the ship's gangway. "What a unforgettable Christmas. That was an amazing divine appointment," Lori Beth said.

"I know. We were just walking, and then the guys showed up, and then we just happened to go to their house, which is where God needed us! It was perfect. And we didn't even know it!" I wasn't making much sense, but Lori Beth knew what I meant.

As we walked up the gangway, we nodded to the watchman. I asked Lori Beth a more serious question. "If Helen was pregnant, that means they have slept together. How can they do that if they are Christians? And they were planning a family, so it wasn't an accident. I don't get it." I was counting on Lori Beth's missions experience once again to fill in some cultural gaps.

"Well, it is not an excuse because it's still sin, but the Latino church is shy about teaching on sexual matters. Maybe they were never taught that sex outside of marriage is sin. Their parents are pretty much out of the picture, and they only have each other. They desire to have the family they have always wanted, so they are going to make it themselves. It's sad, but true."

I was so quick to judge, but little did I know I'd soon be falling into my own temptation. And I did know better.

Carlos liked me from the first time we played one-on-one together. I had to admit I was very attracted to him, too. He had asked me several times to be his girlfriend, but I always told him no.

He'd ask me, "Is it because I'm not a Christian that you won't date me?"

I'd always say, "Yes," and I would try to explain using the gospel.

We became good friends, and most of the time he just joked around with me. In his joking he would always say, "Just one kiss." I'd laugh him off, and the next day he would ask me again. He was always very nice to me, bought me ice cream, and introduced me to his mom and sisters. He even went to church with Lori Beth, Patty, and me one Sunday.

I knew I was playing with fire, but I kept telling myself it was for ministry. Justification is easy to come by when you really want something. We usually spent time in groups, playing basketball, going to the waterfall, or hanging out at the park. Then one day, while heading back from the waterfalls, we stopped at Carlos's house, which was on the way. Cesar, Piero, and Lori Beth all took a taxi back into town because Lori Beth had to work.

Soon I realized that everyone was gone, and Carlos and I were left watching TV. I knew I should get up and walk home, but the justifications were there. I made the wrong decision by staying, and Carlos got his one kiss. I'm not sure how it happened, but I had known that it would from the time everyone had left ten minutes before.

How does your body have a premonition about what is going to take place? Is that why they call it chemistry? I knew what was going to happen, I didn't leave, and I didn't stop it. I knew I was in big trouble with God. I left and walked back to the ship.

I found Lori Beth that night. She knew something was up. We had spent so much time together by this point that she could read me like a book.

I confessed to her what had happened. "I messed up with Carlos after you guys left. I let him get his kiss finally."

I expected her to be kind and understanding. I should have known better, because Lori Beth is not the reserved type. "What the heck were you thinking? That was so dumb. You'd better get it together!" She looked at me sternly and then walked off.

I was a little mad at first, but I loved my friend more than ever as God impressed Prov. 27:5-6 on my heart: "Better is open rebuke than hidden love. Faithful are the wounds of a friend." I knew that she loved me too much to just let my sin slide.

Later that week I talked to Carlos. "I know you are not going to understand, but what I did was not right. I'm sorry."

"You're right, I don't understand. Please be my girlfriend. I'll be good to you; I'll provide for you."

"No, Carlos. It's not about what I want; it's what God wants. And we will never be happy if you don't know God the way that I do. I'm sorry for leading you on."

"Please." He looked at me with his dark eyes. He was on one side of the door frame, and I was on the other. Looking up at him, I felt the premonition again. My flesh wanted to give in so much. It was as if I couldn't even stop what I knew was going to happen again.

But I had been convicted and was committed to what I knew what right. I pushed the door frame behind me with my hands and flung myself to a wall three feet away. I felt as if I had physically cut a spiritual chain in two. The premonition was gone. I breathed a thank you to the Holy Spirit for helping me have the strength to obey, because alone I would have failed.

Carlos smiled and started to laugh. "You are such a freezer, Sarah!" He laughed harder. "You're so cold!"

I laughed too, relieved that I had done the right thing. I would much rather be called "cold" than "easy."

Back in my cabin, I cried to God. Though things ended okay with Carlos, I had still sinned, and the consequence of that was probably that my witness to Carlos and others was gone. Why would they believe anything I told them? I had blown it. Stumbled and fallen. I begged God to redeem my ministry and still use me.

Lori Beth and I continued on in our sports ministry, and God did still use us. But we left Guatemala without ever seeing our friends personally accept Christ. Lori Beth and I sat on the boat deck as we sailed away from Santo Tomas that evening. The sky was purple, orange and yellow as the sun disappeared behind the mountain.

I prayed aloud for our friends, "God, keep your promise that Your words will not return void. Even if our friends forget us, help them to not forget You. May they find salvation from sin in the cross and know the Prince of Peace who can calm their storms."

Please visit my website, www.my-onceuponatime.com/, to see pictures and videos from each chapter.

109

Chapter Six

The Prince Pursues the Princess
2001

El Salvador, Honduras, Belize, Florida, Texas,
Dominican Republic, Puerto Rico, Florida, Virginia,
Georgia, South Carolina, New York

I had survived Guatemala, but not without a few bumps and bruises, on my skin and on my heart. By the next port, Satan was already trying to tempt me with guys who were not right for me. I stood strong, but I knew I needed a plan. I decided to put some thoughts in my journal and make a commitment in writing. I wrote:

2/13/01

I've mentioned that I've made mistakes, and I'm going to be honest. Sarah, you totally suck at relationships! You will always remember how your received your first kiss from Adam, then you pushed the limit with Hugo. These encounters are permanent and will always be there.

You must guard your heart better and let God control the situation. It is the day before Valentine's Day, and it is most fitting to write a list of things you want in a husband. Not to say God will give me all the qualities, but at least I will have a goal and not be easily distracted by the others. I have faith beyond all that God will bring me the perfect mate. And I will not marry anyone who does not qualify, who does not help me love, glorify, serve, seek, see, hear, praise God more.

Dear God, I pray for a husband. I pray for my husband. I commit him to You. He's in Your hands, and I know You can and will bring him to me.

Qualities of that Man—
Absolutely sold out for God!
A totally awesome Christian who can lead me and our household in a Christian walk
Someone who makes me want God more
Humble
Servant
Leader
Loves missions
Likes living in other countries
Speaks Spanish

Taller than me
Respected by all
Loves adventure
Plays basketball and other sports
Active
Can keep up with me
He could be Latino because I love their culture
Very handsome and strong
Has good boundaries in dating
Trustworthy
Creative and passionate lover
Pure

I stopped looking for love and let God be in control as I continued my term on the ship. Over the next couple of months, we traveled to the Dominican Republic, Puerto Rico, and several states in the southeastern United States.

There were many more adventures in these ports, but too many to put into one book. I will note, though, that I got to see Tiger Woods and other great golfers on the PGA tour when the ship was in Jacksonville. Just another example of the exciting things I got to do because I was following God's best for my life.

God's best for my life next was to attend a Discipleship Training School, better known as a DTS. Youth with a Mission has schools like these all over the world, but I wanted to join the class that was starting on the ship. All of our classes were in the International Lounge, which was also where the ship had all of its congregational meetings. We had different lecturers every week or two and learned about everything from the Father heart of God to how we could die to self.

The lecture period of the school was three months. I became very close to my team, especially to four other girls in my small group. I told them a lot about Hugo and how I still liked him, but that God would have to make our paths cross again if we were going to get to know each other. They knew everything and prayed with me about God's plans, especially about if I should go to Bible school next.

In my 11 months on the ship, I had learned that the world has questions and they want answers, fast. There is no time to say, "Wait, I'll go ask my dad; he's a pastor." They would not wait for me to get the answer and come back. DTS had some teachings on how to study the Bible, but there was nothing on deep theology, so I knew I needed more if I was going to do full-time missions.

As I thought through my options for Bible school, I made the best of what DTS had to offer. One great thing about it was the emphasis on knowing the Father heart of God and His "devastating passionate love" for each of us. I kept a journal full of spiritual truths that I still cling to today and share with others.

One thing I wrote in it was a book report that was a requirement for the DTS. I read *Is That Really You, God?* by Loren Cunningham.[1] He is the founder of Youth with a Mission, and his book explains how God spoke to him. In my report I shared:

Loren says, "Practice hearing God's voice and it becomes easier. It is like picking up the phone and recognizing the voice of your best friend... you know his voice because you have heard it so much." God is challenging me to know Him like this. To obey the quiet whisper instead of asking God the obvious. It is so easy to follow the fire or strong wind, but the power is in the gentle whisper of my Lord.

One last challenge deals with trust and letting God. Loren writes, "Put your dreams on the altar. They will be resurrected into something even grander." I guess all I can say is, "Amen to that!" It is something that I pray I can do every day and fully in every area that He asks of me. My comfort is that He is my loving father and has even wilder dreams for me than the ones that I lay down!

A half poem, half prayer I wrote in my DTS journal illustrates the intimate relationship I shared with my Lord during those precious months of learning at His feet.

No Breath
When I'm with You, I don't have to breathe.
You breathe for me and sustain my life.
I rest on Your breath, and I feel You fill my lungs with peace.
I rely on You to provide my life.
I feel Your loving arms hold me close; You put Your lips on mine and breathe assurance and provision.
I give up my hopes and dreams to You, and I feel You puff new, sweet air that exhilarates my mind to unfathomable possibilities.
God, I breathe out all of my life in brokenness, and I feel You blow a deep penetrating breath of new life into me . . . but what I enjoy most . . . is the sweet lingering taste of You."

Looking back, I can see how God used DTS to lay a spiritual foundation that, in His omniscience, He knew I would need someday. I see that now, as I read in my journal:

Reflecting on my morning devotion in Phil. 3:10, "That I may know Him and the power of His resurrection, and the fellowship of His sufferings . . . " I want to take this moment to say something scary: "I want to know Christ in the fellowship of His sufferings!" How much more can I learn about Christ if I do fellowship in His sufferings? What am I missing there? I love the "power of His resurrection." Will I love the sufferings as well? What will it be like, look like? I pray God shows me and brings me to a new level of understanding Christ.

One of the favorite speakers during the ship's DTS was Rob Morris. I looked forward to him coming. I had heard about him but had never met him. He showed up with his ears pierced and with spiky hair. He might have looked crazy, but he had a serious message to bring us. I furiously wrote pages of notes while he spoke. Some of the notes I took are as follows:

God won't give you more than you can handle? Bull! You will get more than you can handle so that you can realize that you need God! God can handle our honesty, our tears, our screams. There are times in your spiritual life when you can't depend on feelings, only faith. There is a maturing and growing up that takes place. It is a good thing. He sees in you a maturity that can handle Him removing the emotions and feelings. He can let go of your hands and you can walk. There is a purification of love. Are we in this for the backrub or are we in it for God? Are you a Christian for heaven and blessings or God? Christianity is not about me! It is about Him! It is because He is worthy to be praised! Victory is the person that is in the midst of struggle and turmoil, and problems, and can still look up at God and flowing out of their lips is love towards Him. That is victory! Only if you want to go deep with Him, if you deeply want intimacy with Him, then love Him for who He is and not what He can do for you. It is a beautiful ache for God. It is a depth beyond anything. God makes beauty out of ashes. But, we make the ashes most of the time. Life happens and it sucks, but God makes good out of it. He redeems the situation. Embrace the struggle, don't let it become your identity, but embrace it. Life is like that in our fallen world.

My heart burned inside of me with each phrase he said. He was so passionate about God's love for me. I was tired of sucking the wonder out of God. I just wanted to be astonished by Him more, and to know that He was not meant to be grasped by me. His love is too extravagant. Rob said, with fire in his eyes and passion in his voice, "We are grasping for air under the thick blanket of boredom, when we should be breathing free in intoxicating air of astonishment!"

I also had fun pages in my journal. I glued in a phrase from a magazine that said, "A knight in shining, double-sided, galvanized steel." Next to it, I wrote, "I love this saying because it speaks my heart's desire. I don't just want a 'Knight in Shining Armor.' I want so much more than that. My desires and dreams are so much more than that. That is why this saying is awesome. It cries out for so much more!"

I also glued a picture of a guy and a girl lying on a bed together. They had on comfy clothes, and the girl's head barely peeked out of a blanket on top of them both. The guy's jeans could be seen, but he had his head under the blanket on the other side of the bed. I wrote a caption under the picture: "Looking Forward to What's to Come." Then I wrote an explanation for why I had included it: "I love this picture because it is so fun! Like the best part of getting married is hanging out every day with your best friend. Just chillin' on the bed, talking about everything and nothing all at the same time. Just being yourself, and loving who he is, and who you are with him."

The last class we had on the ship before we had outreach time in Honduras was on spiritual warfare. I had a difficult time with parts of the theology taught in this class. However, in the end, I still felt that God would be glorified by what I had learned. In my journal, responding to the question, "How are you going to use this class in your life after your DTS?" I wrote, "I will forever be in intercession for non-Christians and showing them how to bridge the gap. Always fighting Satan for souls. Defeating him in every area. Claiming God's victory!"

I decided to go home to Kansas for my friend Danielle's wedding. She had asked me to be a bridesmaid. She was marrying Steve, who was in our TFC youth group. Who would have thought that God would bring them together? The wedding was beautiful. After the wedding, Steve's best man, Cody, and I dropped Steve and Danielle off at her apartment.

She was the first of my close friends to get married, so it was a new and strange experience. Steve's dad had put all of the wedding gifts on the bed and around it. He also put folding chairs and other heavy items against the sides of the bed. It was really funny, but I don't think Steve was as amused. He made Cody and me help move all the gifts to the kitchen.

Then, I hugged Danielle goodbye and waved to Steve at the door. Cody and I walked to the car. I turned and waved bye to them once more. They were contentedly standing in the doorway together, Steve's big arms enveloping Danielle. As Cody and I drove back to the reception to help clean up, I thought about how fast life was changing. Despite my global ambitions, I hoped I'd always stay close to my hometown friends.

For the rest of the evening, I felt pensive and spent time praying. God was pressing on my heart. I could almost hear Him saying, "Hays is good, but I have bigger dreams for you. You need to trust Me for that dream. It will require giving up your family and the hope of living close to them. You will also have to give up living in Hays and having your friends here close."

I was saddened by this impression that God gave me, because I treasured the closeness I felt with my family and friends. But I also felt peace knowing that, when the time came, I was prepared to give up those things for God's call on my life.

God's call for the present was to return to my team and finish DTS. We were all ready for the practical part of our training, when we would put into practice the Biblical concepts we had learned in the classroom. The outreach would be in Honduras. The ship sailed to Honduras, but our team had to fly because otherwise the ship would have been overcrowded, with not enough life vests for every passenger in an emergency.

We flew into Tegucigalpa, Honduras, which was a life-threatening experience in itself! I'd heard it had the highest accident rate of any airport in the world. When we were landing, I began to see why: There was no landing strip in sight, just row after row of houses. It seemed we would land right on top of them, but just when I thought for sure we were going to crash, we hit the runway. The plane had to slow down quickly, because the runway was so short, and all the passengers' heads flew forward in unison. When we did come to a stop, everyone cheered. I felt as if we had just escaped death and was happy to have survived. I know now that a round of applause is customary at touchdown in Latino countries, but I think this group of passengers felt more relieved than excited.

It was early evening, and the ship had sent a bus to pick us up. My friend Oscar drove, and he helped us load the luggage. We still faced an eight-hour bus ride to Puerto Cortes, where the ship was docked. Catching as much sleep as possible during the bus ride, I woke when we arrived at a restaurant called Casa del Rio. Still groggy, I entered the restaurant, then froze. Surely I was still on the bus dreaming.

There sat Hugo.

My friend Tressa bumped into me from behind. "Oh, sorry. Where's the bathroom?" She walked past me and worked her way through the tables and chairs to a sign that read "Baños" along the back wall.

Katia and Albert, who were sitting with Hugo, noticed him staring at the door, at me, and turned to look, too. I went to hug them.

Then I turned to give Hugo a hug and said something dumb like, "It's really good to see you. How's your family? Okay, see you around." I shot like a bullet towards the baño sign.

Oscar came out of the men's room. I grabbed him and pulled him aside. Oscar and Hugo were both Salvadorians and watched each other's backs. "Oscar, did you know Hugo was going to be here? Why did you not tell me?"

I was reeling! I had not seen Hugo in a year and 10 days. I had always imagined what it would be like to see him again. Me freaking out was not a part of the plan, but I thought I would have a little bit more time to prepare. Seeing him unexpectedly at a restaurant following a day of traveling and sleeping on a bus was not part of the plan.

Oscar saw my panic and knew he'd better play dumb, or I would wring his neck. "No, I didn't know he would be here. He must have just come today."

I went into the bathroom. All my small group girls were in there talking. I closed the door and leaned against it. They knew I was not prone to being dramatic. They all looked at me with blank expressions on their faces.

I blurted out, "It's him!" Their expressions didn't change. "It's Hugo. That guy I just hugged. That's Hugo!"

They were all as confused as I was. "Which Hugo? Your Hugo? *The* Hugo?" one of them said.

"Yes! THAT Hugo!"

Another butted in, "But what is he doing here?"

"I don't know. Working with the ship, I guess." I started to calm down. "Okay, it's okay. We just have to be normal." We all piled out of the bathroom. I think Tressa was the only one who actually used the facilities.

Normal, we were not. We would talk in hushed voices, and then one of my friends would turn to look at Hugo. Then we would talk again.

Finally, I went over to Hugo and sat down. My Spanish was a little rusty after having been in the States for three months. Hugo used a little of the English he had learned, but Albert and Katia did a lot of the talking for us. Mostly we made fun of Albert. He's Cuban, born and raised in Miami, but his Spanish could be really bad sometimes.

I found out that Hugo had joined the ship for the Honduras outreach, so I'd be seeing him around. I was a little upset by this, because I did not want to be distracted by a boy during DTS. I just wanted to focus on ministry and finish my time well.

Over the next couple of weeks, I did not get to see Hugo much, because my team was living in a house in town, involved in ministry. We had two outreaches going. The first was working with a people group living along the coast called the

Garifuna. They were descendants of Carib, Arawak, and West African people. Their first language was Garifuna, which is primarily derived from Arawak and Carib, with some English, French, and Spanish. We were glad to see that all of them also spoke Spanish, and a few knew English as well.

We found that the Garifuna in the village we worked in, Travesia, liked the Catholic Church in their town. They claimed to be Catholic, but none really attended church. Instead, most were involved in other spiritual practices that were more voodoo in origin.

One of the men with whom we worked was known as "Cappuccino." He owned a thatched-roof bar right on the beach. In my Kansas mind, he was what I imagined a Rastafarian to look like and be. He had long hair and would make us beaded necklaces, using only red, green, yellow, and black beads. He also had a picture of Bob Marley in his bar.

Cappuccino was one of the first people we met in Travesia. We soon found out that everyone knew and respected him. He was very nice to us and helped us gather groups of people together for different events. Partway through our time in Honduras, he actually received Christ and stopped selling alcohol.

My team's second outreach was to families in a garbage dump. This was a challenge for all of us. Waving constantly to keep the flies at bay became second nature. The families who lived there no longer batted at the flies, for they no longer noticed the nuisance.

We spent most of the two months simply visiting the dump every couple days, trying to get to know the people there. We prayed for them and invited them to a nearby church. At the church, we held a breakfast program for the kids before Sunday School, reasoning that the children would hear better if their hungry tummies were quiet.

Most days, they would look for meals in the trash that would come in from the dump trucks. It was heartbreaking to see how excited the kids got every time a trash truck came down the road. The bigger boys would jump on the truck as soon as it made the turn into the dump. Mothers and old men would slowly come out of their makeshift huts, grab a bucket, and make their way to where the truck was unloading the day's provisions. Everything they needed to survive was retrieved from the city's trash.

During my outreach, Hugo was back on the ship starting his job with the deck department. He spent a lot of time as a gangway watchman, controlling who was allowed onto the ship. Many people would come to the ship seeking doctor appointments or even food, and Hugo would direct them to other locations where we were meeting those needs.

Hugo told me later that when my team would come to visit the ship (mainly to buy Dr. Pepper!), everyone on the team would be friendly and say hi to him. However, the one person he really cared about would simply walk by him without even a nod. I don't think I was *that* bad, but I do remember my desire to maintain on the DTS outreach, with no boy distractions.

After a week or so, Katia found me and told me, "Sarah, you have to stop ignoring Hugo. He really wants to talk to you. You're killing him!"

"But I have to stay focused."

"Just go for a walk on the dock later and visit for five minutes. It is not going to derail you. Just talk to him."

"Fine."

Later that evening, after dinner, I saw Hugo in the dining room. I walked up to him and said in English, "Do you want to go for a walk?"

"Sure," he said and jumped up.

We took the spiral stairs to reception, signed out, and went down to the dock. I knew I would have to switch to Spanish. For some reason this made me mad, or maybe flustered. I think I was embarrassed by my Spanish. I really did want to talk to him, so I was upset that the language barrier was still a problem. Not that he could do anything about it. He was trying to learn English as best as he could, but it takes time.

I started with the basics to break the ice. "Como esta tu familia?" (How is your family?)

"Bien, Febe se caso con Carlos." (Good. Febe married Carlos).

And then we were off, speaking Spanish and catching up on life for the last year that we had not seen each other. It was so good to finally talk to him, even though I had been avoiding it. I had missed him so much. He was just as I had remembered him. Compassionate, gentlemanly, and so good-looking!

After that chat on the dock, our friendship was more normal. I'd actually say hi to Hugo and chat with him when my team would come to the ship. Once, he wasn't at the gangway when I got there. I looked all over for him. I was distracted, just like I didn't want to be, but DTS was almost over. I had plans to go to Guatemala to visit friends that Lori Beth and I had made in the sports ministry. I would stay at Patty's house. Then I'd head home and begin the search for a Bible school.

This particular day I had looked for Hugo all over and was getting a little impatient. I knew he hadn't left the ship, because we were required to sign out in case there was a fire. Hugo had not signed out. Where could he be? I asked myself why I cared so much to find him if I was not interested in him, like I had told all my friends.

I finally decided to go swimming with my small-group girlfriends. There was a small pool next to the ship for crew to enjoy, so I joined my friends there. Just as I climbed the ladder and was about to step into the pool, a truck drove by. Inside I could see Albert driving, Katia in the middle, and Hugo in the passenger's seat with a girl on his lap. I glared at them to see who the girl was. Hugo's eyes caught mine. He waved. I didn't recognize the girl, just as I didn't recognize this burning in my heart and this unfamiliar twist in my stomach.

I got into the pool and hunched down in the water near the wall. I was thinking and trying to figure out what I was feeling. I was perplexed for a moment, but then it hit me. Jealousy. That's what I was feeling. I had never felt it before. It was an eye-opening experience for me. I thought, "I think I like Hugo even more than I'm willing to admit to myself."

I happened to be on the ship the very next day. Hugo found me right away and explained about the girl. "She was a new nurse on the ship. Albert and Katia wanted to take her to a movie and asked me to come along. They couldn't get a bigger vehicle from the ship, so she had to sit on my lap."

I waved him off like it was no big deal. "You don't need to explain to me." But, deep down, I was glad that he had.

He asked, "Do you want to go to a waterfall with Albert, Katia, and me later on this week?"

"I'll ask the team leader if I can have some free time, but that would be fun. Thank you."

I did get permission to go the next week. Albert, Katia, Hugo, and I left in the Frontier truck to go to Pulhapanzak Falls. It was difficult to find, and we kept stopping to ask villagers on the side of the road to point us in the right direction. From Pena Blanca we got off at San Buenaventura. From there, we had to follow the trail to a signpost. Eventually we found the falls. It was kind of an out-of-the-way tourist site, but well worth the fear of getting lost. The waterfalls were beautiful, much more so than I thought they would be.

We paid a guide nearby to lead us to the small caves that could be found behind the waterfalls. The hike down was tricky, because the rocks were slippery and a little hard to traverse. But once we got to the caves, we were well rewarded.

For me, it was a spiritual moment. I was right behind the guide. I could tell he had years of experience. He told me, "Foot here . . . foot here." He'd point where I had to put each foot as to not lose balance and fall. He knew where all the rocks and holes were.

The Holy Spirit was already showing me how this was like me following Christ. Then, when I was crossing the water trying to make my way to the caves on the other side, I lost track of my guide. The water was all around me and I could barely open my eyes. I didn't know which way to turn to get out. My heart fainted in fear. The sound of the water crashing against my body and all around me was deafening. I couldn't hear any voices. I felt alone. Through my squinted eyes, I could just make out a hand thrusting itself in front of me. I recognized the guide's hand and grasped it tightly. He pulled me into the calmness of the cavern. In the security and calm of the cave, I wondered at how Christ was leading me in the same way.

Being behind the waterfall was so much fun, but Hugo and I decided we wanted to jump off the cliff. The guide led us to the safest spot to jump. It was about a 30-foot drop into the rushing water near the base of the waterfall. The guide showed us where to stand and how to jump. Then he headed downstream so he could help us get out of the water. The water was flowing fast enough that he did not want us to miss the exit. I jumped first, because I wanted to show Hugo that I was not afraid. Then Hugo jumped, not wanting me to show him up.

Even though we hadn't been there long, at that point we had to leave. I had been given a time to return to the ship, and it had taken us so long to get there that our time was really short. We quickly changed in a line of changing rooms by the parking lot. After I had gotten my dry clothes back on, I noticed a little eye peeking in at me from the stall next to me. A little native boy had been watching me change. I was so mad that I just got into the truck. I didn't tell my friends. There was nothing I could do, and I just wanted to enjoy the ride home.

There were several other times when Hugo and I hung out and just got to know each other. We were becoming really good friends. We knew we were just friends, but there was something special about our friendship. It just felt different from my other guy friendships. Hugo seemed to feel that certain something too.

One evening, I was playing two-on-two basketball with three guys on the dock. I loved playing basketball with guys, because they made my game a lot better.

Hugo was at a birthday party on the ship's deck, and he called down to me, "Hey, Sarah!"

I looked up, squinting in the sun setting behind the ship. "Yeah, what's up?"

"When you're done, come up and hang out with me."

"Okay, we have a couple more points to go, and then I'll be up." My teammate and I quickly finished off the competition. We shook hands and promised a rematch soon. I bounced up the gangway and climbed the stairs to the deck. Hugo smiled as I came and sat with him at a table. We chatted with Katia and Albert. Katia took our picture.

Then Hugo said, "Come on, let's go talk."

"Okay."

Hugo led me along the starboard side of the ship, past the lifeboats, past the stairs to the lower decks, and up three small stairs. That put us beside the bridge. Instead of entering the bridge door, he sat down on the little landing. It was a spot where the deckhands stood during a sail to look for small boats or lights in the distance. I took a spot next to him on the old wooden floor and leaned against the iron wall of the ship. We sat silently for only a moment. Hugo started in quickly on a speech in Spanish that he must have been rehearsing for quite some time.

"Sarah, I don't tell you this to pressure you in any way. But I have loved you since the first time that I met you. And I just want to ask you: will you be my girlfriend?"

I sat quietly. I looked at him. Why did he have to be so cute? This was going to be so hard. I took a deep breath. "Hugo, I like you. I like you a lot. I have prayed about this. It is just not God's right timing. I am going back to the States in a few weeks, and I'll mostly likely be going to college for the next four years. How am I supposed to study and serve God while I am there, if half of my heart is here with you? It would be so hard. It is just not God's timing, yet."

"Okay." I could tell he was really disappointed and that, although my logic was true, it was not the answer he wanted.

"Hugo, you are one of my best friends. You mean more to me than any other guy friend that I have. Anytime you need me, just tell me and I will stop whatever I am doing to help you. You can count on me to pray for you, but I just have to follow God's will in this area, despite what I want."

"I know. You are right. And you are more than a friend to me too. I will be here when you are ready. Anything you need, let me know. I will drop everything to talk to you any time."

"Okay." I nodded.

"Okay." He nodded.

From that time on, anytime I needed someone to chat with, I'd walk to his post on the gangway and look at him. He'd come right over and ask me what was up. We became even closer friends. He even sang a karaoke song to me at Casa del Rio one night, "Amiga Mia."[2] He was so good, but he made me laugh.

Then Katia said, "You know he is singing that to you, right?"

I looked at her. "What?"

"Yeah, it is a romantic song, and he is singing it to you."

I protested, "I thought the song was about a friend who is a girl."

She responded, "It's a little more than that."

I felt a twinge of pain. I wanted to be with Hugo more. I knew Hugo still cared deeply about me, but I just was convicted of God's will on my life. My mind wandered back to the day I was shooting hoops, when I promised God I would not let any boy get in the way of His will for my life.

My time in Honduras was just about ending. DTS was over. The director's wife wrote in my class journal to sign off that I had done all the required work. She wrote:

> Sarah,
>
> As I have reviewed your journal, I couldn't help feeling pleased in how you have submitted your life to Christ during your DTS and seeing the progressive growth and changes within you. One can really see and hear the desires of your heart seem to be drawn to preaching the good news, whether it be in missions in a faraway land or serving in your local church and community. Your heart is for winning others to Christ. My prayer for you is that the Spirit would continue to empower you and guide you clearly into what all the Lord has for you.
>
> —Janet

With DTS over, I'd be traveling to Antigua, Guatemala, to study Spanish at an immersion Christian Spanish academy for three weeks. I was going to stay with Patty first, then travel to the capital and hang out with same friends from the ship, Byron, Hector, and Marco.

Hugo took me to a carnival in Puerto Cortes the day before I left. We were both sad that I was leaving. Once again, we didn't know when, or even if, we would see each other again.

I said goodbye the next day and took the bus across the Honduran-Guatemalan border to Santo Tomas. I took a bus from Santo Tomas to Guatemala City. Byron, Hector, and Marco picked me up there in Guatemala City and took me out to lunch. They were always nice and paid for me. They drove me up the curvy mountain highway to Antigua. Hector worked in Antigua with a Christian organization called Students International (SI). He showed me where he worked and told me I could walk to his office if I needed anything. SI was in an old monastery and seemed to be a fun mission group.

The guys also took me by the central park and introduced me to a guy washing cars in the street. As I shook hands with him, I noticed a bandage across his neck. I started talking with Marco, while Hector and Byron talked to the bandaged guy. I watched as the man removed the bandage to reveal a huge gash from the right side of his neck near the jawbone all the way across to his left collarbone.

When we turned to leave, Hector explained, "The man with the cut neck got into a heated argument with another car washer about whose territory was whose. The other man pulled a knife and tried to kill him."

I scoffed, "They know this is just car washing, right?"

"Well, yeah. But it's more than that for them. It's their livelihood. Washing that one car could mean food on the table for their kids that night. For them it is life or death."

"I see." I had a lot to learn about life on the mission field.

Hector continued, "I wanted him to meet you so that he would tell the other guys not to rob you while you're here. He'll keep an eye out for you." He smiled, but he wasn't joking.

"Okay . . . well . . . thanks, I guess," I said, thinking that this was one conversation I would not be sharing with my parents.

Marco patted my back reassuringly and explained, "As you have seen, Antigua is a popular tourist attraction, and people from all over the world visit here. It is the perfect place for pickpockets and petty thieves. It's not a big deal, but we know you have to walk to and from the school to the host house. Plus, if you go out to the market to buy souvenirs, we just want to be sure that you are extra safe."

They drove me to my host house and dropped me off. It was now dark. The hostess showed me to my private room on the second floor. I had my own key to the house and my room, so I could come and go as I pleased.

"Breakfast is at 7 in the morning." The hostess spoke to me slowly in Spanish. She knew I had come to learn the language and wasn't sure what level I was at. I asked her about lunch in Spanish so she would know I could carry on a basic conversation.

I woke the next morning feeling so excited to get started. I walked out to the open-air hallway that connected my room to two other student rooms. I was the only resident for this week. As I walked, I looked over my shoulder. The view caused me to stop short.

I could see three large volcanoes dominating the horizon around Antigua. The most commanding, to the south of the city, is the Volcán de Agua, or "Volcano of Water." It stands some 12,356 feet high. It became known as Volcán de Agua after a mudslide from the volcano buried the capital. To the west of the city is a pair of peaks, Acatenango, which stands 13,045 feet high and last erupted in 1972, and the Volcán de Fuego, or "Volcano of Fire," which stands 12,346 feet high. Fuego is famous for being almost constantly active at a low level. Smoke issues from its top daily, but larger eruptions are rare.

I leaned out of the open hallway and looked around the building to my right. From there, I could see Cerro de la Cruz (Hill of the Cross), another popular tourist attraction in Antigua. I took a deep breath of exhilarating fresh air. I took a quick shower and got down to breakfast at 7. The hostess had prepared a Guatemalan breakfast, which included black beans, eggs, coffee, and maize tortillas.

I walked the three blocks to Christian Spanish Academy (CSA) and began three weeks of intense learning. CSA was set up so that all my classes were unique to my ability and learning style. I was paired up with one professor first for personal testing, and he was also my one-on-one teacher for the weeks I was there. The school was beautiful, and I learned so much. I took eight hours of classes for the first two weeks I was there. I decided on only four hours for the last week, because my brain was fried.

Besides, I wanted to get out and enjoy the sights of the town a little bit. I finished my last week without burning too many brain cells. I bought an Alejandro Sanz CD to celebrate. He's a singer from Spain that my Latino friends had introduced me to.

I flew home to Kansas a week before Sept. 11, 2001. That morning, I was asleep in my waterbed when my dad flung open the door to my room. "Sarah, an airplane hit one of the World Trade towers."

Maybe because I'm from Kansas, I pictured in my mind a small crop duster plane. Or possibly a private jet. I got up and dragged myself to the TV to see what Dad was so worked up about. As a family we had visited the Twin Towers once. I remember eating French fries that looked like waffles in the café at the top. Because of this small connection, I was interested in what was going on.

I quickly saw that the situation was worse than I had expected. I started praying that not too many people would get hurt or die. It was horrible. Then the second plane hit. I screamed "No, no, no!" I started crying. My heart grieved, and I prayed on my knees for the people involved. I watched in horror as they showed people falling or jumping from the buildings. I clasped my hand over my mouth, closed my eyes, and prayed aloud, "Lord, no. Please, not this. God be with them. Comfort them." Then the Pentagon was hit, and another plane crashed in Pennsylvania. It was like a movie, but it was real. I kept checking to see that I was really awake and I was really hearing and seeing this on the news. It couldn't be true! But it was.

Then the broadcaster mentioned something about the towers falling. I scoffed. They couldn't fall down. I had seen them. I remembered standing in front of one of the Twin Towers and looking straight up. It was huge. There was no way a building that size could just fall down. The broadcaster was probably just being dramatic. But then one tower did fall, straight down, and then the other. I cried out again, "God, how? Why? Who?"

I felt so powerless to help but knew that praying was the best thing I could do. I prayed survivors would be found and the death toll would stay low. I cringed every day as the number continued to climb. It was devastating, but I prayed that God would use these people's stories for His glory. I was also grateful to have gotten home when I did, because it took the airports so long to reopen and get stranded travelers on their way.

Hugo, however, was still on the ship. He had seen the same images when he entered the dining room for breakfast that morning. He saw everyone watching TV. He watched for a while, then asked, "What movie are you guys watching?" It took some convincing before he was willing to believe that this was real news.

By September, the ship was almost done with the outreach in Honduras. Hugo had committed to those four months, mainly because his finances would not stretch any further. The ship asked him to stay and offered to help find supporters to pay his crew fees. They wanted to use him on the evangelism team because of his excellent music and drama skills. The ship took him to the U.S. Embassy in San Pedro Sula and helped him get a U.S. visa. He would need it, because the ship would be leaving Central America soon and heading to the southern United States for a public relations tour.

As much as I missed the ship and Hugo, I set my mind to finding a Bible school to attend. I applied first to Moody Bible Institute in Chicago, because I'd always thought of it as the "Mecca" of Bible schools. I sent in my application and waited.

At church one Sunday, I connected with a high school friend of mine, Asako. When I first knew her in high school, she was an exchange student from Japan. She was two years ahead of me. She hung out with our youth group and really fit in with us. She was so nice, but the guys joked around with her a lot because she was so gullible then. She was smart, though, and quickly learned their tactics. They tried so hard to get the best of her.

I commented to Asako about my desire to get into Moody. She told me, "I went to a Bible school up in Schroon Lake, New York, called Word of Life Bible Institute. Just check it out online and if you don't get into Moody, pray about Word of Life, because I thought it was really good."

"Okay, Asako, I'll check it out." When I got home from church, I sat down at my Dad's computer right away and looked it up. I scrolled through the classes they had to offer. I was impressed that there were a lot of the classes that I was looking for, including Bible Survey, Theology, and Bible Exposition. That afternoon, I submitted the same application I had sent to Moody. Two weeks later I received my acceptance to Word of Life.

I was happy but still wanted to hold out for Moody. Not long after that, they wrote to me explaining that their housing for female students was full. I decided that

God was closing that door, and I made plans to start at Word of Life as a January student at the beginning of 2002. I had already missed the start of fall classes.

I had read the ship's itinerary and saw that they would be in Galveston, Texas, soon. How I wanted to see Lori Beth, Kristy and some of my DTS friends who had stayed on the ship. I especially wanted to see Hugo. It was only a short 13-hour drive from my parents' house in Hays – a short distance considering the fact that I wouldn't have to cross any oceans to get there.

Soon my prayers were answered when Kristy called me and told me that her commitment with the ship was up. She wondered if I could drive down to the ship, hang out with everyone for a couple weeks, and then drive her back to Hays. I jumped at the chance and connected with a DTS friend, Melissa, to carpool with me. I didn't want to make the drive alone. She would have to leave earlier than I, but her boyfriend would drive back with her. I would be driving back with Kristy.

December came, and I set out on my long trek to meet Melissa and her boyfriend at the designated spot. When I got there, I did not find her. I called, and Melissa said, "I got sick and I'm not able to travel today. Sorry. We'll be coming down in a couple days."

I called my parents and told them I'd be traveling alone. Dad explained the route I was supposed to take over the phone. It was a straight shot south from Wichita to Galveston. I'm pretty good with a map and directions, so I was confident I could do it alone. I popped in a book on tape and cruised down the highway.

I was so into my book on tape that I didn't realize that I needed gas. I caught it just in time and got to the pump right before the car died. I made good time, and soon I was with my friends on the ship. I hugged Kristy, Lori, Tressa, Katia, and Albert as I kept a keen eye out for Hugo in the lineup. Sure enough, there he was. We smiled and blushed at the same time. I was frustrated that I could act normal around every other guy except for him.

I spent most of the week trying to ignore Hugo, while simultaneously trying to be on top of where he was and who he was with at all times. Once, I spotted him in town with a girl from the ship that I did not know very well. He knew I had seen him, and later he told me that he just went to the beach with her to talk about her ex-boyfriend.

It was weird how we weren't in a relationship, but still felt the need to explain these things to each other. We did not spend much time having deep conversations. I didn't want him to fall in love with me while I was there, so I tried to keep him at arm's length. But then I would want to see him, and I'd cave and ask him to watch a movie with me. I kept going back and forth, and I'm sure I tortured Hugo as much as I was torturing myself. I spent the whole two weeks bellyaching to Lori Beth, "I like Hugo so much, but I am going to Bible school in a month, and I don't see how we could keep a relationship going."

Since I had driven my parents' car down, all my friends were excited to be a little more mobile than normal. We'd all go to the movies or to the store and hang out as a group. I almost always invited Hugo. He was fun to be around. Since it was close to Christmas, we watched "How the Grinch Stole Christmas," with Jim Carrey, on the big screen in the International Lounge.

Hugo laughed so hard I could hear his voice booming all the way back in the dining room area where I was popping some popcorn. I laughed too, because I doubted that he even understood all the dialogue. He just wanted to laugh and make other people laugh too.

Once Hugo and I went to a museum about oil rigs that was right next to where the ship was docked. We talked a little bit then, but still nothing very deep. Finally, the last night I was on the ship, I decided I would allow myself real time to spend with Hugo. Lori and I invited a few of our guy friends to a special meal that we prepared in the crew galley. After that I went with Hugo to his cabin. We left the door open and listened to music. He had to go on gangway watch soon and wanted me to listen to something first

I knew Hugo played guitar, but I was not aware of his great love for music. He'd play one song for me, then switch to another song, then another. Finally I said, "Wait, don't you ever listen to a whole song, DJ Hugo?"

"Not usually," he confessed sheepishly. "My philosophy of music is: 'There is a lot of music and not enough time.' So I rarely listen to a whole song. I know my favorite parts and just listen to those."

"I see," I responded, questioning his sanity.

He started another song. It was in Spanish, and the words were too fast for me to pick up, so he translated it for me line by line. It was a beautiful story. This singer was famous for songs that told stories. Hugo played though several of them and translated them for me. He was like a little boy. He eyes would light up and he'd say, "Listen to this part …wait … it's a simple piano in the background." As that section passed, he'd pretend to play the piano section too. I could barely make out the piano part myself, but his ears heard every instrument and every subtle note. The music loved him, and his smiled showed that he loved music.

He had to dress for work on the gangway. He had the 10 p.m. to 4 a.m. shift. I told him I would be in the TV lounge watching a movie with friends.

"Okay, I'll check on you later," he said.

I walked to the lounge and started the movie. About five minutes later, Hugo slid open the door. I was on the couch right next to the door, so he sat on the arm to be next to me. He stayed for a while, but knew he should check the gangway again. He left, but not for long. He came back again.

I knew my friends would kill him if he kept opening and closing the sliding door, letting in light and noise and distracting them from the movie. I decided I should go to the gangway and hang out with Hugo there, because it seemed like that was what he really wanted. I figured we only had a little bit more time together, and he couldn't fall in love with me in one night. I leaned over and told Lori Beth the scoop. She nodded and I left.

I found Hugo at his post at the gangway. The tide was so low that the ship sat really low in the water compared to where the dock was. This made it necessary for the gangway to be connected to the ship on the "A" deck, instead of where it normally attached on the "B" deck.

Hugo was standing with one foot balanced on a chair, playing the guitar that a Korean friend, Induk, had given to him as a gift. Hugo was so proud of that guitar. I could hear that he was playing "I Can Only Imagine,"[3] by Mercy Me. I slowed my assent of the circular stairs, so I could watch him before he noticed me. He looked very handsome in his watchman uniform.

He looked up. "Hey . . ." He smiled and blushed because he knew I was watching him. I could tell he really was shy, though most of the time he covered that over with jokes. He looked down at his shoes, turned in his right foot slightly, and dug at the carpet with his shoe. I smiled at his shyness and decided to give him a break by starting the conversation.

"So, I just wanted to come and keep you company."

"I thought you were going to watch the movie."

"Well, you came back so many times, I figured you really wanted to hang out with me, so I decided to come to you."

"Yeah, thanks. I hate having to work nights when there is a party going on."

"I know. That is the bad part about deck department. Oh, I especially hate when it is at the end of your shift, and it's 3:30 a.m. and you can hardly stay awake, and you body hurts so much because you just want to go to bed."

"That is the worst," Hugo said.

"I once pulled a triple shift," I said, trying to impress him and get the conversation flowing with common deck duty horror stories. "Yep, on one sail I was on the last shift before we got to port, from 4 a.m. to 8 a.m. Right about the time my bridge shift was over, we got into port. I had to report to the bow to help with the mooring lines and dock the ship. That took about two hours of being on the deck and some hard labor.

"Then right after that I was told they were switching to the new gangway watch schedule and I was first up from 10 a.m. to 2 in the afternoon! I was beat, but I went and changed into my watchman uniform and got to the gangway. I was miserable. Luckily the guy next on the schedule knew I was tired, and showed up early. I don't remember my head hitting the pillow when I got to my cabin. But I do love working on deck. There's something new to do every day and so many interesting things to learn."

"The schedule is the worst in the deck department. I hate getting up at 4 in the morning and having to go to work," he said. "Sometimes I hit the snooze button and just show up late. Hey, do you know what the worst lie of the devil is?"

"No." I raised my eyebrows and looked at him closely. I still could not read him well enough to tell when he was joking and when he was serious.

"The worst lie of the devil is, 'Just five more minutes.'"

"Huh?" I said, confused.

"When you wake up in the morning and think, 'Just five more minutes,' it is never just five more minutes. It is the worst lie of the devil."

We laughed together. It was a much-improved joke compared to the little red marble. I was still smiling when I asked, "You're changing teams, right? To the evangelism team, Esperanza?"

"Yeah," he replied. "I really liked deck. But now they are switching me over to the evangelism team to help with music and drama, which I really love to do, too. I will miss some parts of working on deck, like my boss, Kathy. I respect her so much.

"Once, there were four guys pulling on a mooring line trying to get it tight, so that the ship would not move too much next to the dock. She was yelling at us, 'Tighter! Tighter! Pull harder!' I was new, and did not know her well yet. I got mad and yelled, 'That's as much as it goes.' She came over, looked at us, grabbed the line the four of us just tried to move, and heaved it tighter.

"She is super strong and really smart to be a first mate, since they're usually men. Ever since then, I respect her a lot, and we are friends now. But Cindy Lou needs a lot of help with the Esperanza Team."

"Yeah, you're going to do awesome there," I told him. "You are so good at guitar."

"Can I play for you?" he asked me.

"Sure." I sat on the floor in front of him. He put his foot up on the chair again, and propped the guitar on his knee.

"I just helped the Esperanza Team, along with some DTS guys on the ship, to record a CD at a recording studio. See what you think," Hugo said. He started singing "God of Wonders."[4] He had such a great voice and played guitar with such passion.

Our conversation, with interspersed guitar solos, lasted until 4 in the morning. Hugo finally forced me to go to bed, because he knew I had to drive 13 hours in the morning. We had talked about seemingly everything, and it was all in English. He had learned so much during the four months that I had not seen him.

When I asked him about it, he said, "When I was on gangway watch twice a day for four hours each, I'd get out my notebook and study. I'd ask people going by how to say things. People would stop and visit with me, encouraging me. Especially Captain John's daughter, Loren. When other people would be too busy to help, she'd sit and answer all my questions."

I was very impressed. For the first time, I felt that I really, truly communicated with him, that I was able to express my feelings about issues and be able to listen to his heart about life.

When Hugo convinced me to leave, I gave him a long hug goodbye. It was more than just a "we are good friends" hug. It was a "there is so much more to say, we've been through so much, I'll be waiting for you" hug.

"I'll wake up early to see you off at 7," he promised.

I walked slowly to my cabin. My heart was skipping beats. I was deep in thought, but I wasn't thinking anything in particular, my brain was just humming non-stop.

All of a sudden, it was as if God spoke to me and said, "Yes, he does have all the qualities you want in a husband. You have just not understood it before."

I stopped short. I let the thought sink in. "You have not understood it before."

God was right. I had never taken time to really hear Hugo's heart. I had not heard his true heart, because we had struggled with a language barrier. Before, we knew simple phrases and topics. Tonight, we had connected on a totally different level. I got a real glimpse of his love for God, missions, and people. I had known this before, but now I knew it in my heart. I felt he was real in his pursuit of God.

By the time I got to my room, I knew something was different, even though I wouldn't have admitted it. It wasn't Hugo who had fallen in love in one night; it was me. I was totally swept off my feet.

Kristy and I drove back to Kansas the next day. Hugo did not wake up and say goodbye to me as he had promised. I tried to understand, because he was up all night on gangway watch, but I still felt a pang of hurt. He'd done a lot more than roll out of bed to be with me for a few extra moments in the past, so I was disappointed that he didn't go out of his way again to say an extra goodbye.

He called me when I got home to explain. "Sarah, I'm so sorry for not waking up early to say goodbye. I did wake up at 6 a.m., when my alarm went off, but then I thought, 'Five more minutes', and I went back to sleep."

We both laughed really hard, because he was serious. He had believed the lie once again.

"That will get you every time."

"I know. I'm telling you, it is the worst lie of the Devil."

"Okay, I forgive you. I'm kind of glad you weren't there, because it was really hard to say goodbye to everyone. Especially Lori Beth. I'm going to miss that chicken so much. Having you there would have made it that much worse."

"Well, anyway, goodbye, and say hi to all your family for me."

When we hung up, I went to the computer. I wanted to write to Hugo, tell him all my thoughts and feelings, and profess my true heart for him. I knew I had to keep my emotions under control and keep waiting for God's timing, but I wanted to write him something. What could I write? Something that would give him hope for us, without giving away too much. I wrote six words and clicked send. Satisfied, I went to wrap some Christmas presents. I had written, "Hugo, I'm thinking and praying. -Sarah"

A day later I got this e-mail as a response to my coded message:

You know, when you were here on the ship I really wanted to tell you so many things that I had in my heart, but out of fear that you would say no, I told myself not to. But . . . believe me I miss you too, and a lot. You know that I will always feel something in my heart for you. Whether you are my friend or something more, I don't know! I wish you a beautiful Christmas with your family and those that you love.

With Much Love!
Hugo

With those words ringing in my heart, I went to Word of Life in Schroon Lake, New York, in January. I knew it was where God wanted me, but I only knew about Word of Life from what Asako had told me and what I had read on the Internet. I didn't know anyone, and I didn't have any idea what to expect. All I knew was that the January term started with some sort of missionary conference.

When I got to the campus, I grabbed my duffle bag from the back of the bus and followed the signs into the cafeteria to check in. I signed in, and someone pointed in the general direction of my cabin. All of the cabins were named after countries where Word of Life had a missionary presence, and I would be living in Bangladesh. It was already dark, but I just slung my duffle over my shoulder and trudged through the cold snow. I passed the laundry room and mail room, but I didn't see my cabin.

I asked a girl walking by, "Where's Bangladesh?"

She pointed straight ahead of me. "Right there. You already made it."

It looked like a log cabin of sorts. It had a little wooden porch out front. I looked down the road to the right. There a few big cabins and a lot of little ones all along the road. I could see a lake off in the distance. It glimmered in the moonlight. Beautiful. I breathed in a cold breath of clean, crisp air. I could smell pine trees. Living in Adirondack National Park would be very different from Kansas.

I wanted to settle into my room before the opening conference session. I met the four other girls who would be my roommates, and with whom I would share a bathroom. They pointed to which closet was mine. It seemed gigantic after the few inches of space I had in my cabin on the ship. I hung up my stuff, and it barely made a dent. I was so excited to have some breathing room.

My roommates seemed really nice. They explained to me that I had to wear a dress or skirt to the conference. And nylons. Conference dress code. I knew that I'd be under some strict rules for a year. I just got over it right then and decided to follow along. I knew I could survive for a year. It would be worth the Bible knowledge I'd gain. Plus, I had told my parents that if I did not like it after the first semester, then I would just come home and figure out something else. I headed off in the night chill to the conference. Nylons and all.

I met a girl on my walk to the gym where the meeting was held. She was really nice and invited me to sit with her. I readily agreed, because I felt so lost about what was going on. We found seats near the front next to some of her friends, and she introduced me. All the students were so nice, but everyone assumed that I knew who was who and what the deal was. The speakers talked about Jack Wyrtzen, Harry Bollback, and Joe Jordan, as if I were supposed to know who these people were.

The girl that had befriended me quietly whispered to me, "Jack Wyrtzen and Harry Bollback founded Word of Life. Joe Jordan started Word of Life in Argentina."

"Okay, thanks," I whispered back.

I started to get more comfortable with my surroundings, and began looking around to take in the room full of people I was with. There were about 100 students in first year with me and about 50 students in the second-year program. Only about 15 of us had started school a semester late in January. We'd be making up the first semester of the course the following September, but with the new class that would be coming in. It wasn't ideal, but I still had my back-up plan: leave after a semester if I didn't like it.

I glanced down the aisle. A face caught my eye. I leaned back quickly.

"What?" my new friend asked me.

"Oh my gosh, I can't believe it."

"What? What happened?" she asked quietly.

"I think I know that guy."

"Who? How?" She looked down the aisle to see who it could be. I casually looked too, not wanting to disrupt the speaker or the people listening.

"Yes," I said, "it is definitely him."

"Who?" She was so confused, but I couldn't believe what I was seeing.

"It's Aaron. I went to Africa with him in 1998. That was four years ago, and I have not heard anything from him since. I am really surprised to see him here."

"Wow! That is so cool."

I was excited to talk to him, and at the break time I went up to him. "Aaron," I said, to get his attention.

He looked at me. Then he looked at me again. He hadn't forgotten me, he was just so surprised to see me. "Sarah Breeden? What in the world are you doing here?"

"I'm a January student."

"Wow, this is so amazing," he said, still in disbelief.

"I know, but it's God. I was nervous because I have no idea what is going on, who is who, or what I'm supposed to be doing most of the time. I prayed God would provide friends to help me, and He answered my prayer by sending a friend I already knew."

"Yes, I'd love to help you. You can meet all my friends too!" he exclaimed. He started to explain all the dynamics of the school and point out key leaders. When the second session started, I was so relieved to have a good friend near. I sighed a prayer of thanks to God.

After three days of a powerful missions conference, I called my parents and told them, "I am staying all year! This school is amazing. It's exactly what I need to train for full-time missions."

"Wow! Praise the Lord, honey," my mom said.

I continued to talk a mile a minute. I was so excited to know I was in the right place for the next season of my life. "I met this guy, Ron Blue, and he used to be a missionary with Central American Missions, and he knows about SETECA, where Carlos and Febe are going to seminary in Guatemala. Word of Life has a Bible school in Argentina where all their Bible classes are in Spanish! How cool would it be to learn the Bible in Spanish? That would be so good for me before going on the mission field in a Latin country. Maybe I can do that next."

"Sounds like you are where you need to be," Mom said.

"Totally. They set up all these mission booths in the gym, and we got to check out a lot of other mission boards, like Wycliffe and New Tribes. You know, all the big ones. But there were others that I did not know about, too. It was so interesting. I also found out that Word of Life has a Spanish ministry. I picked that for my ministry requirement, so I get to go to the Bronx and Philly to preach the gospel in Spanish to Latino neighborhoods!"

"That's good you get to practice your Spanish and keep it going."

"I know. I'm so happy to be here. And this weekend we start Snow Camp. We are going to have 300 junior and senior high teens here every weekend for seven weeks to be involved in camp. The students are going to be counselors for the teens, but we'll also be in charge of working the tube hill, dog sled run, ice-skating, and all the other awesome games, plus help with cooking, dish pit, and cleaning.

"I am on the transportation team, so I get to drive a tractor pulling a train. Our team shuttles teens from one side of the campus to the other because the grounds are so huge. Good thing Grandpa Jackson taught me how to drive a tractor, and I got lots of practice that summer putting up hay.

"My job is so fun. What college does this? It is so refreshing for college to not be all about me, my degree, and my success in life, but about people and helping them find and follow God! Last night we were having a 'practice snow camp,' and the whole student body was out practicing the games to make sure they work the way we planned. It was so much fun to be running around like crazy people, but knowing it was for a real purpose. The kids who are involved with those games this weekend are going to have a great time, and God is going to impact their lives."

That was the beginning of a wonderful year of deep study in the Word of God. We even had Charles Ryrie, who wrote the notes in the *Ryrie Study Bible* and several other books, teach us eschatology. (The *Oxford English Dictionary* defines eschatology as "concerned with 'the four last things: death, judgment, heaven, and hell.'")

Word of Life had two permanent professors, but there were two guest speakers each week teaching different books of the Bible. I could fill a book just with things God taught me that year, in classes and otherwise. I filled several notebooks of notes from each class. We had required study hours, which a lot of people complained about, but I loved it. How often are you required to spend hours reading the Bible? It was awesome.

I was so glad just to be learning, because I had been on the mission field. I knew the shame of being asked a question about the Bible and not having an answer, or even knowing how to use my Bible to find the answer.

A professor said once, "You may be the only Bible someone will ever read." I wanted to be that person, so I studied as much as I could. I knew I would make friends eventually, but socializing was not my highest priority. I had to utilize my time and learn as much as possible before I went back to the mission field.

There were other students who were fresh out of high school, or their parents had sent them to get "straightened out." I just ignored those people and their complaints about the rules and the food. I connected with people who wanted to learn and be changed by God.

In all of my excitement and learning, Hugo was still heavy on my mind and heart. After a couple of weeks, I started to ask a few professors for advice. I also talked to my resident assistant. I was claiming the verse that says, "There is wisdom in the counsel of many."

I sought the same advice from all of them: "I just want to know if I am rushing God's will with Hugo. I feel the time is right to see what God wants in our friend-ship, but we are not going to be around each other for most of this year. I need to focus on Bible school."

They all responded in about the same way: "Just seek God, and He will lead you. Focus on the most important thing, and He will show you which way to go."

It didn't seem to help much, but I felt better knowing I was on the right track. I would keep asking questions of adult, Christian people I respected, staying in the Word of God, and praying moment by moment. I took my time and was patient. My life, my surroundings, my walk with Christ, everything about my maturity of mind and spirit were very different from what they were when I first met Hugo.

Hugo and I e-mailed frequently. We talked a couple times a month. He had been sailing a lot with the ship recently, but a month and a half after I got to school he called. I wrote the following journal entry after we hung up.

February 2002

Hugo, I just got a phone call from you! I love to hear your voice and talk with you. I can't believe how good your English is! You make me laugh when I hear a new English phrase out of your mouth! "Just chillin' like a villain'! Kickin' like a chickin' with a little bit of penicillin, listenin' to Bob Dylan!" You're so cute speaking slang!

I can't believe that you get to go to DTS! That is so awesome! Praise God!

You ended the phone conversation with "I love you" and hung up. You don't know what that did to my heart! I don't remember you ever saying that in English before, especially the way that you said it. What beautiful words! I had to remind myself not to say them back, because it is not the time yet. But, oh how I desired to say those words. I hope only to say those words to you when we stand face to face, and I know deep in my heart that you are God's purpose for me. Why must I be in such torment over this, why can't it be easier then this? Why must I be so divided in how I feel towards you?

I wanted to call you back and ask you why you said you love me. Why? Why me? What drives you to always seek me, to pursue me as a knight that fights for his princess locked in the tower? Is that God? Does God drive you to love me so? Your faithfulness is commended. I have seen it and been honored. I love that you love me. I know that I could turn to you at any moment and you would be right there with all that you are. That is part of what drives me to get to know you. I want to invest my life into you, but I feel I have to wait until the Lord has worked in us both.

I wanted to call you back and tell you I'm waiting for God's timing with us. That there are things that God has to work out first. How do I let God control and take a chance on love at the same time? Where is the balance? I don't want to mess up God's will for my life or your life.

My journal entries clearly show the struggle my heart was going through. I was in agony over the whole thing. The next day, I spent time praying. I e-mailed a missionary couple I knew in Mexico and asked them what questions I needed to ask myself before I committed to a cross-cultural and cross-language marriage. He was from the States and she was from Mexico.

One issue they stressed was that I needed to decide if I could give up my heart language and only speak Spanish, if Hugo never became fluent. I prayed hard and finally decided that I could give up English, if God asked me to do that. I had to give God full control of my life, knowing that Hugo might be God's perfect plan for me. I was planning to read in bed, but my mind could not focus. I only thought of Hugo. I wrote him this letter:

> Hugo,
>
> I wrote you after I got home from Texas that "I am thinking and praying." I'm writing you today because I want you to know a lot of what I have prayed and thought about, and maybe one day I'll tell you everything. I'm not sure all I want to tell you or how to do it, so I'll just start.
>
> Hugo, I can't get you out of my mind. As much as I have fought it, somehow you remain in my heart. I don't know what God has planned for us in the future. I pray every day that God will make it clear to us. I have not wanted to date you again for several reasons. First, we have tried dating before and for many reasons it did not work out. I also know you like me, and I fear hurting you more if God does make it clear I am not to be with you. Also, I'm afraid of letting another person come into my life. I'm afraid I'll let that person affect my relationship to God. Especially deciding what's God's will for where to go next and what to do.
>
> Hugo, sometimes I get so frustrated and cry because I want to tell you all the little details about my life. But, I can't find the right words in Spanish. And I want you to understand everything so I don't want to say it in English. This is probably the biggest thing that I struggle with in my relationship to you. I know God has a purpose for it, but it is really hard.
>
> With all of that said, there is my heart laid out for you to decide. Hugo, I deeply care about you and want to get to know you more. We are and forever will be friends, but I want to be able to discuss openly with each other all areas of life. Especially about how we feel about each other. I'm not sure how this actually changes our relationship, because we are thousands of miles apart. But, just know my friendship is always there for you in the same way it has been. Please pray about all of this. I'm open to what God wants in YOUR life.

After writing all of that, I read the letter again and decided he would hardly know I was really trying to say I wanted to date him again. I decided to call him and talk to him on the phone about it. I needed to communicate with him.

Before I called, I prayed fervently to God about all I had in my heart that I wanted to say to Hugo. I prayed that He would keep this call from happening if it was not His will. I knew it would be pretty miraculous if I was able to reach Hugo either way. The ship was in dry dock in Mobile, Ala. The telephone lines were constantly down, and there was no receptionist at this time to take calls. If someone happened to be passing by the ringing phone, he might answer it. Plus, everyone was very busy with repairs and upgrades. Hugo might be working and not able to talk.

I reminded God that I had prayed for Him to get Hugo out of my mind or show how I could not marry him. But Hugo had remained a big part of my life. At this crossroads, I felt I had to go down this road and see if it was God's will. Otherwise, I'd regret not knowing for the rest of my life. I was shaking all over as I called. I was so nervous because I knew this was a pivotal moment in my life. No turning back.

Hugo was there—in the cargo hold, of all places. He was lying on some boxes taking a quick snooze while he waited for his boss to come back with his next instructions. He was almost asleep when, from high above him in the ship's hallways, he heard the intercom system, "Hugo Liborio, dial 101, Hugo Liborio, 101."

He sat up and looked around him. He would never make it up the cargo hold's treacherous ladder in time to pick up the phone. He spied a phone on the wall, tucked behind the boxed milk. He picked it up and dialed 101.

"Hi. Hugo? This is Sarah."

"Hi," he said, confused. We only talked every couple of weeks and I had just talked to him the day before. He was quite surprised to hear from me. The first thought that came into his head was that I was dating someone else, and I was calling to politely tell him to leave me alone. He did not say anything.

I said, "I needed to talk to you."

He immediately said, "I will drop work to talk to you. Whenever you need me to talk, I am here for you."

I told him some parts of the letter that I wrote to him. I knew he was confused by what I was telling him. I clarified things by saying, "I've prayed a lot, and if you want to pursue a relationship with me, you can."

He started speaking slowly, disbelievingly. "Are you saying what I really think you're saying? I don't understand you."

"I can tell you in Spanish if you want."

"No, I understand your English. I just don't understand you. I've wanted to date you, but didn't want to lose your friendship if I asked you again. So, you are saying even though I have asked you before to be my girlfriend and you've said no, I can ask you again now?"

I said, "Yes, you can."

He paused and asked, "Sarah, would you be my girlfriend?"

I said, "Yes." I really couldn't believe what was going on. I was so scared to be doing this, but somehow it felt right.

We were so excited for a moment, but then he got serious and told me, "I do not want our relationship to be a game like it was before. 'Yes' today and 'no' next week. I just want to spend a lot of time getting to know you, without thinking about marriage or any of that. I just want to open my heart to you, so you can know more about me, and I also want to find out all about you."

I responded, "I'm sorry for what happened before. This time it's not a game. If I am saying 'yes' this time, it is because I know that I could marry you someday, if it is the Lord's will. I will open my heart to you, and I want to know everything about you."

As soon as I hung up, I turned over on my bed and asked God for feedback on what I had just done. He told me a few things.

First, He showed me that I had been the one saying "no" all this time, and He was trying to show me "yes." I had brought all these logical reasons before God for why it would not work. He in turn showed me how He could overcome those issues. The whole time that I had tormented myself about it, God just wanted to have control over my life, Hugo included. I was trying to get all my ducks in a row and God was saying, "Let go!"

God gave me such an indescribable peace in that moment. I had finally given control of my future and my future with Hugo over to God. Since then, I have not planned and debated over the future like I did before. I was trying to figure out, step-by-step, how Hugo fit into God's plan for my life. I hadn't realized before that I needed to stop figuring and start trusting. From that moment, I have trusted all my life to God, because who am I to figure it out?

Within the first week of Hugo's and my new relationship, God answered several important prayers. First, I really wanted Hugo to do a DTS, but he did not have the money to go. On Feb. 5, I wrote, "Hugo DTS money" in my prayer journal.

When he called me the next day, he told me, "God provided a way for me to do my DTS! Someone donated my tuition, and I am going!" I was so excited for him.

A couple of nights later, I was thinking about how there were a few things in Hugo's life that I really wanted God to fix. I was contemplating which verses I could send to him to "help" God. I was almost worried about it. What if God did not iron those things out? God assured me that He was working in Hugo's life, and that I shouldn't worry. Also, his DTS would be really effective in refining his life. God told me that.

The next day, a DTS friend who was still serving on the ship, Tressa, e-mailed me and wrote, "I heard Hugo and you are dating. He is a great guy, but he has a few areas that worry me." She added, "But I think his DTS will really help him with those areas!" I viewed that e-mail as a confirmation from God, especially since Tressa had not written me in a long time. It was perfectly on target with what I was already thinking.

God also showed me that He was at work through Hugo's growing desire to be honest with me about his struggles. Later that same day Hugo called, which was weird because we had talked the day before. He said in a serious tone, "I have to tell you something."

I knew he had to tell me something heavy. "Okay, wait a second." I shushed my wild roomies. "It's Hugo," I mouthed to them. I took the candy I had been sucking on out of my mouth so I could concentrate better and said, "Okay, shoot."

He started his story. "The day before you called me about dating, another DTS had just left the ship. There was a girl I spent a lot of time with, and she even broke up with her boyfriend because she liked me. She told me that she might be coming back to the ship."

He stopped to see if I had something to say. I just said, "Okay," so that he would know I had not hung up on him.

I already knew about the girl, because Lori Beth had told me about her. Lori Beth also told me that one night Hugo confessed to her, "I do not feel for her like I felt for Sarah. But I do not know what else to do. Sarah is not interested in me."

I never told Hugo what Lori Beth had shared with me, and I let him continue. "I am just friends with her, because she is great girl. I did not ever feel toward her what I feel toward you. I do not love her as I have always felt love toward you. I knew that I needed to tell you this and be honest with you. I did not want to you hear rumors from other people on the ship. I want you to know everything, but I do not want to lose you. That's why I didn't tell you all this right away. I did not want something stupid I did in the past to affect how you felt or thought about me. But, I knew I had to be a man for you and tell you everything."

I reassured him, "Hugo, I am here for you and it will take more than that to lose me. Actually, I'm beginning to think that nothing could deter me from you, unless God specifically showed me."

"Thank you for your commitment to me."

I think he was beginning to learn how much I really cared about him.

Please visit my website, www.my-onceuponatime.com/, to see pictures and videos from each chapter.

136

Chapter Seven

The Prince Wins Her Heart
2002

Mississippi, Alabama, Honduras, Haiti, Dominican Republic, Maryland, North Carolina, Kansas, New York

In March, I decided to spend my spring break from school in Mobile, Ala., so that Hugo and I could get to know each other more. The ship was leaving Gulf Port, Miss., and would be in Mobile soon for a dry-dock time to work on some major repairs.

Spring Break at Word of Life didn't feel much like spring. We had just wrapped up our last weekend of Snow Camp, and the sledding hill and ice chute were still fully functional. But despite the frigid air and frozen ground, my heart was nearly bursting with warmth and joy – in just hours, Hugo and I would be reunited!

When I landed in Mobile, my heart was pounding so hard it seemed like it must be showing through my shirt. I hurried away from the gate, scanning the signs, searching for the way to baggage claim. I had spent enough time in airports that I could get pretty much anywhere I needed to go without a lot of effort, but for some reason this airport was testing my intelligence a bit.

The signs I was following kept pointing around corners until I felt as if I were walking in circles. I could feel frustration rising in my throat and was just about to grab the nearest employee to ask for help, when all of a sudden baggage carousels stretched before me.

"Sarah!" Hugo's lilting voice lifted above the din.

I turned, and he was rising toward me on the escalator, floating up like something out of a dream. His famous grin looked as though it would split his face, and he clutched a single white rose in his fingers.

He approached me timidly, showing the shy side of himself. Looking back, I think he loved me so much and was so excited that I was there that he forced himself to be reserved so as not to break me. He did give me an awkward but tender hug. It was awkward because, after months of e-mailing and talking on the phone, this was our first time together in the flesh as a seriously dating couple.

Then he pulled away and held me at arm's length. "You look so beautiful to me right now," he whispered.

I laughed. "You look beautiful, too," I said with a wink.

His laugh was nervous as if his mind was racing for more questions to ask me so he could prevent uncomfortable breaks in conversation. He asked me about my flight as we walked toward the baggage carousel. When my suitcase came around, Hugo lifted it off for me and set it on the ground. "Here we go," he said. Even though he carried my luggage, he still managed to open doors for me.

I was relieved to have him close to me and to be in the same country, much less the same city. I was already starting to think of next week when I would have to leave, but I forced that thought out of my mind, determined to enjoy every second that we would have together.

When we reached the car, Lori Beth was leaning out the window, waving frantically. She looked as if she might fall to the pavement any second, so I dashed to her and threw my arms around her.

"You're here," she shrieked into my ear.

"Okay, that's my eardrum," I laughed, pulling away and squeezing her shoulder affectionately. "Let's get out of here, you guys. We have way too much to do."

Hugo tossed my bag in the back of the car and opened the front passenger door for me. Ah, chivalry! I really missed this part of having him close by. American boys did not get it all the time, but, in my experience, Latino males have chivalry in their blood, and they can't help but be gentlemen.

When we arrived, I had to give another round of hugs and hellos. I was happy to see everyone, but all I wanted was to be alone with Hugo. We kept catching each other's eyes as I greeted people, silently saying what we couldn't say out loud. Finally, I felt that I'd done my duty, and I grabbed Hugo's arm. "Vamos?" I whispered in his ear.

He nodded into my hair, and his breath was warm on my cheek. "Okay, we're going for a walk now, and none of you are invited," he announced to the group. "We'll be back later."

There were a few groans, but everyone understood.

We walked through downtown Mobile, standing close to each other but not touching. I wanted so much for him to put his arm around me, but I knew it wasn't a good time for that.

Hugo pointed out some of the main sights to see – Mobile was no metropolis, but it had its charms. We turned into a quiet little park beside the convention center. I was hoping we would sit on a bench and whisper sweet nothings to each other, but instead Hugo pointed at a bench on the other side of the lawn. I could just make out a man sitting on it, his back to us.

"Let's scare him, Sarah," Hugo said, putting a finger to his lips.

"Ha, ha, very funny," I replied, rolling my eyes.

He looked at me innocently. "No, I want to; it would be so funny." He wasn't smiling, and I started to worry that he was serious. Why couldn't this guy ever be predictable? He always managed to do something I didn't see coming.

"Hugo, don't!" I pleaded, holding onto his arm. "That is so mean! You'll give him a heart attack."

Hugo twisted away from me without a word and began to creep silently toward the man. I looked frantically around to see if anyone else was in sight, but we were alone. I didn't know what to do. Should I follow Hugo? Run and hide? Try to find someone else to protect us in case the man got angry? My heart was beating in my throat.

Hugo was right behind the man now, and he slowly stretched his arm out.

"Yaaaaahhhhh!" he yelled, smacking the man on the shoulder. I cringed. I wanted to disappear from embarrassment, but there was no place to hide.

After a second I realized that all I could hear was Hugo's laughter. What was going on? Had he scared the old man to death? Why was he laughing? Slowly, I opened my eyes wider. In the darkness it was hard to see. Hugo was sitting on the back of the bench, his hand on top of the man's head, laughing uproariously. I squinted now and tried to understand what I was seeing.

Wait a minute. The man was a statue! At first he had looked real but, moving closer, I could see that he was made of a weather-worn metal. Hugo looked like he might die laughing over the fact that I had fallen for his joke. I couldn't believe he had fooled me like that. I hadn't been around him enough to know when he was joking. I punched him in the arm to help ease my hurting pride.

Hugo howled and rolled over the back of the bench, faking great pain to cover the real pain that he did feel from my socking him. I pouted, but suddenly it occurred to me that this was one of the things I loved most about Hugo. Life with him was never boring; he was constantly looking for ways to make me smile and laugh. He was always full of surprises, and yet he loved people too much to ever do anything truly cruel or insensitive. He had a balanced humor. I fell to the ground and laughed until my sides ached, knowing that I wouldn't change one thing about Hugo's funny bone or about that moment.

The next day we went to church and to a barbeque with the rest of the gang, and then were off to a Third Day concert. I was so happy to have the chance to see a band I loved with people I loved – one person in particular – and especially because Hugo was so into music. We stopped at a gas station and everyone else got out of the car to get snacks. Hugo and I were alone in the backseat.

"Sarah?" he said quietly. "Can I hold your hand?"

"No," I said sheepishly, as I wanted to play hard to get, and I was feeling a little shy. Plus, I was buying time to think. I had talked with the Dean of Women at Word of Life about going to visit my boyfriend and she said that, given my age and circumstances, she would leave it up to my discretion on PDA (public display of affection). I wanted to be sure this was the right choice.

He was silent. I looked at him and he was looking out the window. I could see that he was upset. He always had the utmost respect for my physical boundaries, but I knew it was really hard for him. I really wanted to hold his hand. What could it hurt? And yes, I had agreed to use discretion, but I was justifying this by the fact that I would be away from Hugo for a long time after this trip, and I didn't think God would mind if we showed each other a little bit of affection. I unfolded my hands and slowly extended my left one towards Hugo.

He didn't see it at first, but then it caught his eye and a slow grin spread across his face. "Sure?" he asked, keeping his hands on his lap until I gave the go ahead.

I nodded. A giggle escaped as he laced his fingers through mine. Our hands fit together like nothing I'd ever felt.

After I said yes to the hand holding, it was hard to say no again. Hugo kept my hand in his all during the concert and walking back to the car, which was amazing. I didn't have the heart to pull away from him. We had perfected the perfect handhold. Our fingers were intertwined but offset, so that his thumb and first finger were both wrapped around my thumb, and my last two fingers were both wrapped around his palm.

I did let go briefly to take my first Krispy Kreme doughnut. "The light was on"; my friends explained to me that meant fresh donuts. The best kind of Krispy Kreme doughnut you can get. I took a bite; it was like a miracle in my mouth.

I licked my fingers and quickly gave them back to Hugo. He smiled a private smile just for me. I was happy to be with all my friends, but they might as well have not been there. I had eyes only for Hugo and he for me.

In the car, I let Hugo hold me against his chest. I had waited so long to be near him like that. We whispered to each other all the way back.

"Remember the last time we sat like this?" he asked.

"Um . . . " I knew exactly when, but I wanted to hear his chest vibrate on my ear as he told me.

"El Salvador, on the way back to the ship." He nuzzled the top of my head.

I sighed contentedly. So much had changed since that time, but Hugo and I were still the same, still in love. I didn't see how life could be any better as long as we were together.

The next morning, we went to community devotions after breakfast, and then I did my personal quiet time. We left for the park at about 10:30 a.m. It was a small park, and we had it mostly to ourselves. There was a fountain and white pillars, tables and chairs, and a flowerbed. Hugo and I sat on the edge of the flowerbed, and he talked for about two hours. I didn't know he liked to talk so much, but he did. He told me all about his life before I met him, what he was like, and how God had changed him up to that point. It was very good to hear all of that.

We were getting hungry, so we took our conversation to the sidewalk and walked to a fast food place. He bought me lunch, and we stayed there for an hour or more. I finally got to tell him the whole story.

"Hugo, I've never told you this, but I feel I need to confess how much I liked you all this time. I have struggled with God back and forth to get to the point where I could date you again. Sometimes I was waiting on God, and sometimes I think He was waiting on me. But, I've always liked you."

He looked down at the table. "Wow," he said softly. "I never knew that you liked me that much. I thought you just wanted to be my friend. I never imagined you liked me more than a friend. You never let on. Actually, when you called, and I first heard your voice, I thought you were calling to tell me you were dating someone else. I never imagined you were calling to date me again. I never knew until now how much you thought about me and prayed for me."

I looked straight into his big brown eyes and said, "If you only knew how much I have sought God's will about dating you, and all the tears I've cried and prayers I've prayed."

"I feel very special knowing that someone has thought about me that much."

We walked back to the park. He had brought along a guitar, and now he showed me some new chords. Soon, he pulled a paper from his backpack. It was the Franco de Vita song, "I Love You."[1] Hugo began to strum his guitar and sing. During the first verse I was mainly trying to keep up with the Spanish and listen to this beautiful song he was singing to me. As he started the chorus, my heart beat faster, and my palms got sweaty. He was using this song to tell me he loved me for the very first time. I cherished every word of the chorus in my heart as he sang:

> "I love you
> since the first moment I saw you . . .
> (E)ven though it's not so easy to say,
> and define what I feel,
> with these words.
> I love you"[1]

It was very romantic, and I'm sure I blushed through the whole song. Hugo had such a great singing voice, and he played guitar like an angel. I just sat there, in awe that this man loved me so much. He really did love me. We stayed at the park until about 4:30 p.m., then went back to eat dinner on the ship.

Later that night, Tressa, Roberto, Sara, Hugo and I played the game Twister. It was a lot of fun.

Once, while Hugo's and my heads were close, I whispered in his ear, "Te quiero" (I like you). It was the first time I had told him that in Spanish. My heart had been bursting to say it for so long. We wrestled a little bit, but we both know we had to stop that, and we did. He ended up with his head on my stomach, then mine on his. We chatted and laughed.

He said, "I'm going to name you 'Mapache!'"

"Mapache? What does that mean?"

"You know, the little furry animal that has a mask on his face. What's it called?"

"You mean a raccoon?"

"Yeah, a mapache!"

"Why are you going to call me that?"

"Because you left your sunglasses on all day in the sun, and now you have a white mask."

We laughed and talked endlessly about the weirdest topics. He finally escorted me to my room a little after midnight. I had missed his birthday the week before, so I gave him a hug then to make up for it.

The next day, we set off for the park again. We threw the football around first, and I was surprised by how well Hugo threw it. Apparently, he had asked an American guy to show him how to make it spiral. Most Latinos have never touched a football, let alone thrown a perfect spiral. I tried not to show that I was impressed.

Then we brought out the soccer ball and played a little one-on-one, but I wasn't very good. The ball kept rolling into the fountain. It was really hot, so when Hugo went to get the ball out of the fountain, I tried to push him in. He hardly got wet at all, but he got me soaking wet. I had a great time.

Then we just sat and chatted for a long time, drying off. He told me the whole story about the earthquake in El Salvador in February 2001.

Hugo, Febe, and Carlos had driven home right away after the earthquake. Everyone was running out from his neighborhood, but he was running in to find his mom. He kept trying to take shortcuts down streets, but they were all filled with dirt. He had to stay on main roads and take a longer route.

Finally, he got to his own street. He felt some relief to see that the path to his house was free from dirt. His heart still pounded in fear as he ran down the path to his house. He flung open the gate, and his mom immediately came to the door. His heart finally calmed down as he wrapped his arms around her in a big hug and thanked God she was still alive.

Irma said, "I'm fine, but two of your friends are missing."

After he got a quick update from his mom and was sure she was fine, he left to help find his friends. He ran down the road and turned onto his friends' street, but dirt filled the street about 10 feet deep or more. He ran to the next block, more dirt. He could not get through; the streets were filled with dirt. His mind started to grasp the magnitude of what he had heard from others, the whole side of the mountain had fallen onto the houses below. His mom had told him that because their neighborhood was the epicenter, people saw the mountain "jump" and flatten all the houses.

He couldn't see any of the houses, so he climbed on top of the dirt and looked both ways. For blocks each way, dirt covered everything. He heard a man talking with a police officer behind him. He turned and saw his friend's dad, who was looking for his whole family. The father had gone to run errands and was not at home during the quake. When he returned, he could not find his family.

Hugo and the man found shovels and started digging at the place where they estimated the house had once stood. Emergency workers and neighbors were digging too. The quake happened on a Saturday morning, and nearly everyone had been at home. Hugo didn't tell me much else, just that they never found his friend.

They found her mother and two children, all dead. The children where clutched in their mother's arms.

He also told me that he saw the girl's boyfriend just staring at the mountain. Hugo went over. The guy kept repeating, "She is gone, she is gone." Hugo just held him in a hug and tried to assure him God was in control, though in his heart he felt the same pain.

They did not find the body of his other friend either. He lost six close friends and about 300 people from his neighborhood. I cried while he told me this. I couldn't imagine going through something like that.

Soon we went back to the ship to eat, but some friends wanted to go to the Seaman Center and play soccer. We decided that sounded fun, so we got a ride there. We played ping-pong a while, simply batting the ball back and forth. Then the competition began. Hugo won a pool game against me, and then I won a game of basketball and a game of pool. Then he won several games of ping-pong, but I won the last game of basketball. This kind of friendly competition became a hallmark of our relationship.

We went back to the ship to eat, but that evening went to the Seaman Center again with others from the ship. Hugo wanted to beat me in basketball, but I put off the game. I hung out with my girlfriends instead. Maybe I was trying to make him miss me a little. I hate to admit I'm a girl who secretively plays those silly mind games. But it was so cute when he would call my name and throw me the football, just so I knew he was thinking about me.

I left early to go with Lori Beth to pick up another friend. While driving and talking with her, I had to really concentrate on listening to her, because I wanted to be with Hugo so badly. It was a strange feeling that I had never had before.

After we picked up our friend at the airport, he wanted to eat Chinese food. I told him I needed to get back. We finally stopped at a fast food drive-thru, which felt like the slowest thing ever. My heart was pounding to get back and be with Hugo.

We finally parked next to the ship, and I ran to find him. I found a note saying that he was in his room or in the TV lounge. I found him in the TV lounge and, as I sat down next to him, I was finally able to breathe again. I loved being with him. We stayed up until almost 3 a.m. He kept singing "Barney" in Spanish, and we laughed about a lot of stupid stuff. It was funny, but only to us. I wouldn't be that crazy with too many other people, but I felt comfortable with him.

I slept in a little the next morning, but made it to community devotions. I loved walking in and knowing my place was next to Hugo, and I could take his hand or put my arm around him. At the end of the service, we broke into groups to pray. I loved listening to him pray in Spanish. Then we watched the film, "The Emperor's New Groove." Hugo had never seen it before, and it was one of my favorites. We laughed a lot.

In the afternoon, we went shopping with some friends. We were not buying anything, but mostly tagging along and visiting between ourselves.

I asked him, "What is your deepest secret?"

He avoided the question and never really answered me. We did, however, end up talking about past relationships and first kisses. Painfully, I divulged my mistake with Adam. He also told me some of his mistakes.

Later, we changed clothes to take black-and-white pictures in the park. We went for a walk and hung out together, talking about a little of everything, and a friend of ours took candid pictures of us. While sitting on the park bench, Hugo looked at me and kissed me near my mouth.

He said, "I almost kissed you just now. But, I know you don't want me to."

I explained to him, "I just need to prove to God and myself that I am not going to make the same mistake again. Also, because of where I'm in school right now, I need to try and be as picky as possible about when and why we start any physical part of our relationship."

"I understand," he said, nodding his head. "It is just really hard to keep from kissing you!"

"I'm sorry. And just so you know – it is really hard for me too!"

He looked down, smiling for a moment, and then seemed to switch gears as he looked up at me with a sober expression and wide eyes. "I have something serious to ask you. I might laugh because I'm nervous, but it really is serious."

My heart was beating wildly.

He repositioned himself on the bench and asked, "How serious are you about me?" He stopped, but then continued before I had a chance to answer, "Do you just love me, but could never marry me? Or is marriage a possibility if God leads us to that?"

I was quiet for a moment because it was so cute and sweet for him to ask me. I took his hand in mine and told him the core of my heart. "Hugo, the reason it took me so long to decide if I could date you again was that I had to know I could marry you if God led us in that direction. I had to be sure I would be willing, and I am willing to marry you if that is in God's will."

We talked for a while about life, and then started walking back to the port. I wanted to ask him how far he had gone with a girl, but I never got the chance. We ate and then called my parents. Hugo got to talk to them for the first time ever. It was very cool.

That night, we started watching the movie "Armageddon" in his cabin with the door open. We stopped it to get a drink from upstairs, and we ended up just sitting on the couch and talking. I asked him what his church believed in and his personal beliefs. We talked about theology, and it turned out that he really enjoyed those kinds of discussions. I was really happy to find that out. We agreed on a lot of doctrinal points.

Neither one of us had studied enough to be dogmatic or remember all the exact conclusions on every topic, but we decided that our churches, and more importantly we ourselves, believed in the same doctrinal truths. We went to bed at midnight, which was a mistake, because we had to wake up early to work in the deck department.

The next morning, we dragged ourselves out of bed. We were assigned to paint an anchor chain at another dry-dock. We got a ride there, even though it was not that far away from where the ship was currently docked.

We talked about a lot of topics as we painted. Hugo finally asked, "What was the question you've been meaning to ask me?"

I dodged it for a while, because it was a hard question. I wasn't sure how to put it without seeming insensitive. Finally, I knew I needed to have the courage to ask. I said, "Is kissing the only thing that you've done with your past girlfriends?"

He kept painting and said slowly, "Okay, I understood the question." He did not answer right away. I waited.

After a few minutes, he took a deep breath. "The answer is no." He laid down his paintbrush. "Do you want to hear the short story or the long one?"

I breathed a quick prayer for wisdom and said, "Tell me only what I need to know, or what you think you need to tell me."

He said sadly, "I just never knew I wasn't supposed to. I knew my mom hated her and that somehow it was wrong. But all my friends were doing it, and I lived to please my friends. Since a young age, I have always tried to fit in and have a reputation as a rebel. I want to go back to El Salvador someday and show people how I've changed. I want to witness to them and use my mistakes for God's glory."

The whole time I was quiet and let him speak. Then I picked up my brush and returned to work. I didn't say anything for about an hour. I knew it was hard for him that I didn't say anything, but what could I say? I had to think and pray about it.

Months before, I would have told myself that I could never marry a man who had been with a woman before. I would have said it would be too hard to forgive him. But here we were, and he had just told me that he was not a virgin, and in my heart God was revealing a grace I never thought possible. I tried to be mad, to stop loving him because of his dumb mistake. I asked God to give me the wisdom I needed to deal with this.

Hugo finally broke the silence. "What did you expect me to say? What do you want me to say?"

I confessed my ignorance. "A month earlier, I told my mom I thought you were a virgin. But in the last couple of days I had begun to question that, as I've been learning about other stupid stuff in your past. And that's why I asked. I wanted to hear you say that you have never had sex, but that did not happen.

"But listen," I went on, "before you get upset, I've been praying, and I feel God has given me the ability to look past that mistake. It is hard for me, because all my life I have heard many lectures from my dad about failed marriages because of premarital sex by one or the other person. So I am really trying to seek God and not be led by my emotions. But God is telling me, 'Sarah, who are you to withhold forgiveness? I've forgiven him and put his sin as far as the east is from the west. I am God, and I will give you grace to overcome this if you marry. Who are you to say this will ever affect your marriage, if I put you together and bless your union?' He will be faithful."

Hugo had stopped painting as I spoke, and was now standing a few steps away from me. I had been sitting down, but now I stood to be face-to-face with him. I was scared to take this step, but I knew that I was not mad at him, that I had forgiven him, and that I still had deep feelings for him.

He said in a husky voice, "Thank you for loving me, despite the stupid stuff in my past. I prayed you would still love me even after you knew all my secrets and bad decisions."

"I really do. God is bigger than all of that."

We painted together the rest of the day.

After showering, I walked upstairs to eat. As soon as I walked into the dining room and saw Hugo, he let out a low hiss. I was wearing my red tank top under a white stretchy top, and it was so cute to know I affected him like that.

We went to pick up the pictures. Hugo was standing at the counter waiting for someone to help him, so I left to look at CDs. Later, he told me that while waiting for the man to give him our pictures, a beautiful woman caught his eye. His first thought was, "Wow, she is so beautiful!" Then he realized that it was me. He thought I was in a totally different spot and didn't know I had moved.

He said, "I feel so lucky to have such a beautiful girlfriend." Then he went on and on about how beautiful I was. He leaned over and said in my ear as we walked to the checkout, "Have I ever told you how beautiful you are? Or how much I love you?" He always asked me this question. It was a special game between the two of us.

"I don't think so," I would say. "I must have forgotten. Please tell me again."

"Well, Sarah, you are so beautiful and I love you so much." he'd say. It was very cute and so romantic.

After we got back, I went to put my purchases in my cabin. Then I found Hugo on the couch, lying down and playing his guitar. I crawled in next to him and he played while I put my chin on his arm and stared at his face. I couldn't stop looking at him. I wanted to remember every curve of his face. I knew in my heart I would always love him. All I wanted to do was lay there on the couch with him and look at him.

We went to the community meeting that night on the ship, and then afterwards we watched a movie in the TV lounge. I had to put a pillow between us for a while because we were getting too close. It was a good break, but I was cold and wanted his warm arms around me again.

Friday's work day proved to be challenging. We had to finish up the anchor chain, and we painted quickly because it was cold and windy. I wanted to work on the ship instead of at the dry dock, so after lunch we worked in the housekeeping storage area. It was fun, even though we didn't talk much. We painted primer on the rust and listened to music. He had this dumb joke with me where he would pretend he liked Limp Biskit, a group I did not care for at all. When he went to change the music, he told me he was putting their CD on (he was really putting on something different).

I told him, "We are in the pit of Sheol anyway; we might as well listen to their music." It was funny, and we laughed.

After he put the CD in, he stood up, and I was standing too. There was no flooring in this room, so we stood on a wooden beam. Our eyes locked, and we paused. He stepped across the space that divided us and put a foot on my beam.

He kissed my neck and whispered softly into my ear, "It's so hard not to kiss you." He leaned back and returned to the safety of his own beam, saying, "Every time you leave the room because I'm about to kiss you, or the other night when you put the pillows between us, it is like you kissing me. I really appreciate how hard you are working to help keep me pure, and I'm very happy with hugs and your beautiful neck."

We finished and went to a cabin to paint there. My friend from DTS helped us for a while, and I asked her, "What is God teaching you in your relationship with your boyfriend?"

She thought for a moment and responded, "Even when we've been fighting, he still serves me and loves me."

"Cool. It is interesting what we can learn about God's character through relationships," I said. "Do you know what I have learned about God while being friends with Hugo?" I asked.

"What?" Hugo asked, curious.

"What I've learned about God's character from Hugo is His faithfulness. In the two years I've known Hugo, I always knew he loved me, and at anytime if I asked him for anything, he was there completely and wholeheartedly. It's like how God is always loving us and faithful to us even when we say no right to His face. And as soon as we turn to Him, He is there with all His heart."

Hugo did not say much for the rest of the hour of painting. I think he was shocked that anything in his life could be compared to God after his rebellion. But, as he would always tell me, he had been protected from so many things, and God had shown faithfulness to him even as he rebelled.

After work Hugo wanted to play basketball again. We walked to the Seaman Center and played really hard. It was a very serious game, but Hugo won.

Once, while I was checking the ball, he was standing hunched over with his hands on his knees, breathing hard, looking at me. I stopped, put my hands on my knees, and looked at him. His eyes were so soft and beautiful, I felt like I could see his soul. I felt so much love for him. I said, "Hugo, I love you." I checked him the ball, and it crossed my mind that I would love to have a marriage where we could always play together and have fun and stay fit. Laugh together, but be competitive. That would be a fun marriage.

We finished the game, and I sat on the floor, while he walked around the gym. He came and sat down, facing me, but leaning on my knees. I knew that he wanted to kiss me.

"I really want to kiss you again," he said, "but I will wait until you tell me it is okay. I know you love me a lot when you can separate yourself from me."

We sat for a moment more, but decided we had better start doing something to distract ourselves. We played a round of pool, and it was close. An older couple from Denver visited with us, and then they went to the other table to play pool together, too. They were so cute to watch. My mind drifted back to my thoughts about having fun together even after years of marriage.

We started to play another basketball game to 21, but some people showed up to play volleyball, so we only went to 15. Hugo won again. I was determined to beat him eventually, but it wasn't going to be today.

We joined the volleyball game, with Hugo on one team and me on the other. It was a lot of fun. I got to dive and hit, which I hadn't gotten to do in a long time.

Hugo said, "You're really good."

"Whatever," I joked back. I was cut from my sophomore volleyball team, which is a pretty accurate indication of my skills. Being tall is my only advantage.

After a while, we switched up, and Hugo and I got to be on the same team. One woman jokingly threatened, "Hey! I'm going to break you two up if you can't concentrate. Hugo, keep your eye on the volleyball!" Both teams were laughing.

We left because Lori Beth had told me that she wanted to talk to me. As we walked back, Hugo and I discussed how we wanted to have a good balance of time together and time with friends. We seemed to be on the same page in a lot of areas and communicated really well, even with our language difficulties.

He held my hand and balanced on the curb of the sidewalk. "Did you notice the older couple earlier? They were playing pool together." He looked at me out of the corner of his eye. I nodded so he could keep talking without me interrupting him. "That is how I want to be all though marriage until the end—always playing together."

That was exactly what I'd been thinking earlier. But I didn't tell Hugo that; I just agreed and let him think it was his awesome thought.

Hugo gave me a piggyback ride part way home, and then I gave him one part of the way, too. We got to talking about how much we weighed and how tall we were. Once on the ship, we went to the boutique to weigh ourselves. He weighed 164, and I weighed 166. Then we stood back-to-back and had three different people check our height. Hugo was a tiny bit taller. I was so excited. As a six-foot-tall woman, I had always wanted to find a taller man to marry. I used to think Hugo was a tiny bit shorter, but he was actually taller by about two fingers. I was so excited that I called my mom later to tell her.

I showered and met with Lori Beth in her room. We talked for about an hour or so. I loved talking with Lori Beth, but I was happy to find Hugo again. He was in the TV lounge waiting to start "Armageddon" with Roberto, Sara, and Tressa.

I was so excited to be with him again, and I curled up on his chest as we watched the movie. He whispered to me that he now had everything he had ever wanted or needed in life – salvation and me. I was really touched, and then it hit me: That was true for me, too. I could really be happy, without needing anything else in life, if I had God and Hugo. I knew I could be content with only God, but with Hugo added to that, wow, what an awesome thing that would be!

He fell asleep during the movie and started snoring. It was so cute. I thought that maybe I would hate it one day, but not then. I sat up and repositioned because I was getting a little too comfortable. I dozed off once, but managed to stay awake for most of the movie. I rubbed Hugo's feet a little bit.

Sara left the room, then Roberto. I was glad Tressa stayed until the end. Hugo woke up for a while, and I laid my head on him again. I cried, as I always did at the end. Tressa left soon after the movie ended. Hugo got up and went out, then came back in and lay on the other couch next to the one I was on. We were holding hands and talking about nothing.

He said, "We need to go."

I said, "Yeah, we need to."

He said, "You move first."

I got up off the couch quickly, before I lost the momentum in my heart.

He said, "Man, you are so strong." He stood and backed me against the pole in the middle of the room. He told me again, "I want to kiss you so much, but I feel your love when you walk away from me."

"That is why we were going to bed, now."

He walked me to my cabin. We would always walk to the cabin with him in front of me, my right arm draped over his right shoulder, and my left arm holding his waist or wrapped around his left shoulder. We didn't want to say good night, but we knew that we had to give each other the gift of walking away.

Friday was my second-to-last day with Hugo on the ship. This key week for our relationship would be over when I left for the airport the next day. Of course, we would continue to date, but doing so long-distance would be much harder and would have a different growth pattern than face-to-face did.

I had learned so much about Hugo, his background, and his convictions on this trip. Despite the seriousness of some of the things Hugo revealed to me, I still felt Hugo was whom God wanted me to wait for.

This was the week we really fell in love; I mean a true, informed love. Before, we knew we liked each other a lot and were attracted to each other, but we only knew superficial facts about each other. This week, we had been led to reveal the dark and horrible secrets of our pasts, and also who we were as people – the good, the bad, and the ugly. We had revealed ourselves deeply and still found a way to love what we saw.

That afternoon, we watched "Forrest Gump" in Lori Beth's cabin. I could sense "a kiss moment" coming, but I didn't know if I was getting that vibe from Hugo, or if I was the one wanting it so much. I kept thinking about it, weighing the pros and cons. I stood up and nonchalantly grabbed my toothbrush as the movie played. I thought, "Hey, if we do kiss, I don't want to have bad breath." There was a sink in every cabin, so I just pretended that this was something I did every day while watching TV.

I sat back down next to Hugo, and we continued watching the movie. I was still thinking to myself and barely paying attention. I wanted to be sure that I was consciously making the decision to let Hugo kiss me. I'd be leaving tomorrow and not seeing him again for six months.

My concern had been that if we started kissing at the beginning of the week, it would have escalated by the end of the week. But here we were at the end of the week, and the door to the cabin was open, so we were protected from going overboard. I had made my decision, so I just relaxed and watched the movie.

Soon, Hugo kissed the left side of my neck gently. I'd normally tilt my head to the right for a moment, so he could snuggle his face into me better, but instead I turned to face him. This caught him off guard. At first he looked surprised, but then his eyes seemed to ask if this was okay. I nodded my response. We both leaned in for our first kiss. Again. Only this time I knew it was in the plan and timing of God.

Hugo took me out for dinner that night. While I was getting ready, I was so nervous. I was in Lori Beth's cabin doing my hair and I asked her, "Why am I so nervous? I've spent so much time with him already."

She said, "You crazy chicken. It's because you're all dressed up and about to go out with a guy you really like."

When Hugo came to the door, Lori Beth opened it a crack and told him, "Bring her back by 11 and be nice to my best friend." Then she opened the door all the way so we could see each other.

He was just as nervous as I was. It was so cute. We walked upstairs to sign out, and everyone said we looked great. I had on a little black dress, and Hugo was in a shirt and tie.

Just as we were about to walk down the gangway, Hugo said, "I forgot my camera, and I need to go back to my cabin to get it. Do you want to come with me?"

"Sure."

We walked towards his cabin, but he cut up the back staircase towards the kitchen.

I asked him, "What's up?"

"Roberto is up here with mail from a little girl I gave a soccer ball to, and I want to show you the letter at dinner."

I had sorted the mail, so I knew that was true. I followed him up the stairs.

At the top of the stairs was a little room set up with a small round table and two chairs. This room was normally the "dish pit," but at the moment it was empty of the sink and counters, because they were being redone. So far, everything had been emptied out, cleaned, and painted, but the new equipment hadn't arrived. It was the perfect romantic spot.

Lori Beth and Hugo had put up white lights, plants, and Mexican-style furnishings. We were supposed to go out to eat at a Mexican restaurant, but Hugo surprised me with this instead.

As we sat down, Hugo said, "I'm so nervous!"

That broke the tension, and we both laughed and relaxed.

Hugo had made huevos revueltos and frijoles. Roberto made tortillas. We had Dr. Pepper in nice glasses by candlelight. Roberto was the waiter, and Tressa took pictures. We talked about all that we had done that week. Then, after we ate, we walked around the ship and saw more people. We took some more pictures together. We changed and went for a walk with Tressa, Sara and Roberto. We went to the park with the statue and Hugo tried to scare them with it, too.

Hugo and I separated from the group and stood inside a giant circular monument. We put our heads together.

"I wish I didn't have to go tomorrow," I said.

"I know," he said. "I'm going to miss you so much."

Our lips instinctively met. Then we left the monument and followed the voices of our friends in the dark. I felt strange because I couldn't think or walk straight after kissing him. My mind was really spinning. It was the strangest feeling ever, but in a good way. I had never been so affected by someone before.

Then we all went to a nice hotel to see the view of the city lights from high up in the glass elevator.

On the walk back, Hugo and I talked about how we were both really laidback people and didn't care how someone squeezed the toothpaste, or which way the toilet paper rolled. Neither of us was very picky. We talked about how we had never argued and wondered when we would and what it would be about.

We went back to the ship and watched "The Lion King." I realized that Hugo made a lot of spiritual connections with every movie he watched. He also told me he always cried during "The Lion King." He had such a great heart.

The next day, Lori Beth took us to the airport. We stopped at a fast food place for breakfast, and when we got back in the van, we heard Vanessa Carlton's song "A Thousand Miles."[2] It was the first time we had heard that song, and we talked about how it applied to us. At that point it became "our song," and we'd always think about each other when it came on the radio.

Then we were at the airport, and the inevitable was about to happen. Lori Beth took some last pictures of us, and then she told me her personal goodbye. She knew we wanted some time together before I left.

Hugo and I played some video games in the arcade for a while, and then we stopped playing, rested our chins on the table, and just looked at each other. I looked into his big brown eyes, because I never wanted to forget how they looked at me. I could see his love and see him. I loved him so much, and I knew in that moment that it was going to be harder than I thought to leave. I never wanted to let him go.

He walked me to the security check. We hugged goodbye and he asked me, "Why do you love me?"

I told him, "I don't have enough time to answer you right now, but I will soon." Then I just left, because that was all I could do. I went through the security check and looked back to wave. I walked away and saw him walking, too. I walked a few steps, then ran back to the window to see if I could catch his eyes one more time. I wanted to see him to tell him I loved him. He had already left for the van. I cried as I walked to the gate.

When I got back to school, it was hard to get focused on studies again. I forced myself to get back into a groove. I was also dreading talking with my parents. As much as Hugo and I were on the same page and everything was great, I knew my parents would have a lot of questions.

I finally called and talked to my mom. I told her about all the fun stuff that Hugo and I were able to do in Mobile and updated her on my other friends on the ship.

After a while, Mom finally asked me, "Sarah, is Hugo a virgin?"

I was quiet. I knew this was a big deal for her and for my dad, because it was something they treasured so much in their own marriage, and it was something they had prayed for me to have since I was a baby. I didn't want to burst this huge bubble of expectation they had for my future mate, but now was the time.

"No. I hoped he was, but as we talked more about his past, I finally got up the nerve to ask him. And no, he's not."

"I see. Your dad is going to want to know."

"I know. Hugo and I talked about it. You can tell him."

After this conversation, phone calls with my parents spiraled out of control. Dad and I went in circles about our convictions on this topic. I was so discouraged. Why was God taking me through this pain? It hurt me so deeply that my parents did not see Hugo the way I did. I needed to confront my hurt and deal with it.

One night, I was on the phone with my parents for hours. After we hung up, I was not able to sleep. My heart ached because of the helpless feeling that I had in my entire being. I would never be able to change my parents' hearts about Hugo.

I finally took my pillow into the bathroom and knelt down, not before the porcelain throne, but before the heavenly throne of grace, and poured my heart out to God. I cried hard and deep, with tears that started in my gut and shook my whole body. My heart churned with earnest prayers and complete surrender of control to God. It was one of the most honest times that I'd ever had with my Savior. I cast all my cares on Him. That was my greatest step toward having peace without understanding what God was doing.

Hugo started his DTS. He wrote me some letters, but mostly e-mails that I no longer have. One letter said:

> Bebé, I miss you a lot, and I know that this is hard for us both. But, even if you don't believe it, it is harder for me here in Honduras because we were here together before. So, the majority of things remind me of you. But, don't worry; you are not too much of a distraction for me. You know, last Sunday we went to the same church that your DTS went to. There are many people there who remember you, and when I said, "Yes, Sarah is my girlfriend," they were surprised and were really happy! And I was too!

I soon wrote to Hugo to tell him why I loved him, as I had promised him at the airport. On the envelope, I wrote a verse in Spanish: Prov. 16:9 "El Corazón del hombre traza su rumbo. Pero sus pasos los dirige el SENOR." (In their hearts humans plan their course, but the LORD establishes their steps.) Inside the envelope was a card, which was completely covered with the outpourings of my heart.

Hugo (a.k.a. Bebé) ☺

Despite all of the madness, I love you so much and am really crazy about you! Yes, some days it is very hard to be away from you. But, Hugo, I choose to love you every day. My teacher says, "People don't fall in love, people fall into holes." Love is a choice you make and a commitment to another person. I studied your face for hours while on the ship, trying to memorize every last detail. Your eyes communicate so many words to me. There is a popular song that says, "Sometimes you say it best, when you say nothing at all."[3]

Your eyes tell me a hundred times over how much you love me. Hugo, I don't understand it. Why you would pursue me over all the women in the world? I love you for loving me. I love you for not giving up on me when I told you no. I love you for not listening to other people telling you to forget about me. I love you for encouraging me through e-mail for the last two years. I love you for praying for me. I love you for loving God with all your heart, soul, & mind. I love you for being a gentleman with all people, especially with me. I love you for being crazy & easygoing. I love you for being adventurous! I love you for seeking God no matter what. I love you for being good at sports! (We're still tied!) I love you for being patient with me. I love you for understanding me.

I love you for talking with my dad. I love you for doing whatever possible to see me & spend time with me. I love you for giving me things that are special to you. I love you for being creative. I love you for wanting to know about me. I love you for being willing to share about your life with me. I love you for learning English. I love you for listening to God's will for your life. I love you for being bold enough to step out of the box people wanted you to be in, to be who & what God wanted you to be. I love you for loving to praise & worship my Heavenly Father. I love you for your faithfulness. I love you because you are not afraid to be yourself. I love you for being humble.

I love you because you care for your mom & sisters. I love you because you love your dad despite his mistakes in life. I love you for your honesty with me. I love you for your jokes and stupid stuff you say. I love you for following your heart. I love you because you speak Español! I love you because you are 100 percent Salvadorian! I love you for being a lot like me. I love you for being totally different from me. (You are both!) I love you. I love you. I love you. I can never say it enough. I love you . . .

With All My Heart,
Sarah

Dad also wrote me a letter that month. I gulped as I opened it. It said,

Dear Sarah,

I think often about our long phone conversations last month. I have many things I want to write to you, things that I believe in very, very devoutly. These are things that I wouldn't write just to you as my daughter but to any young women in your situation. Yes, I would write the same thing to your daughter also. Whatever you name her and wherever you wind up living. I have studied Scripture in the integrated areas of love, sex, and marriage for many years now. This is the area of burden/passion/vision/ministry that God has blessed me with.

But as I sit here thinking about my responsibility as a father and as a mature disciple, to warn my daughter and other younger believers about what Scripture says about the integrations of love, sex, and marriage, I also realize that in any area of spiritual belief, whether it is evangelism or something like this, the believer needs to have the personal permission of the one he desires to share Biblical truths. I remember something you said on the phone during our long conversation. You said the more that I talk about it, the more difficult it is for you to forgive and forget about it. So if I do write what I would like to write to you, I might just do more harm than good in your personal life. That is something I truly want to avoid at all costs. I love you! I truly love you a lot. I love you so much that I want God's awesome best for you every moment of your life.

In Christ,
Your Dad

I was somewhat relieved to see that my dad seemed to be coming around. I knew he would come around the rest of the way if it was God's will.

Soon I started my summer ministry on Word of Life Island, The Rock. I supervised four high school girls who worked under me during our daily kitchen shift. I worked closely with them and also discipled them individually when we were not in the kitchen. I had hoped to be back on the ship for the summer, but Word of Life had not approved my request. I was not happy to be on the Island at first. However, this summer turned out to be one of my greatest spiritual journeys.

God sent me a friend who bunked next to me, Michelle. She was in charge of the girls on the other kitchen shift. She helped me to grow and pray though my longing to be with Hugo and my love for him versus my parents and their unmoving hearts toward him.

The start of my time on the Island is marked by a journal entry:

6-16-02
I've been on Word of Life Island for two days now. It is good, but it is going to be challenging. I need strength from God so much. The first couple of weeks are going to be the hardest. But, that is not what I want to write about now. I am very tired, so my thoughts are probably not clear, but I need to write what I think and feel.

Of course it is about Hugo. I miss him a lot right now. I just got an e-mail from him, and also three messages on my voicemail. He is trying to call me, but I have no phone here on the island and I have no minutes on my phone card right now. I also got an e-mail from him that said that he got my letter to him, but the ring that was with it got stolen by the post office.

I'm so mad about that. Mad that it happened, and mad at myself for sending it to Honduras. I know that stuff like that gets stolen. Why didn't I just send it to the ship? That was so dumb of me. I want to talk to Hugo so bad. I want to be with him even worse! I know that I'll be fine and make it, but I just want to be weak for five minutes and confess that I really desire to be with him. I want to see him face to face and look into those beautiful, loving eyes. I want to hear his voice tell me about his day and what God is doing in his life. I want to sit with him while he intently listens about anything I want to tell him. I want Hugo in my life. I pray and desire it so.

In his e-mail tonight he wrote something like, "No puedo negar estoy enamorado de ti." (I can't deny I am so in love with you.) That moves me so much. It really speaks to my heart. He is so in love with me, and I love him so much. I really want to be with him forever. My biggest fear is that God will take me away from him. Why do I have this fear? God doesn't give me something to take it away. He doesn't give me a snake when I asked for a fish.

Maybe I'm on edge because there are so many unknowns between Hugo and me. And I also know there are a few things that God needs to teach Hugo before I will marry him. I'm afraid that God won't teach Hugo those things and then I can't marry Hugo because I know that I need those things in my husband. That is why I pray hard for Hugo every day, because I really want God to be moving in Hugo's life and for him to be learning so much.

I've been praying out of the prayer book that my dad wrote and gave to me. It was really awesome that Dad gave that to me because I thought that he would send me all this stuff on marriage and all the reasons to marry a virgin. It really spoke a lot to me about how much my father loves me and wants the best for me. He knows that God's best will only come through prayer. He saw the importance of prayer over what he thought and extended that to me first. What an awesome show of trust. I use it almost every day to pray in-depth and from scripture for Hugo. I'll close here, with these last words to Hugo.

Hugo,

I love you so much and pray God's best, ultimate, perfect will to be done between us. I miss you immensely!

Love Sarah

The friendship ring I mention in my journal I had sent to him by way of a Honduras address that he had given. The ring was stolen in the mail. Fortunately, no one found my letter valuable enough to steal, so that made it all the way to him.

Hugo, I'm not sure how many pages it would take to tell you all the reasons I fall in love with you every day. Or what I see in you that makes me love you. I pray to God I will have a lifetime to tell you all the ways and reasons I love you. So for now I'll say, "to be continued . . ."

But, you'll notice in this envelope I sent you a ring. I thought of the idea of buying you a ring a while ago, but I wasn't sure if you like to wear jewelry. When you mentioned on the phone that you were wearing a ring to fight off some of the girls down there, I decided that if you were wearing one already, it would be awesome to have one from me & a nice ring at that!

So, I prayed before I sent this ring to you, because it is a ring and in relationships rings can mean a lot. And people are going to ask you who is it from? And what does it mean? And what's up? So, I want to tell you what it meant to me.

Sending you this ring means that I love you enough to wait on God's perfect plan and timing. It means I love you enough to pray for you faithfully every day. It means I believe in you. It means that you, Hugo Liborio, mean a LOT to me, Sarah Breeden.

Te Quiero Mucho ~
Tu Amiga,
Tu Novia,
Con total de mi Corazón,
Sarah

The next day, I still hadn't had a chance to talk to Hugo, but I did get a letter from him. I was amazed to see that he had sent me a ring, too! Our rings had crossed in the mail, and neither one of us had told the other. The thought was really sweet. I say "thought" because the ring he sent me was broken into four pieces. It was a green ring made out of really hard plastic, but it had not survived the long journey to me.

I was sad, but I also got to thinking, "God, are You telling us something? His ring gets stolen, and my ring gets busted. What's up with that? Please, God, let it be just sin in the world and not a sign that things won't work out between Hugo and me."

In the end, I decided that one could take any information and bend it one way or another, so I focused my thoughts toward being patient and waiting on God. I knew only God could give me wisdom in my relationship with Hugo. Time was my friend, because God was not ready to show me the next step yet.

A couple of days later, I finally got hold of Hugo at the hotel where he was staying with his DTS. He picked up the phone, and I knew it was him the moment he said, "Hola?"

I was so excited. He gave me his phone card number and PIN, so that when my card ran out I could call him back. We had a great time talking, and I enjoyed it so much. I loved that he liked to listen to me talk and that I could ramble on about anything. I asked him a bunch of questions about what he was up to in Honduras.

We talked about the rings that we had sent each other. Neither of us knew the other one was sending a ring, but we did it at the same time. Very weird. We also both wrote that the rings were friendship rings. We marveled at how we thought so much alike.

He told me, "I saw your friend Cappuccino, and talked to him. He remembered you and was very excited when I told him that we were dating. Also, I saw your friends from the Zion Church, and they were all jumping up and down when they found out that I was now your boyfriend."

"That's so cool. It's funny to think that when I was there in Honduras, I really wanted to be your girlfriend, but didn't know how that was possible since I was going to school soon. And now, here we are!"

"My DTS might go to Guatemala for outreach. My team voted for where we should go, and I wrote down New York or Kansas."

"Oh, Hugo. You're so silly."

"Yeah, my team all rolled their eyes at me."

We visited some more, and then at the end of our conversations he got more serious. He said, "Sarah, I've never told you this before, but thanks for staying with me."

I said, "Thank you for pursuing me, even when I said no to you. It really means a lot to me." And I meant it. It moved me so much that he could be so faithful in his love for me.

The last thing he said was kind of a confession, but in a good way. "Do you remember the girl who was in Honduras just after you left?"

It was a vague question, but I knew exactly whom he was talking about because he had already told me about her. "Yeah, I know who you are talking about. What about her?" I said, curious to see where this was going.

"She has called me a couple times, and the other day she e-mailed me to ask if I had a girlfriend again. She also said something about 'me and her.'" Anyway, I e-mailed her back to let her know that I did have a girlfriend, and I was very serious about her and loved her."

"Well, that is great. Thanks for letting me know."

"Yeah, I just want you to know about these things. I also wanted to tell you that there are several girls here in Honduras who keep talking to me about going out with them. I tell them that I have a girlfriend, but they keep telling saying, 'She's not here, she'd never know.' I just keep explaining to them, 'It does matter, and it is important to me because I love her.'"

We hung up, and I got to thinking about our last conversation about other girls. My thoughts were, "Hugo is a very good-looking guy. Everyone I've ever shown his picture to has said so. It's weird that my boyfriend is desired and in popular demand from other women. He could really have any woman he wanted, but he chose me. Why me? Why is he so enamored with, in love with, excited about, captured by, and passionate about me? Who am I to be loved so dearly? I've done nothing to deserve his love. Why has God given him such a capacity to love only me?

"God, I pray if we do marry that he will always only love me. With all the other pressures from other women, let him never be led astray. I also realize how happy I am when I talk to him. He makes me so excited to be alive and serving God. We think so much alike, but differently enough to enjoy learning from each other. I realize again today how much I love him, and really pray that he is God's will for my life."

I decided to write him a letter about how much I was praying for him, and also to update him on the situation with my Dad.

One of the biggest reasons that I wanted to write to you today was to tell you how much I pray for you. Every day I pray a verse of Scripture for your life. My dad actually sent me a book he wrote on praying for your future husband. It was really awesome to get that from my dad, just because of all the talking that we have done over you. He knows what he thinks, and his fears are not going to win in the end. I thought I would share with you one of the lists I pray over your life. That way you too can be seeking God in prayer over these things and be thinking about how God wants to work in your life in every area.

Qualities I pray for in your life:
1. Spirit-Controlled Christian (Eph. 5:18)
2. Jesus is #1 in your life, not just an ornament. (Mk. 13:30)
3. Broken; understand how to rely totally upon Jesus. (Ps. 34:18)
4. Ministry-minded; wherever you are, you are available. (I Cor. 4:2)
5. Motivator; man of vision, concerned about lost souls. (Rom. 10:14)
6. Sensitive spirit; in tune to the needs of others. (Gal. 6:2)
7. Understand the awesome responsibilities of a husband to his wife. (Eph. 5:25-31)
8. Humble enough to be a disciple (teachable) & able to disciple others. (Matt. 28:19-20)
9. Man of prayer; you know the key to success is in your private time with God. (Col. 4:2)
10. Family man; you desire to have children & raise them properly for God's glory.

33333

11. Put the needs of others ahead of your own. (Phil. 2: 2-4)
12. Rejoice in your relationship with Christ. (John 15:11)
13. Maintain proper relationships. (Heb. 12:14
14. Refuse to jump ahead of God's own timing. (Ps. 37:7)
15. Seek to meet the practical needs of others. (Eph. 4:32)
16. Stand for what is right (Rom. 2:9-10)
17. Follow through on your God-given responsibilities (1 Cor. 4:2)
18. Understand the importance of feelings & emotions. (Col. 3:12)
19. Flee temptations to compromise. (Prov. 25:28)
20. Practice the principles of rejoicing. (I Thess. 5:16)

So, that is one of the many ways that I pray for you daily. I know God has put us in each other's lives for a reason. I hope that the ship does go to Baltimore, so that we can see each other while you are there. Especially for my birthday! I so hope that I can go out with you that night. That would be the best birthday date ever!

Not only did I show Hugo that I cared by writing him a lot of letters during the summer, I also decided that I should call and talk to Hugo's mom. I called her home in El Salvador, praying my Spanish would not fail me. It was really nice to talk to her. She was very talkative and friendly. She had just had an operation less than two weeks before and was recuperating well.

She told me in Spanish, "I'm praying for you, your ministry, studies, and activities." She also said, "I'm praying for you and Hugo and what you do together."

I said, in the best Spanish I could manage, "Thank you. I was calling you tonight so we could pray for Hugo together. He is going through an important learning time right now in his DTS."

She agreed, so I prayed first in English, and then she prayed in Spanish. It was very exciting.

After we prayed she said, "I am very excited and nervous."

I said, "Me, too." I told her I was praying for her and her ministry. I had a bit of trouble telling her I hoped she'd heal quickly, but she finally understood me. I loved speaking Spanish to her, and I was glad I could understand her. I was shaking when I hung up the phone, but I felt so happy that I'd talked to her.

I got an e-mail from Hugo halfway through the summer. He said he had a crazy question to ask me. He wanted to know whether, if we got married, I would be interested in having a wedding on the ship with two other couples. Oscar and Roberto were also in relationships, both with girls from my DTS, and apparently the three guys had been scheming together.

I thought about what a disaster it would be if three girls tried to share their special day, but then I was struck by the thought of actually marrying Hugo. I felt a tug-of-war in my heart. On the one hand, I liked him a lot. I loved his personality and character. But, on the other hand, did I trust that we could stick together through the rough times? Would he be dependable and unchanging in godly character?

Again, time was my friend, because I needed to observe him more before I could see these traits in his life. I was loving him on faith that God would show me if Hugo was the right one. But I worried about God telling me no. That would be a huge heartache for both of us, because I did love him, and I would hate myself for breaking his heart.

I prayed, "God, you must show both of us Your will; either yes or no. It will hurt too much any other way, but I pray that I will have the strength to do whatever You want me to do to remain in Your will."

Hugo e-mailed me back the next day. I had responded to him and carefully laid out my concerns about sharing my wedding day. He said that I was right. The ship would not work for all the friends and family we would want to invite, but that maybe we could spend an anniversary on the ship someday.

On one of my days off from the kitchen, I got a pass to leave the island. I gave my permission slip to the barge operator, another WOLBI student, and sat down on the bench. As we started out across the water to the mainland, I looked back at my summer home. It was such a small island when you got far enough away from it.

I mused at how an island was such a great place for a summer camp. It was small enough that I was able to run the entire perimeter in ten minutes the one morning I decided to get out and exercise. At the same time, it contained all the activities a teenager could possibly want. There was a paintball range, a beach, a giant blob for kids to dive onto, and plenty of sports to play. I wished I'd been able to see what it was like as a camper.

Michelle let me borrow her car for the day, so I was going to drive and listen to music for a while, then go to a friend's house and watch TV for the day. I had given Hugo the phone number at the house, so I was praying he would call soon. In the evening, my friend got home from work, and soon after that Hugo did call.

I ended up talking to him for a long time. Usually he was busy with his DTS, or I was working in the kitchen, so there'd be a lot of background noise and we couldn't have really in-depth conversations. I was so excited to have a quiet place to finally visit with him. It was strange, though, because after the normal, "Hi, how's it going, what have you been doing?" we didn't have much to talk about. We were not accustomed to unrushed conversations.

I hated it when there was silence, especially when he was paying for the call with a phone card. I tried to wait until he thought of something to talk about or a question to ask. I didn't always want to control the conversation. But then I got impatient and started talking again.

Finally he said, "It will be interesting to see what problems surface between us that we will have to work out when we finally can be together. You know, I've always thought couples should have a really good fight before they get serious."

"Oh, really?" I said, surprised, although this was something I had always thought too.

"It will help us to know each other more, even when we might not agree. One of the speakers was talking about this today in my DTS. Oh, that reminds me. I was going to tell you that I think it would be fun to be a speaker at some point in my life."

"Oh, really?" I said again, but this time I was genuinely surprised, because I had been thinking the week before that I wanted my man to be able to speak to people, and even travel to teach the Word of God. I really marveled at all the men of God who came and spoke to us at school. They knew so much and had studied the Word. I wanted someone who knew the Word of God, so I could go to him and learn spiritual truths. I really thought Hugo had that capacity. I had just not given him the chance. He was so much more than what I had given him credit for. He was just growing his wings to fly. I needed to be patient and let God work in his life.

As Hugo continued to share with me his passion and vision for a speaking ministry, I thought back to a paragraph in a leadership book that I had been reading which said, "So when God calls you to a task, let neither a sense of inadequacy nor a 'poor background' hinder you from following his lead. For it is God who works in you to will and to act according to His good purpose." (Phil. 2:13)

After reading that and hearing Hugo's passion on the phone, I was confident that, in Christ, Hugo would achieve great spiritual depths and be mightily used by God. I knew that believers did not have to be limited by their background or what they had been through. God could use anyone in any way that He desired. I had seen so many great leaders in full-time Christian service around the world who had come from bad families or out of lives of sin, and now they were taking this world for Christ.

That night I laid my head on my pillow and prayed for Hugo. "I'm confident that he who began a good work in you will perform it to the day of Jesus Christ."

I wrote him another card and encouraged him with my words. The message on the card read:

Love, joy, peace, patience, kindness, goodness, faithfulness, gentleness. I love you for the joy in your smile. The peace you bring to my world. Your patience when you listen. The kindness in your touch. The goodness of your heart. Your faithfulness to me and the sweet gentleness of your soul. I love you for being the LOVE of my life and my very BEST FRIEND.

Inside the card, I wrote:

Hugo,
    As soon as I read this card, I knew it was the one my heart was saying to me. It is a card of truth because you do bring such JOY to my life. Whenever I'm having a bad day or stressed out, thinking of you can brighten the darkest day! I do have so much PEACE and contentment right now in my life, because I know I'm in God's will. And right now you are part of God's plan for my life.
    One of the things I admire about you is your PATIENCE to listen to all my random stories. No one else really cares to hear them. You've also shown great patience in waiting for when we can be together and patience through times I can't e-mail or call. Thank you for that. You've shown KINDNESS in the way you treat me and hold me. You are kind with your actions and words, which is something I respect in you. You have GOODNESS in your heart, which desires to seek God. The pursuit of God is the highest honor a man can find. You have goodness in the way you give of your time, energy, and anything you have.

Your FAITHFULNESS is amazing! It is an awesome feeling to know that you are there for me, loving me all the time. I have so much trust in you because you have proven your faithfulness to me time and time again. You have taught me a lot about Christ's faithfulness to me. You've shown me GENTLENESS in opening doors, walking on the street-side of the sidewalk, helping me off buses, and giving me a hand of help when I need it. Now, I know that this card ends with gentleness, but I'm a big believer in being biblical, and the fruit of the Spirit also has self-control.

Thank you, Hugo, for having SELF-CONTROL, and respecting me in that area. For asking me before holding my hand or kissing me. I am proud of you for that. I know that we both have a lot of growing to do in this area, and I trust God for that. But, for now, I'm thankful for all the many times that self-control was shown.

The quote on the inside of this card is a saying that comes from my heart. Hugo, I've never in my life told a man, besides my own father, that I love him. You have captured my heart and my love in a way no man has been able to do. I do love you very much and pray every day that my love is of God and not my own desires. Because real, true love can only come from God who IS love.

And finally, thank you for being my best friend who cares about me, and prays for me. Who encourages me and helps me grow stronger in the Lord. You're a great friend because you want to know what is going on in my life & are excited when I'm excited, you're sad when I'm sad. You also think a lot like me, which is neat. We understand things and do things in almost the same ways. I can't wait to have lots of time to get to know so much more about you.

With All My Heart~
Sarah

At about this time, as Hugo was finishing his DTS, friends were writing goodbye letters to him. After six months of living, ministering, and sharing together, they knew Hugo pretty well. I think these letters are important to share because they give other people's views of Hugo, not just a love-struck girl's view. They also show how my relationship with Hugo was already being used by God.

Dear Hugo,
Thank you for being a wonderful friend and for sharing your life on this DTS. Your passion for God, your enthusiasm, your testimony, your love of music, your worship, your love for Sarah, your mum, your dog ☺, your struggles, your victories, and your dreams. You are an awesome man of God and I am so looking forward to see what God is going to do through you. You have such a passion for the gospel and a love for the lost, that you can't help make an impact on the world. I'll never forget your grin-split face, your cowboy hat, your laugh, your humor, your playfulness, funny tired walk, and stories (I'll find that hitchhiker in the dollar note one day ☺).

You have taught me so much through your love, generosity, and humility.

Adios mi amigo,
Love Hayley (From Australia)
P.S. Remember to invite me to your wedding.

Dear Hugo,
You are a leader of men. I first realized that fully in El Salvador and have become more and more convinced of the fact since. The ability to take charge of situations is one God has

given you and one he plans on using now and in the future. Don't ever be afraid to take on the responsibility that comes with this gift.

You are a man who shows his emotions. I appreciate that you are touched emotionally, even to the point of crying. You are a passionate man; about life, about love, and about God. That is a beautiful quality.

Your Friend,
Karabo (South Africa)

Hugo,

I admire you a lot. First of all your relationship with Sarah. It is awesome. If I ever get a boyfriend I would wish that we will be able to love each other as you and Sarah do. And don't worry, Hugo, her dad will love you just as we do. So don't start getting these thoughts that you are not worthy for his daughter because you are. And Hugo you know that yourself. You know that you are forgiven and that you are a new person, the old is gone, He has forgiven you. And don't believe what the devil is trying to tell you. Hugo, I pray that you will be strong and say no, when you need to say no. And remember, Hugo, when you are weak, then He is strong.

Hugo, I admire, how you are able to give things away, both material things, but also things from yourself—like love, a smile, a song etc. I have gotten to enjoy your smile, your time, your listening ear and your songs and playing together a lot. Thank you for all you have given to me. I pray and hope that you will continue to listen to God. He has something really big for you in the future. You have awesome talents you can give to others, and I know that you already are using them. I pray that you will continue to listen to God and what he has for you. I know that you love Sarah, but I pray that you still will be able to put Jesus highest.

God bless you Hugo,
Your friend Maria (Denmark)

At the end of the summer, I wrote Hugo one last long letter from the Island about a lot of what I had done and experienced over the summer. The highlights of that letter are:

This summer has been awesome! God has taught us both so much, which in turn makes us closer together even though we've been far apart all summer. It's like a triangle: We are on the bottom points of the triangle, but as long as we are focusing on God and drawing close to Him, we grow closer to each other. Focusing on each other only separates us more, and does not glorify God. God is amazing! I love Him so much! And I love you. I love that you have placed our relationship before the cross of Christ.

If we cannot stay focused on God with our relationship at the cross, we have no business being together! Seriously, if we can't glorify God together, I don't want it. That is why I'm so glad that God had taught us so much this summer. I can see how God is being glorified in our lives and see Him working in our relationship. I love you for being patient despite hard times and lonely nights staring at the wall. Sometimes I think if I stare at the wall long enough and pray hard enough, I'll have the answer; I'll have you.

But, then I realize the answer is to wait. God tells me that every day. "Wait, Sarah, be patient for My perfect plan and perfect will. You won't be sorry, just wait and be faithful to what I have you doing now."

While on the island, I decided to spend a month focusing on writing and finding God's will in my life, especially pertaining to my relationship with Hugo. I somehow knew that in the process, I might uncover more than I had bargained for.

The first issue in this process pertained to the fact that my parents were disappointed that Hugo was not a virgin. But before I go on to that, I want to share my quiet time from the first morning in my "Will-Finding Adventure." It was from Ecc. 5:1-15. Alongside it, I wrote: "God is in Heaven, I am on earth. His ways are not my ways, His thoughts are higher than my thoughts. For this reason I let my words be few before such an awesome, good God.

"God, I love you with every breath in my body. You know my heart much more than I know it. God, search me and know me, tell me if there be any offensive way in me. God, I've given you my life to love and serve You. Use me as You will. I am Your humble bondservant. I honor You with all my life."

Then, I knelt before the couch and prayed to God. I prayed claiming the promise that the earnest prayers of the righteous man avail much.

All this happened around 5:30 p.m. About 6 p.m., my mom called. I had talked to her a little the night before about Hugo, but nothing big enough to shake me up emotionally. This time, she had talked to Dad, and now she was telling me about the conversation they had had.

Needless to say, it was really hard to hear. As much as I didn't want Mom's words to shake me, they did. Especially when she said, "What if Hugo goes to Dad in a couple of years and asks to marry you, and Dad says 'no'? What then? We need to iron out this issue when you get home so that Dad and I can be excited for you. We want to be excited you have a boyfriend. Things cannot continue how they are."

I was so frustrated by the whole conversation because I could not see how they could ever start to like Hugo until they had a chance to meet him. They couldn't understand or trust someone they didn't know. Anyway, the conversation ended when Mom told me that Dad had decided we should all search the Scriptures for God's will, and then when I got home we would pray and make a decision together.

As I hung up, I purposed in my heart to fill my journal with thoughts and Scriptures that confirmed what my heart felt about this delicate issue. In this way, I knew my heart and mind would be prepared to go home. Not prepared to fight, but to have wise, true answers based on the Word of God, because He was the only one with the power to move in my parents' hearts—or, if need be, in my heart.

Despite my determination to seek the truth, I was crushed. Crushed because I felt the decision had already been made. Mom had said again, "It is a non-negotiable for your future mate to be a virgin."

I told her, "I will not marry Hugo without God's blessing. But, can you prove from the Scriptures that a non-virgin cannot marry a virgin? I would obey that, but as far as I have found, that is not the case."

She simply answered with, "We still need to pray and talk about it."

When I got back to my bunk that night, Michelle knew something was up. She used some quotes from a book she was reading to help me understand why I was going through this.

She said, "I agree with you, there is forgiveness and purity again." She looked at me very seriously. "But it is good you've chosen to honor your parents. Continue to commit to honoring them in your heart. Sarah, you must come to a point where, if your parents to tell you, 'No way' when you are at home, you can make good on that promise and end things with Hugo."

I took a deep, long breath. I silently prayed, "God, may I never have to do that."

Michelle continued, "You have to honor your parents in what they say, because they are good, Christian parents who listen to God. God could be using them to close the door on your relationship with Hugo, to keep you for something else, or someone else. Do you trust God to bring you someone better, if God closes the door on Hugo?"

"Yes, Michelle. I honestly believe that, but it will still be so hard."

I fell back on my "wisdom in many counselors," and asked my unit leader Ruth's advice. She had just talked to a professor's wife, Ellen, about some questions I had involving the whole Hugo issue. Ellen was very qualified and knowledgeable in this area. She had a lot of godly wisdom. Ruth passed on Ellen's wisdom to me at our meeting time.

Ruth said, "I explained your situation to Ellen, and she said you don't need to be involved. It's for Hugo to talk to your parents and explain your relationship, his walk with God, his heart, and his guidelines for your dating, engagement, and marriage. He needs also to explain his forgiveness from God and ask forgiveness from them because he has offended them. The Bible talks about going to the person you've offended and asking for forgiveness."

This was a lot to think about. After that conversation, I wrote in my journal.

7/22/02

It's so weird, but awesome how I have peace and joy about this. Yeah, it scares me to death to have been left with no control over the situation, but it's not my fight. It's God's. Now, only He can work, only He can change my parents' hearts. God has rendered me helpless in order to teach me so many things. I can already see how this is God's awesome plan. Good or bad outcome, God is big enough to have His will be done. In the end, I need to know that I did not convince my parents of what I want, but instead they truly see God's best. I need to know Hugo will take the lead and fight for me. You treasure and take care of what you've earned. The pressure is off me and put where it is supposed to be.

Two days later, I wrote a 10-point "Plan of Action to Obey God."

7-24-02

1. Talk to Hugo about the whole thing. Explain to him the importance of him taking over the responsibility of talking with my parents. Suggest he call my parents and ask them to talk face-to-face when he's there in December, but realize that it is all on him to convince my

parents he is God's best for my life. He needs to ask forgiveness from them, and explain his heart towards God and me.

2. Continue to faithfully pray for Hugo and my parents.
3. Continue to fill my mind with Scriptures relating to the situation.
4. Continue to seek wise counsel from a variety of places.
5. Continue to seek Christ's face and ask Him to reveal His plan to me.
6. Explain the plan to my parents again and see how they respond, but only after Hugo has called and talked with them.
7. Continue to encourage Hugo with this added stress, not telling him what or how to do it, but just fill him with Scripture and positive thinking.
8. Once home, hand a copy of "A Lady of Conviction"[4] to my father and tell him that this is what I'm holding out for in my husband, guidelines for him to follow.
9. Spend quality time listening to whatever information my parents would like to give to me, listening patiently and also calmly adding my own Scriptures to the conversation. Not proving a point, but adding truth.
10. Sit back and watch God work. It is out of my control.

So many times during this season of my life, I had to learn again to "let go and let God." In my friendship/relationship with Hugo, this was the fourth or fifth time that I had come to this point: Don't try and get all your ducks in a row, just give control to the One who is really in control anyway. I started to understand that I would probably have to reach this point over and over again throughout my life, as I released control of different things to God.

I stuck to my plan and, as bullet two pointed out, I needed to stay in communion with God. I kept up my Bible studies and also Christian book reading. I journaled briefly about my findings in a book I was reading called *Secrets of an Irresistible Woman*.[5] I understood that for a good Christian man to be able to marry me, I had to be a good Christian woman. I sought Christ in order to be who God wanted me to be as a woman, married or not.

I had just heard a sermon at school on I Thess. 4:3, "It is God's will that you should be sanctified." The professor said, "What is the will of God? We are always looking for the will of God. The Bible says clearly here being holy is the will of God. It is not about finding the right person, but being the right person." This tied into the book I was reading, and I wrote concerning this:

8/6/02

"On the way to matrimony, many of us only have ourselves in mind: How this state of being will make me happy. Complete me, provide me with the stability, love, and validation I've been looking for. Give me the child I've been wanting to have. But what are you bringing to the party? What do you have to offer? What are you planning to give? Are you coming with a couple of marbles to exchange? Are you willing to bring a casserole and leave the plate?"[5]

My prayer about this quote:

Dear Heavenly Father, help me to be who You want me to be. Continue to prepare me to be a blessing to the man You've created me to help. Deposit in me everything I need to pour into his life. Help me to be an oasis for him, a place of refreshment. Help me to equip him to serve and glorify You in every area of his life. Give me Your love and care for him. Help me to serve him and be a gift to him all his days. Help me to be not only his wife, but his friend, companion, and lover. Help me to be all that You've ordained me to be for him, in Jesus' name. Amen.

Summer finally ended, and when the first anniversary of the September 11th attacks came, I was starting my resident assistant training for the fall quarter at Word of Life. It would be my last quarter, but I was excited to have the extra responsibility of being an RA. I was also excited about doing basketball as my ministry that quarter.

I had seen how much Hugo had grown over the last few months. It was awesome to watch God work in his life and to see Hugo respond to what God was teaching him. A few weeks before I ended my summer ministry, Hugo told me, "I am going to stay and work on the ship. God has confirmed to me that this is what I need to do. I would like to be with you, and would like to follow you where God takes you next, but I know I need to stay here until God tells me differently."

I was so impressed to find out that he was willing to sacrifice time with me to serve God. I needed to know Hugo's priorities, and I now knew Whom he was seeking. That was so reassuring for me.

We talked twice the week before RA training. I had more time on my hands than usual.

In the first phone call, which lasted two hours, we talked about his past. Not what it was, but how he feared how it might affect him later. He shared different situations recently when he had to stick to his convictions and stand up to temptation.

He told me, "I'm not sharing about this to prove myself to you or to show you how great I am, but only because I'm your friend and friends share these things."

I started to wonder when it would be my turn to be within earshot of Hugo and be able to cultivate a deep friendship. I enjoyed our deep conversations, but I wanted to spend daily time with him so that we could have the kind of conversations that only come through sharing life. The one person I really wanted to be with was thousands of miles away for at least another month, if not more.

I had been conspiring a way to see him. His ship was going to be in Baltimore, Maryland, soon, and I was planning to go and surprise him there. My cousin, Erica, was going to a school near Baltimore, so I'd be able to see her and meet up with Hugo, too. A perfect plan. I couldn't wait to be with him.

I was also beginning to think about the month of December. Hugo was planning to come to my house, to spend Christmas with me and meet my parents. I was thinking about what a blast that time would be if I didn't have to involve my parents. As harsh as it sounds, it was what I was thinking. They were uptight about everything. I wanted them to just kick back and love the guy. I wanted to have fun and not have to stress out about it.

In the end, I decided that this was life, and I needed to be patient with it. I hoped Hugo meeting my parents would not be as weird as I thought it would be. I also prayed that God was working in my parents' hearts. I really cared about Hugo a lot and wanted to pursue what God had for us together.

I really wanted to see the ship, my friends, and Hugo. I went to the Dean's Office to get permission to go to Baltimore on October 2nd, when the ship would be there. I didn't know how it would all work out, but I knew it would some way or another.

It had been about six months since I had seen Hugo in Mobile. That's half a year. I couldn't imagine going all next year without seeing him; could it really be possible? I wondered what God was up to.

I only told one friend, Tressa, my plans to come to the ship, in hopes that my visit would be a surprise to everyone. I couldn't wait to see Hugo's face.

I got permission from the Dean's office, and on October 2nd I was on my way to Baltimore. Erica picked me up at the airport. We drove to the house where she was staying and hung out with her school friends for a while. It was really nice. I also got to go to class with her the next day.

At 1 p.m., we left to drive back into Baltimore. I was so excited and couldn't believe I was an hour away from seeing Hugo. When we were close to the water, I got really excited and had to have my seatbelt off. I leaned forward as far as I could in the car and scanned the faces of the people walking on the waterfront. I told Erica, "If I see him on the street, I'm going to take off."

"Just don't forget to shut the car door if you get out."

We drove past several other ships that were not the Mercy Ship. I was getting anxious because I did not see it in port. Then we passed a tall building, and finally I saw the ship. I was even more on the edge of my seat. I told Erica, "Park anywhere."

Erica heard the panic in my voice and quickly obeyed. She whipped into a five-minute parking spot in front of a hotel, and I got out. My heart was pounding so hard I almost lost my nerve. I said, "I don't know if I can do this. Maybe you can go and page him at the reception and then bring him out?"

Before we could put that plan into action, though, I spotted Hugo. He had not seen me because he was practicing with the evangelism team on the dock. I started to run towards him. My flip-flops were clicking loudly. Other friends saw me and yelled out a hello, but I did not stop or even look at them. My eyes and heart only wanted to be with Hugo.

Hugo had heard Rueben say, "There's Sarah." He thought I must be on the phone so he turned to go to the ship and pick it up. He looked up. I was running towards him, less than fifteen feet away.

He did a double take. All he could say was, "Oh my gosh."

I ran full force until I was wrapped tightly in his arms. I almost knocked him over, but I had to get to him and I couldn't slow down. We held each other for so long. I shed a few tears because the wait was finally over. Everyone saw the dramatic reunion, and all commented later, "It was just like a movie. In slow motion and everything."

Hugo and I hugged tightly for a long time. He said, "How did you get here?" He started to pull away so he could look at me, but then decided he preferred to hold me. Before I could answer, he said, "Well, I don't care. You're here." He held me tightly again.

Finally, we looked at each other. It seemed so strange to finally be with him, like a dream. I couldn't believe I was actually looking into the face of the man I loved and had waited six long months for. We looked into each other's eyes, then held each other tightly again, lest the dream escape us. Finally, we were able to step back and stop being rude to the world around us.

"I'm sorry. Erica, this is Hugo. Hugo, this is my cousin, Erica."

"Nice to meet you," Hugo said.

"And it is very nice to finally meet you," Erica said. She then looked at me and said, "Sarah, we have to move my car now. I had to leave my keys with the hotel, and they told me to come right back."

"Okay!" I waved and said hi to my other friends who were standing around. It was good to see everyone and feel at home again.

After the weekly community meeting that evening, Hugo and I went for a walk. I told him that I had found a song I wanted to play for him. We took the guitar out on the pier and sat under a light post. I played the song that I had written for him.

"In His Hand"
I would give you the moon, my darling
And all the stars in the sky.
I would give you the sun, my sweetheart
But, God holds them all in His hand.

Chorus:
But, Baby, Baby I love you
I love you, Baby
Bebe, bebe te quiero
Te quiero, Bebe

And I would give you all my heart
And I wish to give you all my love
I could give you my life forever
But God holds them all in His hand.
        (chorus)

Darling, you're my Angel
You are so worth the wait
So, I wait in perfect peace
Until that one day God gives you to me.
But, today God holds you in His hand.
        (chorus)

I will seek God and trust Him forever
Because I trust the plan He has
He knows best, because He loves us
I know I will always follow Him
Because I rest in the palm of His hand.
        (chorus)

I didn't tell him that I'd written the song for him until after I played it. Hugo liked it a lot, and he thanked me over and over for writing him a song. I was so glad he loved it.

We hung out there for a while, and he played some more songs and taught me some new guitar tricks to practice when I got back to school. We went for another walk later and came back to hug in front of the gangway.

Hugo said, "This beats the world record for the longest hug." Then we danced together slowly while we talked about the next year and where I might be.

During community meeting, I had been thinking about how much I loved this place, and how I'd be so happy to serve another term on the ship. Even thinking about the possibility was getting me really excited.

I thought, "I would rather be there than anywhere!" I prayed, "God, I pray my parents are up for this plan of me going back to the ship after school, and really see how this is a good decision. I trust You are in control of their hearts and understanding."

Hugo really wanted me to come. He didn't know how he could last another year away from me. He said, "I want you to do what God wants you to do, but my heart wants you to come to the ship."

I prayed diligently that the Lord would guide and direct me.

While I was there, Hugo gave me a note that some of the girls from his DTS wrote to me, to encourage me. The words they wrote really spoke to me; I was not the only one who could see the greatness in Hugo. They wrote:

Dear Sarah,

Hello! We are Hugo's DTS buddies and thought we would write to the famous Sarah. Hugo is an awesome godly fellow who adores you so much, and we thought we'd write and encourage you and tell you how faithful Hugo is to you. He received your ring and cards yesterday and hasn't wiped the grin off his face yet. He has showed EVERYBODY and we mean EVERYBODY on board the ring-several times, demonstrating its wonderful spinning capabilities.

Anyway, you sound like an awesome woman of God, confirmed by both Hugo and Aresa, and Hugo is the perfect match for you! It is fantastic! To have him on the team, he is a huge encouragement because he is so humble, fun-loving, generous, solid, passionate about God and GENTLEMANLY, which we girls really appreciate. Having such a solid, faithful relationship as you have, would be a terrific thing. Know that you have such a faithful boyfriend who loves you with all his being. Keep going for God Sarah!

Maria, Julie, Hayley
P.S. We love all your photos

He also showed me another note from Hayley, which said:

Hey Sarah! This is Hayley! We just thought you'd be encouraged to know that your boyfriend is so faithful to you, but still treats others with respect and brotherly love. He is truly the most wonderful guy on the team. We love him heaps, and are waiting for the day to hear that you guys are married. We've already had to give our opinions on rings. We feel like we know you and have seen lots of photos, and we hope we have encouraged you, and not scared you! You sound so wonderful, we just wanted to write and say hi. Hugo sat on the couch in the crew lounge yesterday reading your cards, grinning like a fool! It was so cute. You guys are fantastic, God bless you,

Hayley(from Australia!)

My time in Baltimore was amazing, and I was especially happy that someone from my family had met Hugo. Erica told me later, "I like him! I like that he asked me questions and looked at me while we visited. He seemed to really care about getting to know me. I was impressed." I was so grateful that she liked him and that I was not just blindly in love.

After I went back to school, God started teaching me about being patient and dwelling in His faithfulness. I liked Ps. 37:3-4, as well as Psalm 84 where it said, "No good thing will God withhold." From that verse I determined that, if it was good for me, God would not withhold it from me. This included Hugo and decisions for next year, like going to the ship. Whatever the case may be, God would not withhold a good thing from me. If Hugo was a good thing in my life, my heavenly Father would know, and would, in perfect time, give him to me to love and to hold until death parted us. I trusted my loving Father for that.

I also prayed, "If this is not to be, please God, close the door to this relationship. I don't want to walk the whole way to find the door is closed." I asked God many times to close the door if it was not His will. I asked Him many times if it was okay that I was in this friendship with Hugo, traveling in the direction that we were. God lovingly assured me that I was abiding in Him and doing His perfect will. I learned a valuable lesson about my constant need for permission when Hugo told me this story he heard in DTS:

"There was a little boy at the water park with his dad, and he asked, "Can I go down the waterslide?"

"Go ahead, son, have fun," the dad replied.

The boy asked again, "Really, I'm serious, can I go down the slide?"

"Sure, go ahead," said the father.

The boy started to walk towards the slide, but stopped and returned to the father. "Dad, are you really sure you want me to go down the slide?"

"Yes, my child, I want you to go down the slide."

The boy walked all the way to the slide and climbed up the ladder, but once he got to the top he paused, went back down the steps, and returned to the father.

He asked, "Daddy, I really want to go down the slide, but are you sure you want me to?"

Patiently the father replied, "Son, I love you, I want you to enjoy the slide."

I felt like this little boy. I was learning that God's will did not have to be such a guessing game. God was big enough to be small enough for me to hear Him. I was open to anything God wanted to tell me, and I would do anything for Him. He only needed to let me know what that was. God knew my heart and that I did my very best to remain open, sensitive, and available to him. I wrote out a verse and a prayer in my journal as worship to God. I could have never predicted how this verse would be used again in my life.

Ps. 73:25
Whom have I in heaven but You? And there is none upon earth that I desire besides You.
Vs. 26
My flesh and my heart fail; But God is the strength of my heart and my portion forever.

Lord, I love You. You are my portion now and forever. Make me clean today and please use me. I love You . . . I love You . . . I love You.

I talked to Hugo on the phone the next night. We had a really awesome conversation. I told him about some of the topics I was learning in school. We ended up talking about points of doctrine, which was kind of my plan because I wanted to see again how easy it was to talk about God and the Bible. I noted that he loved to talk about these subjects, and I could hear the passion in his voice.

It got me more excited about being at Bible school and learning more theology. I knew he'd love to go to Bible school, but it had to be the right balance of studies and hands-on ministry. I asked him, "What would you tell Christ if you died right now and were standing before the gates, and He asked you why He should let you into heaven?"

He said, "Because I believe that Jesus Christ died on the cross for my sins and I received this gift of grace from Him, the only one who is able to save."

"Good answer," I thought. I guess I wanted to ask him because I didn't want to assume his salvation. Only God can judge the heart, but we humans can never assume that because a person is serving God he or she is saved. But I had seen the work of Hugo's hands and heart, and was more than satisfied with his answer.

We went on to talk about Hugo's second passion after God: music. He explained to me how Ricardo (a ship friend from Mexico) had told him that he planned to record some music, and he really wanted Hugo to sing and play guitar. Their plan was to record two CD's in Mexico, and then go on tour to promote the CD's.

Hugo said, "If I go to Mexico, I really want you to go with me."

"Wow! That would be awesome," I said.

"Yeah. Which reminds me, if you do come to the ship next year, I don't want to be apart from you again. I don't think I could handle that."

"Okay, I just don't know God's plan right now."

"I know," he said. "After this year, I don't know about marriage, only God knows, but I know I don't want to be away from you again."

I said, "God will prepare us if we need to be apart."

"Yeah I know, but now I can't handle that."

"I understand. Let's just change the subject."

We went into a deeper conversation and I asked him, "What about disciplining children?"

He laughed and said, "That scares me because I can't even discipline my dog!"

We talked more seriously about it, and I determined that he did have it in him.

He said, "I want to explain to my son what he did wrong, then tell him, 'Because I love you, I am going to discipline you.' Basically, I want to do everything my dad did not do. I also would not undermine your authority in front of the kids, even if I did not agree with you right then."

After I shared what I thought with him, he remembered something else he wanted to tell me.

He said, "First, I don't know how to explain to you how great I feel about being with one person my whole life."

We took a moment to muse over that thought, and I said something profound, I'm sure.

Then he said some of the most romantic, but real, words I had ever heard him say. I could hear in the tone of his voice and how he carefully formed his words that he meant was he was saying and had thought and prayed a lot about it.

He said, "Sarah, when we are talking about all of this stuff – kids, marriage, and life – I really see all of this with you. I don't know when or how for sure, but I know, I feel for sure, that you will be my wife."

This time I had nothing profound to say, just complete silence. I was trying to let these words sink in and somehow try to understand why this man loved me so much. Finally, I regained enough composure to say, "That is so awesome."

He went on, "It would take seeing angels, the waters and heaven to part, God's voice, and a burning bush to convince me that this is not true."

Though everything in my soul wanted to reciprocate, I formed my response carefully, "That is what I want and desire to tell you, but I'm guarding myself and not jumping in with both feet, because I don't want to get hurt and I don't want to hurt you."

"Don't worry about it. I understand completely and know that you are also waiting on your parents." Hugo had more on his heart to share. "Sarah, you don't know how much you have affected my life. You have no idea how you've changed my life and brought me closer to God." He used a joke I'd made earlier and said, "I'll explain it to you when you are older."

He went on and said, "When I tell you that you are my angel or my blessing, I don't just say that because it sounds nice. I say it because it's true. When I think about God, I think of you and when I think about you, I think of God. I don't know if that's right, but you have helped me so much, you have no idea. And when I tell you that I love you, I don't just say that; I really mean it. Sarah, I love you so much. You have no idea how much I love you. You probably only know a little bit of how much I love you,"

"Yeah, Hugo, I know. I know you love me. I don't know why, but I know you do. And you're right; I have no idea how much."

Right before we hung up I told him, "Hugo, thank you for loving me."

He tried to thank me for something, but then opted to say nothing, which was better. We both knew I didn't, couldn't love him the way he loved me. He loved me wholeheartedly, without reservation. I wished I could love him in that way, but there were too many unknowns that God had to iron out for me. I needed to continue to guard my heart and wait on Him.

Hugo also said, "One thing I really like about our relationship is that we are willing to follow God either way. No matter how hard it is, God will give us peace if we are to be together."

"Exactly," I said. "I like that, too, because we want to only glorify God in our lives, whether together or not."

"But, like I said," Hugo laughed, "it would take angels."

At school that week, I overheard my friend Rachel tell someone that she was going home that weekend. I knew that she lived in Baltimore, so I asked if I could get a ride. She said, "I just need to ask a few people that were supposed to go with me, and I'll let you know at basketball practice."

When she told me yes, I jumped up and down. My coach raised her eyebrows at me, but I didn't care. I was so excited to be with Hugo a couple more days.

That weekend was such a blessing because I didn't think I would be able to see Hugo again until December 12th. We'd been having a lot of good talks on the phone, and I was really missing him, so it was so awesome that I got to go back to the ship another weekend.

On the nine-hour car ride down, I had lots of time to pray. First, I prayed that Hugo and I would have time for some good talks. There was a deep conversation about "the line" that I wanted to have with him. I really hoped to raise our standards, because I wanted to be an example to people in everything. If I desired my marriage to be an example and a way for people to see Christ, then my dating relationship should be too. The goal was to be separated from the world to point people to Christ. If I could date in a way that would help people see Christ and God's holiness, then that was what I wanted. I wanted to be different from the normal.

I compared it to the reading I had been doing for school in Leviticus. God gave the Israelites rules and weird ways to do things because he wanted them to be different. He wanted His people to be different from the nations around them so that they could be a living testament to God. Holiness gets people's attention. I wanted non-Christians and Christians to feel and see the difference in my relationship with Hugo, so that they would ask why. This, in turn, would give us the opportunity to tell about God's holiness and faithfulness to us. It was all about God's glory!

Of course, Hugo took it upon himself to make sure my time in Baltimore was a blast. From the time he picked me up at Rachel's house until the time he took me back, we had a lot of fun together. The ship was docked in the downtown boardwalk area, so there were lots of fun things to do and see. We went to Barnes and Nobles and wandered around. It was there that we fell in love with a cartoon called "Get Fuzzy."

Hugo said, "I can totally see you as a cartoon! If I could draw, I would make tons of money drawing you as a funny koala!"

We also bought the Vanessa Carlton CD that had our song on it, "A Thousand Miles." It was the song we had heard on the way to the airport in Mobile. We listened to it a thousand times while I was in Baltimore, too, and it was always on the radio. We spent a lot of time hanging out and talking. We did talk about "the line," and I thought it was a topic we would have to go back to a lot, because the flesh is weak and needs lots of reminders.

It was good to just be together and get to know Hugo more. I found out he really liked magic tricks. While we were walking by the river, there was a man doing a magic show. We stopped and watched. Afterward, Hugo said that he had a trick for me. He opened my hand flat and put a quarter in it. He told me to try to close my hand as fast as possible, before he took the coin out of it. He positioned his hand above mine. His hand started to move, so I closed my hand as fast as possible. His hand had touched mine, but I could feel the coin in my closed fist.

He held my fist closed and asked, "Do you still have the coin?"

I could feel the coin, so I said, "Yes!"

"Are you sure?" he asked, giving me a wink.

I started to open my hand. "Yes, I have the . . . " I stopped. I was shocked to find that I had opened my hand to reveal a penny, not a quarter. I looked up, smiling. Hugo showed me how he did it, but he made me practice with him until he could do it more smoothly. That was one of the first of many tricks he would learn and use when he gathered crowds in order to preach the gospel. In fact, not long after this, I remember going bowling with Hugo and, in no time, he had a small crowd of adults around him as he did this trick.

We celebrated my birthday together on the ship, even though it was not the exact day. He bought me a pair of great brown pants, which I spilled ice cream on later that night.

I returned to school before my actual birthday, October 29th. That day, Hugo called me at 6 a.m. so we could talk before my class. Unfortunately, I had already left, so he left me a voicemail in Spanish. He had promised to call me at 5:45 a.m., but when the night watchman, Oscar, came to his room to wake him, Hugo thought to himself, "Okay, five more minutes." The worst lie of the devil. He called me back later that day so that we could actually talk. I'll never forget what he told me.

He said, "Sarah, I really, really, really, really love you. And I've really fallen in love with you."

I said, "You're crazy, and you need sleep."

"No, I need you."

After we hung up, he called me again about half an hour later from a store. He had rounded up two clerks to help him sing "Happy Birthday" to me. It was so crazy, but very funny.

On most days, my heart felt split in two concerning Hugo. I ached to be with him but, when I was with him, there were constant physical temptations. I loved him and hated him all at the same time. I loved him because of who God had made him, and I hated him because he confused me, and because it was so hard to balance life and know which way was right.

I loved him and cared for him so intensely, but I was so reserved and cautious at the same time. I hated that I didn't know for sure that he was the one I was supposed to marry. I hated that I wanted to marry him so badly, but was worried that I would get hurt or mess up my life. I hated and loved that I just wanted to fall completely in love with him. Was God holding me back, or was I holding myself back?

I talked to my roommate, Rachel, that night about why people get married. That particular weekend I had started to ask myself that question.

"Why do people feel like they want or need to get married? Why do I need to get married?" I asked her.

Rachel gave me the best answer that I could actually agree with and live by.

"God gives us a unique opportunity to minister to one person in a special way. It is something extraordinary, and you won't be able to minister to anyone else as you will to your husband."

Lying in my bed, I thought about what she said. I stared at the glow-in-the-dark spray paint my friends had used to write, "Hugo loves Sarah!" on my wall. I mulled it all over in my mind, Hugo, marriage, love, me . . . a unique ministry . . . and I finally decided, "The 'ministry' would be all about how God could be glorified in Hugo's life, and how I could be a part of that, and how God could use me to work in Hugo's life. Now, I could get married for that. I could get married to glorify God, and to be a living example of Christ's love for the church."

As heaven would have it, I was blessed to spend another weekend with Hugo before I planned to see him during Christmas break. On November 10th, my friends Panin and Monica were going to travel to Panin's sister's house in Philadelphia. Hugo met me in Philly, and a friend of his, Greg, dropped us off in New York City while he went to a meeting. This day became one of our favorite memories as a couple.

It started when Greg dropped us off near the Statue of Liberty ferry dock about 10 a.m. He gave us a tour book of New York, a bottle of water, an umbrella, and his wife's cell phone. When they were done doing all they needed to do that day, they would call us and pick us up wherever we were. It was an awesome plan, because no matter how far we walked, we would not have to walk back, nor would we get lost.

The best memory of the day happened while we were walking to Times Square. Hugo said, "I have an important question to ask you. I want to know how you really feel about the future." I was kind of at a loss for how to respond, so he explained further, "In December, I want to talk to your parents about marrying you, but I want to know what you think first."

He stopped, pulled on my hand, and gently spun me around to face him.

"Sarah," he continued, looking into my eyes, "all I want to know is, will you marry me?"

I looked at him and smiled, "Yeah."

It was all so casual that it took us a second to realize what we had just done. Then we both broke out into enormous grins and hugged for a long time.

We walked to Times Square and took some pictures. We stared in awe at the flashing lights and displays. It was so surreal to be there. Neither one of us could believe that we were there, especially together.

We decided to eat at McDonald's so that we would remember this day every time we went to a McDonald's. It was a two-story McDonald's, so we ate upstairs. Later, we went to FAO Schwartz and played with some of the toys. Then Greg called on the cell phone, asked us where we were, and told us the corner we should stand on for him to pick us up. Again, it was great to have him find us and not have to walk back all those blocks.

Hugo and I were really excited when we got back into the van. I felt like we were talking a hundred miles a minute about all that we had done and seen. It was so funny. I was tired, but I wanted to stay awake to spend more time with Hugo and to remember our moments together better. He laid his head on my lap and I massaged his shoulders and back, and then we switched. After walking for about nine hours, it felt really good.

We stopped to get some food and I sat up. Hugo leaned over and kissed me, but I pulled back. It felt so good to not give in, but it was hard at the same time.

After getting our food, we piled back in and I fell asleep on Hugo's lap. About an hour later, I knew we were close and I woke up, wanting to spend the last few moments close to Hugo. I put my head on his shoulder and slid my hand across his waist. He said he loved it when I did that, and at that point, I really wanted to kiss him.

I moved my head, and we had the most amazing kiss. It tasted so good. It was purposely short, though. We were so close to Panin's house, where I would have to get out and leave Hugo, and I wanted just one more. I turned again, but Hugo just gave me a quick peck on the lips. He said something to me, but I couldn't hear all of it. The only part I heard was "someday." I was astounded. I never thought I'd see the day that Hugo would refuse a good kiss from me, and keep me accountable to my convictions. I was so amazed and proud and excited all at the same time.

Later, on the phone, I told him how excited I was about that. I really knew how much he loved me because he chose to help me show self-control. It was so awesome, and it meant so much to me. He also told me on the phone that the first kiss was so good and he really, really wanted to kiss me again, but he knew that he couldn't. He had made his mind up to respect me the whole time.

Once at Panin's house, I said goodbye to Hugo and started back to school with Panin, David, and Monica. David asked me if I had ever been in love.

I said, "Do you mean, have I ever loved someone, or have I ever been *in* love with someone?"

"Both."

"Yes, I love Hugo."

"But have you ever been *in love*?" he asked.

I had to answer, "No." My heart broke as the words came out of my mouth, and I wanted to take them back. I had always told myself that I was not in love yet because I did not totally know God's will yet, and I needed the permission of my parents. Somehow I knew that I was in love, but I didn't want to admit it. It hurt me that I had said no to David's question.

I called Hugo and told him I made it home. We didn't talk long, but I was so distraught over the question David asked that I had to call Hugo back. I asked him what he thought was the difference between loving someone and being in love. We had a deep conversation about why I was holding back. Why I was scared to love with my whole heart.

He pointed out to me how hard it was to have this conversation in English, and that made me realize what he went through to communicate with me and love me. I told him I couldn't imagine having this conversation in Spanish. I know the poor guy was confused by me most of the time, because I could hardly understand my own feelings and thoughts. But somehow he helped me, and the Holy Spirit worked in me.

I told Hugo I needed 45 minutes to talk to God first, and then I would tell him if I could love him with my whole heart and pursue marriage with him, trusting God to work out any details. Then we hung up, and I began to cry out to God. These are the notes I took:

> These are the verses and encouragements God gave to me tonight as I decided to love Hugo completely and trust God to work out the details. I do believe this is God's will and He will bless it.

> -Like the little kid that keeps asking his father if it is okay to slide the slide.
> -Psalm 91:
> -He shall cover you with His feathers
> -His truth shall be your shield and buckler
> -You shall not be afraid
> -Keep you in all you ways
> -Don't worry about tomorrow; today has enough worry of its own
> -It's not who you marry. It's who you are while you are married to them. Are you doing God's will? (Yes! I can do and be in God's will married to Hugo— He is seeking and loving God.

> -Psalm 61
> -Hear my cry, Oh God; Attend to my prayer

> -Job 42:2-3
> I know that You can do everything, and that no purpose of yours can be withheld from You . . . Therefore I have uttered what I did not understand; things too wonderful for me, which I did not know.

-Psalm 2:12
Blessed are all those who put their trust in Him.
-Phil. 4:6-7
Be anxious for nothing.

After I prayed and read my Bible for a while, I wrote the following to Hugo, in Spanish, so that I could tell him straight to his heart what I felt.

Hugo escúchame bien. (Hugo listens to me well)

Tu eres mi mejor amigo en total el mundo (You're my best friend in the whole world)

Por eso te quiero (And that's why I like you)

Tu eres honesto y fiel (You are honest and faithful)

Por eso te quiero (And that's why I like you)

Tu eres divertido te gusta sonriendo (You are fun and like to smile)

Por eso te quiero (And that's why I like you)

Pero mas que total es te amas a Dios primero (But, more than anything, you love God first)

Quieres servirle por total tu vida y con total tu corazón. (You want to serve Him with all your life and with all your heart)

Y tu eres Hugo Amilcar Liborio Gómez (And you are Hugo Amilcar Liborio Gomez)

Y por eso te amo mucho. (And that's why I love you a lot).

Y quiero ser tu esposa cuando Dios quiere. (I want to be your wife when God wants).

I called Hugo and read him what I had written. He didn't really say much, but I could tell that it really impacted him and that he couldn't believe what I had said. I had to go soon after, but I received an e-mail in Spanish the next day that said this:

How are you babe!

I hope that you are good and that God is blessing you a lot! Before I knew that you loved me but now it is like I have never heard you say it. To say te amo, well, really you have never told me that before. Only in English, I love you, and I thought this was "te amo", but now I know that it was, "I like you." Which is also awesome! Now I am just left to pray to be the best for you!

Te Amo!
Hugo

After this e-mail, I was glad that I had waited at least this long to tell him "te amo." I told him "te quiero," which was a more friendly way to say that I loved him, for the first time while we played "Twister "in the Amazon Café. The first time I said "I love you" in English was in Lori Beth's room, while we were watching "Forrest Gump." But I knew "te amo" would really speak to his heart, so I wanted to wait to say it until I really meant it. I was glad I had waited, because I really did mean it now. I knew I wanted to marry him someday.

I talked to Pastor Schenke at Word of Life. I told him that I wanted to talk to an unbiased sounding board before I went home and my parents shot my ideas full of holes. I said that jokingly, but that was what it felt like sometimes. I loved my parents so much, and I was so thankful that they cared enough to help me through this time. But it was nice talking to Pastor Schenke. He helped me get it all in perspective again, and I was more confident and comfortable in the decisions that I had made. He helped reassure me that I wasn't totally off the wall or doing something stupid.

He told me two important things. First, he said that I shouldn't be pressured by time. Time would keep me from making a big mistake, and ultimately I'd have a better marriage in the end. At the moment, I just needed to enjoy my friendship with Hugo and continue to gather data about how he worked and responded to life. Second, Pastor Schenke said that he would like to see continual, consistent spiritual growth in Hugo's life. I just needed to observe and remain objective. This was important because the man of the home sets the spiritual thermometer for the relationship and the family, so I needed to see how Hugo would behave without pressure from me.

On the other hand, Dad and I were still going round and round on the phone. We got to the point where we were just having the same conversation over and over and not getting anywhere. Dad came to the same conclusion and thought of a new plan. We would both talk to a mutual counselor friend, Richard. Not because we didn't want to talk to each other, but because we needed an unbiased, wise sounding board to help us resolve some issues.

I called Richard the first chance I got. Basically, he assured me that I was not crazy to love Hugo. But he also helped me filter my desire to marry Hugo through Scripture. He used Colossians 3 to help me think about my decision.

He said, "To know who God wants you to marry is the cake. But will you be patient for the icing? That is your parents' blessing."

I started to take notes on our conversation, and later I wrote them in my journal:

"Cake Questions"- Col. 3:15-20
"And let the peace of God rule in your hearts"
1. Do I have peace, from the Holy Spirit, in my heart, about marrying Hugo?
    ~ Yes.
"To which also you were called in one body"
2. Do other people, who I highly respect in the Lord, agree with my decision?
    ~ 99.5% Yes.
"Be thankful ... with thankfulness ... giving thanks" (Three-Fold Thank You).
3. Does the decision to marry Hugo make me say, thank you, thank you, thank you to God?
    ~ Yes. Yes. Yes.
"Let the word of Christ dwell in you richly"
4. Is the Spirit dwelling in me richly as I make this decision?
    ~ Yes.
"Do all in the name of the Lord Jesus"
5. Is my decision an obedient decision to the Lord Jesus?
    ~ Yes.
"Icing Question"
vs. 20; "Children, obey your parents in all things, for this is well pleasing to the Lord."

6. Do my parents approve and bless this decision?
　　　　　　~ I need the icing!

In talking with Richard over several weeks, I was fairly certain of God's will concerning Hugo. I was on a mountaintop, but most mountaintop experiences are followed by a valley of trial. Mine was about to begin.

At Thanksgiving, I stayed at the Word of Life Inn with some friends instead of going home both then and also a couple of weeks later for Christmas. I should have just paid the money to go home, because it was the worst Thanksgiving ever. Not just because I wasn't with my family; mostly because I got a call from Hugo. We had been chatting on the phone a lot because I had so much free time, but as soon as I picked up the phone this time, I knew something was wrong.

"Sarah."

"Yeah?" was all I could say, but my mind was racing with what could be wrong.

"I have to tell you something." Hugo said. He sounded calm, but I could hear his heart breaking.

I thought for sure he was going to break up with me, and I started to panic. Why would he break up with me? But I forced my mind to get it together and I spoke again. "Hugo, you can tell me anything."

"Are you sitting down? Are you alone?" he asked.

I was in my room at the Inn, which I was sharing with three roommates. Panin had lupus, and she needed to stay in bed. The other girls were keeping her company.

I glanced over at them and told Hugo, "Just a second." I knew it would be impossible to take the call somewhere else in the Inn or to get the girls to leave, so I opted to shut myself into a small closet.

I sat down on the carpeted floor and took a deep breath. "Okay, I'm alone. What do you need to tell me?" My voice was shaking with nervousness and fear. I felt a chill run up my spine, despite the hot room.

Hugo paused. I knew he did not really want to tell me. Either he wanted to lose me but he didn't want to hurt me, or he didn't want to lose me but knew this was going to hurt me and might make him lose me.

"I'm not on the evangelism team anymore. I mean, they took me off the team."

I felt kind of lighthearted, because it was not nearly as bad as I had thought it was going to be. But I knew I had to dig deeper. "Why? Why would they take you off? You're amazing at guitar, drama, everything. Why would they move you? Where did they move you?"

"To the galley department."

"Why? That makes no sense. It's just crazy. What happened?" I was talking so fast, trying to ask all my questions at once.

"I'm on discipline," Hugo finally said. I stopped short. My questions were no longer important, except one.

"Why are you on discipline?" I asked. Then I waited. I could hear him breathing. He was fighting with his heart; he knew this could be the end of us.

"I was caught looking at pornography."

He started to cry. I tried to take a breath, but couldn't. The air was totally knocked out of me, and I was in shock. I could not believe what Hugo had just told me. He was sobbing now. Tears rolled down my face, and I smacked them away in anger.

I wanted my life to be the way it had been an instant ago, not so complicated and unfair. I desired to marry this man, and I didn't see why God had brought me this far only to rip it away from me. I had asked for bread in my life and God had given me rocks.

I thought back to the conversation I'd had with God about two years earlier, when I told Him that I never wanted to go through the pain of losing someone I really loved and wanted to marry. But, there I was, possibly going through the exact pain that I never wanted to feel. I wanted someone to fix the pain and the problem. I wanted someone to just tell me what to do, because obviously I had tried following what I thought God wanted. But I didn't know if I could forgive this, so I might end up with nothing.

Hugo and I both cried for a long time, and neither of us spoke. What could I say? I was broken, angry, and felt abandoned by God and Hugo.

"I'm sorry, Sarah. I'm so sorry. I didn't mean . . . It's no excuse . . . " he didn't know what to say. He took a deep breath and started over.

"My DTS director, Tim, told me I had to tell you. I wanted to, but I was scared. I didn't want to have this problem. It's no excuse, but I was exposed to porn through my friends with I was young, maybe eight years old. I didn't know that it was wrong until a few years later. Then I thought there was no harm to anyone else, so it didn't matter. Then, when I rededicated my life to Christ and missions, it was too late; I was addicted and I was too embarrassed to tell anyone to get help. I'm so sorry to have hurt you like this. But Tim is going to help me to control my eyes and my mind and to make them obedient to Christ."

I was still crying; not so much in anger now, but more in sadness. Sadness for myself, that God had not given me the pure, virgin man that I had waited for and prayed for so long. "Hugo, thank you for telling me. I've had a long, hard day, and this Thanksgiving has been horrible away from family. I will call you in a couple days. I need to pray about this."

As I hung up, I knew I was being cruel, and that waiting to hear from me for two days would probably kill him. But I was mad, and I thought he deserved to sweat it out. He had been so stupid, and hurt me deeply, so he could have a little pain in return.

Plus, I really did need time to pray this through. Could I still marry him? Addiction to porn is pretty much a lifelong struggle to keep the devil from taking a foothold again. Did I really want that in my life? How would this affect our love life, or our marriage in general?

I stopped thinking and started praying. "God, please. Please show me. Can I still love him? Speak to me."

I got out my Bible and, as I read, God spoke.

God said, "Why are you mad at Me? You can be if you need to be mad at someone, but I am sufficient for you. I am faithful, just, loving, and good. I have a hope and future for you, plans that do not harm you. There is no need to be angry at Me because I love you, and I have your best interest in mind. The Bible tells you to wait on Me and know that I am God. 'Those that wait upon the Lord shall renew their strength, they shall run and not grow weary, they shall walk and not faint' (Is. 40:31)."

In fact, after that, God gave me many Scriptures to read and hold onto.

Ps. 73:25-26 "Whom have I in heaven but You? And there is no one on earth that I desire besides You. My flesh and my heart fail. But God is the strength of my heart and my portion forever."

Rom. 8:28 "And we know that all things work together for good to those who love God to those who are the called according to His purpose."

Rom. 8:18 "For I consider that the sufferings of this present time are not worthy to be compared with the glory which shall be revealed in us.'"

Ps. 55:22 "Cast your burden on the Lord, and He shall sustain you; He shall never permit the righteous to be moved."

God used these verses to speak great truths to my heart. I learned that I should have not been angry at God because He is perfect, righteous, and good. I knew that I should wait on the Lord – not in anger, blaming Him for taking away my best friend, but in peace. I knew that He was in control and He still had a perfect plan for my life.

The verses showed me that what happened had already been to the throne of grace, and God was allowing this to happen in my life. In His own way it would come together for good. I needed to ask God to use this to glorify Himself in my life, because the pain was only temporary, but the glorification in my life and in Hugo's would be eternal. I needed to seek God, know God, and trust Him, casting this burden upon Him, so that I would not be shaken to anger or lack of faith.

I also thought about how God's ways were higher than my ways. He sees eternity and what He needs to do in my life to accomplish His will. Maybe God wanted me to go through this fire in order to prepare me for a harder battle later. Maybe He was testing my love and devotion to Him and His call on my life. I didn't always understand God's ways, but I would trust Him because He was good and His love would be faithful to me.

My heart broke again. Not in pain this time, but with compassion for Hugo. I didn't think I could forgive him yet, but compassion was a start. I felt compassion for the little boy who had been shown a lie about love. And for the same little boy who had lived in fear, not knowing where to get help to be free.

I called Hugo two days after he told me. I hadn't been able to bring myself to call him any earlier. Not because of any bitterness, but because I really thought I was crazy-sick in love if I was going to forgive him this time. If this was not a red flag, than what was? I wrestled with God over and over in my quiet time. He continued to say, "Just wait and see; time is your friend." So in the meantime, until God said no, I needed to follow up with Hugo. I made the call as promised.

"Hugo." I started seriously, because chit-chat would have seemed painful at this point.

"Yeah, it's me," he said. His voice was sad and tired. I was quiet, still making sure I was doing the right thing by continuing this relationship.

Hugo broke the silence first. "Sarah, can you forgive my stupid stuff?"

"Yes, Hugo. I forgive you."

"Will you still be my girlfriend?"

"Yes, I will. You haven't lost me."

"Thank you, Sarah. You don't know how much it means to me to have you stay with me through all the sins I have in my past. And I promise you I will do everything to be a better man for you. I know the Holy Spirit can help me change and be the man I need to be for you. Sometimes I feel like a guy that is dirty and smelly from playing basketball, and then someone walks up to him and says, 'Here put this on,' and hands him a perfectly white T-shirt. I don't feel worthy to be with you."

"Hugo, we all have sin. Even me. I'm selfish and prideful for a start, and God sees our sins as the same. There are no greater or lesser sins in the eyes of God. I'm just as nasty." I quickly added, "But a lot prettier."

We both laughed. It was so nice to laugh together again. We took our minds off this deep conversation and began to discuss our plans to meet in Kansas for Christmas. Hugo needed to meet my parents, and my parents really needed to meet him. I felt that it would help them start seeing him like I saw him. If they just knew him, they would see my point of view better, and it would ease their fears. Hugo and I visited briefly about his ticket and how God was providing the money for him to come.

I got to Kansas first, and a week later I picked Hugo up from the airport. We were happy to see each other, but both deeply pensive on the two-hour drive back to Hays. As we entered my parents' house, I subconsciously held my breath and pushed aside a conversation I'd had with Dad a few days before.

Sitting in his big oversized easy chair in the living room, he had leaned over to tie his shoes, getting ready to leave for work. I had sat down on the floor close to his feet. We had chatted about what he had to do today. Dad was the manager of a Christian radio station, KPRD.

"I have to go up to KPRD and do some voice tracking," he had said. "The radio station is practically on auto-pilot during the Christmas season, but I have to record some announcements that will play over the next couple days. What are you up to?"

"I'm not sure. Maybe gift shopping and wrapping some presents. I need to catch up on some e-mails, too. Can I use your laptop while you're gone?"

"Sure, it's in my office on the desk."

Then the mood had become sober as I said, "You know, Hugo is coming in a couple of days."

"Sarah, as your father, because I love you ..." Dad tended to start his sentences several times and back up the story each time he started again. He continued, "You know God has put fathers into place to protect their daughters. I am not going to be really nice with Hugo, because being nice might be understood as giving permission and I am not giving permission."

I had looked down at my own shoes, realizing that, as excited as I was to see Hugo, the difficult talks we had planned with my parents were the goal of this visit, and it would not be all fun and games. Talking to my dad gave me an idea of just how hard these conversations would be.

He had looked at me, practically in tears. "Don't make me walk you down the aisle and give you to this man. You will make me leave behind all the convictions I have about marriage. Don't make me do it."

I had felt crushed. I couldn't feel anything. We had sat in silence for a moment, and then I had stood and left. After I had prayed for him and talked with him all year, he was not even an inch closer to understanding the forgiveness I had chosen that day in Mobile.

I thought about the possibility of not being able to marry Hugo at all. I started to cry; it seemed to be an impossible situation. I knew I would not marry Hugo without Dad's blessing, because I truly believed God had put Dad into my life to help me and not to harm me. Dad was in tune to the Holy Spirit's voice. I was confident that Dad would eventually hear God's wisdom, but I was confused about why it seemed like God was telling me one thing and my dad another.

I had wiped my tears that day and decided that I just needed to be patient and wait for God to reveal His ultimate plan. I would deal with my fear of not marrying Hugo if it became a reality. I had prayed I would not have to confront that nightmare.

So now, finally, here we were, face-to-face with my parents, the polite greetings made. Mom told me later she thought, "He is handsome; I can see why Sarah likes him."

Hugo soon picked up my guitar to mask his shyness. Playing and singing were a way for him to ease the tension of the situation, but it was also an important part of him that my parents needed to see.

We had fun hanging out for the week. We went snowboarding with some friends in Colorado. I gave Hugo the grand tour of Hays, and we even saw the local buffalo herd. Hugo stayed for Christmas, but Salvadorians celebrate Christmas by having the big celebration on New Year's Eve. Their Christmas is celebrated on Christmas Eve. I decided to give Hugo a little gift on Christmas Eve with a card that read,

Hugo,

First, I have to tell you how much I love you. I love you so very much. Really Hugo, te amo muchísimo! More than you know! Also, I wanted to write you and give you a special Christmas present on the day that I know in your heart you are celebrating Christmas!

I'm so happy that you are here at my house for Christmas. Thank you for coming so far to make my Christmas one of the best ever! (That's why I love you!) I hope that you enjoy experiencing Christmas in a totally different way than you are used to and are not too scared of my family! I know that you will be awesome and have fun no matter what! I'll really pray this year that next Christmas we can chill with your mom and family in El Salvador. I would love some tamales and pupusas! I know God will be directing us concerning details of the near and far future! That's why I love and trust Him!

Hugo, also I want to thank you for being honest with me, and being open about what you're really thinking about. You don't know how much it means to me to have you share your deepest heart with me. Thank you for being real and for being who you are. Thank you for being so funny and for loving to laugh. I loved so much watching TV with you tonight and resting my head on your chest and feeling you laugh! ☺ You love life and you're not afraid to enjoy it to the fullest! Your humor is hilarious, and I love to laugh with you!

Thank you for spending the time to get to know my family and also my friends. I know they have all enjoyed getting to know you! I'm so glad they finally got to meet the man who has stolen my heart and that I fall in love with dozens of times every day! You know I could go on forever in this letter about how many ways you bless my life and how I love you and why I love you, but I'll save that for another mushy love letter. This is a Christmas card, and I need to stay focused—which is always hard with you running through my head!

Christmas was fun, but it was not the point of why Hugo had come to Hays. Several nights later, before Hugo left, we all sat at the table. I remember what followed very clearly.

This was the moment of truth; I had prayed for this discussion many times over the last year while at Word of Life. Would my dad finally see how God had forgiven Hugo? Had the Holy Spirit changed my dad's heart?

Hugo had asked me in Times Square about whether he could ask my dad for my hand in marriage that December, but he quickly realized how firmly that door was closed, so he simply asked my dad to bless our dating relationship. My dad spoke for about an hour in response to that question. I knew it hurt him to say these things. He was not angry; he said them as a father truly protecting his only daughter. He cried. Hugo cried. Mom and I, too, fought tears.

Mom had told me when this whole cycle of discussion started, "I wish I could just be happy for you. He is your first boyfriend, and I just want to talk to you about it and congratulate you. But I have to support my husband and keep praying that God will work it out."

So Mom sat by him supportively, understanding Dad's points, and aching with me at the same time. Dad talked a long time; I think he had a year of thinking that he needed to get off his chest. He wanted to have his say, so we all listened and only interjected when we felt we had to.

As a pastor and counselor, Dad had seen so much, maybe too much, of how past sins could affect a marriage later on in life. In recent years, he had counseled many couples that, from the outside, looked like they had it all. Couples who were very good-looking, had a house, cars, and money to spare. Some had grown up as good Christians, sometimes even as pastor's kids. The other spouse had grown up religious, but very promiscuous sexually.

In all of these marriages, hidden behind the beauty of the exterior, was a dark interior. They were riddled with thoughts of jealousy, doubt, resentment, and a lot of fear that the spouse would leave for another or commit adultery. In these particular marriages, the trust needed for a biblical, Christian marriage never had a chance to bloom because of sins committed before marriage.

My dad did not want that pain for me later in my marriage. He used the verse from I Cor. 6:18: "All other sins a man commits are outside his body, but he who sins sexually sins against his own body." Dad explained that he was also afraid of sexually transmitted diseases, which, in my innocence, was an issue I had not even considered. Hugo promised to get blood testing and send the results to Dad.

Later, Hugo told me that at one point he hung his head and thought, "He's right; I am those things that he says I am. She is better off without me. I am not good enough for her." But when he looked up, he saw my face and how I stood up to my dad for him, fighting for him. It was then, he said, that he started to understand how much I really loved him and wanted to be with him. For that reason, he did not give up. He sat there and listened to Dad condemn every sin Hugo had ever committed and tell us how those sins would destroy our marriage in the future.

At the end of the conversation, my dad said no. He said we could date if we wanted to, but he would not bless our relationship. Hugo told him that he understood. If he had a daughter and someone from another country came to him to ask permission to date her, and Hugo didn't know that man's culture or language, he would be very untrusting, too. But Hugo continued with words I will never forget. My heart beat wildly at the love, passion, and determination in his voice. He said it slowly, so that he would be understood and not make any mistakes.

"Sir, if you tell me 'no' today, I will be here to ask again next year, and the next year, and every year if that's what it takes."

Dad looked down and slowly nodded. "Fine. My answer is still no. You may continue to date if you want to, but I will not bless it. Sarah can go to the ship in January if she decides that is God's will for her. I would ask you not to pray and read the Bible together, because a deep spiritual bond should be shared only with your future mate. That's it. Those are my wishes."

Hugo had to leave for the airport soon after the conversation was over, and as he walked out the door, my mom told him, "Hugo, I am very proud of you for sitting there and listening to my husband. I think if I were you, I would have gotten up and left." She hugged him, squeezed his arm in encouragement, and then Hugo and I left for the Wichita airport.

We had just pulled onto the interstate when Hugo pulled off to the side of the road. I had been looking down, going over everything that had just been said. I had a heavy heart and neither one of us was talking. I looked over at him, puzzled why he was pulling off on the shoulder. His eyes were full of tears. He put the car in park and hid his face in his hands. My heavy heart broke, too, and I silently cried with him. Moments passed, and we just quietly sat. There was so much to say, but no strength of heart to say it.

Finally, Hugo managed to say, "I hate that the greatest consequence of my stupid stuff is that it might keep me from marrying the woman I love." In his sadness, he seemed almost angry. Not at my dad, but at his younger self, who had known better, but had decided to play the world's game anyway.

We talked a while more, but we knew we had to get to the airport so Hugo wouldn't miss his flight. During the drive to the airport, we talked about my plans to join the ship in January. The ship would be in Puerto Plata's port on the North Atlantic shores of the Dominican Republic. I knew that things with Hugo were nowhere near resolved, but at least I could look forward to more time with him in the near future.

Please visit my website, www.my-onceuponatime.com/, to see pictures and videos from each chapter.

Chapter Eight

The Prince Proposes
2003

Dominican Republic

Through much prayer and talking with my parents, I decided that rejoining the ship was the best next step for me. My year of intense Bible study at Word of Life was over, and I had completed my classes feeling anxious to use my knowledge and ministry skills on the mission field.

Going back to the ship would allow me to do just that, but would also provide the opportunity to observe Hugo in a more ordinary, day-to-day setting. I needed to fully pursue this relationship, trusting that God would guide us to get married or lead us in different directions. This was the breaking point. Would God draw us together finally, or would the final red flags be waved?

Hugo was still in the galley as part of his discipline on the ship. He accepted it for what it was and attempted to do his job well. He really loved his boss, Tyron, from Alabama. Tyron was funny and laidback, so he and Hugo got along well. The other two chefs continually bickered back and forth, and no one could ever tell if they were joking or serious.

I was put on the Community Development Services Team. My team went out to teach villagers, especially in the poor Haitian communities on the sugarcane plantations, how to develop their environments to make them more suitable for daily living. We taught them to build latrines and shower houses. We taught classes on simple water purification, solar cooking, construction, and gardening.

We also built two churches during the three-month outreach in Puerto Plata. One of the guys on my team, John, and his wife, Amy, worked with Hugo in the galley. Hugo and I really got to know and love them. We learned a lot about marriage from them, through their words, but mainly through watching them interact. He loved her, and she respected him. We found out they loved to have fun like us too. We would all go to Fun City outside of Puerto Plata and enjoy bumper cars and go-kart racing. Hugo would tell jokes the whole time, and we always had a blast.

Ship life was as grand as I had remembered it. Tiny cabins with two to four bunks and a sink, bathroom, and shower in the hall to share with 20-plus people. The occasional queasy stomach when the waves were knocking the boat up against the dock. But it was an adventure every day, and I loved it. Hugo and I were joined together at the hip when we were not working. If I was working dockside, instead of out in a village, I would try and sneak away to say hi to Hugo in the galley now and then. When Hugo had the day off, he would come out to the villages and work with me.

Once, he helped my team cut PVC pipe and fasten it to the ends of the corrugated roofs. This would help collect rainwater into a huge holding tank, enabling the sugarcane village to have a water supply other than from the plantation owner. The owners never seemed to provide nearly enough for all the villagers. We taught the villagers how they could put the water from the tanks into clear plastic bottles and then put these on the roof to bake for a day. That way, they could save their firewood for cooking rather than wasting it to boil water. The sun, at the extreme temperatures found in the DR, would kill many of the bacteria that might be in the rainwater.

Soon after I arrived and we were both settled into the routines of our jobs, Hugo told me, "My day off is Friday, but I can't hang out with you. I'm going into town. I have some stuff to check into."

"Okay, you can be mysterious," I replied jokingly, but decided to change my response after I saw his serious face. "Okay, no problem, I'll see you after work."

I wondered what was up, but I trusted him and knew he would tell me when he wanted to. Hugo wasn't normally the strong, silent type. He loved to tell me every little detail about almost everything. He would even think of bizarre questions to ask me just to start up an intriguing conversation. Such as, "Who's the best superhero?" or "If you had all the money in the world, what would you do with it?" So for him not to tell me what he was up to was very odd indeed. I fretted about it for a while, but then pushed it out of my mind.

Then, a couple weeks later, the same thing happened. Hugo told me again that he needed to run into town on his day off. After work I wanted to take a quick shower and then talk to him to see if he'd let me in on the secret. I hurried as best I could, but it was hard to maneuver in the tiny shower. Once I was done, I tossed my dirty clothes into my cabin, took a quick brush through my hair, put it up into a pony tail and then walked three doors down and over to the port side of the ship to Hugo's cabin door. I knocked our secret knock on his door; "Shave and a haircut, two . . ." The secret part was to pause extra long for the last knock, "bits."

Hugo opened the door. He smiled at the use of our secret knock. He took my hand, pushed past me and said, "Let's go to the hammock."

We often went to the hammock on the lower aft deck to watch movies on a laptop, or sit and talk. This lower deck was still outside, but was kind of a storage area for different things, boxes needing to be broken down by the galley staff, old mooring lines, scuba equipment for underwater boat maintenance. The hammock hung over all of this. Not perfectly romantic, but on a busy ship, it was one of the few quiet places we could find.

Hugo started in right away, excited to tell me something, "Remember when I had to go to town on my day off?"

Of course I remembered. I wanted to tell him to hurry and get to the point, but I patiently said, "Yes, I remember."

He continued, "I went to get the blood work done that your dad was concerned about. You know, the HIV test and all that."

I had kind of forgotten that my dad had asked Hugo to get STD testing. I was really impressed that Hugo had remembered and had already taken care of it. But I was also curious about the results.

"I didn't tell you because I wanted to know before I told you, but here you go." He handed me the half sheet of paper the results were printed on. My eyes sped through a bunch of mumbo-jumbo, scanning to find what I was looking for. Wait, there it was. Negative. I looked up at Hugo.

"Negative." I said. "That is wonderful, congratulations."

"Now I just have to call and tell your dad."

"Yes, let's just do it now, and then you will have it done." I tried to sound encouraging and upbeat. He agreed, and soon we were on the phone with my parents. I talked with them first to let Hugo warm up to the idea of talking to my dad. I told my dad that Hugo wanted to talk to him.

"Fine, put him on for me," Dad said. I passed the phone to Hugo. "Hi, David. How are you?"

"Good, what's up?"

"Well, I just wanted to inform you that I got the testing done that you were concerned about. The results were negative."

"Okay, thank you. We'll talk to you later; keep in touch." They hung up without saying much more. Not because they were upset, but because it was just an awkward phone call and both of them wanted it to be over as soon as possible. As hard as that moment was, I was glad it had taken place. I knew it was another step in the process of my dad accepting Hugo as part of God's will for my life.

Now that Hugo had done this testing and had the courage to call and report to Dad about the results, I felt something changing in Dad. I couldn't put my finger on anything specific, but Dad seemed to be coming around. When I talked to Dad on the phone he seemed quieter, as if he were thinking. Before he was always trying to get his point across or tell me a book to read. Again, I couldn't be certain, but I felt God was moving in Dad's heart in a way only The Spirit can.

The next morning I woke up early to pen a letter to Hugo. The card had Prov. 3:5-6 on the outside: "Trust in the LORD with all your heart and lean not on your own understanding; in all your ways submit to him, and he will make your paths straight." I wrote,

The verse on the front of this card has given me so much hope and comfort in my life, especially now in my relationship with you. I don't know the future, but I know that I trust my God. I trust Him to show us both the way that we should go, to give us wisdom and discernment. Last night God proved His love and faithfulness to me. I trusted God to work out this detail, if I would love you with all my heart. I took that step of faith, trusting God. And He opened another door. I just wanted to tell you how thankful, excited, elated, grateful I am that everything went well with your test.

Thank you for spending the time to share with me about it in the hammock last night. I really appreciate your thoughtfulness to include me in you excitement.

Bebe, I'm so glad that I'm here on the ship with you. There is no place I'd rather be right now. I hope that we can be a light somehow here in the DR. You and I are a great team for ministry.

I was relieved to sense small changes in Dad's attitude, because Hugo and I had been dating for a year now and everything seemed to be going better all the time. Dad had stopped sharing any negative comments with me about why he might disapprove of Hugo. And even I could hear a glimmer of excitement in his voice about the ministry we were doing together on the ship. I wrote Hugo another mushy love letter to celebrate.

Hugo, thank you so much for this last year. It's been awesome to get to know you more and to find out who God made you to be. I know how hard this last year has been, but it has also brought me so much joy! Being your friend makes me so happy. My life is so much better with you in it. Thank you.

I want to share with you the poem that Rachel, my roommate from Word of Life, wrote a couple of years ago and gave me as a Thanksgiving Day gift. She said that our relationship fit her poem, so she wanted us to have it. Here it is for you too.

To know a hint of love
Is to hold someone in your heart
Peering through eyes that see faults,
But remain dazzled by beauty.

To gain a taste of love
Is to cling to stubborn faithfulness
Delighting in the simplest words or deeds
But wanting to give all in return.

To feel a touch of love
Is to brush soft eyes with your own
Fearing the strength of your deafening heartbeat
But losing air at nearness of heart and body.

To glimpse a shadow of love
Is to ache to heal another
Savoring sweet moments past
But guarding hidden dreams to come

To hear a whisper of love
Is to be captive to hope and trust
Begging for a heart to be laid open to you
But unconditionally baring your own.

To shelter a spark of love
Is to blaze with a fire of feeling
Melting in the grasp of another
Softening under their fingers
Burning in tender arms.
January 3, 2000, Rachel Fetterholf

Hugo, I really love you. Thank you for the memories of this past year. I look forward to many, many more!
I praise God for you.

Lovingly Yours,
Sarah

Being together so much acted as a fast forward button on our relationship, but Hugo had always told me that he did not want to get married until we had a really good argument. During the romantic weekends or ten-day stretches we were used to having together, it was really easy not to get into arguments, and so our relationship wasn't always realistic. About a month or so after I joined the ship again, we finally had the fight we'd been waiting for.

We had joined a gym that was only a couple blocks from the ship so we could lift weights. It was small, hot, and I felt out of place, but Hugo went with me and we exercised together. On the walk home, he jokingly pinched at my small but sensitive rolls. Then he tried to hold my hand, but I shrugged him off and walked two steps in front of him for the last block back to the ship.

Once we had walked up the gangway and signed in, he told me he wanted to talk to me. We found a quiet walkway on the portside of "B" deck. We didn't really have a place to sit, so Hugo sat on the inner railing and put his feet on a mooring hitch. His legs totally blocked the walkway. I stood facing him, leaning against the outer railing, arms crossed and a bad attitude written all over my body and face.

He started to explain to me that he hated that other people could tell that we were upset with each other. Maybe it was cultural, but he didn't want me to shrug him off and act mad in public. He did not think people should look at us and think that we were fighting.

Now I understand why Hugo felt that this was disrespectful, but at the time I thought that if I felt emotions, I should wear those feelings on my sleeve. I wasn't going to put on a fake face just for other people. We got into a pretty heated discussion about it. I was too prideful to accept that I had wronged Hugo, and so the discussion dragged out longer than necessary. I was ashamed at my childish actions, but it felt like it would kill me to apologize. I finally did, though. And Hugo did too, several times.

Oblivious to characteristics we had displayed that would mark future discussions, we settled our disagreement. Our first argument was over and, when all had been said, Hugo looked at me and gave me a goofy grin, eyes gleaming.

I gave him a flirty, "Wha-at?" I was smiling, but trying to pout at the same time.

He knew my game though, and revealed his thought. "Sarah, do you realize this is our first argument?"

The thought had crossed my mind at the beginning, but the novelty had worn off once I got so mad at him. But now it was exciting again to ascend to a new level of our relationship. We stood and hugged tightly. We had survived our first heated discussion, and I think we both walked away from that experience satisfied with the softness of the other person's "boxing gloves."

The *Caribbean Mercy Ship* was like our home, and as such everyone was always in everyone else's business. Hugo was constantly pestered about when he was going to ask me to marry him. He felt extremely pressured, so much so he did not know if he wanted to marry me or if he just wanted other people to stop telling him that he did. He pushed aside any thoughts of popping the question. He wanted to look back and see that his motives were pure and not pressured.

A different sort of pressure was applied after my mom and brother decided to visit. Hugo started out uptight, but quickly realized that their dependence on him for language and culture worked to his advantage, and he relaxed into his own element. Mom and Mark were able to witness Hugo's natural leadership abilities when we planned an outing for a group of friends to go surfing and play in the waves.

No one from the group of ten young people had said who was in charge, but for some reason everyone asked Hugo questions and followed his lead anyway. Maybe it was because he spoke the language, but it was almost hilarious how people would instinctively look to Hugo to lead them. It was like they wanted to follow his smile and charisma. When people watched him they thought, "Hey, he looks like he's having fun. I want to follow him and do what he's doing."

Another instance that divinely became a turning point in my dad's heart revolved around an evening worship session. Hugo had invited Mark to play drums for the worship, and Hugo would be playing the guitar.

After practice that day, Mark confessed to my mom, "The practice was so horrible. I'm kind of embarrassed to play tonight. I don't know why, but nothing is clicking with the worship team, and it sounds bad. I think I'll tell Hugo I'm not playing."

Mom worked her magic as only a good mom can do, and she encouraged Mark to follow through with his commitment to play drums. He did play, and something awesome happened. It was as if the Holy Spirit flowed through Hugo as he played his guitar.

The other musicians instinctively followed him, feeling that he had his finger on the pulse of the worship. Hugo's leadership was so natural and the transitions between songs were so seamless that people didn't even notice. And that's the point, to lead people to God and get out of the way. The worship time was a powerful, close encounter with God, and the Holy Spirit had used Hugo to get us there.

Later that night, Mark confided something deep that God had lain on his heart: "Mom, I told you the practice was horrible, but somehow, during the real worship time, Hugo made everything flow together." He looked her straight in the eye, with a serious passion in his voice. "We have to get on board with this guy. I can see how God is using him in mighty ways."

After the week of work, ministry, and fun, Mom and Mark left. After they relayed their stories to my dad in Kansas, I could literally start to feel the Holy Spirit peeling back the layers of his heart.

I patiently waited for God to do the work that I could not do, praying for His will to be done in my father concerning my future with Hugo. Little did I know that thousands of miles away, God was answering my prayer. The Holy Spirit was revealing to my father that it was God's sovereign plan to bring Hugo and his daughter together. It might not be what he'd always hoped for me. But God's ways are higher than our ways.

In another jolting prayer time, God spoke to my father about grace. Dad had started to live out his Christian faith at the age of 18, when he got involved with Campus Crusade. It was only through God's grace that his experiences prior to meeting his spouse were what they were, and that he was still a virgin when they met. He saw how his story could easily have been the same as Hugo's: wanting to marry the woman of his prayers and dreams, but possibly losing her because of past bad decisions. God showed Dad that the grace that had protected him from those sins had also set Hugo free from those same sins.

I sent Hugo verses to encourage him. He was still on discipline with the ship for his computer activity dealing with the porn, and Satan wanted to keep that sin constantly before him and make him believe that he was unworthy for ministry. I knew that only Scripture could renew Hugo's mind.

I gave him Rom. 12:2: "And do not be conformed to this world, but be transformed by the renewing of your mind, that you may prove what is that good and acceptable and perfect will of God." I also shared 1 Thess. 2:12: "Encouraging, comforting and urging you to live lives worthy of God, who calls you into His kingdom and glory." Then I wrote,

> Hugo, remember as you walk through this life, to do it worthy of God. He's called you and saved you for a reason. Now everything you do reflects His character to the people around you. I love this verse because it reminds me that my life is not about me. It's about glorifying God. What a huge responsibility to try and live up to! Thank God for grace! He knows we're not perfect, but our responsibility is to simply follow Him.
>
> Simply follow! Live a life worthy of God and the calling He has for your life!
>
> Let me know how I can help you!

Love you,
Sarah

We did a lot more than think and talk about serious things. Adventures in the Dominican Republic were many. Where to start? How about at the bottom of a mountain that had a cable car attached to it? Hugo and I were in the parking lot with eight friends, and I was begging Hugo to pay a guide to take us up the path.

"No, Sarah, it's no big deal. We just climb straight up. We'll just look up and follow the cable car wires. We can't get lost."

"Fine. But, if we get lost, I will say, 'I told you so.'"

We started to climb, having a good time with our friends. We made it to the first big tower that the cable car was attached to, about one-third of the way up the mountain. We continued on, and soon the path disappeared. We veered right off into the forest and found a new path. We followed that for a while, but then it too disappeared. We looked up to find the cable car wires, but the trees were too tall to see where they were. We kept climbing up as best as we could. Two hours later, Hugo and I came to a clearing that we thought was the top of the mountain. I burst out laughing. Everyone gathered around us and looked over the trees too.

"We climbed the wrong mountain!" I announced to everyone, if they had not figured out our predicament yet. We were on the smaller mountain to the right of the cable car mountain.

The whole group grumbled as we went back down the "wrong" mountain. We hadn't climbed where we planned, but no one was really mad about it. We reached a ravine that allowed us to climb back over to the "right" mountain. Most of the group decided that their hiking day was done and went back to the ship. But two other guys, Hugo, and I were determined to climb what we had set out to climb. Starting out seemed innocent enough—a hard climb, but nothing grand.

But soon, I found myself on a ledge thinking, "My hand does not want to move to go up, and I definitely cannot go back down." We climbed several rock walls that were almost completely sheer. Once, one of the guys knocked a rock loose with his foot, and it fell and hit the guy below him in the head. The lower guy was only dazed but I thought, "If one of us gets hurt or dies up there, there is no way to get a body out." There were foot-long centipedes crawling everywhere. The vines had thorns on them, so any exposed skin received a sound lashing.

Time passed, and we climbed on and on. We hadn't brought much water, and were now down to one bottle of soda. It was foggy and starting to rain a little, which made the leaves slippery and gaining solid footing more of a challenge. It was so late that we thought the cable car would be closing soon, and we would not be able to ride down as we had planned. We decided that if there were no cable cars going down, we would just sleep on the mountain until the cable car service opened the next morning. We picked up our pace as best we could under the conditions. I prayed that God would not let me die on this mountain.

We reached a section that was full of trees, but very steep. We had to put a foot at the base of each little tree to keep from slipping. It was exhausting work. Finally we reached a clearing, and the cable car house was right in front of us. We crawled up onto the cement slab and lay down, kissing the cement.

The guards and workers who were there looked at us, puzzled. "Where in the world did you guys come from?"

We explained our expedition. I don't know if they were impressed or thought we were crazy. We were just glad the cable car had not closed yet. They had one more car going down in fifteen minutes. The two guys, Hugo, and I gathered together, like in a football huddle. We started to pray and thank God that we were okay. Hugo started and then stopped. I was already shaking and crying, and when I shot a look at Hugo, he had tears on his face too. We just stood together for a little while, praying to God silently. We were all really shaken up.

Someone said, "Amen."

We gave each other hugs, then stood to get on the cable car. We were the only ones going down. The operator must have thought we looked like we needed a break, because he let us go down for free. We marveled at the jungle and the sheer heights we had just scaled.

One of the guys asked, "Why did we think this was a good idea?"

I answered, "Hugo convinced us all it would be fun." I smiled and punched Hugo a good one in the arm. "And, I told you so." He just laughed. It took six hours to climb up the mountain, and a whole six minutes to get down.

Later, I wrote Hugo a card about some thoughts I had had on the mountain.

> That mountain was crazy yesterday! You know, I was praying a month ago about you and thinking a lot. And I was telling God how you have this crazy heart that I love so much, but it scares me sometimes. It scares me that in its wildness, you will lose focus. I was praying to God about this and how it could affect my life. God told me that He needs that wild, crazy heart in you to be able to accomplish His will in your life. He needs that spirit in you so that you will not fear the places you will be led to minister to. God told me that I need that heart in you too, so that I can see you pursue me and love me in extreme ways. Ways God knows that I love to be loved. God made us both perfectly, including crazy hearts that love to climb the highest mountain, whether it leads to the cable car or some new depth in our relationship to Christ.
>
> Hugo, I love you so much and love that you love me.
>
> I'm praying for you!
>
> Love,
> Sarah
> P.S. Thank you for ALL that you are!

The very next weekend, Hugo and I got into another life-or-death situation. We went to the beach in Cabarete with a big group from the ship. It was an organized ship outing. Hugo and I decided to rent a two-person kayak for an hour. We easily rowed out past the reef.

The water was calm out there, so Hugo suggested, "Let's get out and swim a little."

Even though I'm deathly afraid of swimming in deep water, because I am afraid of sharks, I said, "Sure, let's do it!" Looking back, I think I wanted to impress him.

We played and splashed around for a while until Hugo looked at his watch and said, "We need to get the kayak back. It is going to take a little while to get there."

The current had carried us past the point we had gone out from. "Okay," I said, as I boarded the kayak.

Hugo tried to get on, but we tipped over. We tried again, same result. We tried Hugo getting on first, or both of us at the same time. Nothing worked. Finally we figured out that the kayak had a small hole in the back where a metal piece used to be attached to a rope. The haul, which housed some air to help float the boat, had slowly filled with water, and though the kayak was fiberglass and would not sink, it could no longer sustain weight. We put the paddles in the kayak and started to push it to shore.

The current carried us further to the right, and Hugo told me, "You stay with the kayak and push it, it will be safer."

"Okay," I replied. I had been a state swimmer in high school for the two years I was on the swim team, so I knew I could swim hard. I thought Hugo was close behind me. I looked back once and I could only barely see his head now and again. I knew more or less where he was, so I was not too concerned. The shore was not that far away. I reached the shore first, but the wave I rode in on was brutal and slammed me into the beach. I lost my sunglasses.

The kayak went one way and both the paddles another way. Two young Dominican boys saw my situation and ran to help me. One grabbed the kayak and started to heave it onto the beach. It was water-laden, though, and he could not pull it very far. The other boy had scrambled for both the oars, but was now helping pull at the kayak.

I saw the situation was under control and looked back to the water to see where Hugo was. He was just getting to the shore about 30 feet further down the beach. I talked with the little boys and thanked them for saving me. Hugo reached me and gave me a big hug. I knew we had had a pretty eventful experience, but he seemed really traumatized by it. He was panting heavily, and his muscles were shaking. I pulled him back, holding his shoulders, and asked, "Are you okay?"

Panting and choked up he said, "I have never yelled for help in my life. But I was really close just now. I wasn't sure if I could make it. I'm not a strong swimmer."

"What! Hugo, you know I'm a good swimmer. Why did you have me stay with the kayak?"

"Because I wanted you to be safe."

"Hugo, you're so dumb. You can't be nice when your life depends on it."

"I know. I planned to stay with you, but somehow we got separated in the waves."

Then Hugo got mad. I mean, really ticked off. "That stupid guy who rented us this kayak, he almost killed us. I am so not paying for this." We were about half a mile from where we had rented the kayak. "Just leave it here. I will tell him where he can come and get it. Besides, it is so full of water, it is impossible to move."

We walked back to the rental kiosk, and Hugo gave the guy an earful. We left and were not required to pay. The guy did feel really bad. Needless to say, we stayed on the ship the next weekend and watched movies.

One safe and productive thing that we did was help a friend, Ricardo, from Mexico, record some music. Ricardo asked Hugo to play guitar and sing, in Spanish and English. Hugo hated the way his voice sounded, but Ricardo convinced him. Ricardo wrote the lyrics and the music, but wanted Hugo's voice on the CD. So Ricardo, his wife Citlali, Hugo, and I would go to the recording studio whenever we got a chance. We'd go in on our free time and after work and record into all hours of the night.

The recording studio was right in Puerto Plata, within walking distance of the ship. There was no sign, no indication that it was a business of any sort. No one would know it was a recording studio by sight. We'd walk though some residential houses, then we'd turn into a narrow space between two buildings, walk 20 steps, and go up metal stairs attached to the side of a house. At the top was a pretty decent recording studio. One guy ran the whole thing. He was pretty talented.

Hugo always said, "This guy specializes in recording Bachata music. If you can pick up on and mix the detailed sounds that are heard in Bachata, you can record just about anything."

The recording artist struck a deal with Ricardo: $100 a song, no matter the hours we put in at the studio. What a break. We spent hours in the studio. They wanted me to do a back-up vocal for a song called "24 Hours a Day."

At 2 a.m., Hugo woke me up. I was sleeping on the floor of the studio. "Okay, Princess, it's your turn."

"What?"

"We're ready to record your back-up vocal now."

I got up groggily, but shook it off to be able to record. Though I was not normally a singer, Hugo and Ricardo assured me it would just be to add extra "fullness" to the song, and that people wouldn't really hear my voice. Hugo, on the other hand, did an amazing job. His voice had a very natural feel to it. He sang with heart in a way that made the things he sang about seem very believable. I loved to watch him in his element. It was beautiful. He was like a little boy in a candy shop, wide-eyed and full of non-stop energy.

He and Ricardo would brainstorm creative music possibilities. "Let's add an egg shake here and change the drums to this beat." And Hugo would beat out on the table how he imagined the section should sound. Or, "We should use a nylon guitar for this song; it gives it a warmer feel." Or, "Isn't there a girl on the ship who plays saxophone? Let's get her in here to play with this section."

It was an amazing experience, and the result was a 7-track CD called "Once Blind." Ricardo paid Hugo by giving him the rights to make any copies he wanted and to sell the CD himself. Hugo and I invested in the CD and started selling Hugo's voice wherever we went.

Soon, God showed Hugo and me that it would be wise to finish our time on the ship. I think in the back of Hugo's mind, there was a desire for a change in environment, so he could really seek God's will for marrying me without the pressure from all our shipmates. Together we discussed an opportunity we had heard about to help lead a DTS in Jarabacoa, Dominican Republic. We thought we would love to do that because we had enjoyed our own DTS's so much. Hugo was a natural leader and was great with groups, while I loved doing personal discipleship.

We rented a motorcycle and rode down the coast through Sosua, taking the winding roads up into the mountains to visit Youth with a Mission (YWAM) at its land base in Jarabacoa. We loved the cool of the mountains and the lush, green landscape. The base was nice and very quiet in its off-the-beaten-path location. On returning to our floating home, we talked with our authorities and arranged to move to the YWAM land base when the ship left at the end of March.

I called home to share with Mom my plans to leave the ship with Hugo and serve on the land base up in Jarabacoa. Mom had visited that base during her stay in the DR, so she was excited for us. She also confided in me, "Sarah, your dad prayed for Hugo last night." She stopped and then said again, "Dad prayed for him! I can't believe it! This is huge, Sarah. You keep praying. God is working on your father's heart."

I hung up with a huge, "Thank you Jesus!" sigh. I was elated that my heart's desire might come true.

As the ship left Puerto Plata, Hugo and I stood on the dock and watched it go. We continued to wave as the tugboat pulled the ship out to deeper water and the port's own pilot stepped off our ship onto the parallel pacing watercraft. He looked proud that he had expertly taken the ship out of port, one of the trickiest parts of sailing. Our arms ached as we waved more furiously, to be sure they could see us. It was a very sad day for us. Hugo had lived on the ship for two years straight; I had lived there for three years off and on. We had met, fallen in love, and had our first kiss on the ship, and now she was gone over the horizon.

Friends took us to the capital city, Santo Domingo, on the south side of the island. We stayed with my friend Ada, whom I'd known at Word of Life. We planned to relax at her parents' apartment for two weeks as a vacation, before getting back into ministry in Jarabacoa. Her parents owned an apartment on the top floor of a five-story building, so they also owned the roof of the apartment building. Ada's mom had some potted plants and flowers up there around a metal gazebo.

About a week into our stay, Hugo and I were watching TV when he got up and left the room. I assumed he was going to the bathroom. I was into the program I was watching and did not calculate the time he was gone, so when he came back I suspected nothing. He cuddled up with me on the couch.

A little bit later he said casually, "Let's go for a walk."

"Okay," I said, and headed for the front door, which led down the stairs to Abraham Lincoln Street, one of the main drags of the capital city. I figured we were walking to Blockbuster or Haagen-Dazs.

Hugo quickly said, "No." Then he added, with a secret smile, "Let's go this way." He indicated through the kitchen, which led to the stairs up to the roof.

He took my hand and led the way. I love surprises, so I changed my direction to follow his lead. My mind pondered what this crazy guy was up to, but my heart sighed and thought, "Ahhh … he did something special for me."

By the time we got to the roof, I was totally euphoric. "Let's dance," he whispered.

"But there's no music."

"It's okay, just dance with me." He took my waist and hand, and we slowly danced in the bright moonlight, the city lights all around below us. Since we were about the same height, I looked directly into his eyes and he in mine. We were so comfortable with each other and knew so much about each other; he truly was my best friend. But I saw something beautiful in his eyes that night. I studied him a moment more, but I wasn't able to identify what I saw. I rested my head slightly on his.

"Let's sit down," Hugo said, barely above a whisper, but with such conviction that I did not think to suggest differently.

But there was only one chair. We looked around for another one we could pull up to the one already in the middle of the gazebo.

"That's okay. You sit down. I will stand." Again, the way he spoke made my body automatically obey his commands, even though it did not make sense to have an intimate conversation with one person standing. Hugo was behind me as I walked to the chair and sat down, and as my body naturally turned back to face him, I saw that he was one step away from me.

In the next moment, he was on one knee. My mind started to pick up speed as it tried to comprehend if this event was a dream or real. Slowly, I realized that Hugo was proposing. I quickly refocused my mind to try to record every word and detail of this fairy tale proposal.

"Sarah, I have loved you since the first day that I met you. I thank God every day for bringing you into my life. You are my angel, and over the last couple years you have become my best friend. I want to spend the rest of my life with you. Will you marry me?"

I didn't have to think for a second. "Yes!"

I stood, and we hugged. He kissed me on the lips. "Oh, I brought something up to celebrate." He revealed two champagne glasses filled with orange juice. He knew that I didn't like alcohol, and orange juice was all he could find in the fridge at the last minute. We made a toast and then continued our music-less dance. Now I understood the look in his eyes. It was the look a man gets right before he asks the woman he loves to marry him.

I didn't want to spoil the moment, but the next day I had to ask Hugo an important question. "Hugo, did you ask my dad if you could marry me?"

"No."

We had talked about how important this was to me, so I was disappointed in him.

"I figured we could ask him today, together," he said pleadingly. He still doubted his ability to speak English, especially over the phone and on such a deep topic. I still thought he was taking the easy way out, but I agreed we would call my parents that day.

We sat on the hide-a-bed in the office where I was sleeping, and I dialed my home number. Both of my parents got on the phone and, after some chit-chat, Hugo hit the punch line.

"David, I asked Sarah to marry me last night, and I would like to make sure that is okay with you, sir."

Silence. I felt my stomach turn. Dad finally spoke, and his voice sounded more positive than I had thought it was going to sound. "Before I give my blessing, I would like you both to spend a week in prayer. Mom and I will be praying too. Then in one week, Hugo, you call me back and tell me for sure if this is God's will for both of you. Debbie and I will have our decision then."

We hung up, and I was so relieved that he had been so positive. He hadn't said no. Not yet anyway.

Hugo and I prayed, separately and together, if getting married was truly God's will. We moved to our ministry position in Jarabacoa during that week, and when the day came for us to call my parents, we had no way to get in touch with them. We had to wait all day, as we worked around the YWAM base in the morning.

Finally we could leave to go into town. Thankfully, my used Honda motorcycle started right up, but the motor wasn't very strong, so we painstakingly climbed up the hills, making our way to the main highway. We were way up in the mountains, so internet and cell phones were slow and had spotty coverage. This was 2003, just a few years shy of Skype and other internet resources designed for easy communication. Plus, we were new to this area and had limited contacts. We got to the edge of town and prayed about what to do next. We went to the first open store we could find. Hugo worked his charm on the teenage girl behind the counter.

"Okay, I have a weird question. Can I use your cell phone? I'll buy a phone card from you to call the States, but we are new here and don't know anyone else to ask, and we really need to call her parents today." He motioned towards me, and then we both smiled at her with pleading eyes.

"I guess so," she said reluctantly. She handed her pink cell phone to us.

We quickly bought a card. We found a deserted aisle in the store and sat on some iron circular steps. We anxiously checked our pockets to find a coin to rub off the numbers on the back of the phone card. In a panic, thinking we were going to miss our date with destiny, I resorted to using my fingernail. Hugo punched in the million numbers it took to make the call, and we each pressed one ear each to the phone, trying not to breathe as we listened to it ring.

"Hello?" Both my parents were on the line in an instant.

After a few pleasantries and details of our move to Jarabacoa, my dad got right to the heart of the matter.

"Well ,Hugo, did you two pray this week?"

"Yes sir, we did. And we still feel that God wants us to get married."

"Okay. Debbie and I prayed as well . . . "

My heart faltered as I strained to hear Dad's words reach from Kansas to the Dominican Republic. I pressed my ear to the phone even harder to block out the voices in the store.

Dad's voice lightened, " . . . and yes, you two can get married!"

"Congratulations! Yeah!" I heard Mom exclaim.

Hugo and I looked at each other excitedly, and the air in the room instantly became lighter. We talked a few moments more, but we knew the phone card was almost up and we wanted to call Hugo's mom as well.

Then the phone went dead. We thought it was the phone card but, come to find out, somehow we had broken the girl's phone. Later that week, we had to pay her for it.

We found an internet café, borrowed another cell phone, and stood in a closet in the back of the store to call Hugo's mom, Irma, in El Salvador. Hugo talked to her first, but then I got on and asked her if I could have permission to marry her son.

She said yes, of course. We knew from the beginning that Irma loved me. Even when Hugo and I were not dating, Irma would ask Hugo, "Cómo está, Sarah?" (How is Sarah doing?) And at night, before bed, she would say, "Oramos para Sarah, su vida, su ministerio y procteccíon." (Let's pray for Sarah and her life, ministry, and protection.) Of all the girls Hugo had dated, I was the only one that Irma had approved of. So my heart did not beat as hard because I knew what the answer would be. She said that I didn't even need to ask, but she was thankful that I had. She would love for me to marry Hugo.

Soon we left the Internet café, and we were on cloud nine as Hugo drove the motorcycle back to the YWAM base. I wrapped my arms snugly around him and laid my head on his back, content that we were heading in the right direction and had turned a huge page in our lives that day. He took his left hand off the clutch and patted my hands as if he was having the same thoughts and feelings. We slowly drove up and down the hills, then turned on the dirt road, which led to another dirt road, which led to the final dirt road back to the base.

Though our lives together were just beginning, little did we know that another marriage was ending. Several weeks later Hugo called his mom on our cell phone, and she revealed that she and Hugo Sr. were officially divorced. They had not lived together for years, but now it was reality.

I held Hugo in a tight hug as he shared with me what had happened, and tears ran down his cheeks. I could see the pain in his eyes of years of seeing his parents fight and not being happy with God or each other. Soon I also saw determination and he looked at me and said, "Never Sarah. Divorce is never an option. Okay?"

"Okay." I hugged him tightly again.

We turned our thoughts to planning our happy union. We were to stay through the DTS, which would last until December, then come home to Kansas in January, plan the wedding in a month and a half, and get married on February 14, 2004. Hugo and I bought some fancy paper and velum, took a romantic picture, and then a few designs and a borrowed laser jet printer later, we had our wedding invitations printed.

We thought we could plan a wedding from the Dominican Republic, knowing that my mom was amazing with details and planning. We quickly learned that this would be harder than we thought, as mom asked my opinions on bridesmaid dresses, colors, flowers.

After one phone call, I broke down in tears. I felt like my wedding might get planned without me, and that is not what I had had in mind when I was little. The reality of what I was giving up started to set in. Hugo and I prayed about what we should do, because we had already committed to help with the DTS and we really wanted to do that as well.

God soon revealed his plan. After three months of serving in Jarabacoa, YWAM asked us not to be leaders for the upcoming DTS. There were many reasons for their decision, and Hugo and I debated each one. Several days went by, and we still did not know what God wanted us to do

Then one day, as we were out for a drive on the motorcycle, a crazy idea came to me.

"Hugo, what if we go home now? There's no reason to wait for December. We could just go home in June."

We talked about it more while we took in the beauty of a waterfall near the base. We prayed about it a little bit, but it just felt right. We were so confused about every other possibility, but we both felt peace about this decision.

Hugo and Sarah share a movie (*John Q*) and a hammock on Valentine's Day 2003

Sarah and Hugo's engagement picture, taken in Dominican Republic
and used on their wedding invitations

Hugo's huge smile when he opens his first music CD that
he recorded with Ricardo Hernandez.

Hugo and Sarah enjoy a motorcycle ride in Jarabocoa, Dominican Republic, in 2003

Please visit my website, www.my-onceuponatime.com/, to see more pictures and videos from each chapter.

Chapter Nine

The Kiss
2004

Kansas, El Salvador

Hugo and I decided to surprise my parents with our homecoming, so we called my brother Mark in Wichita, Kansas. My parents were planning a bike trip, so we asked Mark to pretend that he and his girlfriend wanted to go along. Then Hugo and I would unexpectedly show up and go instead.

When we appeared on my parents' doorstep, it was two in the morning. My parents were excited to see us, but it wasn't until my mom asked how long we were staying that she burst into tears. She thought we were just there for a quick visit, but I explained that plans had changed and we were staying in Kansas for the next nine months to plan the wedding.

Those months passed in a blur. We did work on wedding plans, but we also involved ourselves in ministry. We helped my youth group leaders, Ken and Mary Ann, with activities at Teens for Christ (TFC). We also assisted with a prison ministry through First Baptist Church. We took a special class that gave us clearance to enter into the cellblocks.

Once inside, we invited the men to First Baptist's church service at six in the evening. At first it was very intimidating, but most of the guys played cards together, and Hugo viewed that as an "in" for himself. He'd strike up a conversation, and then ask them if they wanted to see a card trick. A few guys would gather around and, after showing them a few tricks, Hugo would look up and invite them all to church. This always worked pretty well. We laughed at the one time that it backfired, though. A prisoner took the cards and started to whip out the coolest tricks we had ever seen. He told us he had worked at Vegas at one point in his life. Hugo was mesmerized.

Our ministry during the service was to meet with Latino prisoners who wanted to learn about the Bible, but we also helped them with their English. It was through this ministry that we met a 25-year-old man named Luis. He had been busted for drugs, but had gotten saved in prison. Luis was about to finish his sentence and would soon be deported to El Salvador. This was not the last time we would see Luis.

Hugo made fast friends with several of the kids in TFC and even taught guitar lessons to a few of them. He was hot to sell as many of his "Once Blind" CD's as possible, because he really wanted to get that ring on my finger. We still had not chosen wedding bands, nor did we have the money to pay for them.

While we were visiting my Grandma on her farm near Dannabrog, Neb., she brought out the 40th anniversary wedding band that Grandpa had given to her. She explained that now that Grandpa was gone she did not wear it, and wanted to offer it to us to help us in the ring department. She also offered us 1/8 of a karat diamond that she and Grandpa had won in a promotion at a jeweler's.

Hugo and I had talked about finding a small stone for my engagement ring for two reasons. First, I am not a big jewelry person. I like simple and small. Also, since we were going to be living overseas, Hugo had a fear of getting robbed or, as horrible as it sounds, of me getting my finger cut off for a huge sparkling rock. Being from the violent, post-war country of El Salvador, Hugo was always using his street smarts.

Even with the tiny diamond from Grandma, he would often turn my diamond into my palm and hold my hand to cover it. We looked at settings together so I could see what I'd like to put the diamond in. I chose several different looks, but told him to decide on what he liked and surprise me.

One Sunday, we were running late to get to First Baptist Church in downtown Hays. I hate being late, so I was a little perturbed when we left the house. I said nothing as we set off, trying to bite my tongue. But when Hugo turned left on Vine Street instead of crossing the intersection and going straight, my flesh got the best of me, and I had to say something. I tried to sound lighthearted. "You should know the quickest route after living in Hays this long."

Hugo said, "I know. I just want to go this way today."

I brushed it off. As long as we get there soon and don't have to walk in late, I thought. Just as I was finishing that thought, Hugo pulled into the turn lane. Very few cars were out on the street because it was Sunday morning. I sat up and started to protest, because I thought he was going to turn into the grocery store and get gas or something. But before I could say anything, he put the car into park. That's when I saw that little box sticking out of Hugo's chest pocket. All thoughts of church and arriving on time vanished.

"Sarah, this is the third time that I will ask you to marry me: first in Times Square, second in the Dominican Republic, and third here in Kansas. This time I wanted to pick a familiar place, so you will always pass by and remember that this is where I proposed to you with an engagement ring. So, Sarah . . . I love you with all my heart. Will you marry me?" He opened the box to reveal the shiniest, most beautiful ring I had ever seen.

"Yes," I answered, as he slipped the ring onto my finger and we leaned across the car to hug each other. We arrived at church late and sat in the back. Hugo sat on my left with his arm around me. We didn't hear a word Pastor Jerry said because we couldn't stop looking at my shiny diamond.

By the time September rolled around, Hugo and I were starting to wish we had set an earlier wedding date. But we had printed the invitations in the Dominican Republic before we knew when we would be coming back to Kansas, and we were too poor to have them printed again.

So, we fought every day to keep our hands to ourselves. Hugo was living in a guest room at Ken and Mary Ann's house, and it helped to have a little distance between us at night. But it made for tiring days, as we tended to stay up as long as possible talking or watching movies, so that we could have maximum time together. The crazy things we do when we are in love. This card I wrote to Hugo during that time tells of the struggle that we endured in that time of waiting.

> Hugo,
>   Thank you for who you are. Thank you for trying so hard to become the man God wants you to be. Thank you because you were right. I do hear, see, and feel the difference, the difference between our way and God's way. Your kiss was amazing before. But back then, it felt like you were saying, "You're beautiful and I <u>can't</u> wait to be with you." That's not bad, but now when you kiss me it feels like, "Wow, you are such a precious gift from God, beautifully made by Him, and I <u>can</u> wait for you because I love you so much."
>   I hope you understand what I've said. It is hard to put into words, but I'm pretty sure you feel the difference too! It is definitely from God!
>   Thank the Lord for His strength and guidance for you! Thank you for doing His will! I'm praying for you and am so, SO proud of you!
>
> Love You Forever,
> Sarah

We had so much time on our hands that Hugo spent a whole week planning an elaborate scavenger hunt for my 23rd birthday in October. He typed up all the clues and hid them in different places around Hays. He set it up so that the first clue led me to my friend Danielle, so she could be with me to help and to take pictures. The clues led me to places like the park, the library, and the church where our reception would be held. The second to last clue was in the cemetery, which seemed a bit odd. The clue was under a rock next to a memorial shaped like a beautiful double heart. Hugo had written, "Like this couple that grew old together and finally were buried here together, I pray to be married to you until the day that we can be buried side by side. I love you 'until death do us part,' as I will promise to you very soon at our wedding."

The last clue led me to Hugo, waiting for me at Ken and Mary Ann's house. He would be taking me out to dinner. We drove up to the house, and he was waiting outside. I ran up to him and he picked me up in his arms. I wrapped my legs around him and kissed him. Danielle snapped a picture. "I love you too," I exclaimed. "Thank you for the awesome birthday present. It was so creative!"

This was also our last date before Hugo was going to be laid up for a while. On Halloween, Hugo was going to have surgery on his right knee at Hays Medical Center. The left would be done in January. We were not exactly sure why, but both of Hugo's knees had ACL and meniscus damage.

My theory was that weak knees combined with playing basketball on concrete his whole life did him in. He said he blew out one knee on the basketball court when he was a kid. The other knee popped and swelled after he lifted a piece of luggage at the airport. By the time he had his surgery, his knees had gotten so bad that sometimes we'd simply be walking and a knee would pop out of place.

He'd have to stop, pop it back in (yes, I could hear it), and then we'd be on our way. It was not natural. If his knee would pop out while he was playing basketball, it would swell up for a day or two. Since we had time in Hays and he still had insurance from the ship, it seemed like a good time to get the damage repaired.

Unfortunately, the insurance company backed out two days before the first operation. I made Hugo follow through with both surgeries, despite my feeling that our marriage had a better chance if we could go into it debt-free. But God apparently decided to teach me that our marriage would make it because of His grace in our lives, not because it began under ideal financial circumstances. Before Hugo and I even tied the knot, we were $50,000 in debt from his surgeries. But, God was faithful to us and provided for us in many unique ways.

The orthopedic doctor saw that we did not intend to run up a bill and offered his part of our expenses as a wedding gift. That deleted $10,000 from the bill. The hospital also qualified us for compassion help, and that took care of another $13,000, but we still owed a fortune compared to the couple hundred dollars we had to our name.

Hugo's surgery went well. The right knee had been much worse than the left, which was good because he had to more time to recover from that one before walking down the aisle. He spent part of his recovery time making little flags people would wave when we left the sanctuary. He sat in the lounge chair with the hot glue gun—very dangerous.

Hugo was still on crutches when we were interviewing photographers for the wedding. One photographer gave us a particularly colorful experience. He was insistent that we could not take pictures on a flight of stairs because Hugo was still not going to be able to walk (even though we told this man several times that the doctor had said Hugo would be fine).

Hugo and I shared a look that meant, "Loco!" The photographer kept asking where the wedding was going to be, even after my mom had told him several times. Then he started asking Hugo about how he got hurt and a slew of other questions. He even had the audacity (or stupidity) to ask if there were telephones in Hugo's country. This put Hugo over the edge. He was not in a cooperative mood by this point and started to tell his joke about getting hurt in Vietnam!

The meeting was going from bad to worse. Mom was dumbfounded, I was practically in tears, and Hugo was angry. I cringed in my chair because it was so awkward, and I didn't know how we were going to get out of here without Hugo punching this guy.

Fortunately my dad saved us. He said, "Well, it looks like we got all the information we need. Thank you for your time. We'll call you." We all stood at the same time and rushed out the door.

As we left, the man shouted, "Call me for the wedding. We will have fun!"

Once we all cooled off in the car and the tense moment passed, we began laughing hysterically at the memory. From that time until the day of the wedding, whenever life got a little too stressful, one of us would ask, "So, where is the wedding?" Or we'd put on a crazy face, bug our eyes out, and shout, "We will have fun!" That helped keep us laughing, and to this day it remains a family joke.

Even though it was a torturous time to wait, the nine months we spent in Hays before the wedding created a unique dynamic for our wedding day. Hugo got to know all my friends and family so well, and they him. On the day of our wedding, everyone was excited for both of us. It wasn't just me marrying some guy that I had found on the mission field. It was their friend, Sarah, marrying their other friend, Hugo.

A lot of people from Hugo's home church attended as well. Hugo's mom, Irma, and sister, Febe, were there. Some longtime family friends, the Pinos, came with their kids, Roberto and Karen. And Febe's in-laws, the Morenos, flew into Houston where their youngest son lives and drove with him to Kansas.

Hugo and I decided on a fiesta with dancing the night before the wedding, so that we could take off for our honeymoon and not have such a long reception. We planned a trip to Kansas City, because after living on the ship for two years we were done with islands and sand. We wanted cities and concrete. Hugo had not seen much of the States yet, and we did not have tons of money, so KC was within our budget. We were already planning to go to El Salvador for a month after we got back from our honeymoon. And from there we would be traveling south to Bible school at Word of Life in Argentina.

Let me backtrack to how we ended up in Argentina. God started pointing us in this direction when I was at Word of Life in New York, seeking where to study the Bible and theology in Spanish. Hugo was also trying to figure out whether he should go to a Bible school and, if so, where and when. When I first arrived at Word of Life, I told Hugo everything about it. I was going on and on, "…and they have a Bible school in Argentina…"

He cut me off, and then, as if really listening for the first time asked, "What is the name of the school?"

"Word of Life Bible Institute. Palabra de Vida in Spanish. Why?"

"Palabra de Vida? That is so weird. Palabra de Vida came to my church once and talked about the Bible clubs they wanted to integrate into our church. One of my best friends, Eric, does ministry with them."

"Wow! That's a coincidence. Anyway, they have a school in Argentina that would be fun to go to. That is one of the options I am praying about."

We hoped to go to Bible school together at some point, but didn't have enough guidance from the Lord into our future yet to make the decision. We considered Word of Life, SETECA (a Spanish seminary in Guatemala that Hugo's sister and brother-in-law had attended), and others. A journal entry of Hugo's reveals this combination of desire and lack of clarity.

In Spanish, Hugo wrote,

7/15/02

With Oscar we went to the basketball court where my DTS team was praying. There, I started to pray a lot of things, especially for a decision I need to make. Sarah already told me that she did not think she wanted to come with me to the worship school I was interested in. She prefers to go to SETECA and is asking me also if I would possibly decide to go with her there. This is a huge decision because I don't want to go just because she is going to be there, but because God wants that for me. It was good to pray for this and give it to God, so that He can do what He wants.

So God had already set us on the path toward Bible school. We had been in ministry long enough that we knew people expected us to answer their biblical questions. We wanted to have the information at our fingertips, so we would always be ready to share. We looked into SETECA some more, but Hugo had visited there several times and he said it felt too "convent" for our style. We didn't want to sit in class all the time and just learn about theology in books. We wanted exciting, hands-on experiences to put into practice what we had learned in class. With my experience at Word of Life in New York, combined with our love for Latino culture, we felt Instituto Biblico Palabra de Vida in Argentina was the best fit for us.

We had the conviction that God had called us both separately and now together into full-time missions in a Latino, Spanish-speaking country. I don't think there was anything too profound in our decision to minister to the Latino people. Basically, we loved the culture, and I had spent so long (off and on for six years) learning Spanish. I really wanted to use it in ministry. For that reason we wanted to learn the Bible and theology in the language in which we would be ministering.

But before any of the plans for Bible school could be realized, we had to get married first. I wrote what I was feeling about my impending marriage in a fresh journal from my cousin Erica.

2/09/04

I'm getting married in 5 days! I am so excited! People ask Hugo and me if we are nervous, and really we aren't at all. We actually think there might be something wrong because we are not nervous! Not really, but I wonder if I will get nervous or not. Hugo has made me promise to be happy no matter what goes wrong the day of the wedding. Right now I think I will be, but it is hard to tell how I might feel then, especially if it is something major, like my dress!

Hugo has not seen my dress, but I tried it on for my dad when I had my hair practice on the 6th. I had my veil and tiara on too, so it was really close to the real thing. My dad wanted to see me to try and get the tears out before the wedding day. He has been crying off and on and thinks he might cry a lot at the wedding. I pray he does okay. Hugo might be in tears too! ☺

I am just so happy for being this close to being married! I love Hugo so much and can't wait to be his wife and be one flesh with that man. I want to be a better woman; I want to be closer to God, so I can really serve Hugo the way he needs to be served and ministered to. Marriage is set up so that you can minister who God is to one person in a totally unique and personal way. Only through marriage can we get a closer glimpse of God's love and compassion for us. I'm determined to give Hugo the best taste of God's love I possibly can, with the help of the author of that LOVE!

The wedding plans are falling into place, just like everyone said they would. My mom did an awesome job getting it all done, though. I haven't had to worry about too much. She should go into the business, but I fear she might die an early death!

Hugo also took a turn to write in my journal, but only after much cajoling from me. He wrote in Spanish,

I'm still not nervous yet, but in truth have a huge desire for us to be together. These last few days are the most difficult to see Sarah and not want to attack her! (☺) Ha ha. But, I have to wait.

I also wrote two days before getting married,

2/12/04
Sometimes I forget I'm about to make one of the most important decisions of my life. Well, I guess I've already decided and it is all being played out and set into motion in two days. I'm so sure about this, though. I'm so sure that I want to spend the rest of my life with Hugo. I'm so excited to be his wife. I'm very relaxed about the wedding and being married. Hugo is my best friend, and it is just natural for us to be together forever.

The big celebration started with a fiesta the night before the wedding in an old one-room schoolhouse outside of town. Finding a decent price for a party room proved otherwise impossible. My good friend Michelle, whom I'd met on Word of Life Island, flew out from the University of Georgia to share in our big day. Here is her take on the festivities the day before the wedding:

2/13/04
After the rehearsal we went to the fiesta! That was fun. It was at a school several miles north of here. After we ate we had praise and worship, which was really neat. Mark and Sarah and Hugo were leading it. Hugo is a great worship leader. I can already tell the Lord has great things for him in that. We sang English and Spanish songs. Then Mark sang this song he had written for them. It was so cute. The last verse goes: "Today we come from two different worlds. Tomorrow united by this boy and girl. If you don't believe in God's perfect plan, just watch my sister hold Hugo's hand." Isn't that precious? I have been blown away by the amazing miracle that is the union of these two cultures. Just the love these families already have for each other and how welcoming and accepting Sarah's family and church have been to Hugo's family. And I know Hugo's family and church will do the same when they go to El Salvador. It's such a beautiful picture of the family of God. Hugo and Sarah have broken a lot of barriers through this marriage. I think the neatest thing has been watching Irma and Debbie. Irma speaks about

three words of English and Debbie speaks about three words of Spanish. But they have just opened their arms to each other. It's incredible to see them love. There's been so much love this weekend.

Afterward, as we were driving home, Sarah said, "Baby can you believe we're getting married tomorrow?" And Hugo said, "It just feels like I'm going to camp with my best friend for the rest of my life."

We had posted a sticky note countdown on our kitchen wall. Slowly we peeled off each little yellow reminder until 0. Finally the day came, and it was like a dream come true.

I put on the wedding dress that mom and I had prayed to find. We had found it for half off in Downs, Kansas. It was a discontinued dress, so it had to fit perfectly. I had tried on many that day and had narrowed it down to three. I tried on the first two again, and they were stunning. Then I put on the last dress, and my mom and I both started to cry. This was the dress. It was the "aha" dress that we had prayed for in the car before we came in. The lady said that since I was six feet tall, this was the first dress that they did not have to hem up or alter. The dress was made for me.

When I was ready, Hugo's best man, John, positioned Hugo at the front of the sanctuary. We wanted a private, intimate time to see each other before the pictures and ceremony. I entered the double doors at the back of First Baptist's sanctuary. Hugo's back was to me. I set my mind to record all the details of this long-awaited moment. I took my time, gazing at the pillars on stage which overflowed with ivy and white flowers. I loved how the tall candleholders in the middle of the aisle looked; their long white ribbons flowing down were elegant. Mom had worked hard on two banners that hung on either side of the stage. The left banner said, "The two . . ." The right one said, ". . . shall become one flesh." Today was the beginning of my one-flesh, biblical marriage, which would glorify God and speak to the nations about Jesus Christ and his bride, the church.

Once I took in my surroundings, I was ready to move toward Hugo. It felt like eating a gourmet meal and saving the best bite for the last. As I passed the long wooden pews on my right and left, the only sound that could be heard was the soft glide of my gown on the red carpet. The whisper of my impending arrival to Hugo seemed to carry on forever, but finally I stopped two steps away from him.

"Baby," I whispered.

Hugo turned to look at me. He took a moment to really look. "Wow, you are beautiful," he said softly, looking deep into my eyes. "You are so beautiful." He gave me a tight hug, and started to tear up. He told me later that he couldn't believe that God had blessed him this much, with a woman that he did not deserve to have.

I took a step back to show him the cute flat sandals I was wearing. I had chosen them so that I would not look taller than him, which I felt was important.

Hugo didn't care either way; he had always wanted a wife who was his height or taller. He complimented the sandals and said, "Your toes look like little candies." Then he said again, "You look so beautiful."

I should have counted how many times he said that, because that was about all he was able to say the whole time.

"You look handsome, too," I said. He looked so good in his classic James Bond tux, complete with the bow tie, that he had told me he had always dreamed of getting married in.

The tux still wasn't complete, however. As we were taking pictures in a nearby bed and breakfast with a picturesque wooden stairway, Hugo said disappointedly, "This tux does not have a handkerchief in the pocket."

My mom picked up on the statement and asked, "Hugo, is that important? Do you need a white handkerchief in the breast pocket?"

He didn't speak, but his face said it all. My mom sent my dad out to buy a handkerchief. Hugo's face was brighter than a million lights as the last piece of his dream tux was added to his breast pocket.

After pictures, we went back to the church to wait for the big moment, hidden away in the downstairs area of the church. The wedding party included my parents, Hugo's mom, my cousin Erica, my best friend Danielle, Hugo's friend John from the ship, my brother Mark, and Pastor Jerry Sprock. We were waiting for the clock to strike 2 p.m., and then the pianist would begin playing the processional music.

At few minutes before two, we decided to circle up and pray. While we were praying, the music began. We quickly said amen, and everyone rushed up the stairs. The wedding was starting, ready or not.

Hugo walked in with the guys and Pastor Jerry while "I Can Only Imagine"[1] played. When it was my turn, I barely had time to get in place while the white carpet was being rolled down the aisle. As my music began to play, I hurriedly adjusted my dress and my bouquet, grabbed my dad's arm, and reminded myself to smile. The doors opened, and I caught a quick glimpse of my mom before the standing guests blocked my view of her.

The ceremony was nothing extraordinary, except that it was. God was in it. People said later that they could literally feel Hugo's excitement to marry me. They commented about how he spent most of the service patting or stroking my hand.

During the lighting of the unity candle, we were supposed to pray, but as soon as we took our two candles and lit the middle candle, signifying that we were now one flesh, Hugo leaned over and said, "So, have you heard the joke about the dog?"

Just then, Pastor Jerry leaned over to us. I kind of thought we were in trouble, but he said, "Were you going to blow out the single candles on the side?"

We sheepishly ducked our heads to blow out the candles, and then Hugo did take my hands, lean his head into mine, and pray for our marriage and future children. The congregation was singing "Trust and Obey," the same song that had been played at my own parents' wedding. Hugo never did tell me the joke about the dog.

My parents and Irma had recorded on a cassette tape marriage blessings that were played, during the ceremony.

Dad went first: "Sarah and Hugo, in Ephesians 2:8-10, God says, 'For it is by My grace that you have been saved through faith; this is not from yourselves, it is My free gift, not by good works, so that you could never boast.' For Sarah and Hugo, you are God's workmanship, created in Christ Jesus to do good works that He has prepared in advance for you to do.

"Sarah and Hugo, I do not know all of the things God has in store for you in your future ministry of music, evangelism, and discipleship on the mission field, but I do know that one of the reasons that God created both of you and Jesus Christ died on the cross for you is for the ministry of marriage to each other He has entrusted you with today. God has used most of us gathered here today, your parents, grandparents, and siblings, aunts and uncles, friends, teachers, and others to develop character qualities in you that you will find extremely useful in your marriage ministry to each other. Even though we are still here to provide wise counsel when you ask, the only real maturity in a marriage ministry will come from the Holy Spirit using Scripture to illuminate your minds and hearts to God's principles of marriage.

"Your ministry of marriage that you are beginning today will touch countless thousands of lives. Some of those will be young unmarried people; others will have been married for many years. God tells us in First Timothy 4:12: 'Let no one look down on your youthfulness, but rather in speech, conduct, love, faith and purity show yourselves to be an example of those who believe.'

"Today we commission you, with these words Jesus Christ gives us in Matthew 28:18: All authority has been given to Me in heaven and on earth; therefore, Sarah and Hugo, go together as husband and wife and make disciples of all nations, baptizing them in the name of the Father, and the Son, and the Holy Spirit teaching them to observe all that I have commanded you to, and I promise you I will be with you always, even to the end of the age.

"Let your marriage life shine before everyone everywhere, in such a way that they may see your good works of love for Christ and each other, so that they may glorify your Father in heaven by trusting Him for their salvation.

"And now, in closing, I want to give you one more verse, Acts 20:32: 'I now commend you to God and to the word of His grace, which is able to build you up and give you the inheritance among all of those who are sanctified.'"

Mom's recording followed Dad's, and she said, "How long have I prayed for today? A little over 23 years, and look what God has done. Who would have thought that I'd be praying for a man growing up in Santa Tecla, El Salvador. Two languages, two cultures, two countries. God does so love to bless His people beyond what we could even think or imagine. And I do believe He is doing just that! Sarah, your outward beauty today is totally amazing, and is a bright reflection of the precious inner beauty God has grown within you.

"As mom and daughter, I think we have done it all. The past several months, I will always treasure in my heart as some of the best. Thanks so much for coming home. And if I may paraphrase Proverbs 31:29, there are many wonderful daughters, but as my one and only, you surpass them all.

"Hugo, muchas, muchas gracias for coming to Hays to let us – friends and family – see the character qualities and talents God has given to you. We have done many things, gone many places, laughed until it hurt, shed tears, worshipped together, shared hopes and dreams, played Uno, and have grown to love and appreciate your heart and your life. I have no doubt that you have been chosen by God to become Sarah's husband, leader and protector for the rest of your lives. It is with great joy and love for both of you that I say congratulations, and may God richly bless your lives and ministry together.

"Hugo, Sarah, gracious, God has been so good to give you life together."

Then Irma's recording began in Spanish. She said, "Hugo, Sarah, God has been so good to give you the blessing of knowing each other, the same dreams of having missions as your ministry, and above all to be the complement one to the other. Thank you for being so special to God and to the family, and for giving us the gift of being united together in holy marriage this beautiful day, February 14, 2004.

"Sarah, you are a gift from God to Hugo, me, and our family. We receive you with all our heart.

"Hugo, 'He who finds a wife finds what is good and receives favor from the LORD,' Proverbs 18:22. Son, take care of what God has given you this beautiful day.

"I wish you much happiness, my dear ones, in all of your married life."

We didn't have a lot of music, but the songs we sang were songs we really loved, and they meant a lot to us. They told the story of who we were as a couple. One of Hugo's passions was music, so that was an important part for him. One of his favorite songs was one that we listened to after we exchanged rings. It was recorded by Marcos Vidal, a musician Hugo loved, because he told stories in his songs. The song is called "Una y Carne."[2]

It was appropriate for us because it is funny, but deep. The chorus touched on the fun side that we love, but the verses talked about things what were very personal to us—such as the fact that Hugo loved his ring. I loved my ring too, but Hugo was fascinated with his and so excited about wearing it. The song also spoke to us about how God made us so perfectly to compensate for the craziness in the other. We identified a lot with this song. Here are some of the words:

"Because we're not two, we are one forever . . .
Like the fire and the volcano, like a magnet to metal,
Like cloud and mountain, forest and eagle . . .

"Each day be able to see on my finger
The ring that united me to you.
God designed you wise and talented to be able to
Compensate this crazy heart that does not know how to
Love without you."[2]

My favorite moment in our wedding came when I whispered to Hugo, "You can keep it."

I was referring to a game that we had played for many months prior to this moment. Whenever Hugo gave me a hug, he would say me in my ear, "Can I keep it?" He was like a little boy asking his mother if he could take home a stray. I would persistently say, "No, not yet."

So during our ceremony I said, "Hugo, you can keep it."

He looked up and said, "What? I can keep it?"

"Yes, you can keep it," I repeated quietly. His eyes started to shimmer, and John passed him a handkerchief he had brought for just such an occasion.

As soon as Pastor Jerry pronounced us man and wife, we walked back down the aisle. Upon exiting the sanctuary, Hugo and I started hugging and dancing up and down. My heart was saying, "We're married! We're married! We're married! It actually came true, we're married!"

We scrambled downstairs to be hidden until the reception. We ended up in the bathroom, and we thought it was hilarious to be hugging and celebrating our wedding in a bathroom. But soon the fairy tale continued, as we left the church through the front doors, bells pealing, birdseed flying, and little flags waving. We boarded our rented trolley, which was already full of our friends and family, and made our way to the reception. We stood on the back porch of the trolley and waved to our guests as we left the church. Hugo gave me his tux jacket, since the February air was a little chilly on my bare arms.

The reception was great, as we knew it would be. Along with other hors d'ouevres, we had little pupusas, similar to the ones we'd enjoyed together while traveling in Latino countries. We had people tell stories and say nice things about us. My brother, on his guitar, sang a song that he had written for us. Remember, Hugo had knee surgery on both of his knees several months before the wedding. That will help with some of the humor in the words.

"Here's to Life, Here's to Love"
By Mark Breeden
There was a boy who sailed the blue seas
The ship he sailed on was full of mercy
On that ship he met his bride to be
So he moved to Kansas to let the doctor fix his knee!

(Chorus)
So here's to life
And here's to love
Here's to the blessings
From our Father up above
It's a special day
Lord we do pray
As we toast these two
They may honor You

There was a girl so young and free
She traveled the world to see what
God would have her be
In a foreign land, she met a man
So now she is part Salvadorian

(Chorus)

Today we come from two separate worlds
Now we are joined by this boy and this girl
If you don't believe in God's perfect plan
Just watch my sister hold her husband's hand

(Chorus)

I shed a tear at that one. Then, we visited our guests, signed the marriage license, tossed the bouquet (not the one I used, because I was so in love with it), and the garter (my brother caught it). We cut the wedding cake and the groom's cake, which was in the shape of a heart dressed as a tux, and also exchanged our first Valentine's Day cards as husband and wife.

I had picked out a sentimental one. On the front was a black and white picture of a couple holding hands. I wrote:

To My Husband,
My Love,
My Best Friend,
~ This is what I hoped for when I dreamed how love could be ~ and you are all I desired, God's perfect choice for me.
~ We are one because God is so good, and He knew every unspoken desire of my heart even before we met. I'm thankful for the gift of a wonderful man like you, to have and to hold, to love for a lifetime.
I love you Hugo. You're the one and only for me. Happy first really good Valentine's Day. One of many for the rest of your life.

Love Forever and Always,
Sarah

Then on the back I wrote, "P.S., I can't wait to be with you tonight! (wink, wink)" Inside Hugo's card to me, he wrote in Spanish:

Dear Sarah: It is incredible that today we are going to be one person. I love you so much! And I promise to love you because you have God in you. Baby, this is just the start of a beautiful life together. I love you! Hugo

Soon enough, were ready to take off for Kansas City. Honeymoon time! We changed clothes, said our goodbyes, and got into the car. Mom took one last picture of us in the car, all smiles from ear to ear, complete with toilet paper on the steering wheel and a thong hanging from the rearview mirror. My mom told me later that the guys washing dishes in the kitchen were taking bets on whether Hugo would make it to the hotel in Kansas City. I was wearing a long, silky black dress with black sequins and a vine of flowers on the front. My mom had told Hugo before we left to drive slowly and carefully. He said he could not promise anything.

I don't remember reaching 100 miles per hour, but according to Hugo's version of the story later, we did. His version of the story goes like this:

I was going, like, 100 miles per hour or more, even though Sarah's mom had just told me to drive carefully. I was being careful, just fast. I even had in my mind what I would tell the highway patrolman. Something like, "Yes sir, I was speeding, it's my wedding night, so please give me a ticket so I can get going!"

Then when we got to Kansas City, in 3 hours instead of the usual 4 ½, we got lost. I had gotten directions from my uncle and he had written Maine, instead of Main, so we missed the exit we were supposed to get off on. And then, in circling back, we hit all these one-way streets. We could see the huge Westin Hotel, but we could not get there. We even asked a limo driver parked on the side of the road and as he hemmed and hawed directions.

I finally drove off, not willing to wait for an answer. We finally made it to the hotel, parked, and got to the reception desk. Sarah was getting anxious too. She had made the reservation and had the printout, so I let her check us in. I overheard the lady behind the counter say that the room we had reserved had changed and wondered if blah blah blah . . . her voice seemed to drone on forever.

I knew Sarah was not listening closely, and when the lady asked if that was okay, Sarah practically shouted, "Yes." But then she controlled herself to say, "Anything you have is fine."

The bellhop took us up to our room. We entered, tipped him, and then we were alone. We looked around the room and instantly burst into laughter. The bed was folded up into the wall! That was the detail that receptionist was talking about. We lowered it, and for as much money as we were spending on the room, you'd better believe it was the best pull-down bed ever built! Just the fact that our wedding night was on a pull-down bed made our honeymoon memorable.

Before we had our first night together, there was another part to our story. I had found a heavy white cardboard box that had two flaps on the top which, when closed together, could be tied with a white silky ribbon. I retrieved the box from my luggage, smiled as I brushed off the rice my mom had so innocently put in there, and sat on the bed. I motioned for Hugo to come and join me. I gave him the box and he carefully set in on his lap as if he were opening the most precious gift in the world. He eyes were dancing with curiosity.

"Open it," I said, almost afraid for this moment to begin after waiting so long. His fingers seemed so manly compared to the delicate white ribbon. He pulled carefully on each ribbon, so that the lid parted and lay open. Both of us looked intently into the box. I put my arm around his waist and started to explain. "When I was 14, I signed a 'True Loves Waits' card at a Teens for Christ rally. Today I am giving that card to you, along with my lingerie for our first night together."

Hugo's eyes had not moved from the box, where the small purple card lay on a bed of silky white. He picked up the card and looked at me. "This is the best gift anyone has ever given to me." His voice was full and deep. I felt an ache in his heart as he continued, "Sarah, I am sorry that I cannot give to you what you are giving to me."

"Hugo, it's not about that. I just wanted to give you this card." We looked at each other. We were both pure in the eyes of the Lord. Hugo knew his past was not an issue anymore.

His eyes brightened and so did his voice. "I'm going to keep this in my wallet always. Thank you so much, Sarah."

I took the box from him, walked to the bathroom, looked back at him to see his reaction, and smiled as I closed the door on his even bigger smile.

After a wonderful time in Kansas City for the honeymoon, we went back to Hays to pack. We also needed to crunch some numbers and see what we could do about our debt from Hugo's surgeries. We had to get something figured out before we left the country. My Grandpa Breeden had given us a substantial cash wedding gift, and we used that to pay some smaller bills. We wrote letters, filled out forms, made phone calls, and asked questions. We were able to lower some of the amounts we owed. I don't remember now exactly what money went where, but God somehow provided, and at last we only owed the hospital. We set up monthly payments of $100. We thought we'd be paying that monthly for years, but God had other plans.

A week later, we went to El Salvador to spend a month with Hugo's family, friends, and church. We had a second reception and made it as close to the real deal as possible. My parents and Mark came and brought my wedding gown to El Salvador with them, so I wore my dress for everyone to ooh and ahh at. What lucky girl gets to wear her wedding dress twice? Hugo rented another tux and we even had cake.

Remember Luis, the Salvadorian whom we had met in prison ministry back in Kansas? Well, Hugo and I called him, asked him where he lived, and went to visit him. He even took the bus the next week to come to our wedding reception and brought a nice frame as a gift. It was a special moment to fellowship with him in a different setting than where we had first met him, and, more importantly, to see that he was still following the Lord.

One of the other important things we were able to do was sit down and talk with Irma. God had revealed to Hugo that he needed to come clean with his mom in order to start our marriage off on the right foot. I knew the Holy Spirit had convicted Hugo of his past sins and that Hugo had already asked forgiveness and was forgiven. But how many of those sins had he committed and then lied to his mother about? She had prayed for him faithfully through his rebellion, and only got a glimpse of how God was answering those prayers for her before He took Hugo to Mercy Ships. Hugo had been out of her house, serving God, and pursuing me for the last three years.

After dinner one night, Hugo started the hard conversation, "Mom, I know you prayed hard for me all my life. I just want to thank you for your faithfulness and patience with me."

She smiled, lowered her head and said, "Thank you. Praise the Lord."

Hugo continued, "But, Mom, I also want to ask you for forgiveness."

She looked up, "For what?"

Hugo swallowed, "For all the girls, the parties, the alcohol, and the smoking. All the lies I told you, and all the times I disobeyed. I'm so sorry, and I ask your forgiveness." He looked down for a moment, but then looked up at his mom with tears in his eyes.

Irma had tears in her eyes, too. "Son, I always knew the sins that you were committing. The ladies in our church knew that I didn't want to be left in the dark. But I just kept praying and loving you, and I have always forgiven you. But thank you for asking, and of course I forgive you."

"Thank you, Mom. I know I would never have made it if it weren't for your prayers. I would never have met Sarah or be married to her now if it weren't for the example you gave me, taking me to church and teaching me about God. I was lost for a while, but the foundation you laid helped me to find my way back when the Holy Spirit called me. Thank you."

"Gloria a Dios!" Irma said, as she kissed her son's hands.

L-R; Rachel Sprock, Hugo, Sarah, & Michelle Hoag (co-author)
learn to snowboard as Hugo sees snow for the first time (late 2003)

Hugo & Sarah, a "dream come true day", February 14, 2004

The Hays' Trolley carries Hugo, Sarah, and friends to the reception site

Hugo is super excited to finally be able to use his wedding band!

Hugo and Sarah are ready to drive 5 (maybe 4, or 3 ½) hours to the honeymoon suite in Kansas City. How quickly Hugo made it there . . . the truth may never be known.

Chapter Ten

The Extended Honeymoon
2004-2006

Argentina

When our month was up, we moved to San Miguel del Monte, Argentina, to start Bible school at Instituto Biblico Palabra de Vida (Word of Life Bible Institute). We so desired to be on the mission field, especially now that we knew what it was like.

But we also knew that this was the next step God had for us. We did not know where God wanted us in full-time missions, but we knew we needed to be prepared for wherever He would send us. We tried to look at school as an opportunity to learn and grow instead of another obstacle in the way of getting on the mission field. We calmed our hearts for the long haul of Bible school, knowing we would study in the three-year program. But when and where would God finally lead us into the field?

The school was located about an hour and a half south of the capital of Argentina, Buenos Aires. Hugo's oldest sister, Cesia, had moved to Argentina ten years before, after she married Tito. Tito and Cesia picked us up from the airport and took us to their home in La Plata, northeast of Buenos Aires. We enjoyed catching up with Cesia and getting to know Tito; Hugo had only met Tito once, shortly after his high school graduation.

Their driver took us to Monte the day we needed to be at school. There was no room for other passengers because of all our luggage. When we finally found Word of Life, several guys helped us carry our suitcases into our new home, apartment number 4. Even with all the fury of people moving luggage, Hugo still took the time to carry me over the threshold of our first home together.

As a home, it was very simple: one 10' x 10' room that doubled as a living room and a bedroom. We started out sleeping on the pull-out couch that came with the room, but soon found that the springs, old wooden slats, and lumps were not conducive to sleep. Then we bought our own double bed with some wedding money. The bed took up practically the whole room, except for a foot of space on one side that we had to squish through to reach the bathroom, and a foot of space on the other side that we used to get to the couch. We also tried putting the couch in front of the closet, which meant we had to kneel on the couch when we needed clothes.

The kitchenette was in one corner, with a stovetop on the counter and a dining table for two. The bathroom was in the other corner, but we had to be careful how loud we did anything because our bathroom shared a wall with three other apartments, and the ceiling kept no secrets.

Despite the size and discomforts, we were elated to be at Bible school and so in love. We went to our first conference night, which kicked off the new school year. It was so refreshing to hear such deep spiritual teaching. On our way home, a man we had e-mailed with before we arrived approached us. We thought he was going to talk to us about the schedule for the week, or welcome us again to the school.

He pulled us to the side, out of the flow of traffic, and quietly said to Hugo, "Here at Word of Life, our school rule is that you cannot use earrings."

"Oh, sure, no problem, thanks for telling me, I'll take them out," agreed Hugo. We had kind of figured this would be a problem.

"And that black cord on your neck too, you can't wear that either."

Hugo sighed in frustration at this request. "Even though it was from a friend in Indonesia, as a reminder to pray for her?"

"Yes."

"Okay, I will not have it on tomorrow."

That was our first encounter with our new school. For our remaining three years, many of the faculty laughed with us over the first night we showed up on campus. I guess we looked like such a deviation from what they were used to, and it stuck in their minds. Some tall, white girl and a Latino guy with a shaved head and jewelry. What a sight!

Our three years in San Miguel del Monte were like having a three-year honeymoon. We did practically everything together. We were together 24/7 and, surprisingly, never got bored with each other. We were mushy-gushy newlyweds, dressing in matching T-shirts, holding hands, and whispering in class. Even when Hugo had to go to his required sports and work hours for school, he would take a walkie-talkie in case I needed him for something, or just wanted to say hi. He said the guys pretended to make fun of him, but he knew that they were jealous. He was so proud to be married to his best friend.

We made other friends, too. Many of these relationships began during break times from class, drinking *mate* in the commons area. Mate is a classic Argentine drink that is constantly present during times of fellowship with friends and family. It consists of loose herbs that are put into a special cup. Then, a metal straw with holes in it is fitted on the end to filter out the herbs, so only the water comes up through the straw. The water must be very hot, but not boiling. One person, called the server, is in charge of the hot water thermos. The server adds the hot water and then passes it to a person in the group. That person slowly sips out all of the hot water, careful not to burn his lips on the metal straw, and then hands the mate cup back to the server. This continues back and forth until everyone in the group has drunk. Everyone uses the same straw. It is part of close fellowship because most people will not serve a mate to someone who is not their friend or family member. Hugo and I made many friends through drinking mate together.

Drinking mate in the plaza was a great escape from our tiny apartment. But we appreciated the size of our living quarters, because it forced us to cross personal boundaries more quickly, and fuse more tightly as one flesh. We got so close that we even had a joke where we would yell, "Integration!" as we saw areas of each our single lives melting away into the other. For example, when we hung our clothes in the closet, we had to organize them short to long (instead of his and hers) so that we could store shoes underneath.

And then there was the time I accidentally used Hugo's toothbrush before bed. I had already brushed my teeth and Hugo reached the sink to brush his. I was accustomed to his rituals and was listening for him to brush his teeth and then, when he was rinsing his mouth, gag. He always did this because brushing his teeth made him think about the cockroach in his bathroom in El Salvador. Then I would laugh and make fun of him as I did most nights.

But on this night, instead of the familiar sounds, I heard Hugo ask, "Sarita, why is my toothbrush already wet?"

"Um. I don't know. Let me see it."

He showed it to me. I vaguely remembered seeing that red color in the mirror instead of my purple one, as I was thinking about the activities we had to do in the morning.

"Oops," I said. We looked at each other knowingly. "Sorry Teddy."

"INTEGRATION!" we both yelled, laughing at how disgusting it was and also hilarious at the same time. This was not the kind of integration that is really vital to a relationship.

I had started calling Hugo "Teddy" because I decided that I had "upgraded" from sleeping with a normal stuffed teddy bear to a real one. We loved to snuggle and watch movies on our laptop in bed before we slept. We'd get into episodes of "Lost," "Survivor," "Heroes," or whatever series were popular. We especially liked to laugh at the show "Cops." We'd yell, "Use the taser! Use the taser!" And if they didn't, we were always bummed out. For some reason, we thought it was so funny to see these big tough guys get tasered and fall to the ground. This is one of the silly things that helped Hugo and me bond more as a couple.

We were also falling more and more in love with God, which caused our love for each other to grow deeper. One of our favorite things to do was to sit at our tiny table after lunch and talk about what we had learned at school that day, or about passions God was giving us for different things.

For example, we were in a group that spent time praying for Spain that year. We didn't think it was likely that God would send us there, but we wanted to learn about another part of the world, and the spiritual climate there. One of our classmates, Edurne, was from Spain and she told us that she did not hear about Jesus Christ until she was 19 years old. We learned that the southern part of Spain was "in the 10/40 window."

The 10/40 Window is an area of the world that contains the largest population of non-Christians in the world. The area extends from 10 degrees to 40 degrees North of the equator, and stretches from North Africa across to China. Spain still has six unreached people groups, which was a surprise to both of us. It was exciting to become more aware of God's work in other parts of the world.

We shared our hearts and drank deeply from God as he joined us together as a couple. The royalty and glory of God is shown in a marriage that honors Him. I was moved to see Hugo's heart as I read something he wrote in the margin of his Bible one morning after our devotion time.

He had written in Spanish, "A good idea for my tombstone." I followed the arrow he had made back to the verse on the page, Second Tim. 4:7-8: "I have fought the good fight, I have finished the race, I have kept the faith. Now there is in store for me the crown of righteousness, which the Lord, the righteous Judge, will award to me on that day – and not only to me, but also to all who have longed for His appearing." Hugo had also written, "Don't give up! Keep going forward because He is worthy! Let's go!"

On another page, I saw, "You can't watch men, but you can't prevent them from watching you. What example are you giving, Hugo?" We were often told by single individuals on campus that they watched us and that we were an example for them for what they wanted in a marriage. It was nothing for our own credit or glory. It was only by the grace of God that we could seek Him and work out our differences. Because the Bible does say in First Cor. 7:28, "But those who marry will face many troubles in this life."

It was not a walk in the park, but Hugo made it work. Yes, I put in my part too, but it was Hugo's responsibility first to guide us both. Hugo did a few things extremely well that helped our marriage to give glory to God. First, I always believed that Hugo had a heart like King David. When Hugo would mess up, he wouldn't be arrogant and prideful. He would be humble and brokenhearted before God. He would ask forgiveness from God and from me, and then he would ask the Lord to help him to change in that particular area.

Second, Hugo was love in action. It wasn't just words to my face, or to others. He lived it out. He was like this even when we'd be all snuggled down in bed about ready to drift off to sleep. I might mention that my lips hurt, and he would leap right up and go find me some chapstick. He loved to serve me. He loved to listen to me. He highly valued my thoughts, ideas, and dreams.

He understood that God had given me the ability to analyze a lot of data in a short amount of time, and he relied on me to help him make decisions. Even though he would almost always do things the way I had planned, I'd tell people, "Well, Hugo decided . . . " This gave him the honor and respect he deserved for being the head of our family. It also meant that he would take responsibility if my idea failed in any way.

Some women complain about being under the authority of their husbands, but they don't understand that that's the best place. There is freedom under the cover of a husband, not oppression. Our world does not understand that "under" doesn't mean less; it's just a position in an order of command. Jesus is not less than God. Jesus is also God; they are one. But the order that has been established allowed God to send his Son, Jesus.

I found freedom in knowing I was an equal to my husband, and we were one flesh. Hugo loved me enough to consider my ideas as his own, because I was essentially a God-given extension of him. When he made a decision based on an idea that I had, and it turned out to be wrong, he protected me and took responsibility. That is the safe place that God has designed for a woman to enjoy, and we shouldn't take His provision for granted.

It sounds so perfect and glamorous when you group all the information together like this, but we really were just a normal couple in love and enjoying our extended honeymoon. We also got to travel a lot and tour the beautiful landscape of Argentina. Hugo's sister, Cesia, said, "I have lived in Argentina for ten years, and you have seen more in one year than I have in all ten."

A lot of our traveling was done with our first-year ministry group. We were in the "Show Infantil." It was a kids' program, in which I was the queen and Hugo was the herald, as well as a woolly, green bug. Hugo had also helped pre-record the narration for the story in a studio in Buenos Aires. Every time we were about to go on stage, we would hear Hugo's voice start the program with, "Once upon a time . . ."

Basically, the story was about a kind queen (me), who offered a free gift to anyone who would believe and come to the castle to receive it. After the herald (Hugo) had announced this to the townspeople, only the baker believed it was true. The story follows the baker's opposition from the townsmen, Madam Cruel, and her henchmen (Hugo recorded the voice for one of these dopy bad guys, and his inspiration was a Mexican program called "Chavo de Ocho"). The climax is when Madam Cruel and her two henchmen face off in a duel with the woolly green bugs who have come to encourage the baker to believe in the promise of the queen.

In the middle of the epic battle, everyone had to freeze for another character to come on stage, do some narrative, and build some tension. There was a song, too. Hugo and five other bugs had to stand perfectly still. After dozens of performances, Hugo had mastered the art of concealing a needle in his costume. This was Hugo's game to help pass the time while they were supposed to be still. He would lightly poke his friend Mario, who was right in front of him in another huge bug costume. He would try and get Mario to flinch.

This fairy tale was like most others, and good won over evil. The baker went to the castle and received his wonderful free gift: royal clothes, an inheritance, and life in the kingdom forever. At the close of the show, our director, Carlos, would come on stage and compare the details of the fairy tale to our own quest to receive the free gift of eternal life and live in heaven forever with Christ. It was a very powerful witnessing tool, and we ministered to thousands of people.

For the "Show Infantil," we wore costumes that were hand-sewn in Word of Life's costume department. All of the members of the show were required to help out, too. Several other girls and I spent a month sewing jewels onto the queen's dress. Everything had to have sparkle, so that it would be brilliant under the stage lights. Our castle, the backdrop for the production, was made of canvas and measured about 10 feet tall and 30 feet wide. The canvas was supported by a metal structure that had to be constructed at each location. It was an exhausting process, but after so many shows, we got into a rhythm.

That first year, we traveled all over Argentina. We went to Tucuman, Salta and Jujuy into Pumamarca to see the seven colors of earth paint the mountains as rainbows. Those were the hottest shows, and we downed water backstage to try to keep from overheating in our costumes while on stage.

We did performances in Santa Fe, Santiago del Estero, and finally we went into the Córdoba province and performed at 1 a.m. as part of the festivities for a girl who was turning 15. She wanted to mark her quinceañera with a fancy dress, food, and a car, but mostly by sharing the Word of God with her parents' unsaved friends. It was so exciting that she wanted to use our show for that purpose. She didn't even invite her friends from church, so she could have more non-Christians there. As we left, the whole bus took turns trying to imitate the sing-song accent of the Córdoba people.

We also traveled 24 hours southwest by bus to the Neuguén and Rio Negro provinces. Hugo and I were in Bariloche for our six-month anniversary. It was an amazing tourist hot spot, with a majestic lake, mountains, and a chocolate store on every corner. We had just performed for an orphanage and it had started to snow little tiny flakes, when our director told us that someone from the church where we were staying was going to take us into town to have a romantic dinner together. The church had already given me flowers earlier in the day. It was very thoughtful of them to think of us in this way, and we had an enjoyable time together at the restaurant.

Living in Argentina was like living in a different era. Argentina is very European. The clothes and the architecture both point to European influence. I could pick an Argentine out of any crowd, based strictly on clothes. Almost all rode long-handled beach bikes. Between the clothes and the bikes we almost felt like we were living in the 1980's.

Shopping was another unique experience. There were two small grocery stores with three aisles each. But, for the most part, I had to buy meat at the butcher, bread at the baker's, and fruit at another small shop. There was even a store just for cereals and spices. The owners of the store bought items in bulk and then resold them in smaller bags. Palabra de Vida was about two miles from Monte, so Hugo would call a *Remis* (taxi) to take us to town. Then we would walk from store to store and leave our bags at the Remis office as we went along. When we were done, we would wait at the office for a Remis to take us back to our apartment on campus.

The ride out of town, past the lagoon, and into the country was picturesque. The old rowboats floating amidst the reeds along the shore of the lagoon looked peaceful. Often, a *gaucho* could be seen on his horse, wearing the telltale red hand-kerchief around his neck, driving cattle around the lush green pastures. We loved the lagoon. We often walked around it as we tried to memorize Scripture, facts, and dates, all the data we needed for our tests at the end of the week. We'd stuff all our note cards into our pockets and set off for a long, slow two-mile walk, quizzing each other as we went. Sometimes we'd get distracted. We'd stop to look at the great catch a fisherman had, or a tree that was always full of small green parrots with orange bills. They were fun to watch as they flew in and out of the tree. We were not sure why that one tree was so special to them, but it was fun to watch so many nesting together in one place.

My favorite distraction was when we went to the polo field to watch a match. The noise of horses' hooves thundering past us was the most adrenaline-pumping sound in the world. We were really confused about the rules most of the time, but enjoyed taking our mate and going to watch them play. Hugo almost fell over from excitement when the referee asked him to hold his horse's reins while he got some-thing out of his car during a break. Hugo's smile was so huge. It was even funnier for me to watch when he started talking to the horse and patting him like they'd been friends for a long time. Ah, good times, good times.

Hugo and I had a tradition of going on a date the 14th of every month, because we had been married on the 14th, and because it helped keep us accountable to spend quality time together.

Our favorite date was to enjoy the delectable beef the Argentines had to offer. Argentina is famous for its beef, and it is even cheaper than chicken. We loved a restaurant called La Vaca Atada (The Tied-Up Cow). It would serve *bife de chorizo*, which is the same cut used in top loin, sirloin steak, strip steak, and New York strip. The steak of steaks, it is meant for the grill. Rich, meaty, and juicy, it only cuts with a steak knife.

The waiters at La Vaca Atada loved to ask if we wanted our steak *mariposa*. If we said yes, they would cut it open in a butterfly shape. This made it cook faster, but somehow it tasted more tender. When we cut the plate-sized steak, it was like cutting butter, and each morsel melted in our mouths. Hugo would always get fries with his meal, and I would get mashed potatoes. We would also get drinks, salad, and dessert, and only pay about $17 total for both of us.

Hugo made it a point to be as romantic as possible. He bought me flowers every other month or so, especially my favorite, sunflowers. But he also liked to buy me tulips, and then he'd spend several days calling me *Tulipán,* which means tulip in Spanish.

Hugo would try to surprise me in other ways, but he was a pretty bad liar. He was notorious for putting trash, receipts, and any old piece of paper into his pants' pockets without thinking. I'd make fun of him and his *manitas* (little hands), telling him that his manitas had minds of their own, and did things without communicating with his brain. Many times he would leave a receipt in his jeans pocket and, when I would wash them, I would accidentally find out about a surprise he was planning for a special occasion.

Once, he did trick me into thinking his friend, Joel, wanted to sing a romantic song to his girlfriend during class. Hugo told me that he was supposed to accompany Joel on the guitar, so he had to take his guitar to class that morning. He was rarely able to surprise me, but I accepted his explanation and didn't think anything of it when he brought his guitar to class. Even when he went up to the front of the class with his guitar, I continued to think he was helping Joel sing a song for his girlfriend.

I was half listening and half checking my notes for Spanish vocabulary. Then I noticed that Joel was not moving, he was still planted in his chair. He and everyone else in class were looking at me instead. I could feel the unheated room turn uncomfortably warm, and my ears tuned in to what Hugo was saying.

"Sarah, I loved you from the moment I laid eyes on you. I am so thankful to God that he brought you into my life, and that we are able to share this time in Argentina together. You are my best friend and I love you so much, Koala."

Then he started playing the familiar love song that he had dedicated to me. He had originally helped a friend write it for another friend's wedding, but he turned it into his love song to sing to me. He did this on many occasions, and even though I appreciated his efforts, I always felt embarrassed to be the focus of people's attention. This time was no different, and I prayed that I would melt into my desk to avoid the 100 pairs of eyes looking at me to see my response to this romantic gesture. But my heart melted just as much, knowing that this crazy Latino really loved me and didn't care if he looked like a fool expressing it to me and anyone else who happened to be listening. This is the English version of Hugo's song for me:

> When I think of you
> Time stops
> I can't imagine
> Even one second far from you.
> The day that you and I found so much love in life,
> It was such a blessing that joy filled my heart.
> I give thanks to my God,
> To have met you.
> And for so much love in shared moments.
> You filled the illusion that I have always had in my life
> To find a love like you and me in my life
>
> Today we decide to unite our lives
> In a love that will last all of life

God will help us maintain our love,
Growing it and
Demonstrating that there is such a thing as true love
Between you and I

Even though the years pass
May our love never change

When he stopped strumming, the guitar I had given him as a wedding gift still vibrated in tune with his voice. He put it away and sat down next to me again. I was still flushed with heat, but gave him a peck on the cheek, as the professor, Dr. Martin, started our class on Christian Family.

Not all of Hugo's great 14th surprises worked out as well as he planned, though. Once he rented horses from a farm on the other side of the lagoon. He took a friend of ours, Topher, and together they rode bikes to the farm and then rode the horses back to our apartment. Hugo knew I was at home cleaning, so he walked up to our apartment at the end of the sidewalk and knocked confidently. I came to the door, excited to have someone interrupt my cleaning and give me an excuse to put it off again.

He smiled and said, "I have a surprise for you." He motioned toward the dirt road that passed through campus. Topher stood there, holding the reins to two beautiful horses.

I was so impressed with Hugo's creative idea. I had been begging him to take me on a trail ride for quite some time. We took off across the soccer field and out the back gate of the campus with the horses. The first part of our escapade went well as we walked, trotted, and gently galloped the horses around the lagoon back to the farm. We turned off the paved road that circled the lagoon and onto the dirt road which led back to the horse ranch. We were about 200 feet away from the crossroads and the farm's big wooden entrance gate.

As we approached the intersection, the owner of the horses opened the fence quickly, with a panicked look on her face. She was furiously waving for us to get inside the fence with our horses. My heart beat wildly, and my breathing froze. My eyes darted back and forth, trying to see what was going on. My horse was picking up speed, and I had to watch where I was going. I caught a brown image not far down the road to my left. I sneaked a look, trusting my horse not to run into the gate we were quickly approaching. I saw a young horse, wild and strong. There was fury in his eyes, and he was charging right at us.

I passed through the gate first. There was another woman in the yard to help us, and I steered the horse to her. She grabbed the halter and I practically jumped off, thinking the wild horse was right behind me and I needed to run for cover. I looked back and saw that Hugo's horse was finally getting to the gate. The owner tried to shut the gate quickly, using a branch to scare off the wild horse. The movement of the gate was too wide and slow, and the horse too determined to have his way. He pushed in directly behind Hugo's horse. I finally translated in my head what the two women had been yelling at us. My urgency to get in the gate and get off my horse had prevented me from understanding them before.

They were saying, "Get in the gate! Get off the horse! It's a stallion, and he's riding a mare!"

Hugo was riding a mare, and that stallion was going to do whatever he had to do to get what he wanted. Hugo's horse raced to the woman who had helped me off. Hugo didn't wait for the horse to stop to dismount. He raced to me, and together we bolted for a small stable in the middle of the yard. We watched, wide-eyed, as the two women, obviously true cowgirls, bravely waved branches to spook the stallion away from the mare and out the front gate.

The stallion, at one point, darted toward the gate. Then he turned sharply to race back to the mare, but he lost traction on the grass. Hugo and I both gasped as his hooves slid and he fell hard on his side. In a blink he was back up, as if nothing had happened, tail and mane whipping in all directions. He snorted and breathed heavily, but what I will remember most are his wild eyes. Even out of harm's way, I felt I was in danger just looking into his eyes.

The owners finally got the stallion out of the yard, and they put the mare away so he wouldn't be tempted to jump the fence. Apparently he already tried that before. There was another couple riding horses in a field nearby, and the woman was on a mare. The stallion saw them and jumped the fence. He tried to mount the mare the woman was on, and one hoof hit the woman's head and shoulder. She was not seriously injured, but she was shaken up to be sure.

We were thankful we had escaped without injury, and were excited to ride Big Blue and The Little Old Lady (our bikes) back around the lagoon to campus. So, not all of Hugo's romantic notions turned out perfectly, but they always made for a good story to tell our friends at school.

Something we rarely told anyone was the meaning of the phrase "TACTEC," which we often wrote to each other. In a Spanish book of devotionals for couples, we read about a couple who had a personal saying between the two of them. One spouse would write TACTEC on a note in a briefcase and the other would write it on the fridge. Back and forth, they would leave one simple message for the other: TACTEC. It meant, "Te amo con todo el corazón" (I love you with all my heart). Hugo and I thought it was cute, and we started our own tradition.

Once, as I was practically falling asleep in class, Hugo leaned over my notes, one hand covering what he was writing, while his face moved close to the paper so that I could not peek over the top of his hand. Then he lifted his head, turned his hand flat on the paper to cover what he had just written, and smiled mischievously, pretending that he was still listening to the teacher.

"I have something to tell you," he said in my ear.

"What?" I asked. But he just put on his best, "I'm learning, so don't disturb me face." He was trying to get my goat. Flustered, but trying not to let on that he was getting to me, I tried focusing again on the class. But I couldn't focus with his hand on my desk, covering my notes. I tried prying each of his fingers from the page, making sure my fingernails dug into his hand a little, in hopes that he would give it up, but to no avail. I went with a new tactic and pulled out my best Puss-in-Boots face, eyes pleading and lip quivering. He noticed me not moving and looked at my face. He started to laugh, but then covered it up with a cough when he remembered we were still in class. He lifted his hand. He had written those famous letters, TACTEC.

This same scenario played out in different ways many times over the years. My favorite was to write in on the mirror in lipstick for Hugo to find in the morning. Hugo even had it engraved on the back of our ipod. It was one of our most personal gestures of love that only we knew about.

All these stories are mainly about how Hugo professed his love publicly to me. But, I want to share how I felt about Hugo during this extended honeymoon stage. My feelings can clearly be seen in a steamy card that I sent to Hugo using the campus mail. Before I share it, I want to mention that the steamy parts are straight from the Bible, so any comments about Hugo's card being in this book can be taken up with God, because it was in His book first.

My point in sharing this card is to not only show how completely in love with Hugo I was, but also that true, pure, passionate love was created by God and can only be enjoyed when it is in the context of marriage.

The outside of the card reads, "I love the sound of our voices laughing together . . . the sound of your breath as we fall asleep together . . . the sound of our hearts beating together." Inside, the card reads, "There's no one I'd rather share my love, laughter, and life with than you." In my small script, which filled up all the white space in the middle of the card and on the back, I wrote:

Hugo,

Te amo. More than any other person in this entire, whole world I love you most of all. You are number ONE out of a couple billion of others. You are so special. Especially to me! I love everything about you, even the things that seem to drive me crazy sometimes! God is teaching me things through every area of your life. He has made you the way you are to glorify Him, and I would be a fool to change that, but I know God has put me as your helper too, so I am trying to help you be the MAN God wants you to be.

I want to dedicate a song to you and some night, hopefully soon, you can ask me to play the song for you.

The song says, "How can I say; what can I do; how can I show how much I need you? You are my heart; you are my soul; you are my life; you make me whole; you're the sun; I'm the moon; if I shine at all; it's you; all I am; all I'll be; is all you've given me; every word knows it's true; that I am nothing without you; nothing to give; no way to live; my light is you. Where would I go; what would I do? I would be lost if I ever lost you; you are my eyes; you are my voice; I run to you; I have no choice; lost with no love around me; thank God you finally found me."

As Pastor Jerry said in our wedding, through you I see Christ over the Church. I see my life, my light, my soul, my sun. I see Christ in and though you, my Beloved Husband.

I bought this card before our wedding. But I knew some day it would perfect, and it is truer today than ever. And truer and truer every day, because I love you more each day. Every time I get to wake up next to you. I choose you, Hugo Liborio, to share my silly giggles, cute smiles, funny walk, weird thoughts, and my love and life.

My love, which is my deepest and strongest emotion. Song of Sol. 8:6-7: "Place me like a seal over your heart, like a seal on your arm; for love is as strong as death, its jealousy unyielding as the grave. It burns like blazing fire, like a mighty flame. Many waters cannot quench love; rivers cannot wash it away. If one were to give all the wealth of his house for love, it would be utterly scorned."

My life, which God calls a vapor. It is hardly anything, and I should just keep it for myself. But I want to share all that I have with you, no matter how small. Because I love you with all my life and will share it until the very, very end. At the Amen. But, right now I like the beginning.

I remember our first night together. You started from thoughts from Song of Solomon 7, such as "How beautiful your sandaled feet, O prince's daughter! Your graceful legs are like jewels, the work of an artist's hands. Your navel is a rounded goblet that never lacks blended wine. Your waist is a mound of wheat encircled by lilies. Your breasts are like two fawns, like twin fawns of a gazelle. Your neck is like an ivory tower. Your eyes are the pools of Heshbon by the gate of Bath Rabbim. Your nose is like the tower of Lebanon looking toward Damascus. Your head crowns you like Mount Carmel. Your hair is like royal tapestry; the king is held captive by its tresses. How beautiful you are and how pleasing, my love, with your delights! Your stature is like that of the palm, and your breasts like clusters of fruit. I said, 'I will climb the palm tree; I will take hold of its fruit.' May your breasts be like clusters of grapes on the vine, the fragrance of your breath like apples, and your mouth like the best wine . . . "

Then the wife, I say, "I belong to my beloved, and his desire is for me."

The last thing I want to say before I close this love letter to you, my dear Hugo, is taken from the last verse in Song of Solomon. I know this letter is very intimate, but God has made marriage for intimacy, and I want to express my love in the way God has made me. Thank you for letting me be me too!

"Come away, my beloved, and be like a gazelle or like a young stag on the spice-laden mountains."

With all my love, life, and soul,
Your Lover,
Sarah

I think I can best sum up our second year at school by sharing the Christmas newsletter we sent out to our friends and family in 2005. The picture on the page is Hugo and me sitting next to the two-foot tall Christmas tree we bought and decorated. The newsletter said:

What an amazing finish to an already blessed year! It has been icing on our cake to be able to come home this Christmas to see and visit with many of you. Fellowshipping with my Grandfather has been a joy this holiday because we lost Grandma in September, and two months later Grandpa was a step away from eternity as well. He is doing much better now and may even return home.

That is all more recent news, but other highlights of the year include

March- Visiting Hugo's dad in New Jersey

July- Home for cousin Erica's wedding

August-November -Great semester with challenging classes like Historical Books, Soteriology, Homiletics (for Hugo), Women's Ministry (for Sarah), and many more.

September-December 6th- We had the awesome blessing of having Hugo's mom visit Argentina, though she stayed with Cesia mostly.

School life continued, and soon we were enjoying the summer ministry that would conclude our second year of Bible school. We were involved in Word of Life's famous summer camps for teenagers. Every week for seven weeks, 500 to 700 teens would invade our campus, and we Bible students were in charge of every aspect of camp life.

Hugo and I worked on the program team. Our team was awesome, because we got to do different things every day and have lots of fun doing it. We refereed sports games, worked as lifeguards at the pool, and made announcements over the loud speakers. But our most coveted position was facilitating the "Mufa Pufa." A Mufa Pufa is two hours of creative, crazy, hilarious games. I mean wild games that you could never pull off in the United States, because of insurance issues and lawsuits.

The noise level was deafening as the introduction video started. The video department had edited a Batman and Robin spoof, casting Hugo as the "Scarecrow." The kids roared with laughter through the whole video, and then clapped wildly as Hugo came out from behind the curtain to welcome them to the Mufa Pufa. The music changed to a jungle theme as the chosen contestants went behind the stands to change into their costumes. Full size wooden bridges, ropes, and hoops were expertly lowered from the gym ceiling by the program team. All was put into place for the first game.

From behind the stands emerged twenty guys, all dressed as Tarzan. There were ten for the red team and ten for the blue team. The race was on as each Tarzan in turn tried to wiggle his way through the jungle-style ropes course set before him. The Argentines cheered as loudly as they would at a professional soccer game. The blue team won, and the ropes course was lifted back up into the rafters just as quickly as it had appeared. There were already tables in place all over the gym, long ropes dangling at key points, and full-sized jungle animals stampeding out of the changing area. The next game was about to start. Suffice it to say, our summer was a blast.

It was during this summer adventure that we met Ron Bishop, founder, and, at the time, president of SCORE International. In 1985, Ron had left his winning career as a college basketball coach to start the vision God had given him, SCORE (**S**haring **C**hrist **O**ur **R**edeemer **E**verywhere) International. SCORE is a ministry to expose people to short-term missions. The purpose of SCORE International is to evangelize, encourage missionaries, and equip participants of short term trips to do the work of foreign missions.

SCORE had grown to be much more than Ron had ever dreamed it could be. They now had two land bases, one in Dominican Republic, and one in Costa Rica. Thousands of people traveled with SCORE on short term mission trips every year, God was working greatly, and it was only getting bigger and better.

Ron had been invited to come to camp for a week as the keynote speaker. SCORE and Word of Life have many ties because the founder of Word of Life Argentina, Joe Jordan, played college basketball with Ron Bishop at Tennessee Temple. They were friends then and continue that relationship to today, serving on each other's boards of directors.

At any rate, Ron was in Argentina preaching in the evenings to the campers about Christ and winning many souls to the Lord. In the mornings, some of us Bible students had the opportunity to listen to him in a devotional time. He took part of the time to share his vision for SCORE International and its need for more missionaries.

Hugo and I had been in a prayer group for Puerto Rico our second year and had been dreaming about starting an extreme sports rental shop/café on a beach. We wanted to bring teens during the summer between high school and college to help them find their real convictions about life and Christianity before starting college and getting lost in the world. The teens would help us run our shop. We wanted to mix all our passions together: love of sports, teenagers, the islands, Americans, Latinos, guitar—everything into one. This is what we were praying for when I sat in on Ron Bishop's devotional and promotion of SCORE in the Dominican Republic.

Ron said, "Man, I am just really excited about God's work in the Dominican Republic. I want to raise up a team of people to aid the missionaries who are already in place. I especially need a couple who can speak Spanish and English. I need them to have the ability to relate to American teenagers, but also to understand Latino culture so they don't create a stumbling block for our ministry. It would be great if these people have been to the Dominican Republic before and know specifically about their culture. I need people who are young, have a heart for missions, love sports, and are good with teenagers. I also need a leader for our praise and worship times in the evenings. I'm looking for people who want to host American short-term teams, help them spread seed to the Dominican people, and do widespread evangelism. They'll also look to impact the American teams they are hosting. We have got to help these teams take that next step in their relationship with Christ, especially towards getting involved with missions."

I just about fell over in my seat. Every sentence had made my heart pump harder and faster. My hands started to get sweaty, and I glanced out the window to see if I could spot Hugo marking the lines for the soccer tournament. Now I was even more upset that he could not make this morning devotional.

After Ron finished, I raced outside to find Hugo. He was in the field furthest away from where I was in the lunchroom. I ran to tell him the great news, that I had found what we were looking for in a mission organization and ministry. By the time I got there, I was huffing and puffing and talking a mile a minute. I explained everything, but I was so excited I'm sure he only understood part of what I was saying.

"Okay," he said with a smile on this face, one eyebrow raised. This look usually meant he was questioning my sanity.

"Never mind," I said, smiling, questioning my own sanity as I replayed the whole event from his point of view. "Forget I said anything. I'll explain it in detail after Mufa Pufa, but I have to go and lifeguard at the pool right now."

I never got the chance to explain it to him. God did that for me. Before the Mufa Pufa, Hugo sat down with a young guy who, come to find out, had traveled with Ron Bishop and was a good friend of his. Hugo and Scott began talking, and soon Scott was sharing Ron's vision for SCORE in the Dominican Republic and the quest for missionaries.

Just about then, I strolled up and heard the last part of what Scott was telling Hugo. I knew it was the same thing I had been excited about earlier that day, but hadn't really had the chance to explain to Hugo.

Wide-eyed, Hugo turned to me and said, "Hey, you have to hear about this mission group called SCORE? They have a training center in the DR where they host short-term mission teams from the States." I just smiled and nodded as he proceeded to tell me everything I already knew. My heart raced again as I saw Hugo's same passion in hearing about this ministry opportunity on the mission field.

We scheduled a meeting with Ron Bishop for the following day, and he again explained everything again in detail. It was exactly as we had dreamed and more. We also shared with him the areas we had been praying about for a mission assignment, and how we saw SCORE fulfilling each requirement and more. We told him that we spoke Spanish and English, understood American and Latino cultures, loved teenagers and sports. We also told him Hugo played guitar, and that we had lived in the Dominican Republic for six months and knew a lot about the people and culture. We shared our thoughts and our passion to fill this position he had been praying about. We visited a few minutes more and then Ron gave us his decision.

"Well, you have another year of school here, so finish that out. Pray about joining SCORE during the year. I'll be back in September, and we'll talk more then."

Wow, talk about patience. We would have eight months to pray about what we thought we knew after eight minutes. But this was good. Hugo and I got excited about everything very quickly, and even though this time we felt something divinely different, it was great for us to spend time praying about this step and really seek God's will for our future mission field.

While everything was falling into place and life was great, we still had our struggles and issues like any normal couple. Following God does not make you perfect; it just gives you the option for forgiveness when you do mess up. As it says in First John 1:9, "If we confess our sins, He is faithful and just and will forgive us our sins." Hugo and I both made a lot of mistakes, but we kept looking to God every time we fell. I must have been asking Hugo for a love letter like the ones he used to send to me when we were dating, because after one discussion he passed me a note in class that read,

Hey Sarah,

    I remembered that you told me that I should write you a card, and I think today will be a good day to do it.

    I'm really sorry to make you feel sad; it is something that I never desire to do. There are many things that I forget. Like that you are not exactly like me, and if it were like that, you would not be Sarah, and that is not good.

    I have to learn to be nicer in my form of speaking. I am thinking of why all of this happened and the only thing that comes to mind is that I have not been spending time with God lately. That is why I have nothing to give you. That's sad. You understand?

    Well, I just want to finish by reminding you that I love you with all my heart and my only desire is that we are one of the best marriages of our time. I am sure that things like this morning with help us to mature and when we find other couples that are passing times like these, we will be able to help.

    Sorry that this card is not so romantic like it should be, but that doesn't take away from the fact that it was written with the heart. I love you. I love you a lot!

Hugo

Another huge issue we were praying about was my back. I had been struggling with lower back pain for almost a year and a half. We finally decided that I should get an MRI. Our campus doctor agreed and referred us to a clinic a couple of hours away. We had an early appointment, so we could get back for at least part of our classes, so we rolled out of bed at dawn. Thankfully an Argentine friend, Jose Marco, drove us to the clinic, because we would have gotten so lost. The place was a very modern, well-equipped private clinic. One hour and $100 cash later, I had my MRI results in hand as we followed the maze back to campus.

Desperate to find out if something was wrong, I stopped by the school's clinic to see if one of the doctors was in. None of them was, so I left my results with the receptionist and went to class with Hugo. In the last class before lunch, I received word that Dr. Christian wanted to see me. He was the doctor who had referred me for the MRI. During the break, I ran to the medical clinic and found Dr. Christian sitting at the receptionist's desk. He was still looking at the black and white sheets, holding them up to the light to get a better view of the contrast.

"Oh, hi Sarah," he said as he peered at me with one eye, still looking at the sheets with the other. "Well, you will need an expert to look at these, but from what I can see, it is obvious you have a herniated L5 disk in your back. We'll get you connected with a professional who can tell you what needs to be done."

We found an extremely talented neurosurgeon who had done several surgeries for one of the women on staff at Word of Life. She was plagued with degenerative back problems. Hugo and I traveled to Buenos Aires to meet with the surgeon. We showed him the MRI, and he asked several questions about my lifestyle to see how active I was. He also wanted to know if we planned to have children in the future.

He thought for a moment and said, "I would suggest you have back surgery. You are a very active person, still wanting to play sports and do physically challenging activities. If you were older, I might suggest letting the body fuse the disks together, because you wouldn't need the mobility. But you are young enough to benefit from the surgery, and with this particular hemorrhage, it would be excruciatingly painful if you were ever to get pregnant."

We left the office pretty sure that we would decide to have the surgery. But this was a huge decision and we wanted help in making it. Thankfully, my parents were coming to visit us soon. When I first told them about my back and our thoughts on the surgery, they kind of freaked out. Having surgery in another country— that did not sound smart to them. They went with us to our second appointment with the surgeon. My mom's background as an occupational therapist gave her the knowledge to ask all the right medical questions, and she really put him through the wringer. In the end all four of us, Dad, Mom, Hugo, and I, decided that this was the best option for me and we scheduled a day for the surgery in July 2006.

The surgeon told us he would find a nice private clinic that would give us a discount because we were students. He gave me his cell phone number and told me to keep in contact. The personal attention was amazing.

Our winter break had just started, and we wanted to show my parents a good time while they were visiting us. Our first order of business was for them to meet Hugo's sister, Cesia, and her husband, Tito. They had not been able to attend our wedding or the reception in El Salvador, so it was important that my parents meet her.

The World Cup was going on, and the cheering alone was getting serious. Our trip to La Plata landed on a soccer day, which could have been a problem because most businesses shut down when Argentina was on the field. But, thankfully, the bus system was still running. The whole bus had been listening to the soccer game on the radio. Now Argentina was down to penalty kicks. The bus suddenly veered off the highway into a small town. We whipped around a few streets, and then the bus driver stopped at a diner that happened to have the soccer match on. It was obvious what was going on because of the people crowding around the entrance of the diner. Everyone in Argentina was watching the game. The bus driver parked and quickly got out, without explaining himself. But nothing really needed to be said. He was a diehard fan and was going to watch the remaining stressful moments live on TV. He wouldn't miss it even if his job was at stake. And no upstanding Argentine boss would fire a man for wanting to watch this important soccer moment. Besides, the World Cup only comes around every four years.

Once the bus driver left, everyone looked at each other for a moment, and then we all decided to get off too. To our disappointment, France won the game and took Argentina out of the World Cup competition.

When the game ended, the bus driver got back on the bus without a word. Everyone scrambled to get on before the miffed bus driver took off without them.

We had a great time in La Plata with Cesia. She and Tito didn't have any children, but Tito had kids from his first marriage. They were in college and following their father's footsteps into the law. Tito was the glue in his family, and he made sure they got together weekly by cooking his famous *asado*. An asado is an Argentine barbecue. But even comparing it to a barbecue is almost sacrilegious. An asado is a barbecue that we might enjoy in heaven someday. It is a spiritual event that has the taste buds dancing with the angels and thanking God for creating animals for us to eat and savor.

An asado is special because of the technique used for cooking cuts of meat, usually beef. The meat is cooked on a grill (*parrilla*) or open fire. It is considered the traditional dish of Argentina. A true asado, the kind that Tito cooked, uses special wood under the meat as fuel. In one corner of the asado pit, the chef burns the wood until he has perfect coals, and then uses his long-handled shovel to move the coals under the perfectly seasoned meat.

One key is to keep the fat from dripping on the coals, so the smoke doesn't change the flavor of the meat. It is important to taste the true meat, perfectly seasoned with only salt, because the flavor is too good to be ruined by other spices. An asado also includes bread and a simple mixed salad or grilled vegetables. Beer, wine, soda, and other beverages are common. Dessert is usually fresh fruit.

The meats can be topped with sauce called *chimichurri*. Most families make this dressing by hand using a secret family recipe. The basics of chimichurri are chopped parsley, dried oregano, garlic, salt, pepper, onion, and paprika with olive oil. Tito also prepared *morcillas* (blood sausage). When I asked what was stuffed into it, Tito just laughed and said, "You don't want to know."

I looked it up on the internet later, and Wikipedia says, "Blood sausage is a type of sausage made by cooking blood or dried blood with a filler until it is thick enough to congeal when cooled." I'm glad we politely declined that portion.

My parents, Hugo, and I enjoyed a wonderful evening eating with Tito and Cesia in their *kincho* (the smaller house apart from the main house where most Argentines host their asado meals). Only my dad was able to really converse with Tito on any sort of educational level. I think they talked about history more than anything. Hugo tried to translate for both sides, because Tito knew just enough English to fool a waiter into thinking it was his only language, and Dad's Spanish ends at "hola." So Hugo had to pull out all the big words he knew in order to keep the conversation going.

We were happy my parents finally had the opportunity to meet Cesia, and getting to know Tito was a special bonus. We also did lots of fun touristy things while Mom and Dad were in Argentina, including a bicycle ride around Buenos Aires, and a quick ferry trip to Uruguay.

Shortly after my parents left to go back to Kansas, the surgeon called to give us the location of the clinic where I would have my back surgery. When Hugo and I arrived, we were impressed with how beautiful it was. We checked in and were shown a room. We were both trying not to be nervous, to keep the other from being nervous. While we waited, we watched TV and chatted a little, trying to keep the mood light.

A nurse wheeled in a hospital bed. "Okay, it is time to go. Could you please lie down on this bed?"

I stood, and Hugo gave me a big hug and a kiss. "I love you, Koala Bala. You're going to do great. I'm going to see you really soon."

"I love you too." I dared not say more, knowing I would cry if I did. I lay on the cart and Hugo walked alongside me, holding my hand as the nurse pushed the cart down the hall. We stopped at what looked like a service elevator. It was very skinny, and the nurse told Hugo he would not be able to get on with me. The elevator arrived and the nurse pushed me in and squeezed in next to me. Everything was happening so quickly. I didn't feel ready. This was really happening, ready or not. Almost in a panic, I looked up and caught Hugo eye. It was as if there was so much to say, but no time left in which to say it.

"I love you," was all I heard as the doors closed near my feet. I tried not to cry in front of the nurse, but I couldn't help it. My nerves were too high to control my emotions. Instead of a door at my head opening, a door to my right did. The nurse wheeled me sideways out of the elevator. The operating room was right there, and the nurse directed the cart into the room and next to the operating table. There were lots of people, equipment, and lights. I started to think about all the people who were going to see me naked during this procedure. I was now shivering, feeling cold and afraid. The anesthesiologist started to explain to me about his part and what he would be doing.

He put a mask on me, and I asked, "Is this for me to sleep?"

"Yes," he replied.

"Good, because I don't want to be here anymore."

"Count backward, please."

"10,9,8,7 . . . "

Hugo told me later that after he said goodbye at the elevator, he went back to the room we had been in and bawled like a baby. He knew everything would be okay, he just felt so powerless to help me and comfort me. He knew I was afraid from the look I had given him on the elevator, and he just was so mad at the nurse for not letting him go with me. But he knew he had to let me go, even though it killed him to watch the doors close.

After he cried a while, he knew he could not stay there, so he gathered our stuff and left. He went to find the two women who had come with us for support. Fae was a close friend of mine from school, though she was old enough to be my mom. Pam was a friend of Fae's. They were both chatty and worked their magic to keep Hugo's mind occupied during the two-hour surgery.

My first groggy sight upon waking was Fae. I was in the hallway, being wheeled to the recovery room. Hugo had been waiting in another area, but Fae noticed some nurses wheeling me through and sent someone to find Hugo. After that, I don't remember anything until I was in the room, and Hugo was next to me.

"Hi baby, welcome back." His voice was so comforting and his smile so warm.

I was shaking. "I can't stop shaking. I'm so cold."

Hugo asked a nearby nurse about this.

"It's just a reaction from coming off the anesthetic," she said. "I'll bring some warm blankets to help."

Hugo snuggled his nose into my hair. "I missed you so much. I was kind of worried. It took a little longer than we thought. But Fae and Pam kept me occupied." We both laughed a little, knowing how those two together could really get to talking.

Fae and Pam came in to see me, but then they had to leave. Hugo slept in a chair that night and the next. We were so bored most of the time; the only thing we could do was watch TV. The surgeon would come by once a day to check me and redress the incision. Again, we were impressed with his personal attention.

I hated not being able to move around much. My body would ache so much from being in one position for so long, but it half scared me and half hurt me to turn over. Once, when the surgeon was checking my stitches, he had me sitting up in bed. Hugo was looking at my back too. Soon I got a weird sensation as I could feel them touching the edges of the stitches. My head started to spin and I saw the black coming. I knew the signs from one other time I had fainted giving blood. I quickly told Hugo before it was too late. "Hugo, I'm about to pass out."

I came to a moment later, lying down in the bed with Hugo hunched over me and the doctor waving a small flashlight into my eyes.

Hugo laughed at me, but in a nice way. "Sarah, you totally freaked me out. I was like, 'Sarah . . . Sarah . . . Sarah,' and your eyes got all big and black and you were totally gone. It was so weird."

This was not the only time Hugo got some entertainment out of me during my hospital stay. Before I was able to get out of bed, the nurse would bring me a bedpan when I had to go to the bathroom. Arching my back for Hugo or the nurse to put it under me did not hurt too much, but standing and feeling the pressure on the missing disk was not a good thing until I could heal more.

If you have not experienced a bedpan, let me tell you that it is the worst thing in the world to have to use. It is just unnatural and disgusting. I hated it so much. Hugo thought that was funny and tried to give me a rough time about it. In Spanish a bedpan is called a *chata*, and, even years later, if I mentioned something about having to go to the bathroom, Hugo would ask me if I wanted him to bring the chata.

Soon I was released, and a friend of ours, Alejandro, came to pick us up in his car. Alejandro's dad was a co-director of our school. I was so tense that I thought for sure that each bump I felt on the way home would mess up my surgery.

Fae and her husband, Tom, had invited us to live with them while I was recovering, even though our apartment was only across the field from their house. Their house was big, comfortable, and had good food. Stepping into their house was like entering the United States. Chocolate chip cookies in the fridge, air conditioning, DVD's in English, an internet phone to call outside the country for free, comfortable couches, and a big easy chair.

That easy chair became my best friend. I was told I could not lean forward for a week, so Hugo's job was to be my "crane" whenever I needed to stand up or sit down. At first I couldn't even handle sitting on the hard toilet seat, so he would have to hold me over the seat. He was such a tender, caring nurse to me. I wrote Hugo a thank you note to let him know how much I appreciated his help and to encourage him for the short time we had left in school. The front of the card had Snoopy (Hugo's favorite) and Woodstock on it, and it said, "Know how I feel having a friend like you?" On the inside was Snoopy hugging Woodstock and the card read, "Blessed. (That's how.)" I wrote,

> Dear Hugo,
> Thank you so much for taking good care of me these last couple weeks. You have really been good to me and helped me a lot. Not just helping me with caring for my back, but keeping me encouraged when I wanted to cry. You have been my strength and help in my time of great need, and I really thank God for giving you to me! You are a huge blessing in my life, and I would not want to pass through life with anyone else. I am so proud of you for sticking with me, and even if life continues to be rough, I have confidence that you will be by my side, always! I love you so much and appreciate who you are.
> I am praying for you tons and am excited to see how God will continue to work in your life. I am sure He has wonderful plans for your life. I am just grateful to be a part of that plan and be amazed to see it work out though you! You are a wonderfully sensitive man with a huge heart for God, and I know that heart will lead you to be and do the right things in life. Thank you for all you are. Again, thank you for your patience and huge blessing you are in my life. Especially these last couple of weeks! Only four months to go! Aguantamos! It's do or die! We have to finish STRONG! I believe in us and that we can do anything with Christ's strength in us, and working together! Okay, enough pep talk!
> I love you more than any man on this entire planet!
> You're the only man for me!
> I love you Hugo!
>
> Love Always,
> Sarah

Remember that personal attention that the surgeon gave me? A week later, we went to his office in the capital and he took out my stitches for me. I got that familiar sensation and almost fainted again. But by then the surgeon knew how my body worked, and he laid me on my side to take them out.

The other order of business we had with him that day was payment. He told us to pay him personally, and he would divide the money among himself, the clinic, the anesthesiologist, and his surgery team. My parents were paying for the surgery for us since we had no insurance at this point in our lives. But the price was far less than what we would have had to pay in the States: $5,000. That was it, for everything. It was nice to have surgery in a country where lawsuits happen less frequently and doctors don't have to pay as much for malpractice insurance.

We had given the doctor an American check at the hospital the day of the surgery. He thought he could get it cashed, but his bank and every other place had turned him down. Hugo and I had been going to the ATM and taking out 500 pesos at a time, the maximum amount that our bank allowed us to withdraw each day. We told the doctor that by the following week we would have collected all the cash. He agreed to meet Tom and Fae at a coffee shop in Recoleta to pick up the envelope of cash. Hugo and I were back in classes by then, so Tom and Fae drove to Buenos Aires again to make the "drop" for us. Tom jokingly told us that it felt like a drug deal.

The three of them sat sipping coffee as Tom slid over the thick envelope with 5,000 pesos, and the surgeon nonchalantly tucked it into his breast pocket without counting it. They continued chatting, and then he asked them if I had asked for a receipt. I had, so he handwrote a receipt for them to give to me. Life without all the red tape we Americans are used to is great. Who gets back surgery and doesn't even get one bill in the mail? That was awesome!

By September, I was doing quite well. We continued to pray about joining SCORE. Ron would be visiting soon, and we needed to make a decision. But we were also working on a vision we had for bringing some of our classmates to my hometown of Hays, Kansas, to start some sort of ministry with the growing Latino population. We had been pursuing this vision all year. We presented our ideas to our church, North Oak Community Church, had brainstorming meetings with our team, and we were helping the team learn English.

Our team was a family of four, an engaged couple, and three single ladies interested in coming. Hugo and I had a full plate, and we were having a hard time balancing these two dreams. Most likely, we had taken on too much by trying to think about SCORE on the one hand, and trying to help start a Spanish ministry in our church on the other.

As I mentioned before, we got easily excited about many things. When you're young, in love, and fresh from Bible school, you feel as if you can conquer the world. So we worked hard on the Spanish ministry idea, but prayed passionately about working with SCORE in the Dominican Republic.

About this time, God was convicting me about some "anti-baby issues" I was having. I didn't want to tell God no, but I thought I could personally plan out when we should get pregnant, and I counted out months on my calendar. If God agreed, if I could have things my way, we'd get pregnant at the end of 2006, and then we could have the baby in Kansas while we were raising our support for SCORE. At the end of the year, we could be back on the mission field again. I feared living too long in Hays. I thought that if we stayed in Hays too long, we would get comfortable and start to enjoy home too much. Then we might never get to the mission field.

I tiptoed around the baby idea with Hugo because I was a little scared to talk about it. Each time I brought it up, he got weird, almost defensive. His forehead would get wrinkly, and the vein in the middle would shine and pop out. His palms would get wet as he unconsciously wiped them on his jeans. It was actually quite comical: All I had to do was mention the word "baby," and I could watch Hugo's body go into shock. Little did we know that we would have to answer the baby question soon.

Ron Bishop finally returned. We arranged to eat breakfast with him in the Upper Room, which was the name for the cozy apartment above the director's home used for special guests. Our friend and neighbor, Nico, went with us too, as he was interested in an internship with SCORE. We talked about how God had burned a deeper passion within us to work with SCORE, hosting American teams in the DR, and also helping with the worship times in the evening.

Then some words came out of Hugo's mouth that I never expected to hear. "What would you say . . . " He cleared his throat and started again. " . . . um, how would it change our ministry if we happened to get pregnant and we have a baby by the time we get to the Dominican Republic?"

Ron did not pick up on Hugo's panic, as only a wife can read the obvious body language of her husband. Ron spoke calmly. "A baby would be a great asset to your ministry in the Dominican Republic. SCORE encourages families to serve with us on the mission field. You'd be amazed at how having children opens you up to ministry opportunities in the community that you would not have otherwise. SCORE puts our missionary families first, because we know that your first ministry is to your wife and your children. It would be wonderful if you wanted to start a family before you get down to the Dominican Republic."

The meeting ended, and the next step was for Ron to send an application to us. After we sent it in, the board of directors would meet the next month to vote on accepting us. He forgot to get us the application, though. Ron is a multi-tasker, constantly flying all over the world, talking with hundreds of people weekly. There are details that fall between the cracks. Luckily, Ken Lassiter, one of SCORE's board members, was in Argentina the following weeks with his huge church from Woodstock, Georgia. He was able to quickly get an application e-mailed to us.

On September 9, 2006, we received this short and sweet e-mail from the desk of Ron, via his secretary Yvonne:

Dear Hugo and Sarah,
CONGRATULATIONS! You have been accepted as SCORE missionaries. I am putting Dave Marin, vice-president of International ministries, in touch with you. You will need to meet with him. He will walk you through the process.
God bless.

'til the nets are full,
Ron Bishop, President

And with that, we were in! Simple. Now all we had to do was the seemingly impossible task of raising support, which we prayed would take only one year.

I was praying more about wanting to start a family. When Hugo and I had first gotten married, we half-jokingly said that we would wait seven years before we had kids; neither one of us liked kids. I had dreaded babysitting when I was younger, and no amount of payment could convince me otherwise. When people brought babies to church and all the girls my age wanted to hold them, I would avoid any baby contact like the plague. Hugo was the same way. He would hold a kid for a few seconds and then be ready for the mom to take over again. But recently, God had been responding to my "just say no to babies" campaign with a few gentle thoughts.

The first idea that God struck me with was, if the Bible says that kids are a blessing from Him, who are you to say that they are not? Aren't you calling the Bible a liar?

Oops. I felt it hard on that one.

But soon, God struck me with another heavy blow. I heard Him say, "Sarah, you are willing to go to the ends of the earth to serve Me. You would gladly move to Africa and live in a mud hut. But you will not choose to take on what should be the most treasured, coveted ministry in your life. The grandest ministry that I have already revealed to be your calling and blessing in the Bible is raising children to love God."

Ouch. Game over. God won my heart for children.

Now I needed to share my newfound desire to have kids with Hugo. I promptly wrote out a list of pros and cons for having a child within the next year, before we got to the Dominican Republic. It seems tacky to write such a list, but it was the best way for me to organize my thoughts and be able to present them to Hugo clearly.

We sat on the bed together, and I opened my list and told Hugo I wanted to share some thoughts that God was teaching me about having kids. Hugo knew this was the real deal and did his best to not get nervous. He listened intently, nodded, looked at my paper, and wiped away a few of the tears that escaped, despite my efforts to control my emotions. I felt the calluses on the tips of his fingers under my eye as he wiped away one last tear. I looked up at him. His tender eyes were looking back at me, and his hand was caressing my face, which communicated in advance what his response was going to be.

"Sarah, you're absolutely right. God does say that children are a blessing, and we need to pray for His will in starting our family and not stubbornly stick to what our plans were when we got married."

"So, should I go off birth control?"

"Let's pray about it. Finances are a huge concern for me. Having a baby costs a lot, but let's pray and decide soon."

We left it at that, but God wanted to keep the subject in the forefront. That very week, Hugo and I were asked to translate at a marriage seminar. The four couples leading the seminar were from Indianapolis, Ind., and they took turns teaching the different sections of the seminar. Hugo and I traveled with them to present the seminar at a small church.

We got to visit with each couple at different times during the trip, and somehow each couple ended up on the subject of having kids. Hugo actually asked one of the couples what they thought. I almost fell over from shock. One couple's kids were grown and out of the house; the next had only one child in high school; the third had several young kids; and the last couple was just trying to get pregnant, so we had a wide range of experiences to learn from.

God used two key conversations to make an impact on Hugo's heart. The first conversation was with Mark and Susan, the couple with one child, a girl. Mark told Hugo, "When you hold your own daughter in your hands, everything changes. It is not like holding other peoples' children. You'll know what to do. Don't wait until you are ready, because you can never be ready for this experience. And let me tell you, God will give you a boy or girl depending on what you need in your life to make you more like Christ. I bet you he will give you a girl, just like he gave me. God has changed my life so much through her. I am a much more compassionate person now."

Later, we had a chat with George and Cheryl, the couple with several younger kids. Cheryl was Mrs. USA that year. Our conversation turned to birth control. Cheryl said, "When we were ready to have kids, we just trusted God with our birth control. That simply allowed God to control when He wanted us to get pregnant."

I also talked with Lauren and asked if she and Brian had researched how much it would cost to have a baby when they did get pregnant. She told me about a few websites I could look into that might be able to help, but she also said to look into any programs in my state that help pregnant women with hospital finances. Hugo and I had been living on about $250 of monthly income, so I knew we would qualify if Kansas offered such a program.

We got back from our trip excited about our new friends, and with a funny feeling in the pit of our stomachs as we slowly turned the next page to a new chapter in our lives. Hugo told me at the end of September that we would not be stopping by the pharmacy to pick up more birth control patches. Inwardly I clapped and jumped for joy, but outwardly I just nodded an okay, so as to not scare away Hugo's newfound courage to start a family.

We decided to put off our school classes during the month of October, to be made up later, and join a ministry opportunity offered to students in the fall. Fall was the season for senior trips in Argentina. The dream trip for all seniors was west in the Andes Mountains, especially the Bariloche area. Word of Life saw an opportunity to minister to teens on their senior trips, and so it owned a huge lodge in Nahuel Huapi National Park in Patagonia, Argentina. The lodge is named Pichi Traful, and the drive up to the lodge is spectacular, as it is located on the Ruta de los Siete Lagos (the Seven Lake Route).

We were chosen to be part of the leadership team that would host these senior trips. We knew that a lot of the teen groups would be from Christian schools, although not all of the kids were Christians. When one of the rougher schools drove up, three kids got out and immediately lit up cigarettes. Smoking is much more accepted in Argentina than in the States, but we hadn't even had the chance to tell them they were not allowed to smoke on the lodge property. This group looked really hard and tough. All the leaders were afraid of what this week might be like.

But God's word was penetrating, and it ended up to be one of our more fruitful weeks at Pichi. Several of the kids gave their lives to the Lord, and a few others rededicated their lives.

Except for the one week that Hugo and I had to sleep in different living quarters, we were still excited about starting a family. Hugo even let me talk about baby names once while we were walking home from an outing with the seniors. We had taken the whole team to Cinco Saltos. It is a hiking trail that leads up to five waterfalls. Throughout the whole season, we were only able to see the lower two, because the water was too strong from the late snowmelt to climb up any higher.

On the long walk home from the waterfalls, Hugo asked me about the baby names I had been thinking about.

"Well, for a boy I have always liked Justus. You know, there was a guy in the Bible named Jesus, but they called him Justus."

"Yeah, that's cool in English, but it does not sound good in Spanish. Justus said in Spanish is like *Justicia,* which means justice in both languages, so it just doesn't translate well. It has to make sense in Spanish too."

"True. Okay, I like Jonathan, Benjamin, and Silas, but I don't like how Silas sounds in Spanish. See-las; it just doesn't sound right."

"Well, how about girls? What about Guadalupe?"

"No way," I said, wrinkling my nose, but we both laughed. We walked along the dusty road together holding hands; we didn't mind the teenagers around us. We were in our own world. "I really like the name Esther. Did you know Esther means star?"

"Star," Hugo said, slowly rolling it around in his mouth. "I like the name Star."

"I knew a girl named Starr once. She went on my mission trip to Africa with me. She spelled it S-T-A-R-R, with two r's on the end."

"I like it, let's name her Starr!"

"Wait, Hugo, we can't name her now. We are not even pregnant yet!"

"Doesn't matter, you can call her whatever you want, but I will call her Starr."

"Well, maybe as a middle name."

"No, I've decided." He laughed and tickled me. I ran and he chased after me.

Later, we did decide that we liked the name Tirzah Starr. Tirzah because it was the name of the first little girl who ever liked me, and I liked her too. She stole my heart and brought a ray of hope that I might actually want to have kids one day. Plus, in the Bible Tirzah was the name of one of the women who inherited part of God's promised land because she had no brothers. And Tirzah was the name of the city of the Kings before they moved it to Jerusalem. We had several possibilities with boy's names, but never decided on one.

About a week after getting back from Pichi Traful, I was thinking we needed to buy a pregnancy test. At first I thought maybe it was all in my head, but I wanted to be sure either way. I think the woman at the pharmacy was surprised when we asked for a pregnancy test instead of our normal refill of birth control patches. Even though we knew we were supposed to take the test in the morning to get the most accurate results, we couldn't wait. We took the test that night, before Hugo had to go off to music practice. We carefully put the small dipstick into the pee cup and turned our backs to watch the clock together on the opposite wall. We made ourselves watch the clock for exactly two minutes.

"Okay Hugo, on the count of three we are going to turn and look together."

"Okay," he nodded

"One . . . two . . . "

"Wait!"

"What?"

"Is it one, two, three and turn on three? Or one, two, three, now, and turn on now?"

"Hugo!" I yelled desperately. He was always trying to make jokes and be funny. We both knew that we always counted the same way: One, two, three, now! "On the now, you goof," I said. I started again, "One, two, three, NOW!"

We both whirled around and hunched over to see the little stick. Two lines, both horizontal. I looked at the kit's instructions, just to be sure I remembered correctly what this meant.

"We're pregnant." The words escaped my mouth as my brain connected the dots. I guess Hugo had figured it out too, because he was already smiling. He turned me toward him and held me tight.

"Sarah, I love you so much. I can't believe we are going to have a baby. This is awesome."

"I love you too, Hugito. You're going to be a great daddy. But you'd better let me go. You have to get to worship practice!"

"Oh yeah! I forgot. Let's take some quick pictures."

We took some cute pictures of us with our thumbs up, holding the pregnancy dipstick and smiling ear to ear. Then Hugo rushed out to worship practice. Three minutes later the door flung open. Hugo practically knocked me over as he wrapped his arms around me again. I did not say a word. I just snuggled deeper into his arms.

He whispered in my ear, "I got halfway there, and I just had to come back and give you another hug." He held me at arm's length and looked at me. I saw that he had tears streaming down his face. My heart fluttered as I realized how much I adored him in this exact moment. Finding out we were pregnant, and his perfect reaction to the news; God had brought us so far.

Hugo started to speak carefully, choosing the right words for what he was feeling. "I just can't believe that God has blessed me with a wife who loves me so much, and now I get to have a baby with her. I don't deserve this. God is so good to me. I love you so much, Sarah. I am so thankful God gave you to me." He stopped. He wanted to say more, but the tears were stronger. He continued to look into my eyes. "Well, they're going to kill me, I'm so late for practice!"

We laughed. He rushed out the door as quickly as he had entered. I was left in our tiny home to take this precious moment and ponder it in my heart, where I would never forget it. I was living a dream come true. I praised God for his blessings, goodness, faithfulness, guidance, provision, love, grace, and forgiveness. So many of God's characteristics had brought us through to this amazing day.

I never experienced morning sickness or had too many weird pregnancy issues, except for having the munchies all the time. If I got hungry, I felt sick. I was glad I felt good because we only had two months of school left, and I needed to finish up well in my classes, especially the classes and tests we missed while in Pichi Traful. Plus, Hugo relied on me a lot to help him study and pass his tests too. Book smarts were not his strong suit. He had goofed off in high school and had not learned any study skills at all. I would help him set up a system to learn the facts for each test. We would study separately and then together, quizzing each other constantly until we felt we knew the information. I would always say, "Come on Hugo, it's do or die time." I'd smile and laugh and he would groan and complain. I used it before every study time.

School ended in December, and we said goodbye to all of our friends. Everyone was congratulating us on leaving Argentina with a "souvenir." We had about two weeks to kill until our plane left to go back to the States. I think my body knew that it could relax, because I pretty much crashed on Tom and Fae's couch for a week. Hugo and I watched the first season of "24" on DVD. Now anytime I heard those digital beeps, I think about being pregnant in Argentina on Tom and Fae's couch. I also get a little nauseous.

We went to Cesia and Tito's house for a week, too. We wanted to spend some quality time with them before we left, since we didn't know when we would see them again. Tito hosts a big Christmas party for his office every year, so Hugo and I helped Cesia with some of the party prep. We helped set up tables on their tennis court, which was out the back door behind the kincho. I hated walking through the patio to get to the kincho, because I feared their Rottweiler, Roco. I much preferred their fluffy cat, Shaggy, even though she was anti-social and hung out in Cesia's closet most of the time.

We also set up four huge, blue barrels that were filled with ice and water. Then we started to cool the drinks that would be offered that night. Even though Cesia is a chef, this particular meal would be catered. Soon, a gourmet pizza team came and started to bring in their ovens and other equipment to serve the meal.

Hugo and I went out on the tennis courts, trying to visit with people that we didn't know. Cesia was introducing us to people as best as she could while still hosting the event. Soon several people started smoking, and Cesia looked at us knowingly. We'd have to leave because I was pregnant, and it wasn't a good idea for me to inhale the smoke. She set us up in the front room, greeting guests and pointing them in the direction of the tennis court. It worked out great, because we got to watch TV instead of having awkward conversations. We still got to meet everyone as they came in, and explain that we were Cesia's brother and sister-in-law. The best part was that the pizza guys came and brought us whatever variety of pizza we wanted.

It was a good time of fellowship with Tito and Cesia. Now, after three years in Argentina, we looked forward to the next chapter that God would write in our lives. We left Argentina with anticipation for what was to come, praying that the Lord would guide us, and feeling nervous excitement for the upcoming birth of our first child.

We loaded up our five huge duffle bags, said our goodbyes to Cesia and Tito, and flew to Denver, Colorado, where my parents would meet us.

Hugo and Sarah stand in front of the famous Obelisco
in Buenos Aires, Argentina, in 2005

Hugo preaches to the Palabra de Vida student body for chapel
time as part of his Hermeneutics class in Argentina.

Sarah and Hugo's second wedding anniversary. The lights of a small town near Palabra de Vida, San Miguel del Monte, are seen across the lagoon.

Hugo and Sarah in Patagonia, Argentina. The Andes Mountains set the stage for Palabra de Vida's ministry to Senior Class Trips.

The "we're pregnant!" picture with ear to ear smiles as Sarah holds up the proof.

Please visit my website, www.my-onceuponatime.com/, to see more pictures and videos from each chapter.

Chapter Eleven

Love Lived in Normal Life
2007-2008

Kansas

My family still did not know that I was pregnant, so we planned to make the announcement memorable. Hugo had made a video presentation about our adventures in Argentina, but at the end there was a picture of Hugo holding our friends' baby, Fiorella. The next frame showed Hugo and me holding up our positive pregnancy test and giving the camera goofy smiles.

At the end of the video, everyone sat dumbfounded for a second, but then they all smiled and laughed.

My mom said, "Yeah! Congratulations. I knew it." She looked at my Dad. "I told you."

Everyone was so excited for us. This would be my parents' first grandchild, and the first great-grandchild for my grandparents.

On January 1ˢᵗ, we moved into our new apartment. It was upstairs in a big old white house. It was a very unique place. Our address actually included a ½ in it, which was very hard to explain to pizza delivery. The ceiling was peaked in a variety of odd angles. We had to watch our heads when we stood up from the couch.

We had two bedrooms and one bathroom. The second bedroom would be a combined office and baby nursery. We weren't going to decorate that room right away, because we wanted to wait until we knew the sex, and we decided we wanted to be surprised when the baby was born. Hugo thought it was going to be a girl. Even though I had always dreamed about having a boy first, Hugo was so convinced that I think he convinced me too.

Besides our combo office/nursery, another strange thing about the apartment was the huge hallway running through it. Half of our belongings had to be stored in the hallway, including our clothes closet, a big wooden dresser, a bookshelf, a baby changing table, a coat tree, and a DVD rack. The hallway also included a little room for the hot water heater. We laughed about the hallway a lot and actually spent quite a bit of time there.

We put plastic on the windows to keep the wind from blowing through. The new apartment seemed huge after our tiny, one-room place in Argentina.

The first night we lived in our new place, we were watching TV, and I went to the kitchen to get some more popcorn. I announced to Hugo, "I'm going into another room. Don't miss me. I'm leaving this room and actually going into another room."

Hugo just laughed at me. But he did not laugh so much when it was 2 a.m. and my bladder decided it couldn't wait until morning.

I rolled over and said, "Hugo, will you go with me to the bathroom?"

"Sarah, it's across the hallway, like seven steps away. What's your problem?"

"Well, I have to cross the hallway, and I can't see into the kitchen or the living room. I'm used to seeing our whole house at once, and it freaks me out that I can't see into the other rooms."

"Got it." He rolled out of his side of the bed and led the way out the bedroom door, checking to be sure that I had safe passage. "Okay, clear. Come on."

I had a guardian that night, but I made myself get over my fear the next night. I hate being too girly, and I knew I just needed to be realistic. Hugo could not wake up with me every night until the baby was born. Anyway, I was getting used to this "many rooms" thing.

One serious setback to our missions plans happened while we were moving all our stuff from my parents' house to our new apartment. We lost a very important document from the United States Citizenship and Immigration Services (USCIS). We had been working toward Hugo's permanent residency (green card), and this form was vital. We had to get another copy of the document, and the copy cost more than the original form.

Don't get me started about the process of immigration into this great country. The first obstacle is figuring out what you are supposed to do and how to do it. The explanations are like reading Greek. The process is extremely expensive. Even though we could afford to pay the costs of gaining permanent residency for Hugo, the United States government requires that applicants be able to live above the poverty line. Hugo and I did not qualify on that level. We had to have my parents sponsor us and show three years of their tax returns. The whole process took a long time and required divine intervention.

All I'm going to say is: I don't blame those who resort to entering the country illegally. I have no ideas on how to help illegal immigrants, but I walked in their shoes while helping Hugo.

When we finally came to a standstill with USCIS, we were advised by friends to ask for help from our congressman, Rep. Jerry Moran. Hugo and I had hesitated asking him for help because he attended our church in Hays, and we did not want to be asking special favors. But then we were told that assisting constituents is what Congressman Moran's office does. After contacting him, we immediately started to see progress with Hugo's paperwork. Supposedly, USCIS had sent us the replacement document that we needed to move forward, but we never received it. After this mix up was sorted though, USCIS emailed us another copy, we could finally fill out the next part of the paperwork and, of course, send in more money.

Eventually, I had to help one of our classmates from Argentina, Ruth, fill out paperwork when she came to Hays to do ministry for a year. Even though she had a U.S. Visa that was good for one year, the I-95 form she received at the airport indicated that she could only be in the country legally for six months. Ruth needed to stay longer than that, so she had to fill out forms, pay money, and submit an extension of stay. I helped Ruth get her extension, so she would be able to stay the full year she had committed to help our church in Spanish ministry. I was glad I had so much experience from helping Hugo.

Ruth came from the Dominican Republic. She stayed at Ken and Mary Ann's house, in the same room where Hugo had stayed before we got married. She enrolled in English classes and immediately started to look for Spanish contacts. God opened many doors for her. During the year Ruth lived in Hays, she was able to accomplish many things for the Lord. The greatest of these was to see many Latinos saved, as her spiritual gift for evangelism had an impact on everyone she met. Ruth also started a Bible study that was continued by a Spanish-speaking church when she went back to the Dominican Republic.

Hugo was heavily involved with our church youth group, leading worship and making friends with the teens through his crazy antics and huge smile. The kids seemed to gravitate towards Hugo's enthusiasm and joy. I joined him as often as I could find the energy to do so. My biggest side effect of being pregnant was severe fatigue. I also felt like I had taken a "stupid pill" because I could barely remember anything.

At the beginning of the year, SCORE wanted us to travel to Elkhart, Ind., and complete our missionary orientation. There we would also learn how to raise support. We definitely needed some advice on doing that. A man named Dave was in charge of going through all the material with Hugo and me and another missionary couple, Ryan and Megan. They had been married just a couple of weeks.

Ryan had worked with SCORE for several years in the Dominican Republic. He and Megan were moving to Argentina, so Megan could learn some Spanish and take some Bible classes with Word of Life. Ryan already knew Spanish, and had attended Word of Life in New York. Little did we know that, in three short years, Ryan and Megan would be our bosses in the Dominican Republic.

On our way home to Hays, we stopped in Converse, Ind., to visit Monica, a friend from my basketball team at Word of Life in New York. Monica had attended Word of Life in Argentina for a time while we were there, so Hugo knew her, too.

We barely made it to Converse because it really started to snow. We met Monica at a gas station, and she helped us find her house in the blizzard. We huddled down for the night, and in the morning the snowdrifts on the side of the road were at least

5 feet tall. Later, we learned it was the biggest snowstorm they had had in many years.

We left Monica's in the morning, planning to connect with the four couples we'd met at the marriage seminar in Argentina. They all lived in the Indianapolis area, and each one had planned a special treat to help us celebrate our third anniversary.

We drove for a while, and the roads were pretty good, but still snow-covered enough that Hugo was being cautious. Hugo had driven in snow enough during the winters we had spent in the States that I trusted him completely. I called Mark, whose house we were staying at that night, to get directions.

I was just hanging up when Hugo started shouting, "Oh, no! Oh, no! I can't stop! I can't stop!"

I couldn't see the ice on the road, but I could feel the car sliding and knew we'd hit black ice. An intersection loomed directly in front of us. Hugo slowly tried the brakes, guiding the steering wheel as best he could. I looked up at the traffic light. Red. I looked left. Clear. I looked right. A huge SUV was bearing down on us. We entered the intersection. We were going to hit. I cringed, waiting to hear the impact. The SUV passed directly in front of us. The front of our car should have smashed into their bumper, but the crash didn't come. Our car fishtailed, and again I waited again to hear our rear bumper hit theirs. Again, no noise. Now we were headed for a pole on the corner of the intersection.

"No, no, no, no, no," I said, pleading for something to save us. The car somehow found traction, allowing Hugo to swerve, miss the pole, and stop the car on the shoulder. He put the car in park and slumped back against the seat. He looked at me. "Are you okay?"

"Yeah, what happened? We should have hit them. We were so close."

"I know. It was like an angel just put himself between us. There's no other explanation."

We both started to cry, thankful that we were okay and that we hadn't crashed my parents' car.

The guy whom we had almost hit pulled up next to us, rolled down his window, and started to yell profanities at Hugo.

Hugo just nodded and said, "I know, sir. It was my fault. I'm sorry."

The guy left, and we slowly resumed our journey to Indianapolis.

I asked, "Hugo, why did you tell that guy it was your fault? It wasn't your fault. It was the ice's fault."

"Sarah, he was just as scared as we were. He was just mad, and it wouldn't have helped for me to explain to him about the ice. He was not in the mood to listen; he just needed to yell at someone. He did not care whose fault it was."

"Yeah, makes sense. Hugo . . . " Tears started to roll down my face.

He glanced over at me, then put a hand on my leg and gave it a gentle squeeze. "I know."

"I'm just glad the baby is okay."

"Me too . . . Me too." We just sat for a moment, thanking God that we were okay

We began our third-anniversary celebration more thankful for each other than ever. The first night, we stayed in a huge house with a king-size bed, mood lighting, a fireplace, a Jacuzzi, dual showers in the bathroom, and big screen TV. We went out to dinner, rented a movie, and enjoyed chocolate ice cream in the Jacuzzi.

Some of our other anniversary surprises included a visit to the Indianapolis 500 race track and museum and a gourmet meal at a Japanese steakhouse. Even a simple trip like this reminded us of God's great blessings to us.

So many times, Hugo told me, "I'm not supposed to be here. I was the kid everyone said wouldn't make it in life at all. They said that I wouldn't do anything with my life. I never even wanted to come to the States as a kid. But here I am, seeing things I never imagined I'd have the chance to see, with someone I never imagined could ever love me. God has blessed me so much."

When we got home to Hays, Hugo and I were enthusiastic about starting to raise support for our mission work. We put a lot of what we learned in our orientation into practice. We made a plan and started working through it. I kept getting frustrated, because Hugo was shy about writing e-mails, calling people on the phone to make appointments, and directly asking them to join with us in our ministry.

I felt like he was dragging his feet and making me do all the hard work. I thought he needed to be the head of the family and do a lot of the personal contacts. So I pushed him as hard as I could, wearing different hats to do so – the encouraging wife, the mad wife, the reasonable wife, the unreasonable wife.

Finally, I decided to wait. Just pray and wait. Wait and pray.

Soon, at a Thursday morning women's Bible study, God gave me my answer. As we prayed and gave to God the issues that were on our hearts, God spoke to me: "Your expertise is organization, phone calls, e-mails. I have gifted you in those kinds of tasks. Hugo's gift is people. You would not have most of the contacts that you do if it weren't for Hugo's ministry in those people's lives. They support you because Hugo has done his job. He has been their friend. You be yourself, and let Hugo be himself too."

I couldn't wait to get home and tell Hugo. I flung open the door and yelled, "Hugo, I had an epiphany. I have to tell you right away."

He appeared and said, "Tell me."

I told him what God had revealed to me in my morning study.

"That's great, babe. I think you're right. I'm going to try to help you more with phone calls and talking to people about making appointments to meet with them."

"That sounds great. Deal."

Our support raising was much more relaxed after that. It didn't go any faster, but I was not stressed about it all the time. I worked on it when I could and sometimes asked Hugo if he'd mind helping with this or that. Hugo continued his "job" of just making friends and loving people the way he always did.

I was very proud of myself for how I had handled the situation with Hugo. It took me several years to learn how to argue and work out issues in God's way instead of my own. I especially had to learn how to ask for forgiveness, which was a big difference between Hugo and me. I was hesitant to apologize because I was prideful, and it took some time and the work of the Holy Spirit before I learned otherwise. But Hugo was always quick to ask for forgiveness, because it was something he never saw his parents do, and he had vowed to be different. He apologized so often that I was never sure if he was really sorry or just avoiding conflict.

I realized this problem early in our marriage. After one conflict, Hugo said that he always felt like every argument was his fault, because he was always the one to say sorry. I realized that he was right; I always had some justification for why I did what I did, or said what I said, and therefore I didn't have to say I was sorry. I also realized that most of the time I was not mad at him as he thought I was, but mad at myself for acting so mean-spirited. Since it seemed like I was mad at him, however, he always thought he'd hurt my feelings.

Arguing was an art that we learned over time, but at the beginning we weren't very good at it. I remember one argument we had at my brother's apartment in Oklahoma City. Hugo was always telling me to help him not eat so much, so when he went back for seconds or thirds on the lasagna my mom had sent with us to share with Mark, I made a comment about it.

My brother, who was single at the time, said something about how a man can eat as much as he wants, "right, Hugo?"

Hugo went along with that, helping himself to another portion.

I felt humiliated because Hugo did not stick up for me and explain that he had asked me to help him in this area. I was not being a nagging wife, and my feelings were hurt. Strengthened by the heat of my anger, I plunked down the spatula in my hand extra loudly, making it clear that I was unhappy. Hugo got the message, and soon we left.

We did not even get out of the driveway before things erupted. I raised my voice as I spoke to him, and Hugo hated it when I did that. It was one more thing that his parents had done, and he had promised never to do it. I did not intend to raise my voice; I was simply passionate about what I was saying, and I got louder.

Hugo got fired up and said that I needed to control my actions when I was mad. I shot back that he had the same problem, because he had just pushed harder on the accelerator. He was a hypocrite, and he didn't stick up for me in front of Mark.

Both of us let words fly out of our mouths without thinking, neither of us practicing self-control or restraint. The argument escalated so quickly that I told him to park the car because I was getting out. He pulled into a parking spot and stopped so fast, the seatbelt had to hold me back. By the time I got to the curb, I was fuming in my hurt feelings. A million ideas about how to bring him down and win this argument flooded my mind.

Our argument ended in a way that would become the norm for us: Hugo took most of the blame and said "I'm sorry" several times, while looking directly at me with those big brown eyes. I was barely able to mumble an "I'm sorry," while I stared at my lap.

During a women's Bible study I attended while living in Argentina, I heard an illustration that changed my whole perspective on arguing. The illustration considers the plight of a crystal glass if it is dropped. Yes, it can be glued back together, but the cracks will always be visible. The study leader likened it to arguing with a spouse, and explained that if you discuss issues God's way, the glass is not dropped, but if you don't show self-control in your words and actions, the glass will drop and there will be scars in your relationship.

I thought back on my own experiences with Hugo. We rarely had disagreements but, when we did, I observed that if I kept my cool and showed the fruit of the Spirit, it would defuse the argument. Arguing biblically meant that I needed to show honor and respect to my husband with my eyes (by not rolling them), with my body language (by not setting things down hard or slamming doors), with my words (I alone knew the words that would hurt him the most), in my tone of voice and breath (not huffing and puffing or using sarcasm), and with the truth (not insisting nothing was wrong when clearly something was).

When I would pray for Christ's strength to follow through in these areas, then the crystal glass would not drop. I don't think I can recall even one of those arguments, because the glass did not drop and no scars were left. But in those arguments when I let my hurt feelings justify my manners, words, and actions, the glass would fall. Those arguments did leave scars, and I can remember almost all of them.

During my pregnancy, I worked six hours a week with a pesticide company. The owners were friends from church, and they lived three houses away from us, so I would walk over to their house to call the clients they had scheduled to spray in the next day or two. The other part-time work I picked up was delivering flowers for a local florist and cleaning house for a woman in our church.

Hugo couldn't legally work because he did not have his green card yet, but he would help me. We both got pretty stir-crazy in Hays at times. We really wanted to be on the mission field, and we were doing all we could to get there. We were still behind on raising support.

Even though we were still submitting paperwork with the government, we arrived at a point where we were able to leave the country without penalty, so we took the opportunity to visit his family in El Salvador. I was about six months pregnant at the time, so everyone at Hugo's church and in his family were so excited to see me. (Well, and Hugo too, I guess. But, they were more excited that their Hugito was going to be a dad.)

We also got to see Cesia because she was also in El Salvador to celebrate Febe's daughter Daniela's first birthday! A first birthday is a big deal in most Latin countries. Cesia had traveled with Tito's mother, Maria Elvira, so it was very nice to get to know her some more, too.

There were several events that turned out to be very meaningful.

One afternoon Cesia, Febe, Daniela, Hugo, and I squished into Cesia's rental car and drove to Santa Ana to visit their dad, Hugo Sr. He had graciously given the house to Irma and the kids in the divorce. That way the kids would always have a home to come back to no matter where they went. While we were in Santa Ana, we were able to visit with Hugo Sr.'s mom. I had never met her before, so it was interesting to learn more about Hugo's childhood.

She was about 100 years old, but no one really knew for sure, because her birth certificate did not match what she was told when she was little. She was extremely frail. Hugo Sr. played his accordion for us, while Hugo accompanied him on the guitar. The rest of us sang along, and the Liborio family talked about times past. We also drove to a nearby family farm together and gathered mangos to take home with us. This was an important visit because less than a year later, Hugo's grandma passed away.

We were also able to visit Hugo's good friend, Jose Carlos. This was the same Jose Carlos whom Hugo had stuck up for when they were kids. He hadn't lost his humor, but he had lost his health. He had been diagnosed with leukemia and was slowly losing the battle. He was no longer able to get up from his bed. Hugo and I went to his house and sat next to him. His body was just skin and bones. But when he smiled, it was just like old times.

When he saw my big belly, his eyes popped out and he smiled at Hugo. "You're going to be a daddy! Wow! Hugo, I can't believe it. You of all people. Who would have thought?" He looked at me, and his hand shook as he carefully touched my belly. "You look so beautiful, Sarah!"

I blushed and said, "Thank you."

Then Hugo and Jose Carlos were off into a maze of "Remember when . . . ?" stories. Cesia was with us too, and she laughed along with them. I loved hearing the stories. Some I had heard many times, like the time when Jose Carlos was dancing like Cantinflas (a Mexican actor similar to Charlie Chaplin), and everyone rolled on the floor with laughter.

As I sat there laughing with them, I mused at how precious this picture was. Would we ever see Jose Carlos again this side of glory? We finally said our good-byes. We waited until the car ride home to pray once again for a miracle of healing and to cry over the trial our dear friend was passing though.

April, May, and June passed, and we kept busy raising support and waiting for our baby to come. We also decided to join the technology team for Vacation Bible School at our church. Hugo and I were in charge of sound, audio-visuals, and photography.

I was walking around taking pictures of the different classrooms one day when I got a call on our cell phone. I answered it, and it was Roberto, Febe's brother-in-law. He asked to speak with Hugo, and he did not sound happy. I walked quickly to the sanctuary, where Hugo was arranging chairs, and handed him the phone.

He walked off a little ways so that he could hear over the noise. I watched him. He said little, and I could not see his face. A minute later he hung up, turned, and embraced me. He did not say anything at first, but tears ran down his cheeks. I had an idea what had happened so I waited until he was ready.

Finally he said, "Jose Carlos died."

I hugged him tighter. "Oh, Hugo . . . I'm so sorry." We cried together for several minutes, and then somberly got back to work. It hurt so much to lose Hugo's friend, but Jose Carlos had fought so hard and was in so much pain. How joyous to know that he was now with his Savior and pain-free.

July 2007 came, and all support raising, ministry, and immigration work were put on the back burner: this was baby month! My due date was the 19th, but on the 16th I started to feel a tightness in my midsection. It was so light that, as a first-time mom, I couldn't be sure whether it was contractions or just my mind playing tricks on me.

Hugo and I went to bed as we always did. In the morning, Hugo had men's Bible study, so he was up early and out the door by 6 a.m. When he got home two hours later, I was in the middle of cleaning. I was thinking that today might be *the* day, and I wanted the house to be clean when we got home from the hospital. I was still trying to identify these pressures I felt. Where they imaginary? Were they Braxton Hicks (the technical name for false labor contractions)? or real contractions? I had heard that a woman could have light contractions for a week before going into real labor. I did not want to freak Hugo out; I wanted to be sure this was the real deal.

We went to take the trash out to the alley. On the walk back I confided my thoughts. "Hugo, I've been having little pains off and on."

"What kind of pains? Like contractions?"

"Well, I think so." I tried to sound as calm and normal as possible.

"So do we need to go to the hospital?"

"No, they are not strong and very inconsistent."

"But you think today might be the day?"

"I'm not sure. Well . . . yes. I think today we will have a baby."

"Oh, my goodness! Yikes." He looked like a little boy about to get the best Christmas present in the world.

"We have a lot to do today first, though. I told Ruth I would help her with that I-95 extension paperwork, so let's go pick her up from English class, and I can get that done."

I spent pretty much all day helping Ruth fill out the paperwork to get her visa extended until the end of the year. Normally I would have taken a nap during the afternoon, but I worked through in order to get Ruth's paperwork finished.

My contractions got stronger, but they were still really inconsistent. I ignored them for the most part so I could keep focusing on the complex forms and not make a silly mistake. We took Ruth with us to the post office to mail off the paperwork, and then we took her to Ken and Mary Ann's. Hugo and I relaxed for a little while at home, making sure we had all of our hospital stuff gathered and that the house was just right. We drove to my parents' house for dinner. I did not eat much, just a light meal.

The county fair was that week, and Hugo and I had gone the night before to see the derby cars race. Since I am a Wyoming native, I really wanted to see the rodeo that night. Mom, Hugo, and I had all submitted photos in the open 4-H class. We were all excited to see if we had won in any of the categories. Even though I was now really sure I was having contractions, Hugo and I had learned in Lamaze class that the more I walked around and the longer I held off going to the hospital, the better my labor would be. I knew walking around the fair would do me good. So off we went to the fair.

We saw the rodeo from a distance, but I didn't have really time to enjoy it. We headed for the 4-H building. Mom had won a third place ribbon for a nature scene, and Hugo had won second place for a picture of my parent's house during a light snow. I had submitted several pictures, and I won a third, a second and two firsts, all in different categories.

My favorite was a picture I had taken in Argentina on the famous Florida Street. Using computer software, I had turned the three tango dancers black and white, except for the brilliant red hat of the female tango dancer. The picture earned one of my first prize ribbons. I made $13 on my winnings. But I was much more excited by the win than I was the money.

We continued to walk and visit with people we knew, trying to act normally despite the fact I was having contractions, and we would most likely have a baby that night. After about an hour, I had to stop walking due to a contraction. This was a sign that they were getting strong enough to start thinking about the hospital. We drove back to my parents' house and stayed there for a while longer. About 11 p.m., we decided that we should go to the hospital. The doctor examined me and informed us that I was dilated to 4 centimeters.

"So, what does that mean? Do we get to stay or do we get to go home and sleep?" Hugo asked.

"Yes, you have to stay. Go get your stuff; you're spending the night."

I was glad we were staying, but disappointed that I was not further along. Now that I was at the hospital, I wouldn't be able to move around, because I needed to have a monitor strapped to my belly so the doctor could check the baby's heart rate.

Despite less movement, we were delighted and surprised to see that everything started moving along quickly. We had decided beforehand that I would go through the labor process for as long as possible. If I felt that I needed an epidural or drugs, we would decide that in the moment.

My parents came up to visit with us for awhile, and they were amazed at how relaxed we were. We were just smiling, laughing, and talking. When a contraction would come, everyone got quiet while I waited through it. Then, we'd continue the conversation. My back hurt the worst during the contractions. I don't know if the baby's head was on my back or if it hurt because of my earlier back problems. Hugo and I discovered that if I leaned back on him and he held me up, the pain would be less. The nurses commented on how helpful Hugo was and said that some husbands turn on the TV and don't really help at all. I would have kicked Hugo in the head if he had done that. But he never would have let me do it all myself. He helped me through the whole labor. He gave me so much encouragement and strength that I chose to forego the drugs.

About 4 a.m., it seemed like everything just stopped. I was dilated to 8 centimeters and not progressing at all. I was so tired and wanted to sleep. I had not gotten a nap in earlier. Hugo was really tired too, because he had gotten up up early to go to Bible study. We were both exhausted. My contractions never really got closer than 4 to 5 minutes apart. I tried to sleep between contractions.

By 8 a.m., the dilation had not progressed any further. My obstetrician, Dr. Fort, came in to see me, and the nurse explained that the labor seemed to have stopped.

He told her to give me oxygen, because I was looking pale. He told Hugo and me, "You should think about getting an epidural. At this point, an epidural could help just enough for your body to relax. You might move up to a '10' pretty quickly. If that doesn't happen, it will be time to think about a Caesarean section. The way things are going at this point, we are looking at a C-section anyway, and you'll have to get the epidural in that case."

Hugo and I looked at each other. It seemed clear that we needed to choose the epidural. Hugo answered for me, "Okay, let's do the epidural."

Dr. Fort said, "The technician who performs the epidurals is with another patient. He should be here a little after 9 a.m."

"Okay," we said.

The epidural was the worst part of my whole labor experience. For each contraction, I had to lean really far to take the edge off the pain in my back. The doctor had me sit on the side of the bed and lean over the dinner tray so he could insert the needle in my back. He explained to me that he would wait until after a contraction to start, but that if I had another contraction after that I could not move at all. When the next contraction began, I leaned over the table, and he started to insert a small needle. Another contraction started to come. I was holding Hugo's forearms across the table. I just looked at him and squeezed his arms. The pain was excruciating, but the needle was in place.

A few contractions later, and the drugs had done exactly what Dr. Fort thought they would do. My body had relaxed and I was at 10 centimeters and ready to start pushing. Dr. Fort was paged, and, when he finished up with another delivery, he strolled into my room. It was about 10 a.m. The epidural had only been in for a short time, but it must have been the perfect dosage. It eased the sharpest pangs, but I could still feel my legs.

I pushed for 44 minutes, and then at 10:44 a.m. on July 17th, 2007, Dr. Fort announced, "It's a boy!"

He put the baby on my chest. He was perfect. I immediately thought, "He looks like a Mattias (which means Gift of God)." I did not say anything to Hugo, because we had not decided on a boy's name. I didn't want to pressure him in this emotional moment.

Hugo cut the umbilical cord and went with our new baby boy to the little bassinet where the baby is put while the nurses clean him, take vitals, weigh, and measure him. Hugo spoke gently to the baby, "You're so beautiful. You're so beautiful."

Hugo came back to my bed. Dr. Fort was rubbing on my lower abdomen very hard. I guess this was to shrink the uterus and help stop the bleeding. It was very painful after just having delivered a baby. I ignored the discomfort and focused on what Hugo was telling me. I knew it was important, because tears were running down his face.

"Honey, you're so strong. You did awesome. I'm so proud of you. He is so beautiful. Sarah, I think he looks like a Mattias."

My eyes widened. "Mattias is the name I thought, too, when Dr. Fort put him on my chest."

"Okay then, his name is Mattias. Just like the disciple in the Bible who replaced Judas. How should we spell it?"

"Hmm . . . in English it's usually spelled with a T-H, but I want it to be pronounceable in Spanish. Let's spell it M-A-T-T-I-A-S, so all our friends and family can pronounce it, and he can shorten it to 'Matt' if he wants."

"Perfect," said Hugo, kissing my forehead.

Dr. Fort was now filling out some paperwork. "So, what are you going to name him?"

"Mattias!" Hugo said proudly.

"Middle name?" Dr. Fort asked, not looking up from his paperwork

We looked at each other. We hadn't gotten that far. "Undecided," I said.

Hugo went out into the lobby to tell my parents the wonderful news. They had spent most of the night in the lobby waiting, and Mom hadn't seen me since just before I started pushing. Hugo saw them and immediately started crying.

Mom thought he was crying for joy, so she gave him a big hug, but then she started to worry and asked, "Is everything okay?"

"Yes," he managed to say. "You have a little grandson."

The three of them cried together and hugged all around. Hugo brought my parents into the delivery room. They were so happy to meet Mattias. They left shortly after, and handed Mattias to Hugo.

Hugo sat down in the big easy chair next to my bed. Mattias was sleeping soundly, and soon Hugo was sound asleep too. I was the one who had just given birth, and he was out like a light. A nurse came in to take Mattias for a few shots and some tests. I was left to entertain a few visitors who had come to see him. I tried to sleep too, but I think I was too hopped up on adrenaline. I was just so excited to be a mom and relieved that the delivery was over.

We spent the whole rest of the day flipping through my Bible, trying to figure out a middle name for our new son. We discussed several options, but were not sure about any of them. Finally, we made a decision: William. It was my father's father's first name, although he went by Ormond. My brother Mark's middle name is also

William, so we loved that it was a family name. Hugo wrote Mattias William on the white board in our room. It was perfect.

When we were released the next day, my parents came to help us move our stuff home, along with the flowers and, of course, Mattias. Driving our baby home for the first time was like driving with a casserole dish on the floor in the backseat. We turned the corners slowly and pressed the brakes softly, trying to drive as smoothly as possible. Our defensive driving skills were heightened. We just couldn't believe that the hospital was letting us drive around with this fragile little bundle of joy.

Mattias was a good baby and ate and slept well. I only remember one big melt-down on my part. It was in the first week, and we still had not learned Mattias's cries. Most parents can tell the difference between a hungry cry and a tired cry, especially once they learn their baby's schedule.

I was trying to figure Mattias out, but on this particular occasion he had been crying for a while, and I had tried everything. I felt so helpless not knowing what he needed. I nursed him, but he kept crying. I felt sad to think that I did not have enough milk to satisfy him. I lay on the bed and just cried. Hugo told me to sleep, and he was right. I was so exhausted I could not make any wise decisions. I had not recovered from the long night I spent delivering Mattias. Hugo worked some sort of magic to get Mattias to relax for a little while.

Barely an hour later, Hugo woke me up. "Babe, I've tried everything. I really do think he is hungry."

"Okay, let's try that." This time it worked, and Mattias quieted down and slept.

Hugo and I made a good team. He helped me so much with diapers, burping, even night feedings. Hugo would get up with me, and we'd watch the TV show "Friends." We borrowed the DVD's of all the past seasons from a friend, and we slowly worked our way through them while we fed our hungry baby.

Hugo had not wanted to have kids for several reasons, the big one being that he didn't want to make the mistakes he had seen his father make. God had answered our prayers in this area, because Hugo was a patient, loving father. Hugo's other concern was the cost of having and caring for a baby.

Through our friend Danielle, whose job was to help families access available resources, we found a program to help us, Kansas HealthWave. We soon learned that the state of Kansas was going to pay for all my doctor's visits, labor, and baby care for the first three months. It was a huge answer to our prayers. Hugo had given his concerns to God and found that they were not too big for Him to overcome.

Mattias's arrival did not slow us down for long. We wanted to get back in the saddle for ministry, and soon God opened the door to do just that. TFC, my old youth group, called, and they really needed help from Hugo during their summer camp in Alma, Nebraska. They would give us a camper to stay in, so Mattias and I could have plenty of quiet time. It seemed like a crazy idea with such a tiny baby, but we thought it through and decided, why not?

So at three weeks old, Mattias got to join his first summer camp activities. The campers gave him lots of attention when I would take him out for walks in the stroller. But I also loved relaxing in the camper and figuring out Mattias's eat/sleep/poop schedule. It was really an awesome time for me to get to know my new baby more, without having to keep up with house cleaning and cooking. Hugo did a wonderful job entertaining the campers too.

In October, when Mattias was three months old, we got a very special visitor. Hugo's mom, Irma, came from El Salvador to see Mattias for the first time. Hugo went to pick her up from the airport in Denver. I was so excited for Irma to arrive. I knew this was a huge moment for her and for Hugo. Her son had a son. She walked in the front door of my parents' house, where she would be staying. I was holding Mattias as he slept, so I stood up and walked up to her. We both softly cried as I passed Mattias to her. He was asleep and looked like such an angel. She kissed him gently on the cheek. No one said anything. It was such a tender moment.

Irma was able to stay for all of October, and she was even with us when my brother Mark tied the knot with Anne on November 3rd, 2007, in Oklahoma City. It was a beautiful wedding. Hugo and I were so thankful that Mark had finally found the girl of his dreams. She was a perfect fit for him. It was so much more enjoyable to be with my brother for Christmas, now that we each had our "someone special" with us.

Mattias got a Radio Flyer wagon for his first Christmas present. My parents and Hugo and I all pitched in to pay for it. We weren't sure how we would get it to the Dominican Republic, but we would figure it out when we needed to.

We spent the rest of the winter and spring working with the youth at church and enjoying our new little family. Both Hugo and I wondered how we ever thought having children was a bad idea.

We celebrated Mattias's first birthday with a rubber ducky pool party in the back yard, and I even made a yellow ducky cake. A week later, Hugo's dad came to visit us. He had been living in New Jersey, and he took the bus to Kansas. He stayed with us for a week. We showed him a lot of what we were doing with the youth at church and what we had done in Argentina at school. We explained what we were going to be doing in the Dominican Republic.

It was a good visit, and it re-established a relationship between Hugo and his dad that had been lacking. Hugo had forgiven his dad for his mistakes, so the past wasn't the reason they didn't talk very often. I think they were both just normal guys who simply didn't pick up the phone and talk to each other. After enough time had passed, they had become very distant. Spending a week with Hugo Sr. helped my Hugo to bridge that gap.

Hugo helped his dad open his own e-mail account, so after he left, e-mails and phone calls became more frequent. They still didn't talk all the time, but it was better than once a year as it had been before the visit. This reconnection with Hugo's father was a huge answer to prayer for both of us. I really wanted Hugo to have a better relationship with his dad.

I also didn't want Mattias to grow up not knowing Hugo's dad, or to think that there was some big family secret. Everyone makes mistakes, and the Liborio family has done a wonderful job of forgiving the past. I wanted my son to see that those relationships had been mended, so that he could enjoy everyone in his family.

Hugo and I had been raising support as much as possible during all this time. We had decided not to travel all around the country looking for churches to meet with us. We felt that most churches were already overrun with missionaries asking for support. We had a lot more success utilizing Facebook.

Facebook proved to be a vital tool to help us reconnect with many people from our past, people we had ministered to or gone to school with, but with whom we'd fallen out of touch. I don't know what we would have done without Facebook, because before it existed there was really no way to track down old friends. We were reconnecting with all sorts of people, and we were delightfully surprised that many of them wanted to support us.

We found that people we had ministered to, or with, in the past were better at responding to requests to join our support team than people with whom we had other kinds of connections. In general, people who knew us wanted to help, and people who loved and cared for us did so sacrificially. We were so thankful that God was answering our prayer in this way, because we had already been in the States six months longer than we had expected.

SCORE has a general policy that missionaries cannot enter the field until they have 100% of their support. Dave, who did our orientation in Indiana, was the yes or no guy in this area. He was praying faithfully for us and helping us write and rewrite budgets and brainstorm ideas for fundraising. That summer of 2008, Dave told us that our monthly support was coming in well, and he suggested that we start working on our setup costs. We needed nearly $10,000 to ship boxes, buy plane tickets, set up our house with furniture and appliances, and buy a vehicle. Hugo and I asked several people to serve on a brainstorming committee to help us plan some big fundraising events. It was so nice to be able to spread around the responsibility of this huge task.

We hosted an "Un-Banquet" for out-of-town friends and family. The idea was for people to send in the money that they would have spent on a formal banquet. Our team also organized a putt-putt miniature golf event, a car wash, and a bake sale. We also decided to sell water and soda pop at different summer and fall events. We used the same baby pools we had bought for Mattias's rubber ducky pool party. Kentucky Fried Chicken donated the ice to fill the pools. Some water bottles were donated, but we also bought a lot of water and soda pop. Teens from our church youth group came in shifts and helped us sell our drinks to earn a few more dollars.

In autumn, Hays has an Oktoberfest event on the county fairgrounds. Most booths were only selling beer, so Hugo and I capitalized on the market by selling water and pop. We sold a lot during the weekend celebration. We started off outside with the other vendors, but one of the buildings had a square-dance floor inside.

Hugo and I knew we could sell drinks to the thirsty dancers, so we got Mattias's new wagon and set a big cooler full of ice and drinks inside of it. Hugo and I took turns pulling the wagon around the outskirts of the dance floor, while the other person manned the pools outside. It was hard to be the person inside the building. We were making a killing in there, so it wasn't that. Maybe no one else thought anything of it, but it felt weird. Here we were, 28 years old, and pulling a little red wagon around selling drinks.

At one point I thought, "Why am I doing this? I feel so dumb; it's pointless." But then I remembered why I was there. I really wanted to do God's will and be on the mission field in the DR. And I knew I'd do almost anything to get there, even look a little silly and feel out of place, selling drinks for a dollar at the county fairgrounds.

About this time, Hugo and I received permission for him to leave the country for one year without losing the progress he had made on his permanent residency paperwork. Normally, non-citizens have to stay in the country while paperwork is processed, which can take years. Hugo and I talked with Dave, telling him that even though we were not quite at 100 percent of our fundraising goal, we hoped he would approve us to leave soon.

We explained that Hugo could only be out of the United States for a year because of his residency application. We would be able to raise more support when we returned to the States at the end of the year. We were so close to our goal. Understanding the special circumstances, Dave agreed to our request and approved us to buy plane tickets. We were on our way.

Hugo and I were about to buy tickets the following day, but prices seemed very high. There were also a few more issues we wanted to resolve before we bought tickets. We had learned that when we got ahead of ourselves and rushed into a decision, we usually made a mistake, but when we took a step back and tried to go slow, God would do the work.

God did help us out. Two days later we got a letter from the USCIS. We had an appointment in Wichita for an interview to approve Hugo's residence. Had we bought the plane tickets earlier, we would have missed the interview. It was already September, and the appointment was the end of October.

We started packing, because we knew that we could live without a lot of our stuff. Sending it now meant that it would be in the DR when we got there. Lord willing, we'd fly by the end of the year. We didn't own any furniture or big items, but all the small stuff added up. We sent about 30 boxes in a variety of sizes to the DR, through an organization called Agape Flights.

Agape Flights is a Christian service that helps missionaries in the DR and Haiti by flying in their mail and packages. Part of the set-up money we had raised during the summer went to shipping boxes of our necessities to the DR. Mattias was a "big helper" in the packing process. He was 15 months old by this time. He would climb into all the empty boxes which was kind of cute, but he would also take stuff out of boxes right after Mommy had put stuff in. Once Hugo had taped all the boxes shut and organized them in the living room, Mattias would get on top of the mountain of boxes and walk around. I guess this was a good test of the durability of my packing job.

All the boxes were shipped by the time the USCIS appointment rolled around at the end of October. We were again living in my parents' basement. We left Mattias with a babysitter and drove to the appointment, knowing that this was the last step in the long process of getting to the mission field.

We were very nervous, because we had heard lots of stories about how these meetings could be nightmares. The interviewers would want to know everything about us. They would especially try to verify that our marriage was legitimate. We were told to bring wedding pictures and pictures of our life together. I brought two books' worth. We also brought bank statements, electric bills, our apartment lease, and tax forms, all indicating that we were not only married, but also living together as a married couple. I felt frustrated with the people who had tried to cheat the system, making it harder for the rest of us.

After some initial jitters, the meeting went extremely well. Hugo and I sat in silence as the immigration officer looked over the papers and made a few comments under his breath. I tried desperately to assess whether the grunts were good or bad. I held my breath and squeezed Hugo's hand.

The man started asking questions. "Where were you married?"

Hugo answered, "In Hays, Kansas." We knew we should just answer the question and not say anything further.

The man asked, "When were you married?"

Hugo said, "February 14th, 2004."

I wondered if my mind would go blank when I was directly asked a question. I prayed we were doing okay. It was hard to tell.

The man looked at me. Oh, no, I thought.

He asked, "Do you have any pictures?" as he motioned to the photo albums that I had in a death grip on in my lap.

"Yes," I said, handing him the album. He quickly flipped through the pages. "Do you have any copies of these pictures that I can keep?"

Luckily, I had thought to photocopy a few wedding pictures, and I fished them out of my tote and handed them to him. Hugo and I were starting to relax, as we realized that he was not asking anything that we did not know. We were doing all that we could do, and the outcome was up to God.

At the end of the interview the man told us, "You should be getting your green card in the mail soon. Just don't leave the country."

"Okay," Hugo said. "Excuse me for asking, but why can't we leave? We need to fly to the Dominican Republic soon."

"When will you be back?" the man asked.

"We are going to be missionaries there, and we don't plan to come back until next year," Hugo explained.

"How will you get your card in the mail then?"

"The card will be mailed to my in-laws here in Kansas. They will bring it to me in December when they come to visit us for Christmas."

"Oh, okay, that makes sense. No problem; you can leave. You just have to find a way to get your card in the Dominican Republic before you return to the States."

Hugo and I breathed sighs of relief.

We knew waiting on the government to send us something in the mail could take weeks, if not months. We drove home to Hays and looked online for flights. This time, there was nothing standing in the way. We were ready to click and buy. God had brought us to this place of certainty in the timing of our next move. He had gone before us. We bought one-way tickets for the three of us, leaving Kansas on November 8th, 2008.

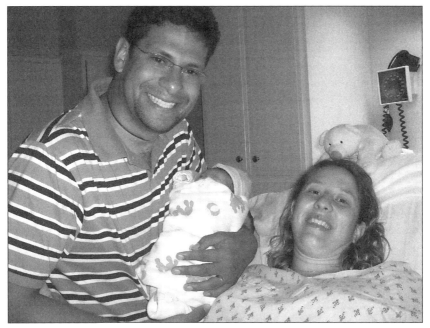

Proud new parents Hugo and Sarah welcome
Mattias William into their family (July 2007)

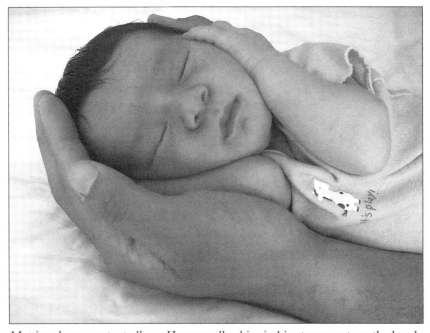

Mattias sleeps contentedly as Hugo cradles him in his strong, yet gentle, hands

Daddy and Mattias (3 months old) pose together as they show off
the shirt that Hugo's mother, Irma, made for Hugo when he was a baby

L-R; David, Debbie, Anne, Mark, Mattias, Sarah, and Hugo
celebrate Mark and Anne's wedding on November 3, 2007

Family Picture of Grandma Jackson's Family. She is in the middle.
To the bottom left is Sarah's cousin Clifford; the couple above him are cousin Erica and her husband, Justin. Uncle Galen and Aunt Rachel are above them, and Uncle Mark and Aunt Ronda are at the top left. The next couple are Sarah's brother Mark, with Anne in front of him. Then parents David and Debbie, Sarah. Hugo, and Mattias (July 2008).

Please visit my website, www.my-onceuponatime.com/, to see more pictures and videos from each chapter.

Chapter Twelve

The Dream Came True: A Perfect Kingdom
2008-2009

Dominican Republic, Kansas

We arrived in the Dominican Republic on the late-night flight connecting through Miami. With our six huge duffle bags maxed out at 50 pounds each, a heavy flat screened desktop computer in a specialized computer backpack, all our other carry-ons and diaper bag, plus Mattias, we were heavily weighed down. Hugo and I both pushed loaded carts.

Nathan and Erica Jude picked us up in SCORE's old beaten-up blue van. We had met Nathan briefly at a staff meeting in September, and I had e-mailed Erica a hundred times, asking lots of new-missionary questions.

Mattias sat in his car seat on the plane, but we were promptly ushered into Third-World life as Nathan informed us, "There are no seatbelts in the blue van. We're so sorry you've been welcomed into the country with such a bad vehicle, but ours is in the shop, and the other van is being used."

"It's no problem," Hugo said, grinning. He was so exhilarated by the lifestyle we were about to embark on. I felt an air of excitement too.

Hugo put Mattias's seat backwards in the middle set of seats, and slid in next to him to hold him down. I sat in front of them in the front passenger seat, and spent the drive asking Nathan and Erica questions about SCORE.

Less than a half hour later Erica said, "There is the front of SCORE, but we are going to go down the back alley so we can unload your luggage into your apartment more easily. All of your boxes from Agape are already there, so you'll have lots of unpacking to do tomorrow. But there are fresh sheets on your bed, and a portable crib Pack n' Play (a play yard for play and sleep) for Mattias, so you can get right to sleep and worry about getting settled later."

Nathan turned left, and we bumped through potholes for five minutes until we arrived in the alley at the back of SCORE. We would be living in a part of the campus that had been built recently. It was hard to get the lay of the land in the dark, but I could see that our section had a small 15'x10' pool and a patio area. Mattias was 16 months old, and there was a pool seven steps from our front door! It was a fine welcome to a place where nothing was baby-proof.

Even though it was late, our new missionary neighbors came out to meet us. Next door lived the Prado family from Costa Rica. Gladys was from Argentina originally, but she had ministered with her husband, Abyzhadwl (Aby) in Costa Rica for the last 25 years. They had just moved to the DR two months before to head up church planting, which SCORE wanted to make more of a priority. Their two kids, Joel and Sophya, immediately took to Mattias. Joel was 15, and Sophya 13.

"Anytime you need a babysitter," Gladys said, "Sophya would love to help. She is crazy for babies!"

I could tell this was the case because Sophya was already picking Mattias up and showing him all the fun things around the courtyard. The guys had finished unloading all the bags and putting them in our apartment around the boxes. Since Mattias was engaged with Sophya, I went in to see our new home.

It was temporary, because SCORE was building new apartments for the Prado family and for us on the other side of the front property. But for the next eight months, what I was looking at would be home.

It was very similar to our small apartment in Argentina, except that we would have our bed in the bedroom and not in the living room. But there was no real eating area. Later we tried different options, but mostly we ended up just sitting on the couch and watching TV while we ate. The kitchen was extremely small, and I was back to just a stovetop on the counter again. This was a downside to our mission field experience for me, because it really limited my cooking options.

Hugo was already ripping tape off boxes and eagerly sorting through the life we had packed up a month earlier. I retrieved Mattias from Sophya and Joel. We all said goodnight, and I brought Mattias back in and put pajamas on him. He laid down in his Pack'n'Play just like he had in his crib at home. Hugo and I sang "Jesus Loves Me," as was our nightly custom, and closed the door. Mattias didn't make a noise—such a good missionary baby.

I looked at Hugo with wide eyes.

He knew what my look was saying, and confirmed he understood me when he said with a sigh and a silly grin, "We're here . . . "

"Yes!" I whispered. Hugo grabbed my hands and danced me around the room. We didn't have much space to work with, but our hearts danced freely. For the finale, we both fell back onto the bed. We were laughing as quietly as we could, but we were elated to finally be on the mission field. I had prayed and waited thirteen years since God had called me to be a full-time missionary, and Hugo had waited nine years.

Hugo became quiet. He was next to me, and I was cuddled against him. He wrapped his right arm and leg around me. His nose nuzzled into my hair. He spoke very quietly, partly because his lips were right next to my ear, and partly because he was humbling himself before a wondrous God. "God, thank You. Thank You for bringing us here. Thank You. Thank You for protection and safe travels to the DR. Thank You for providing everything we needed to finally be able to live on the mission field and serve You with our lives. Please use us. Be with our families, wherever they are. Thank you for Your love and for Your mercy. Thank You, Lord Jesus. Amen."

We dug our pajamas out of our carry-on luggage and went to bed. I slept like a rock, exhausted from traveling all day.

I'll never forget the feeling I had when I woke up the next morning. It was a familiar feeling, one I was used to having from all my traveling: opening my eyes in a new place, and needing a second to remember where I was. But that is not the part I will always remember. The real memory is the exact moment when I did realize where I was.

I don't know how to explain it completely, but maybe it is a tiny bit of what it will feel like when we wake up in heaven. Blood surged to every extremity in my body in the same flash of realization. Instantly the clean sheets felt softer, looked whiter, and the sun filtering through the crack between the curtain and the window frame seemed as pure as joy. I stretched, trying to keep my excitement from exploding within me. I snuggled contentedly up to Hugo.

I mentally thanked God for giving me everything I'd ever dreamed of: life with a husband I loved, on the foreign mission field, and raising our family there.

I had already started praying about when to talk to Hugo about adding another family member, but at this time it was still a secret in my heart.

For the first few weeks there were no teams to host, but we had deliberately chosen a less busy time to give ourselves the chance to settle in and get up to speed with how to do our ministry. We did, however, help with the annual baseball clinic. It is one of SCORE's biggest outreaches in the Dominican Republic every year. Coaches, youth pastors, men, and boys are invited to come to the DR and help run the baseball clinics. SCORE also invites a famous Major League Baseball player to help promote attendance at the clinics.

Mariano Rivera of the New York Yankees came one year, and Albert Pujols of the St. Louis Cardinals came another. Gary Carter of the New York Mets and Montreal Expos taught catching techniques, Eric Stults of the Los Angeles Dodgers shared tips and tricks for pitching, and Andy Green of the Mets came as well. The name-dropping could go on and on, but the point is that the clinics are a big deal for SCORE and for the Dominican baseball players.

In 2008, about 300 baseball enthusiasts came from the States to help with the clinics, and about 5,000 Dominican boys attended different baseball camps over four days. The most exciting thing was that they were all presented with the saving knowledge of the gospel of Jesus Christ! Many professed faith in Christ following the baseball clinics.

I hung out with Mattias, walking around the baseball diamond and taking pictures of Hugo helping. Hugo's job was to translate for some of the coaches who were instructing the players. This was a pretty big learning experience for him, because his sport was always basketball. Since baseball games aren't televised in El Salvador, Hugo had never seen one except in movies.

When we got home, Hugo said, "I learned more about baseball in one day than I did in the first 28 years of my life. I was translating for a pitching class. The man was teaching the guys how to throw a change-up."

I looked questioningly at Hugo. I didn't know much about baseball, either.

He explained what he had learned. "The change-up is thrown with the same arm motion as a fastball, but it reaches a lower velocity due to the pitcher holding the ball in a special grip. I guess it is really famous in the DR because of a Dominican named Pedro Martinez who was very successful with it.

"The man I was translating for told the boys that he learned how to throw a change-up from the same guy who taught Martinez! They listened so intently. Later I asked one of the baseball players who the coach was that I was translating for. He said that he was a pitching coach for the New York Yankees!"

Hugo's and my knowledge about baseball grew exponentially that week. We knew that the Dominican Republic was famous for baseball, but that week we learned that one-third of all Major League players are Dominican. Of the 30 major league teams, 29 have baseball camps in the Dominican Republic, where they grow many of their baseball players from scratch.

Major League teams invest more money in the Dominican Republic than all other Latino countries combined. The town that Hugo and I did our grocery shopping in, San Pedro de Macorix, is the birthplace of more Major Leaguers than any other city in the world. Hugo and I enjoyed the baseball clinics a lot. It was so interesting to learn about a new sport and to see how deeply it was ingrained in the Dominican culture.

After baseball week was over, we spent a lot of time talking with our boss, Tim Craiger, and his wife Ginny. They would be leaving for the States soon, and we wanted to be on the same page with them before they left. They explained our ministry to us and when there was a team, we went along with Ginny in the bus so she could show us what to do.

After the Craigers left for the States for the Thanksgiving and Christmas holidays, we busied ourselves with unpacking and making a list of needs and wants for our home. The Judes made time to take us to get groceries and household goods and to help us learn the ropes of life in the DR. It was a blessing to have them around.

We also met Giovanny and Carolina, Dominican missionaries who lived in Santo Domingo. Giovanny is a product of what God is doing in the DR. Giovanny was born in a Catholic home, and basketball was his god. He started playing basketball when he was five years old, and he was playing professionally by the time he was 16. He played on the Dominican National Team for several years.

In 1995, the men's basketball team from Tennessee Temple University went to the Dominican Republic with SCORE International. While there, the Temple team played against Giovanny's team. After the game, the Temple players shared the gospel of Jesus Christ. Giovanny received Jesus as his personal Lord and Savior that day. After that, God blessed him with a scholarship to play basketball at TTU. After his time at TTU, Giovanny went back to the Dominican Republic.

When he married Carolina, she was not a Christian. She received Christ as her Savior in 2005. Hugo and I soon learned that Giovanny was the Sports Director in the Dominican Republic. He planned and arranged all of the games for the athletic teams that came to play in the DR with SCORE. Giovanny also showed us how to lead a group and facilitate the trip to make it the best it could be.

Eddy Gil, the SCORE Mission Training Center's (MTC) manager, also helped us find our way around. Eddy was Dominican and lived in the capital, but he was in charge of all the Dominican staff that worked for SCORE, including maids, cooks, security guards, and maintenance workers. He did all the paperwork that was required to keep SCORE legal in the DR and maintain its status as a non-profit. He had a huge job and did it well. He was also well-connected. On the island, we found out, it was not who you were, but who you knew.

When Hugo and I decided that we needed to purchase a vehicle, Eddy was our connection to a trustworthy source. We knew we could only afford a used car. We were told by many people that we needed to buy a car from someone we trusted, or we were liable to get a lemon. Most people recommended we get an SUV because of some of the village roads and because Dominicans respect them and would be more likely to treat us kindly on the road.

Eddy met us in the capital and led us to his friend's car lot. We saw some new and some used cars, but there were only two close to our price range. The one we picked was a Nissan Pathfinder that had been the salesman's wife's SUV. It was in great condition with low mileage. Eddy's friend did not charge us his normal commission, so we got a good deal. It was still more than we would have paid for a Pathfinder in the States, but pretty much everything on the island is more expensive. If it is imported from anywhere, it has a higher price tag on it.

Hugo and I decided we could have found something cheaper at a private sale, but it was worth at least $1,000 to us to have confidence in the purchase. The salesman actually handed us a folder with all the paperwork for every repair ever done to the vehicle, including every oil change. Hugo and I continued to take our SUV to the same mechanic, because he knew the car so well.

We were elated to have transportation, especially since my parents were coming for Christmas, and we wanted to be able to take them around town.

As we left the lot, I said, "Never in my life did I think that I'd own such a nice vehicle."

Hugo added, "We are both 28 years old and have never owned a vehicle, and now we have one that is only a couple years old. Awesome! God is so good to us."

Hugo, being from El Salvador, knew how things worked in a country with crazy drivers who did not respect road rules. Still, he experienced quite a bit of "road rage" while learning how to adapt to Dominican driving customs. I would constantly reprimand him for being angry with a car that had cut us off.

I'd tell him, "They are sinners, and they only know how to drive selfishly. Obviously he thinks he is more important and can cut us off."

Hugo would speed up and try to glare at the driver as we passed by. I would shrink in my seat, completely embarrassed by what I considered a juvenile act. However, I did love trying to name the flaws of Dominican drivers.

Motorcyclists were the worst; they weaved in and out of traffic constantly. A motorcyclist would frequently turn right from a side street onto the main road without so much as a glance. I called that the "no-look turn." Instead of using his blinker, he would wave his hand down by his leg on the side where he planned to turn. This was the "I expect you to know what my little wave means and not kill me" blinker.

Then there was the famous "Am I drunk or sober?" game, in which we would try to guess if the person driving the car in front of us was drunk, or sober and just choosing to weave from lane to lane.

Many motorcycles in the DR are taxis called *motoconchos*. It was common to see a family of four or five on one motorcycle. The most any SCORE missionary had seen on a motorcycle was eight (three adults squished together on the main seat, a small child on the front gas tank, and two small children in the arms of each of the two adults in back. It *is* possible.). I actually started taking pictures of motorcycles with odd cargo held precariously on the back. My gallery includes a washing machine and a car frame.

Hugo helped me gain confidence in driving in the DR. We knew that I'd be driving to get groceries, or out to visit him when he was with a team, so it was important that I learn. I also started to write down and memorize the directions to many of the villages. One of the directions to Los Montones was "go past the cow head!" This landmark actually did help, because it seemed like every time I went through Quisqueya, there was an entire cow head hanging in front of a butcher's shop, with ears flapping in the breeze.

The first team that Hugo and I led on our own was from Liberty High School in Anderson, Indiana. It was a group of seniors on their class trip, planning to mix ministry with pleasure. We were both excited, but Hugo more so than me. I knew I'd be going with the team during the morning ministry times and then staying with Mattias while he napped in the afternoon. Hugo would be going solo, and he was like a boy in a candy store.

We drove the big box truck to the airport to load the luggage after we greeted the team, and the bus driver met us there. We strapped Mattias's car seat into the truck's passenger side, and he promptly fell asleep due to the loud engine noise and dry heat filtering in from the outside. There was no air conditioning.

Giovanny and another Dominican missionary, Kiko, had earlier tricked Hugo into thinking there was. There were three vents on the ceiling in the middle of the truck. With the three of them squeezed into the truck, Kiko had asked Hugo, "Are you hot? Do you want me to put on the air conditioner?"

"Sure," Hugo had responded.

"Giovanny, can you put on the air conditioner for our new friend Hugo?"

Giovanny had reached up and opened the vents to let in the hot wind from the moving truck.

"That's it?" Hugo had asked.

"That's it." They had all had a good laugh and driven home.

We met the team as soon as they appeared out of customs. Hugo dove into his task, blocking out his shyness. "Hi! Welcome to the Dominican Republic!" he said with the usual huge smile on his face. "How was your flight? Did all of your luggage make it?"

One of the leaders spoke, "Yes. Thank you. My name is Ernie, and this is my wife Natalie. The other leader, Matt, is over there in the back of the pack, and his wife is Stephanie. And these are all the seniors." He waved his hand over the mass of twenty or so kids, who were talking excitedly and catching the attention of all the people in the airport.

"Good to meet you. I'm Hugo, and this is my wife, Sarah, and my son, Mattias. We're new missionaries, but we will be hosting your team this week. We're glad you're here! You've been here before, right?"

"Yes, the staff has," Ernie said.

"Then you know the drill; come right this way and we'll get you loaded up and off to SCORE."

We met the team back at SCORE and ushered them into the Upper Room for orientation. Even though the DR has a lot of tourist-friendly elements, it is still a Third-World country, and SCORE has rules to keep everyone safe and on the same page. One of the most important rules is, do NOT flush your toilet paper in the toilet. That might sound crazy, but most Third-World countries do not have the same pipe size as we do in the States. Those who forget this rule too frequently find themselves with a plugged toilet.

After Hugo and I had ensured that all the questions were answered, we took the group back downstairs to the reception desk, where we passed out the room keys. Most teams had their first day to settle in, and they almost always chose to go to the beach or the guest pool. They weren't allowed in the little pool in front of our house, which was just for the staff. As our Indiana team was getting settled, Mattias was attracting quite a crowd of senior girls around him. I tried to use this "in" to get to know the girls.

Hugo worked the guys, trying to find some common ground. "Does anyone play guitar?" he asked.

"Yeah," one guy said, "but I didn't bring my guitar."

"You can borrow mine, and I can play Sarah's. Let's jam tonight!"

"Sweet!" the guy said. Hugo had found his "in." And it was his favorite – playing music on the guitar. Hugo's eyes met mine. We both knew what the other was thinking: It was really happening. God, through His grace, was going to somehow use us to impact these teens, despite our failures. It felt a little like the day we got married. We were totally excited and couldn't believe the moment had finally come.

The next morning we set off on our first village trip. In the DR, a village is called a *batey*. This particular *batey* was named La Laura. On the drive there, Hugo decided to try out a joke he had learned from Kiko.

He pointed to the sugar cane factory, and said with a straight face, "This is the Oreo factory."

"Really? Wow!" everyone said.

Hugo continued, "You see, the white smoke is from when they make the middle part, and the black smoke is from making the black part of the Oreo."

Someone snapped a picture and said, "Cool."

The leaders looked knowingly at Hugo. Ernie added, "Yeah, I think we can go on a tour later."

"Yeah!" Hugo exclaimed. "And they have free samples, too!"

Most of the bus was in awe, except for a few skeptics. At first no one questioned aloud, but then one of the skeptics asked, "Is that really true?"

Hugo said, "No! Why would you even believe that?" He laughed loudly at his own joke. I rolled my eyes.

Soon we turned off the main road and drove down a dirt road to La Laura. The bus driver drove through the village and parked in the shade at the edge of an open area, close to the *batey's* public school. The kids began running behind the bus the moment they spotted us. By the time we parked, there was a crowd of about thirty kids under the age of 13 pressed against the door. I was thankful for our experienced bus driver, Blanco. He got out and insisted the kids move back so that the Americans could exit the bus. The kids moved back, but only enough for the bus door to be opened.

I waited on the bus with Mattias to let the crowd get involved in activity first. As the seniors exited the bus into the sea of black hands grabbing for them, I could hear the Dominican kids yelling, "Es mi Americano, es mío!" I laughed as I realized they were "claiming" their Americans by saying, "He's my American; he's mine!"

I had experienced this before and knew that once a kid grabbed my hand, I was his to play with, and other kids could legitimately be punished if they tried to steal me away from him. Most of the girls, especially the little ones, held their Americans' hands the whole time we were there. Wherever their Americans went, they went. Neither could say anything to the other, but smiles, hugs, and laughs ministered to both parties.

Once everyone seemed engaged, I felt comfortable taking Mattias off the bus. Quickly I ended up with an entourage anyway. Mattias just wanted to walk around and explore, but the Dominican girls were so motherly that they wanted to hold his hand and pick him up. Mattias got so frustrated that he refused to be put on the ground. He was totally overwhelmed. Hugo ended up holding Mattias and tossing a Frisbee back and forth with a Dominican boy at the same time.

I retreated to the shade and tried to strike up a conversation with some of the adults looking on. I met a woman named Carmen, and spent most of the time talking to her. She was a mom, too, so we compared notes on raising kids. Hugo brought Mattias over to get some shade. His neck had already broken out in a heat rash.

We watched as the seniors played pick-up games of basketball, soccer, baseball, and Frisbee with the boys. The Dominican girls were now into braiding the American girls' hair. Some teens blew bubbles, painted faces, or jumped rope with the younger kids.

After about an hour of play, Hugo yelled at all the kids to gather under the shade of the big tree. Once the kids settled down (as much as possible), Hugo nodded to Ernie to introduce his team and start their program. Hugo interpreted for Ernie as he spoke. The team had prepared a few testimonies to share, and the teens who spoke were nervous, but Hugo encouraged them by nodding his head and smiling while he spoke.

After the testimonies, Hugo took off in Spanish and re-explained the gospel for the kids, in case they did not catch it the first time around in the testimonies. He pulled three red and white ropes from his backpack and started to tell a story and do a trick with the ropes at the same time.

"You see, there are three sizes of ropes here in my hand; a short one, a medium one, and a long one. These are just like different people in our world. Some are very good and do lots of good things like go to church on Sundays and read the Bible, so they have a short list of sins." Hugo lifted up the shortest rope and showed it to all the kids.

"There are also people who society says are good, but they still rebel or do bad things. They may or may not believe in God. They are represented by this medium-sized rope." Hugo lifted the medium rope as he had the short one, and then he smoothed the two ropes out next to each other so that everyone could see the second rope was a little longer than the first.

"This third rope is for people who are really bad, like thieves and murderers. They have a long list of huge sins." Hugo put all three ropes together in one hand, then used his other hand to manipulate the ropes and do his trick. At the same time, he continued his story.

"You see, God sees all people and all sin as the same. He loves all people the same. He does not see a long or short list of sins. To God, all sin is equally bad, so all the ropes are the same." At the moment he said "same," he jerked the tails of the three ropes, and they all became the same length. A few children in the front gasped in awe. Hugo flashed a smile; he was thoroughly enjoying using his magic trick to share the gospel. He folded down the top half of the ropes on each side, and the bottom half of all three ropes hung below his hand. The red and white ropes now formed a cross.

"God sees all people the same. We are all sinners. The Bible says we are all born with sin. There is nothing good you can do to save yourself, and there is nothing you can do that is so bad you can't be saved. Only through Jesus Christ's death on the cross can we be saved. We need to ask His forgiveness for our sins, and thank Him for dying on the cross." Hugo wrapped up the program time by asking everyone to pray with him.

"If anyone prayed the prayer of salvation with me for the first time, please raise your hand. And remember, it is not the prayer that saves you; it is an honest heart before God. Only God knows your heart. But if you are not a Christian, let today be your day. Don't leave without knowing for sure where you will go after you die."

Several little kids raised their hands to receive Christ. These raised hands were the beginning of a new church plant that Pastor Aby was starting. He would be providing transportation from this village so that new believers could come and grow in the Word.

Soon, we pried the teenagers away from the kids. It was funny how when we arrived it was the kids stuck on the teenagers, and now the seniors were about ready to hide their little Dominican friends in their backpacks. How quickly hearts can be bonded in the name of Jesus. As we left, the Dominican children rode on the back of the bus, or ran next to us until we turned on to the main road.

Hugo turned and kneeled in his seat to address the group on the bus. "Good job, guys. That was fun, huh? Awesome testimonies, too!" He gave a high five to a kid sitting close to him who had spoken. "Several of the kids raised their hands to receive Christ. We don't know their hearts, but something in them responded to the message. Now our church-planting team is in charge of follow-up and discipleship." He turned to sit, but then stood again to say, "Oh, and make sure you watch for monkeys in the trees when we go over the bridge! They are only by the river."

He sat down and looked at me. I shook my head and rubbed my forehead with my fingers. It amazed me how he could be so spiritual and so crazy at the same time. It was like an on-off switch; he went back and forth so quickly that people didn't know when he was joking.

The teens were all discussing whether Hugo was telling the truth, while they pulled out their cameras in case he was. As we passed the bridge, one girl yelled, "I saw one!" and snapped a picture.

Hugo laughed his big loud laugh, cupped both hands over his mouth to stifle it, and then raised his eyebrows deviously. Then the kids understood that he had been joking, and everyone groaned. That tickled Hugo even more, and his laugh, no longer stifled, filled the whole bus. Even though they had been fooled, the kids couldn't help but laugh along.

This was how our ministry played out day after day, week after week. Hugo would mix up his jokes or give the teams mind games to pass the time on the bus.

Making an "okay" line or a "no-okay" line was a group favorite. Hugo would say, "From the window to your hat to my shoe, that is a no-okay line. And …" he would glance around the bus as if looking for more objects "… okay, from the green backpack, to the floor, to this seat, that is an okay line. Why?"

The kids would moan and groan and rack their brains, trying to figure out the difference between the two lines. Some begged for Hugo to tell them, and others spent hours trying to figure it out and did not want to know. In the end, he would tell them if they wanted. The trick was to say "okay" before starting to name the items in the okay line. (For those of you to whom Hugo never told the answer, you can now sleep soundly).

Every team that came would have a beach day, which was our family day off, but sometimes we'd hang out with the team anyway. We would often go to Catalina Island with them and take Mattias, too. Usually, we'd also take the team souvenir shopping in the capital and pass out tracts on a pedestrian-only street called El Conde. We'd also do some historic sightseeing at the old fort, Catholic Cathedral (it was the oldest functioning fort in the western hemisphere), and Diego Columbus's (son of Christopher Columbus) house.

Before we got full-blast into leading teams, we were excited to have my parents down for Christmas. Two days before they got there, I was mopping our apartment, so some friends were watching Mattias in another apartment. Hugo was on the couch with his feet up so the floor could dry, and I was in the back room with the door closed still mopping. I heard a faint, panicked voice cry in Spanish, "Mattias cut his head open!"

"What?" I yelled to Hugo to make sure I had heard right, but he had already burst out the door. I knew Hugo would get to Mattias quickly and comfort him, so I needed to be calm and figure out what needed to be done. I calmly grabbed the cell phone off the counter, his favorite bunny-bear from the couch, and kept walking to the apartment next door as I found Dr. Bob's number on the speed dial.

I took one look at Mattias from the doorway, saw blood on the towel and his face, and clicked send. "Dr. Bob. Mattias cut his head. We need you to look at it."

"I'm over at the clinic, just bring him in," was the response.

"Okay, we'll be right there," I said and looked at Hugo. "Carry him over to the clinic; Dr. Bob is waiting for us."

Hugo was almost in a panic himself. He scooped up Mattias and started walking.

One of the girls walked along with us to tell us what had happened. "He was walking through the room when he slipped on the floor mat and hit his head on the coffee table."

"Okay, thanks," I said. "I don't blame you; it could happen to anyone. That's just life. He'll be fine."

We walked through the SCORE hotel and to the back door of the Fourman Clinic. Dr. Bob met us at the door and opened it wide. Mattias had stopped sobbing and was whimpering softly. Hugo still held the bloody towel to Mattias's forehead. Dr. Bob escorted us into his office.

"Sit down here. Let me see the damage." As usual, Dr. Bob was extremely calm and in control of the situation. The "doctor" title could be a bit misleading, because he was actually a doctor of theology, not of medicine. But he had been an ER nurse and knew what he was doing.

Hugo carefully pulled away the towel. Now that the gash was no longer bleeding, I could see it clearly for the first time. It was like a third eye above Mattias's left eyebrow, halfway between the eyebrow and the hairline.

"Yep, that is going to need about three stitches," Dr. Bob said matter-of-factly. "Let me call Anna (Bob's wife and right hand lady) so she can come and assist me. Just hang out here and I'll start preparing the materials we'll need."

Mattias was not crying anymore, and he wanted to get down and investigate his surroundings.

Dr. Bob looked at Hugo. "I need you to go and get the sound equipment and load it into my car. I have to leave for Monte Largo soon, and I won't have time to do stitches and load up later."

"Okay, got it," Hugo said, getting up to start on his project. I got the feeling that Dr. Bob knew Hugo was stressed about Mattias's injury and impending stitches and needed a task to keep Hugo's mind busy. Dr. Bob could have called another missionary to help him, but he was wise and knew Hugo needed to do something.

I watched Mattias as he explored the clinic. It was funny to see him walking around like nothing had happened, with a gaping hole in his head, holding his bunny-bear with blood smeared on its ear.

Dr. Bob was busily getting all his materials together. He looked at me and said, "I called Pastor Aby. He was out at a church plant and is ten minutes away. I am going to have him hold Mattias during the stitches. It is going to be really hard for Hugo. Mattias is going to fight hard, and I can't have him move. It will just be easier for all of us to have someone else hold him."

"Okay. Whatever you think is best."

Soon everyone was in position for the stitches. Dr. Bob wrapped Mattias's legs tightly with a towel to restrict his movements, and then he raised Mattias's arms above his head next to his ears. Pastor Aby was at his head and firmly held Mattias's arms still. Anna was at the ready to diligently hand items to Bob as he asked for them during the procedure.

Mattias instantly started to resist being held down. Dr. Bob placed a white sterile paper on Mattias's face so the sutures would not get contaminated. Mattias screamed even more with something over his face. I was at his ear and talked to him to let him know we were there. Hugo was helping hold Mattias's legs, but tears were silently dripping off Hugo's chin the whole time.

I thought back to when Mattias was a baby and Hugo had said, "Look at this beautiful, perfect skin. Someday it is going to get cut, and on that day I will cry."

In a few minutes Dr. Bob had finished, with Mattias screaming the whole time. Dr. Bob cut the suture and lifted off the sheet. There were beads of sweat on Mattias's entire face. I picked him up, gave him a big hug, and assured him that we were all done. I gave him his bunny-bear and passed him to Hugo.

Hugo, still with tears on his face, kissed Mattias on the nose. "It's all over, baby. Daddy's here. I got you. I got you."

We thanked Dr. Bob and the helpers. He gave us a few instructions for how to take care of the wound, and we went home. My mopping still lay abandoned, dripping a puddle on the floor.

My parents arrived from Kansas the next day, and we told them all about the big stitches event. Mattias proudly showed his bandage to his grandparents.

We took Dad and Mom around to see all the sights we ourselves had been able to find within the past month. We had a great time. The plan was to have Christmas with the few other missionary families who would be in the DR for the holiday. We had all decided on a non-traditional meal. My mom would cook her famous lasagna. We'd have to cook it in the main kitchen, of course, because I did not have an oven.

Christmas morning, we woke up early and walked down to the beach. We brought cut-up fruit. We sat at a table on the beach that had an umbrella over it, ate our fruit, and watched the Christmas sun rise over the beautiful Caribbean water and small fishing boats netting their morning catches. I love one of the pictures I took on the beach that morning. It's Dad and Mom from the back, sitting in their chairs, looking at the sunrise in their Santa hats.

We went home and opened presents, and then Mom and I started assembling the lasagna with the supplies we had bought at the store the day before. We got the first two layers on, and then we realized that there were tiny white holes in the edges of the uncooked noodles.

I looked closer. "Bugs," I said quietly, not wanting the guys to hear, because they would be totally disgusted. The bugs were tiny, but Hugo's gag reflex would surely keep him from enjoying his favorite lasagna. I was too new in the country to have learned that even when I bought "new" products at the grocery store, sometimes they were already bug-filled or moldy.

"Mom, there is no place open on Christmas to get more noodles and we have to have the main course. What are we going to do?"

"Do you think it is safe to just cook and eat?" she asked.

"I don't know. I'll go ask Dr. Bob."

I nonchalantly walked out of the apartment and found Dr. Bob. I explained the situation.

He chuckled and responded, "It will be fine. You're going to cook the lasagna, so the bugs will be cooked too and will not harm us."

"Okay, that's great. We're just going to have to eat it because there are no other options for the Christmas meal. Just don't tell anyone!"

"My lips are sealed."

I trotted back to the apartment and told Mom the good news. We finished constructing the lasagna and added the special ingredient (besides the bugs; I guess they were the secret ingredient!): brown sugar. We cooked it, and everyone loved it at the Christmas dinner. We all had seconds, including Mom and me.

Mattias got his stitches out the day after Christmas. It was not nearly as traumatic, but he remembered the chair and started crying as soon as we sat him down in it. Still, he did a great job and did not cry much. Hugo and I called him our 30-second crier, because he usually cried for thirty seconds after a fall or bump, and then it was as if nothing had happened.

Two days later, Mattias was in the parking lot playing soccer with Grandpa and, instead of kicking the ball, he put his foot on top of it and fell forward – on exactly the same spot where his stitches had just been removed! It was like his center of gravity was rooted in that spot. It swelled up almost instantly and started to bruise. It looked like he was trying to hide a ping-pong ball in his skull.

We walked up to Dr. Bob, who was close by visiting with other missionaries. "Dr. Bob, Mattias fell again."

"Well, he is all boy, isn't he? If this is how your time here is starting out, I'm a little wary of the next couple of years." All the missionaries laughed. Dr. Bob looked at Mattias in the patio light and commented, "I'm surprised his skin didn't split open again, as fresh as this scar is, but it looks fine. You need to put ice on it and give him some ibuprofen. It is going to hurt for a couple of days."

"Thank you. It's so nice to have you around for this rambunctious boy."

"I'm here any time you need me, day or night," he said. Then he added, "But it couldn't hurt to lay low for a while." He chuckled.

Soon after my parents left, I got up the courage to talk to Hugo about having another baby. Now that life had calmed down from the move and transition to the mission field, I felt that he was ready to consider another life change. Although he was back to the sweaty hands and pale face when I mentioned anything about having another child, I finally sat him down and we talked face to face. Only this time, I really wasn't sure about God's timing on having a second baby. I shared with Hugo my pros and cons list, as I had when we were deciding whether to have Mattias.

"Hugo, I know we've just gone through a big move and this is still a huge transition for us now, but we have to plan for the future. Let's just look at dates, not make a decision yet, but just look at dates. We have discussed before about how I want our kids two years apart like my brother and I were, and you want our kids to be three years apart like you and your sisters were.

"Ideally, we need to plan to have a baby during our time off in November and December. If we have a baby this November or December, Mattias will be two years and four or five months old, almost a perfect middle between what we both want. The big negative for me is that I am not sure I want to be pregnant our first year of ministry. I would love to just enjoy this year and not be pregnant. But, in the big scheme of life, I guess this one year is not going to matter much, and how close our kids are in age is more important.

"The other thing is what we said after Mattias was born, that if we knew then what we know now, we wouldn't have taken so much time to make the decision to add to our team. I am confident that this baby is going to be a huge blessing in our lives, just like Mattias has been."

I had said a lot, and Hugo just sat and looked at me intently, taking in all my words. I feared that the transition of moving to the Dominican Republic, coupled with the new ministry responsibilities of our first year on the field, would make him feel overwhelmed and reluctant to add this extra stress. Even though we had put our luggage away and we felt settled in, there were a lot of unknowns for this first year of ministry. We did not know what life would be like in the long run of doing ministry, day after day.

However, Hugo was not sweaty or pale as he had been when we talked about having Mattias. I think that, when he knew the Lord was moving, he gained courage and felt an unusual peace. His face was thoughtful, compassionate, and gentle.

"You're right. It makes more sense to have a baby at the end of this year than to wait until next year. Let's pray about it and see what God directs."

"But what I am asking you now is, do I have your permission to go off my birth control pill, and we'll use other forms of birth control until God says yes or no? Then we'll be ready if He says yes, and, if not, I can start birth control again."

"Yes. Stop taking them. Let's see what God has in mind." Hugo smiled shyly. I knew that he felt like a little boy making a grown-up choice, but God had molded him into a godly man, and he was more than capable of making this important decision.

"Thank you, Hugo," I said, giving him a kiss on the cheek. "You're a great daddy and husband to listen to me and make a scary decision with me. Thank you for who you are and how you have allowed God to grow you. I am so thankful you are my husband and the father of Mattias and any other children God may give us."

"Thank you for saying that. I don't feel like I deserve it, but thank you. I love you, too and I'm so thankful God gave you to me."

Around that time, we started seeing billboards for a Juan Luis Guerra concert on Valentine's Day. That day would be our fifth anniversary, and it was perfect, because Hugo loved Juan Luis Guerra, who was a native Dominican and had received Christ several years ago. It would be a dream come true to go to one of his concerts. We were planning to drive to the capital, go to the concert, and come home. Hugo tried to buy tickets a week before the concert, but the box office was closed, so he'd have to go in again the next day.

That evening, director Tim called Hugo into his office. I was in the apartment with Mattias and I figured they were talking about schedules or something. Little did I know that Pastor Aby was also there, and this was a more serious meeting than I had thought. When Hugo got home, he looked a little sad.

I looked at him, confused. "What?" I asked.

"They asked us not to go to the concert." I knew how much this concert meant to Hugo, so I was upset for him, even though he didn't appear to be too upset.

"What! Why?"

"I was upset at first, too, but then I remembered all the times in Argentina when God taught us that obeying our authorities was always better in the end, even when it didn't make sense. So I just calmly told Tim and Pastor Aby that it was okay."

"Okay, but why did they say they did not want us to go?" I asked again.

"Well, they don't think that it's a sin or anything. They would love for us to go. But some of the churches that SCORE works with here are more conservative and new to their faith, and if they knew that some SCORE missionaries went to a concert, they might stumble in their Christian walk. Apparently this situation has happened before, and it was not good."

"Oh, well … that makes sense. I'm glad that you were humble about it and backed out gracefully. You're right about what God had taught us about obeying authorities. You did the right thing. We'll figure out some other way to celebrate."

"Thanks for understanding."

We tried to come up with other ideas, but there wasn't much we could afford. I prayed, because I really wanted this anniversary to be special.

A couple of days after we canceled our concert plans, Tim came up to Hugo and me. He had a smile on his face. He said, "I was on the phone with Ron Bishop last night, and I told him about our conversation the other day about the concert. I wasn't sure how you were going to handle it, and it was just so refreshing to see your calm response to confrontation, and your humble willingness to cancel your plans. I told Ron how awesome all the staff is here in the DR. God has really built a unique family, and Hugo's response to my request proved to me that God had brought some great new additions to that family."

Hugo didn't say anything; he just looked down at his shoes.

Tim continued, "After I told Ron that, he told me, 'Well, let's help them out and do something special for them. Make some arrangements and put them up in the Hilton Hotel in Santo Domingo for the weekend. SCORE will pay for it.'"

Hugo looked up, shocked. "What?"

Tim said more slowly, "SCORE is going to pay for you guys to go to the Hilton for your anniversary weekend."

Hugo looked at me. We were both smiling, knowing that God had rewarded us for obedience and faithfulness to our authorities.

"Well, that's awesome, but we are only going to be able to go for one night because Mattias can't be alone with a babysitter for any longer, so we'll just stay the night of the 13th."

"Okay," Tim said. "I'll call and make arrangements."

The next week, we left Mattias in Bethany's capable hands. Bethany was from Buffalo, New York, and had been with SCORE for six months. She loved kids, and was great with Mattias. Once, Hugo and I had to travel to the other side of the island and left Mattias with Bethany. We were gone much longer than we had expected, but Bethany was a pro with kids. She had even written me a list of everything Mattias had eaten and the times he had pooped and peed. Once she got to know me better, she found out I am a more laidback mother than that, and she stopped keeping the "poop list." Hugo and I knew that Mattias was in very good hands for the night we'd be gone.

We left early in the morning for the capital. We wanted to enjoy as much time together as possible. We had some time before we were allowed to check into the Hilton, so we went to the botanical gardens. They were beautiful, and Hugo and I laughed at the trolleys that toted guests around the huge campus. In the brochure they were advertised as "the funny trains." And they really were funny, because they were so old that they trembled going up and down the hills, and we felt like the bolts were going to pop out. Hugo kept saying, "Whoa, the funny train!"

We checked in and took the glass elevator up to our room. When we found our room we looked at the room number and laughed. It was like Tim had played a bad joke on us. It was Friday the 13th, we were on floor 13, and staying in room 1313! We laughed, but as we opened the door, we knew this was no joke. The room was stunning, nicer than any we had ever seen, let alone stayed in. And the view was spectacular.

There were two huge picture windows. One overlooked the pool and the beautiful Santo Domingo skyline, and the other overlooked water – water, water, and more water. Big, blue, and endless. When I looked out across the depths, my soul felt something special: a closeness with God, as if being in a dream.

I lay on the bed, instantly in heaven wrapped in the luxurious sheets. Hugo joined my cloud and said, "This is so much better than a concert, where we'd barely be able to talk to each other."

"Good, I'm glad you think so. I didn't want you to be too disappointed."

"No, this is the perfect anniversary," he said.

"Good, because I have a gift for you!"

"Oh, really?" he responded curiously.

I unzipped my luggage and gave him a card and a small gift. He read the card and then, as he started to open the gift, I explained, "I know that you were sad that your spinner friendship ring broke last month, so I wanted to buy you a new one." He took the top off the little box. It was another spinner ring, with a lightning bolt pattern on it.

"As the card says, you are my lightning and will always strike my heart," I said.

"Thank you."

We had an amazing dinner in the hotel, also paid for by SCORE, and then walked over to a movie theater. There was not much showing, so we saw "The Curious Case of Benjamin Button." It wasn't the best movie ever, but it was a different sort of movie, which I liked.

Waking up in a hotel on our wedding anniversary was a new concept for us, but we loved it. I told Hugo, "Next year we will have to plan to go somewhere the night before our anniversary so we can wake up where we want to be on that day, because it is so relaxing and nice."

"Yes, for sure. I'd love to come back here. Do you think SCORE will pay for it next year too?" We both laughed and gazed out our huge window towards the ocean. We had left the curtains open because it was impossible for anyone to see in, and it was so amazing to look out at the ocean from the comfort of our bed.

After our anniversary, Hugo and I threw our energies back into leading teams. SCORE always had a lot of medical and dental teams at the beginning of the year, and Hugo loved to make them think hard with his mind games. One of the best, or worst, depending on your viewpoint and funny bone, involved a $20 bill. Hugo would pull it out of his pocket and explain to the group that there was a hitchhiker on the bill, and he'd give the bill to whoever could find the hitchhiker first. Then there would be a scramble for turns to examine the bill.

Hugo would give "clues" by saying, "You have to hold it up to the light." Or, "It is in the top right corner."

If people asked me for clues, I'd say, "I don't know," or avert my eyes, because I have no poker face, and I was so embarrassed.

Hugo would draw out the time as long as possible, until everyone was completely frustrated from trying to find the hitchhiker. When everyone had given up, he'd take the bill from them, carefully hold it up to the light, turn it over, smooth it out, and then say, "Huh, he must have gotten a ride!"

Most people wouldn't get it in the first few seconds, but then, as they realized it was a joke and there was no hitchhiker, they'd groan and laugh. Hugo would practically be dying of laughter on the floor. Most people would then want to do the same trick on other friends who were not around for the joke the first time.

Hugo knew how to help the groups have a good time. On the bus rides, especially with youth groups, he started taking his ipod and doing "DJ Hugo" to pass the time. He used his "philosophy of music" (skipping to another song long before the first one was over) to entertain the captive audience. He had confessed to me several times that he had always wanted to be a DJ. The teams loved to play "guess that song," especially during the Disney-themed round. But Hugo also liked to laugh at people's responses as he put on random songs, such as the love song from "Titanic," or a Backstreet Boys song.

Mattias and I would often go with the team in the morning and then stay home in the afternoon. But when it was a medical team, who came to treat the sick in the DR, we didn't think it was too smart to have Mattias around sick people all day, so Hugo would go by himself in the morning.

Then I would drive out to the *batey,* eat lunch with the team, and bring Mattias home. It was a good arrangement, and Hugo enjoyed translating for the medical teams. He was learning a lot, how to take a person's blood pressure, and a dental team had allowed him to pull two teeth. They were the last two teeth the patient had, so it was a pretty easy job. Hugo came home ecstatic at having done something new that day.

He started to become very skilled at identifying medical conditions, because most of the cases were the same illnesses over and over again.

Once, after going out with a team of medical students, Hugo seemed burnt out. This was not normal for him, so I asked him, "What's up? How'd it go?"

"Ahhh!" he groaned, but then he laughed. "The medical students are so slow and too thorough. They ask every single question to find out the problem, and I know what it is in the first two minutes. But I have to just sit there and translate, so they can get good experience. I tried to give hints and help them out, though. It is just so different from doctors or nurses who have been here before and know what to look for."

"You could be a doctor, it sounds like."

"No thanks, too much studying. Anyway, I challenged some of the guys to a chugging contest, so I want to try and break my record of drinking a bottle of water in 4 seconds tonight. They're having Snack Attack down by the back pool if you want to come with me. We can put Mattias to bed and just take the baby monitor with us."

"Sure, sounds good. Also, if we see Dr. Bob, we need to ask him for a pregnancy test."

I said it so offhandedly that Hugo thought nothing about it and said, "Okay, honey." But then he realized what I had really said. "WHAT?" He looked at me wide-eyed, but he also had a huge smile.

"I know. I just feel something's different, and we should check."

"Okay." He looked excited and thoughtful. He looked at me again to scrutinize my sincerity and see if I was joking. "Really?"

"Really," I said, and he wrapped his arms around me. This was a huge moment, but we did not want to get our hopes up yet. I was not sure, so I tried to downplay the excitement I was feeling. We'd have to wait to get a test kit from Dr. Bob, probably the next day, and then wait another day to do the test in the morning. I would have to try to relax and not think about it, so that I could get other normal things done.

After Mattias was tucked into his portable crib, we took the monitor with us to keep tabs on him, and soon Hugo was smack in the middle of a chugging contest. The kids were so impressed with how fast he could drink a glass of water. Sometimes he'd do timed chugging tests, and he'd set his ipod to time each person.

Other times, he'd set up the group of challengers to drink quickly against him, and see who could turn the empty cup upside down on the counter first. Little did the contestants know that Hugo, in his period of sinful drunkenness, had learned the key to winning a chugging contest: he opened his throat and let the drink go straight down the pipe without swallowing. It was an acquired skill, and Hugo was able to use it to the glory of God as he broke down a wall to be able to speak Christ into the teens' lives. Though he did use words when necessary, most of Hugo's "speaking" was done through the example of his life.

Hugo loved his ministry with the teams, especially the teenagers. Almost every day, he'd walk in the door from being with a team all day, and he'd have a smile from ear to ear. He wasn't tired at all. Well, his body was tired, but his soul was soaring. It was as if being with the team actually gave him energy instead of taking it away. He'd even have energy to entertain Mattias for a while.

The next day, just like every day, as soon as he'd walk in the door, Mattias would run up to him. "Daddy! Daddy!"

"Hey, my little bundle of joy. How are you?"

Mattias would try to start untying Hugo's shoes. Once he helped Daddy get his shoes off, he'd pull on Hugo's hand and say, "Bed. Bed." They both knew that meant Mattias wanted to tickle fight on the bed. Hugo also knew that I needed a few moments away from Mattias to regain some sanity after being a mom all day. Soon I'd be refreshed and able to focus on asking Hugo about his day and all the exciting details. I'd encourage him if he needed it, or praise him, or give him ideas on how to handle a situation. My main ministry this first year in the Dominican Republic was to Hugo and Mattias.

Working with female interns was another part of my ministry in the DR, and my first discipleship relationship was with Bethany. Bethany and I would try to get together weekly. I loved to use the light green tea set that Hugo had gotten me for my birthday back in October. I loved it because on the side it said, "God makes everything beautiful . . . in His time." This is a verse I have loved since I was very young, and it has encouraged me with the reminder that God is always working for the good in my life.

I'd make tea, and then Bethany and I would have a tea party and talk. I would keep her accountable to her Bible reading and quiet times. This challenged me to keep my quiet time up to date as well, something I frequently struggled with.

One day, in order to encourage her, I told her something I had read recently. "Reading the Bible is just like eating. You do it every day because you have to, to survive. Sometimes it is a banquet and you remember every delicious bite. Sometimes it is a breakfast that you can't remember by lunchtime. It's not always about having an amazing enlightenment every day. It is just important to be consistent, and open to what God wants to teach you, so that God has the opportunity to move in your life."

Bethany was not sure what God's plan for her life was. She had gone on a SCORE mission trip, and then done SCORE's Gap Year in Costa Rica to learn Spanish and the Bible, and now she was here as an intern, but to what end?

We talked and prayed earnestly about this topic for almost the whole six months. In the end, she left for home knowing that God had called her to be a missionary in the DR. She would soon be accepted as a SCORE missionary, raising support and moving back to the DR to be in charge of child care with the missionary families.

Bethany's ministry would allow mothers to work with their husbands in ministry or accomplish tasks in their own ministries. For example, I was teaching English in a big *batey* called Los Montones. Hugo was often available to watch Mattias because the class was on Saturday when teams were coming or going, but sometimes he was not available and I had to find childcare. When Bethany was in the

DR, she would help immensely with such situations. We were even more thankful to have her once we learned that we were pregnant again!

We made an appointment with the Ob/Gyn that Erica had used when she was pregnant with Mali. The office was thirty minutes away in the capital, and it was nice, although sometimes we had to wait a long time. I was expecting to find out that we had gotten pregnant in February, maybe during our anniversary. But the doctor told us that we were further along than that, and the due date for the baby was the end of October. This was good, because we were further into the pregnancy than we thought, but bad because we were going to have to take off a lot more time than we had planned.

Ideally, we wanted to go home in November and have the baby in December. That was not going to happen. But at least we would be able to spend Thanksgiving, Christmas, and New Years in the States this year, because we had celebrated in the DR last year. And there was no way my family would let me take our new baby away right before the holidays.

We looked at the calendar and counted up the days. My Ob/Gyn in Kansas told me that he wanted me to fly home six weeks before the due date. We counted back, and it was about a week after the annual SCORE staff meeting in Chattanooga, Tennessee, on September 3rd.

Hugo said, "We might as well go home to Kansas after the staff meeting to save money." We counted forward to when we could come back after the new year. Four months.

"Four months is a long time; almost half a year. Do you think Tim will go for it?" I asked.

Hugo raised his eyebrow and said, "What other option do we have? For some reason, God wanted us to get pregnant when we did, so we are just going to have to work with it."

I looked at the calendar again. Hugo would be missing the baseball clinics. I knew that would be a big problem, because SCORE really needed him to translate that week and to help with a ton of other grunt work.

An idea popped into my head. "What if we tell Tim that we will spend the money to buy you a plane ticket to come back for the baseball clinics?"

Hugo thought for a moment. "I think that would be great. That should be the only thing they need my help with, since there aren't many teams in the fall. It will help smooth over our long absence, plus I really would love to see all the guys from last year at the clinics. Good thinking, woman!" He loved to call me "woman" when he was joking around with me. He smiled and gave me a big hug.

As soon as we told Mattias and our families that we were pregnant again, we gathered the staff by the pool and announced the good news. Everyone was so excited for us.

Tim's wife, Ginny, said, "I knew it!" And she was right. The previous week, before I knew for sure about the baby, I was crying to her about something. She asked me, "Are you pregnant?" Not just because I was crying, but because she used to work at an obstetrician's office, and she can sniff out a pregnant lady like a bloodhound.

A month later, Hugo's sister, Febe, and her husband Carlos announced that they were pregnant, too. The whole Liborio family was so excited that there would be two new babies born only weeks apart.

However, the excitement was cut short when Febe found out that her baby did not have a heartbeat. We were heartbroken for them. How could the family enjoy our baby being born when everyone knew that another one was supposed to be born soon after? It would be a delicate situation, but we prayed that God would give us the grace to pass through it.

When I was four months pregnant, we flew to El Salvador for two weeks to catch up with Hugo's family. Hugo's sister Cesia was there, and it was fun to see her at the same time as everyone else. We had no plans to go back to Argentina anytime soon, so if she hadn't come to El Salvador when we did, too much time would have passed between visits. Her husband Tito could not get off work to come with her. But it was great to see Cesia, and we got to meet her friend, Romina, who traveled with her. They were both chefs, so they spent a lot of time cooking, which was good for us.

We also had the opportunity to see Hugo's dad. All of us went to the beach together one day. It was the first family outing that everyone had gone on with both Irma and Hugo Sr. since they had divorced in 2003. As awkward as it was at times, God had done an incredible work to heal wounds in that family.

Irma and Cesia had struggled to forgive him for a long time. Thanks to a lot of prayer, they were doing much better. Febe was the family's peacemaker, and she had suffered greatly in her failure to keep everyone together. She was now praising God to see her family back together again.

It was hard to tell if Hugo Sr. had ever fully dealt with his sins. He was not a man of many words. Hugo and I prayed often that his father would confess his part in the failure of his marriage, knowing that his family had forgiven him and loved him greatly. But if Hugo Sr. had received that forgiveness, he never said.

It was a blessed time with Hugo's family in El Salvador. When we returned to the DR, our new apartment above the Judes was ready, and we could move in. Even though there was no air conditioning yet, we readily agreed to move into the bigger space. After waiting for months for our home to be ready, and with the new baby coming, my nesting instincts were in overdrive. We quickly moved all our stuff into our new home.

Teams continued to come and go each week. Hugo kept up with all of them. Our whole family got sick one week, but Hugo and Mattias were over it in three days. My pregnancy exacerbated the illness, and it took me two weeks to feel like a human being again. When I was ready to go out again, I tagged along with Hugo as much as possible, despite the fatigue I felt.

One of the things we loved about SCORE was that they staff did its best to provide ministry opportunities for all who wanted to come. Regardless of talent or experience, they found a place to plug the team in.

Besides the traditional medical, dental, construction, drama, and sports teams, as well as youth groups and senior class trips, we also enjoyed the help of a foot-washing team, called "Happy Feet," that did nothing but wash feet and give out socks and shoes to people. The Dominicans were shocked to see Americans get down and humbly wash their feet. They couldn't believe someone would pay money to come serve them in this way.

There was also a "step team." If you've ever seen the movie, "Stomp the Yard," you know what I'm talking about. This was a group of college guys from the South who used stomping, clapping, and slapping to make a musical rhythm. Over the top of this beat, they shouted their message. I have never seen a Dominican audience so rapt with attention. Their eyes were glued to the four men before them who called out loudly, "Cristo vive en mi!" (Christ lives in me.)

Hugo was able to get involved with another team that was creative and useful. It was from a church in Woodstock, Georgia, and the members called themselves "Gloves for God." They would accompany SCORE baseball teams to games and perform their ministry there. At the beginning of the game, they explained to the opposing team that if their gloves needed any repairs, the players should bring them over, and the glove experts would look at them. This was a huge act of faith for the Dominican players, because baseball was everything for them.

Hugo once asked a six-year-old boy, "What is your favorite sport?"

He thought for a moment and then replied, "Soccer."

"Really?" Hugo asked, surprised. "What about baseball?"

The boy responded, "Oh, I thought you asked me about my favorite sport. Baseball is my life."

This demonstrates how seriously Dominicans take baseball and shows that they wouldn't let just anyone touch their baseball gloves. But, they could see the equipment the Gloves for God team had brought, and soon the opposing team started to bring over gloves. When they needed to be on the field, they borrowed gloves from teammates who were in the dugout.

The condition of the gloves that the Gloves for God team worked with was terrible.

Hugo joked, "These guys play with their gloves until they disintegrate into the air."

We saw that the original leather laces had been replaced with shoestrings, duct tape, wire, or whatever the players had decided would hold the mitt together. The Gloves for God team would often have to disassemble an entire glove and reconstruct it with matching leather. The team had brought with them a lot of leather string.

The team also conditioned each glove. Some gloves were so bad that they could not be fixed. The team had prepared for this as well and had brought gloves to donate. Team members would bring the owner of the glove over and explain to him that his glove could not be fixed, but if he would like to swap gloves with them, they'd like to make an exchange. The players were almost always glad to upgrade to a new glove.

Hugo saw what Gloves for God members were doing and started to help them. At first they just let him condition and return the gloves, but then they promoted him to doing some sewing with a big needle and leather thread. They taught him along the way, and Hugo loved it. Plus, Wes, Dave, and Bob were a blast to work with. As cool as it was to fix gloves, Hugo was most excited about how they used their ministry to share Christ with the team.

After the game, one of them would speak, usually Wes. Jose, one of the team members who spoke Spanish, or a SCORE missionary would translate. Wes would tell the guys, "A glove on the ground is just a glove. It has no power on its own. But, with the right hand inside it, it has the potential to do amazing things. By yourself, you can't do much, but when you accept Christ, you have the Holy Spirit in you, and He is the hand that can help you do great things and change your life."

He used something known to them to make spiritual parallels that they could relate to. Or he'd tell them, "You could not fix your glove on your own, because you didn't know how or didn't have the supplies. You had to give it to someone who did know how to fix it and had the right supplies. Christ is like that too. You don't know how to fix your life, but God can fix your sin through the cross of Jesus Christ, and He can change your life. The cross is the right supply, and Christ is the right man to fix your life. Trust Him and give your life over to Him."

Hugo loved how the Dominican baseball players connected with these messages. He was so excited about this new way of drawing Dominicans into what he was talking about that he wanted to buy a $100 colored baseball glove. It was kind of like a wordless book for baseball players, with each color representing a part of the gospel story. He was looking at getting one from Gloves for God online.

When he was telling an American baseball team about it two weeks later, a guy named Will pulled one out of his bag and said, "Like this one?"

"Yeah, wow! You have one? That is awesome!" Hugo said.

Will threw it to Hugo and said, "You can have it. I know you will get good use out of it here in the DR."

Hugo's gaze went from the glove to Will's eyes. "Are you serious?"

"Sure, I'd be honored for you to have it."

I prayed that Hugo would not shed a tear in front of these baseball guys. But he held it together and simply said, "Thanks, Will." He hooked the glove on his backpack, and it rode with Hugo practically every day after that.

Hugo's other love in ministry was the guitar, and he got plenty of opportunities to use his talent. He loved to sit and play for the groups while they had an impromptu worship time, or even host a jam session with other people who played. His scheduled playing times were during worship every Tuesday and Thursday, when the teams were invited to the Upper Room for SCORE Night. Joel would accompany him on a second guitar, but he was also very good at playing the djembe, a skin-covered drum played with bare hands, and Joel often chose to add to the worship time in this way.

Hugo always got lots of compliments about his spirit-filled worship time, and he'd always respond with, "Praise the Lord." He wanted to stay humble and knew that his gift was for God's glory, not his own. He also led worship on Sundays for our local SCORE church plant, which met in the Upper Room. It was a bilingual church, so Hugo led both Spanish and English worship songs.

Summer came, and life at SCORE was crazy. At one point we had 300 people in the country working with us. The SCORE mission training center was full, and we were renting two villas and a multitude of hotel rooms. There were thirteen buses going different places every day.

One of our most memorable teams that summer was an all-girls team from Wesleyan High School near Atlanta, Georgia. They chose to do a construction project. They helped a small school in the capital lay concrete block for three more classrooms. The older students from the Dominican school helped carry blocks up to the roof during their break times.

Hugo had to take the guys aside and explain to them, "The American girls are here to work, so despite your urge to help them carry their loads, you need to let them work, too."

Latino men are not used to allowing a woman carry something heavy by herself. Hugo gave the girls on the team a hard time and challenged them to make an okay-line or a no-okay line and to find the hitchhiker in the $20 bill. He also showed them a game he had used a lot called "Mickey Mouse."

Mattias, Hugo, and I went out to dinner with the team one night and, as we waited for our pizza, Hugo decided to teach them the game to kill time.

"I am going to do something with my hands, and you have to do it exactly as I do it," he told them. With his right hand, he pointed to each of the fingers on his left hand, starting with his pinky, while saying, "Mickey, Mickey, Mickey, Mickey...." When he reached the L-shaped piece of skin between the pointer and the thumb, he said, "Mmoouuse." Then he tapped his thumb again and did the whole thing in reverse: "Mouse, Mickey, Mickey, Mickey, Mickey." He made one last motion with his arms and then challenged, "Now you do it exactly the same."

It seemed relatively easy, so the girls tried again and again. Hugo kept telling them, "No. No. No. That's not right." They got frustrated and asked Hugo to do it again. He did it about twenty times. Out of the corner of my eye, I could see Mattias doing it. Hugo turned to look at him. I knew what the trick to the challenge was, but it was so cute to watch Mattias try and do it. He randomly pointed at different fingers and mumbled something about Mickey Mouse, changing his voice up and down like his daddy had done.

When he was done, he crossed his arms. Hugo shouted, "He did it right! My two-year-old got it right! Mattias, do it again!"

All the girls watched him. Mattias did exactly the same hand work and then crossed his arms at the end. Hugo said, "You see? He did it right! The trick has nothing to do with the fingers; you have to cross your arms at the end!"

Another event that happened while this team was in the country tested Hugo's readiness to speak the gospel in season or out of season. Mattias had been sick off and on for a while, so his pediatrician in the capital ordered a test to see if Mattias had any parasites. This test included collecting a bowel movement and taking it into the lab. Hugo was going to the capital anyway to help the girls with the construction of the school. He was translating between the foreman and the girls, plus doing a lot of grunt work.

I did not want to drive into the capital just to drop off the specimen, so Hugo decided that he'd get the girls started on the day's work and then take a taxi to the drop-off point and go back. I gave him the small jar containing the sample in a brown paper bag.

He said, "I feel so dumb carrying poop to work."

I laughed at him. Once in the taxi cab, Hugo was quiet, just wanting to get this miserable task done over with. But the cabbie was friendly or bored or something, and he struck up a conversation with Hugo.

Soon Hugo felt the conversation lead to an opening to present the gospel. He heard God tell him, "Be ready to speak the truth, in season or out of season." This definitely felt out of season because of the "sticky" situation he was in. However, Hugo followed God's prompting and told the cabbie about the saving grace of the cross and the power of the resurrection—all with poop sitting on his lap. The man didn't receive Christ, but Hugo was faithful to plant the seeds. Needless to say, I was rolling on the floor with laughter when he told me about the incident later that night. He did not think it was so funny in the moment, but he enjoyed a good laugh with me.

Hugo joked with the Wesleyan team so much that they were fed up, and one night they conspired to give him a taste of his own medicine.

"This game is called 'Family Tree,'" one girl, Adrienne, said on the bus the next morning. She pointed at different girls on the bus and said, "If she's my sister, and she's my cousin, that makes her my mom. You have to guess how the last person is related to me based on the other clues."

Hugo was on the edge of his seat, excited to learn a new game. He said, "Okay, do it again."

Adrienne began, "If she's my aunt, and she's my niece, and she's my grandma, than that makes her my what?"

Hugo thought carefully. He gave every ounce of brain power into reviewing the facts, as well as comparing the game to other ones he knew. A lot of the mind games were similar in terms of the trick to playing them. He analyzed the clues over and over and made the girls repeat the game every few minutes. They acted as if only a few of them knew the game initially, while others began to catch on throughout the week. The girls told me the answer the night before their last day of work, and

I was sworn to secrecy. The answer was so good, I knew that I would have to keep it from Hugo.

Hugo did not know that the girls had told me the answer, so that night I almost died as we lay in bed and Hugo said, "You know, the girls have been telling me this mind game all week, and I can't figure it out. It is driving me crazy." He explained to me the rules of the game.

I said casually, "Is it based on saying or doing something right before or right after the family tree?"

"No. I've been watching and listening."

"Is it something with numbers or the first letters of their names?"

"No, I am bad with math and spelling, but they said that is not the answer."

"Does it have to do with who talks first after the tree?"

"No, I've tested that theory. I can't figure it out."

We lay quietly, but I could tell that he could not let it go; it was driving him crazy. I knew he'd lose sleep that night, but the fun was too good to spoil. In the morning, Hugo dragged himself onto the bus for the last workday with the girls. They had promised to tell him the secret to the mind game at the end of the day.

When he got back home, he burst into the house and said, "I have to tell you!"

"What, what happened?"

"The girls told me about the family tree."

I stifled a smile and tried to not give away that I knew anything.

Hugo started the story from the beginning. "At work today, the last girl got the game, and I still could not get it. I felt so dumb that I could not get it. They tried to help me figure it out all day. I was frustrated. On the bus ride home, they finally told me. They said, 'If she's my sister, and she's my cousin, that makes Hugo punk'd!' I didn't get it at first, but then I was so mad when they explained that the mind game had no secret. The game was just for me to always be wrong and to drive me crazy all week!"

"I know," I said quietly.

"What? You knew? How could you not tell me? I lost sleep and brain cells over this stupid game."

"Because you drive people insane with all your mind games and jokes all the time. It was a little taste of your own medicine for them to come up with this creative joke on you."

"I know," he said slowly. "It was pretty awesome of them, huh?"

"Best practical joke ever."

Hugo's fun side was known by all, but his tender side was not always as visible. A team from Shelby, North Carolina, got to see this other side of Hugo when he helped the team with a project while they were with us. The team leader, Pastor Tim Sims, had asked Pastor Aby, "What do you need in SCORE's church planting ministry?"

Pastor Aby said, "Another motorcycle so that the disciples can get to all the church plants to help with the services. I am spending so much on gas to transport them to all the places I need them to be. I have two motorcycles for them, but I need one more."

Pastor Sims then asked Hugo, "Where can we get another motorcycle for Pastor Aby, and how much would it cost?"

Hugo started thinking, and then made some phone calls. He tracked down the place where Pastor Aby had bought the other two motorcycles and the price he had paid for them.

"It costs $800 U.S., and Pastor Aby will not know until we give it to him at the service in Los Montones tonight." Many teams bring extra donation money and pray about where God wants them to use it while on their trip. Pastor Sims's team decided this is where God wanted them to donate their money to help the ministry be more productive.

"How can we get the motorcycle out there?" Pastor Sims asked.

"The team can go on ahead with Sarah and start the Vacation Bible School program, and I will follow with the bike. I have a motorcycle license, and I know the roads."

"Sounds like a good plan," said Tim's wife, Angie.

We all left on the bus to Los Montones, past the cow head, over the big bump, down the dirt road, down another dirt road, and 40 minutes later we were there. The team started with their prepared program and for the kids.

Pastor Aby asked me, "Where is Hugo?"

I simply said, "He's on his way." I looked at my watch; he should have been here by now. I waited and watched, looking down the dirt road over and over. But the only signs of life were the occasional chicken or cow. Where was he? My cell phone did not get service in this village. I could do nothing but wait.

Finally, Hugo pushed the motorcycle through the side door and hid it behind the puppet stage. I hadn't even seen him come up the road. I looked around. Pastor Aby was across the soccer field checking on the kids' activity. I rushed up to Hugo and asked, "What happened?"

He rolled his eyes and said, "The motorcycle that we had first chosen wouldn't start. So they had to get one of the other ones out and put oil and gas into that one. But that one wouldn't start, either. They had to call the mechanic, and he came and he started to take it apart. He finally got it started, and they told me that I needed to let it warm up for fifteen minutes. I told them, 'No, I have to leave now!'

"They asked where I was going, and when I told them. they said, 'You're nuts! That is so far away.' I guess they are not used to riding bikes long distances. Anyway, I'm here, the bike is here, and Aby doesn't know. Yohander met me on the road and led me in the back way."

"This is so exciting." I said. "I'm glad you got here safely."

He smiled and then started scheming with Pastor Tim and Pastor Steve about how to give the motorcycle to Pastor Aby. They decided to it "magically." Pastor Steve was an amazing magician and could go three hours doing tricks without repeating. Almost all of the tricks had some spiritual truth that went along with them. So, the plan was for Steve to pretend to do a magic trick, and then the spiritual truth would be about gratitude to God for amazing answers to prayers made in faith, or something to that effect.

They planted a team member behind the stage and three participants were called to the front, including two little kids and Pastor Aby, who reluctantly agreed. At the end of the magic trick, the kids were told to go the front of the puppet stage and ask God for candy. When they did, candy flew over the top of the stage.

Then Pastor Steve said to Aby, "Now I want you to go and pray for a heart's desire of yours." Aby went to the front of the stage, and instantly candy flew over the top. Everyone laughed, and Aby thought that was the end of the joke. Then, something else came flying over the stage. Out of instinct, Aby caught whatever it was that was flying toward him. He opened his hand – keys. He looked at Pastor Steve and Pastor Tim with confusion on his face. No one said anything. The person behind the puppet stage pushed out the new motorcycle, and all was clear. God had answered a desire of Pastor Aby's heart.

I saw Pastor Sims look over at Hugo in the corner, and I looked, too. Hugo had both hands folded like a prayer over his nose and mouth, tears flowing shamelessly down his face. The gift wasn't even for him, but he was so touched by the generosity of the special gift of this motorcycle that he was truly moved. I adored the soft heart that God had given to my husband, and a lump formed in my throat, too. He looked like a little kid on Christmas day, and I loved him for the pure excitement he felt in the simple things of life.

As much as I loved my husband, as a married woman I missed my intimacy with Jesus as my only love. In my pre-marriage days, I understood very well the idea that Christ was my husband and the only man in my life. Maybe not everyone understands this, but I felt as if Christ were next to me, giving me an intimate fulfilling hug.

Now married, I had never completely figured out how to love the two men in my life: Hugo and Christ. I am not sure how it happened, but during this summer God showed me that I had left my first love.

Erica was doing a study with the intern girls that she had written called *The Vintage Girl*.[1] It was based on Jer. 6:16: "Thus saith the Lord, 'Stand ye in the ways, and see, and ask for the old paths, where is the good way, and walk therein, and ye shall find rest for your souls.' But they said, 'We will not walk therein.'"

The study used a lot of "vintage" terms to show readers they needed to ask God for the old, good ways and walk in them. After the study, Erica had all of us write about what God had taught us during the study. I wrote:

> The biggest thing I've learned with "The Vintage Girl" is that Christ is more than my Savior. He is my husband.
>
> Is. 54:5 says, "For thy Maker is thine husband; the Lord of hosts is His name, and thy Redeemer the Holy One of Israel; the God of the whole earth shall He be called." For a long time I have lost this intimate love relationship. I have kept God as my Father and Jesus Christ as my Savior, but have put aside my first man! Rev. 2:4 says, "But, I have this against you, that

you have abandoned the love you had at first." I have struggled with the time and desire to read God's word and be in prayer with Him. I'd fly through my times of communication with Christ, mainly only praying to God. Now I know I'll never smell like Him (2 Cor. 2:15-16) if I don't make some sacrifices.

Now I want to sit down with Him, open my Bible and get to know His innermost thoughts and feelings. I want to find out what He thinks romance looks like.

But to get to this point I had to see that spiritual strength is something that comes from spending time with God in His word. After I was convicted that I needed to power up my life through Scripture, I knew I needed to confess.

This brings me to the third thing that God taught me through the chapter called "Faux Real."[1] I needed to understand that daily confession is like therapy for my soul. I confessed my lack of quiet times to Erica and how I missed Christ as my husband. She listened and helped me work through what I needed to do to get back to my first love.

She shared with me that devotions are not always a half hour in a quiet place, with no distractions. As long as the Word is being opened daily in my heart, it can have different forms. I have felt a Selah in my heart that I had not felt for a long time. Psalm 32:5 says, "I acknowledge my sin unto Thee, and mine iniquity have I not hid. I said, 'I will confess my transgressions unto the Lord,' and Thou forgavest the iniquity of my sin. Selah."

God, thank you for changing me! Christ, thank you for waiting for me and loving me when I did not know how to love You.

As God was teaching me how to fall in love with my first love all over again and as my intimate "hug" relationship with Christ returned, God was laying another foundation. I did not realize how important this lesson would be in less than five months. God knew that I would need my heavenly husband to hold me up, as He would deal in the life of my earthly husband.

Hugo takes a quick picture of himself before
he translates the gospel for a baseball clinic (2008)

Hugo preaches the gospel using a colored baseball glove (www.gloves4god.com) that represents
different parts of salvation to get the Dominican baseball players to listen intently (2009)

SCORE basketball team L-R Hugo, Giovanny Valdez,
Kiko Alvarez, Alex Reyes, and Hunter Bedingfield

Hugo uses a "rope trick" to bring in a few kids. He would then repeat the same trick, but add a
story about sin and Jesus dying on the cross for them.

Daddy and Mattias out on ministry together in a village.

For their 5th wedding anniversary (2009), Sarah and Hugo revisited the same rooftop and gazebo in Santo Domingo where Hugo proposed to Sarah in 2003.

Please visit my website, www.my-onceuponatime.com/, to see more pictures and videos from each chapter.

Chapter 13

The Prince's Heart is Captured by a Tiny 'Dark-Haired Beauty'
2009

Dominican Republic, Kansas

Hugo hosted his last team for the year in August. Tim told Hugo, "Go to the airport and pick up your last team; there are 42 of them."

When the team walked out of customs, we realized that Tim had failed to mention that they were middle schoolers. I leaned over to Hugo and whispered, "It's do or die, baby!"

He just groaned, remembering how I'd always challenged him with that phrase before our big tests at the end of each month in Argentina. This was the last team of the year, and we wanted to give them all we had and more. Hugo dove right in and did just that. He had a great week, but he was exhausted from having to keep up with the energy those kids put out 24/7.

On September 1st, 2009, we flew to Atlanta with Mattias. We were blessed to rest at the home of our friends Chris and Kimberly. Chris and his son, Michael, had come to the DR with their church, Johnson Ferry Baptist Church, on a Fellowship of Christian Athletes baseball team. We had made friends with them and the sports director, Justin, and they had invited us to stay with them in Atlanta for a few days before we went to our staff meeting at SCORE in Chattanooga.

It was a wonderful two days. Their house was on a small pond, and it was so relaxing. We went fishing and canoeing. And their four teenagers were great with Mattias, so we were able to take a break from parenthood. Christian even changed diapers for us! It was so nice.

Justin picked us up from the airport and dropped us off at Chris's house, but he came back with his wife, Jennifer, for dinner. It was an amazing meal. The adults ate on the porch overlooking the pond, while the kids ate inside. The whole trip was like green pastures for tired missionary bones.

During our time in Atlanta, Chris took us over to Wesleyan so we could surprise the girls who had played the funny mind game on Hugo. The leaders knew we were coming, but the team didn't. It was hilarious to watch their faces as they came in the door for their team breakfast and saw us there, too. It was screams, hugs, and tears.

We also stopped by Woodstock, Georgia, and met with the Gloves for God guys. They gave us a tour of their church, which was huge. They told us that Woodstock Baptist Church's new sanctuary was the largest facility in the county. From there, we were off to Chattanooga for staff meeting.

It was a challenge to have Mattias with us for staff meeting. The year before, he had stayed with Grandpa and Grandma in Kansas, but this year we were passing through on our way to Kansas, so he had to tag along with us. Most days we had baby-sitting that SCORE helped us find through the church. But one morning, Mattias was stuck with us in the conference room for a couple of hours. I used a special weapon to keep him occupied – Hugo's smart phone ipod touch.

Mattias was barely two years old, and he looked quite grown up sitting in his car seat, totally engrossed in the game he was playing. Hugo had loaded several kid games and racing games that Mattias somehow knew how to access and play. Sometimes he figured them out through trial and error, but he knew how to get to his "Handy Manny" video without any help. He also knew how to move the screen by flipping his finger sideways across it, and he could enlarge a picture by putting his fingers together in the middle of the screen and slowly moving them out. He loved electronic stuff. Like father, like son.

The staff meeting was great. Hugo and I loved seeing friends we had met the year before and meeting the new missionaries. It was so humbling to be part of a ministry that God was using in so many ways. When all the new missionaries lined up at the front to give a few details about themselves and how they'd be serving God with SCORE, Hugo and I laid hands on and prayed for Ken and Jennifer. They had five kids and were raising support, but they were already recruiting sports teams to travel with SCORE.

As we sat in the meetings and heard about all that God had done during the year and was doing presently, Hugo and I felt as if we should sign up to be a part of this great work. But the awesome thing was that we already were a part of it. It was the same feeling I had when I heard a great gospel presentation, and it made me want to raise my hand and get saved even though I already was. We were so honored and proud to be involved with such an exciting ministry.

The first thing on our to-do list when we got back to Hays, Kansas, was LASIK surgery for Hugo. We'd been saving for it for almost a year. We actually chose a cheaper surgery called PRK. Hugo was a good candidate for both, but PRK was $1,000 cheaper. The healing time would be slower, but the end result was the same. We had time, but not money, so we opted for that.

Hugo and I drove to Wichita and spent the night at some friends' house while they were out of town. We went out to dinner and to a movie that night before heading back to our "hotel" for bed.

Early the next morning, we went to the vision clinic, and the procedure took all of ten minutes. Hugo said he was a little freaked out when he smelled flesh burning and saw the red laser close to his eye, but then all of a sudden it was over. Hugo was shocked by how fast it was, but also by how much money we had spent for ten minutes. The doctor put bandage contacts on his eyes while they healed, but Hugo could already tell that he'd be seeing better. We went back to our friends' house, and Hugo slept for most of the day. I put lots of different drops in his eyes for him.

We were back in Hays by Saturday, and on Sunday Hugo could not even go to church with us. He said it felt like sandpaper in his eyes. He could not stand the light, either, and he wore his sunglasses around the house. He was miserable, but we used the drops when he felt the worst and he took some medicine, and by Monday he felt much better.

The following weekend, he played worship for a men's conference. He loved being able to do all the ropes course activities without having to worry about contacts or breaking his glasses. Six weeks later, we went back for his checkup, and they also took the protective lenses off his eyes.

One eye had reached 20/20 vision, but it turned out that the other was a lazy eye and, because it had not been working as much throughout his life, his brain was causing it to be lazy. They said they couldn't fix his brain. After the doctor left, I laughed at Hugo because his brain was messed up – just as I had always suspected.

After the eye surgeries, we focused on baby time. Two weeks before our baby girl's due date, she decided that her time had come.

The night before, my mom and I went for a little pampering. We got manicures and pedicures, and I felt a lot more relaxed than I had before Mattias was born.

Hugo video-recorded our baby's birth from start to finish. At the beginning, Mattias and I were rocking in mom's rocker. Hugo asked, "How are you feeling?"

"Good. The contractions are about five minutes apart."

Mom waved at the camera and said, "We're excited!"

Later that night, my contractions were down to two-and-a-half minutes apart. We were ready to go to the hospital.

Mom zoomed in on Hugo and me with the video camera, getting one last shot of the parents-to-be. "What are you thinking?" she asked.

"It's going to be great!" Hugo said, looking down at my belly and rubbing it gently. "We'll see you soon!"

Just then I started to have a contraction, which Mom also caught on tape. She and Hugo were laughing and so was I, at first. Hugo started doing our Lamaze breathing. I copied him, but my breaths were a bit more intense.

"I can tell it's getting harder; your arm is squeezing me," Hugo said. "Now it's not joking."

Dad was anxious to get going, but I couldn't get up until my contraction was over. Everyone tried not to disturb me as I breathed through it. Then I sighed.

"She's so good!" Hugo exclaimed.

I rolled my head back and said, "I'm ready for an epidural, I'll tell you that much."

Everyone laughed, and my mom said, "Drugs! Drugs! Drugs!"

We arrived at the hospital and the nurse instructed me to take off my clothes off. "So violating!" I joked after the nurse left. "All right, I guess we don't have any secrets anyway."

Hugo pointed out, "This is the room next door to where Mattias was born. Isn't that crazy? I guess we'll see how this one goes."

By 11:30 p.m., I was dilated to 6 centimeters. I was outfitted with monitors to keep track of the baby's heartbeat and my contractions. I smiled for Hugo's camera and said, "The nurse is coming back soon, and I'll be able to walk around then. And hopefully get my epidural."

Hugo cheered with me, "Epidural! Yeah!"

Unfortunately, I did not get that epidural. I needed some blood work first, and by the time the results came back, I was too far into labor for the drugs to be effective. So I was wide awake and totally with it for this birth.

The nurses ushered me into the delivery room. I had to wait about ten minutes for the doctor to come, which was the worst part because my body was desperate to push. This baby was in a hurry, too. The nurses didn't even have time to break down the bottom of the bed. After the doctor arrived, I had one contraction. The next thing I knew, I was the mother of a little girl.

"She's so beautiful," Hugo said in a tender, tearful voice. "Hi, baby. You're so beautiful." She just grunted, mad at having to be under such bright lights.

The nurse said, "Let's see how long you are, sweet girl." She laid the wriggly baby as flat as possible and stretched out her legs. "She's 22 inches, which is really long. And she weighs 7 pounds, 13 ounces."

Hugo kept saying, "It's okay, baby, it's okay. You're so beautiful."

Dad had gone home to stay with Mattias, but Mom was still at the hospital. She came into the recovery room to meet her new granddaughter. "Have you named her yet?" she whispered.

"No, not yet," I said softly.

Hugo was still cooing, "She's so adorable."

Mom said, "I can't believe you are done."

Just then, the baby sneezed. Hugo was right there with his camera. "Oh, bless you, cosita. Your first sneeze, and I recorded it." Hugo zoomed in on her and said, "How're you doing? I love you."

We chose Layla Elizabeth for our new daughter's name. Layla means "dark haired beauty." Elizabeth is my middle name, so I was happy that both my children had family names.

Later, the camera caught a sweet family moment as Hugo and I sang "Jesus Loves Me" to our little girl. After we finished the song, I told Layla, "That's the song we sing to your big brother every night before bed."

Mattias was not able to come onto the maternity ward, so Hugo recorded a message from me. I said into the camera, "Mattias, I hope Daddy can explain to you about your little sister, Layla Elizabeth. And I'll be seeing you tomorrow morning. I love you. I miss you a lot." I blew him a kiss.

Hugo helped Mattias record a message for me. He coached him on what to say. "Mattias you have to say this: 'Mommy.'"

"Mommy."

"I'm proud of you."

"I pou of ou."

"And I hope."

"I hope."

"To see you soon."

"Soon."

"I love you."

"Love you."

"And now blow a kiss. Let's do it together!" Both boys covered their mouths with their hands and blew me a kiss.

When Layla and I were released from the hospital, my parents brought Mattias to accompany us on our trip home.

After we got the kids situated in the car, I shifted Mattias so he could see his sister better. "What is that, Mattias?"

"Baby," he said.

Hugo helped him by saying, "Baby Layla."

"Yeah, baby Yeaya."

I asked Mattias, "Are we going to take her home?"

He nodded his head up and down.

"Should we keep her?" I asked.

"Yes …" But then, Mattias got distracted with something out the window and said, "Mommy! Tractors!" He pointed out the window at a construction site near the hospital parking lot. It was obvious he loved his sister, but tractors were much more important right then.

When we got home, we laid a white blanket out on the floor. I set Layla on it and took off her tiny blue coat with the pink butterfly on the front.

Hugo gently explained to Mattias, "This is your baby sister and she is really delicate. Isn't she beautiful?"

Mattias said quietly, "Yes."

Hugo said, "Can she use your toys sometimes?"

Mattias whispered again, "Yes."

Hugo lay down on his stomach next to Layla and told Mattias, "You can get down like this."

Mattias took Hugo's exact position.

"See, she's so beautiful. You can give her a little kiss like this." Hugo pecked her forehead with his lips.

Mattias leaned over and copied his daddy. I lay down next to Hugo too. The three of us stared at the beautiful baby God had given to our family.

We talked some more, and then Hugo said to Mattias, "Now you have a job, buddy. You have to protect and love her."

Mattias, now squirming and doing fake handstands, managed to say, "Yes."

Hugo leaned over and nuzzled his nose into Layla's thick, soft, black hair.

I'd never seen any man as passionate about a woman as Hugo was about Layla. He had recently been telling everyone about his plan to protect Layla from boys: "When a boy comes to my house to date Layla, I'm going to be sharpening my knife or polishing my gun when he walks in the door. I had a friend once whose dad would say to boys, 'You look like the guy who killed my parents.' He'd pause until the kid was freaked out, and then laugh and say, 'Just kidding, *I* killed my parents. Come on in!'" Hugo would laugh loudly and then add, "Isn't that great? I can't wait to try that one!"

Hugo and I worked together to help Layla adjust to life in the real world. I tried to nurse her at night without waking Hugo up, so that if she went back to sleep easily, then both Hugo and I didn't have to lose sleep.

She was a little trickier than Mattias was. I finally had to put her crib right next to my side of the bed, because she would spit her pacifier out every five minutes and refused to sleep without it. I just slept with my arm in her crib, so that when I heard it fall out of her mouth and hit the mattress, I'd find it in my sleep and put it back before she started crying.

I didn't want Layla to cry much, so she would not wake my parents. With Mattias, we taught them to sleep on his own by letting him cry in five-minute increments. If Layla didn't go back to sleep after I nursed her, Hugo would stay up with her and help her get back to sleep while I went to bed. She seemed to have lots of gas, so Hugo would hold her up by her armpits and let her legs hang. She liked this position the best. My mom told me that my Grandpa Jackson had held me in that same way when I was a baby. Hugo also bounced Layla, and she liked that, too. He'd bounce her until his arms got tired.

Hugo helped me out at night, but especially in the mornings. He was a morning person and it didn't bother him to get up at 6 a.m. For me, it was torture, and I felt hate for anything that breathed that early in the morning. Hugo would graciously wake up with the kids and take care of them until I was ready to join the living at a saner hour.

Hugo could wake up early so easily that he joined a men's Bible study that met at 6 a.m. I thought he was insane, but whenever we were in Hays he met this "Men's Fraternity" every Tuesday. The Tuesday before my birthday that year, Hugo went to early Bible study. I got up with the kids and was waiting for him to come home. I felt like it was taking forever. I finally got frustrated waiting and called his cell phone.

"Where are you?" I demanded.

"I'm working on something, but I will be home really soon."

I could tell he had a legitimate excuse, so I didn't even question him about it when he got home.

Two days later, on my birthday, he gave me three cards and told me, "At Bible study the other day, the speaker told us, 'Men, when you give your wife a card, don't just sign the bottom. Write something meaningful' So after the study I bought three cards. Then I went to McDonald's and wrote on them. I saw Pastor Ken and some other friends there, and they asked me to join them for breakfast, but I showed them the cards and told them I had homework to do. They understood what I meant."

I opened each card carefully. There was a baby shower card, thanking me for having and loving Layla in several sentences. There was a birthday card from Mattias and Layla, which had a short paragraph written to me on behalf of both kids. Then, as I started to open the last card, he also put a gift on my lap. I smiled, and he smiled his huge little boy smile back. I opened the card and slowly read his beautiful words. I opened the gift and was surprised to see a pair of designer sunglasses that I had been drooling over for weeks.

"Hugo, this is a true gift, because it is something I would never buy for myself. Thank you. I love them so much."

"Well, you're welcome, but I did find a good deal online, so I saved us money too."

"Good job. You're so smart with computer stuff," I said.

"I know. And humble too." Hugo laughed.

Two weeks later, Hugo flew with my brother Mark to the Dominican Republic. Hugo helped with interpreting as he had the year before. Mark got wrangled into shooting video with an expensive, professional camera, as well as helping out with a lot of media stuff for SCORE. The two guys were bedding down in our apartment for the week and getting lots of bonding time.

Hugo was on cloud nine back on the mission field. He tried to Skype with us when he was available. He told me once, "I just wish you could come here with the kids. It is great to be back here at home, and I wish I didn't have to leave again. I know we'll be here again at the beginning of next year, but I just can't wait to be back on the mission field. This is what God has made me for. I love it."

The next day, I had just laid Layla and Mattias down for their naps when I got a call on our cell phone. I looked at the caller ID, and it read "Laptop." This meant that our Skype phone was ringing, but Hugo had not picked it up in the DR, so it had automatically forwarded to our cell phone in Kansas. I figured it was Hugo's family wanting to catch up on life. I answered cheerily in Spanish and was surprised to hear Hugo's brother-in-law on the other end. Normally only Irma or his sisters called us.

Roberto was not calling to chit-chat. "Sarah ... Cesia is okay, but she was in a car accident." My heart froze, waiting to hear all the details. He slowly continued, "Tito was in the car, too." His voice broke. "Tito died." I felt a stab in my heart. Oh no. Not this. Poor Cesia.

"We are not sure of all the details, but Irma and Febe are going to fly to Argentina to be with Cesia. Apparently her elbow is crushed, and she needs surgery. Please, if you could contact Hugo and let him know." I could barely breathe, but I managed to respond in Spanish, "Okay, I will." We hung up.

I called Mom and told her the horrible news. I was upset and crying.

"I'll be right home, honey. Just relax and try to think of how to get hold of Hugo."

By the time Mom arrived, I had concocted a plan to get in touch with Hugo. "I have to call the SCORE office and get Tim's Skype number. Then he can call Hugo's Dominican cell phone and tell him to call me. I can't just call Hugo's cell phone, because I don't know how."

"Okay, sounds like a plan. Go for it," Mom encouraged me.

I called SCORE, and they gave me two numbers. I left a message at the first number, and then reached Tim at the second number. "Tim, is Hugo with you?"

"No, I'm out at Highlands watching SCORE play baseball."

"Well, his brother-in-law died in a car accident, and I need to talk to him."

"Your brother is standing right here next to me."

"Okay, let me talk to him," I said. I waited for Mark to come on the line.

"You guys need to call Hugo and tell him to go back to our apartment and call me, if he can. Tito died in a car accident, and I need to tell him."

"Okay, I'll contact him. He'll call in less than an hour."

At this time, Hugo was driving out to the Highlands to join the baseball game. Mark called him and told him, "Sarah and the kids are all fine, but you need to go home and call her. Cesia is fine, but she was in an accident."

Hugo turned around and drove back to SCORE. Ryan met him at the gate. Hugo was starting to get a little worried, and he quickly ran upstairs to our apartment and called me.

"Hugo?"

"Yeah, it's me. What happened?

"I'm not sure of all the details, but there was a car accident. Cesia's elbow was crushed. Tito was driving, and he did not make it."

"Oh, no," he said. He was quiet for a while. He was breathing hard from running up the stairs. "Sarah, we have to pray hard for Cesia. This is either going to make her totally reject God or draw her closer. God saved her for a reason, and He has a good plan for her life, but I'm afraid she will blame God. We have to pray hard for her. I'm so sorry about Tito, though. He was a great man, and he loved Cesia so much. I'm glad that Carlos, Febe, and Daniela were just there last month. I'm sure Carlos preached to him a lot. I'm just sad that we don't know for sure that he was a Christian. He was very religious in his Catholic faith, but as far as I know he did not profess to believe that Christ died for him. I bet Cesia is so torn apart. That's just so sad. I am thankful God saved her, though."

"Well, are you going to be okay?"

"Yeah, Ryan is with me. I think I'm just going to go back out to the baseball field and play with the guys so I can relax a little bit."

"Okay. Let's Skype later."

"Okay, thanks for calling. Bye."

Hugo went back out to the field. My brother, Tim, and all the other guys knew by then, and they gave Hugo big manly hugs and encouraging slaps on the back. "We'll be praying for you, brother," they said.

That night, during the worship time, one of the songs was "Blessed be Your Name,"[1] by Matt Redman. This was one of Hugo's favorite songs to sing during SCORE nights, and he would always tell the kids, "Do you know these words come from the book of Job?"

But this time, the words hit Hugo so hard that tears ran down his face. Even though his heart felt great pain, Hugo still wanted to worship God for always being in control as he sang:

"Blessed be Your name
On the road marked with suffering
Though there's pain in the offering
Blessed be Your name"

Hugo also said a prayer for Cesia as he thought about the darkness she must be feeling at that moment. He sang and prayed for her that she would also be able to say,

"When the darkness closes in, Lord
Still I will say . . .
Lord, blessed be Your name"[1]

Dr. Bob noticed Hugo, and he moved from his seat across the aisle and put a strong arm around Hugo's shoulder. After the song, Hugo turned, said, "Thank you," and gave Dr. Bob a big bear hug.

Later, we found out the details of the accident. I called Febe and asked, "How did the accident happen? I've only read Argentine newspaper articles on the internet."

According to Febe, there were five adults in Tito's truck. They had gone to buy some furniture for Cesia's new business. Cesia sat in the middle in the back, which was unusual. She normally sat in the passenger seat up front, or behind Tito. Her friend Alejandra was to her right. An investor in the new business was to her left. A doctor friend of theirs occupied the front passenger seat.

It was dark, and they were in a hurry to transport everything to Pina Mar, where the business was located. Cesia asked Tito for his cell phone. He passed it to her, and she called Tito's mom, Maria Elvira.

Right then, Tito yelled, "Noooo!"

Cesia knew it was bad right away. She looked and saw a horse that had entered into their lane from the shoulder. She did not realize it at the time, but if Tito had hit the horse, Cesia would have been thrown through the front windshield and possibly killed. But Tito was a great driver, and he thought he could safely swerve around the horse and get back into his lane before the oncoming truck passed them. Tito swerved, missed the horse, and jerked the steering wheel back, but he didn't get over quickly enough. The truck passing them hit the back door on the driver's side. They went spinning.

When they finally stopped spinning, Cesia felt pressure on her left side. She realized that the business investor was partially on top of her. She rolled out from underneath him, and saw right away that he was dead. Two men helped her crawl out of the window of the truck. She held her arm, because she knew it was in bad shape. She looked back at the truck and saw Tito through the window. He was still looking forward, with his hands on the steering wheel.

She yelled to him, "Tito, just don't move. We've been in an accident, but don't move."

Their doctor friend, who had suffered minor injuries walked around to see about Tito. Cesia was now lying on the ground with her feet on the truck. Alejandra was there, too. She had a head injury, but was still alive.

Cesia heard the doctor yell, "No, Tito, no!"

Cesia did not understand it then, but Tito had died on impact. His body suffered very little injury, but the side of his head had struck the roll bar, and he was killed instantly.

Hugo had to block out his emotions about Tito and Cesia so he could finish his week with the energy that the baseball men needed from him. He and Mark made the best of the week. They had a productive time of ministry, and the baseball clinics again ministered to thousands of Dominican boys.

Hugo and I talked about him going to Tito's funeral in Argentina, but we knew Irma and Febe were planning on going and thought it was better just for the ladies to be together. When Hugo talked to Cesia on the phone she agreed. Mark and Hugo flew back to Mark's home in Oklahoma City, Oklahoma, and Hugo drove back to Kansas the next day. By the time Hugo made it home, I was ready to have him back. I had missed him so much.

We looked forward to Thanksgiving because my cousin Erica's baby, Morgan, had been born three weeks after Layla, and this was the first time we were going to have the babies together. All the families were really excited to see the baby cousins play together and dress alike, and to see how Mattias would respond to two babies.

Morgan was really a miracle, because Justin, Erica's husband, is a kidney transplant recipient and takes strong drugs to keep his body from rejecting the transplant. Doctors had told them for several years that there was not enough research to know if they could get pregnant, or if it would even be safe to get pregnant.

When Hugo and I found out we were pregnant with our second, Erica called her mom and cried, "Mom, I thought we'd be ready to have our first by the time Sarah had her second!" She was really distraught. Little did she know she was already pregnant. Then we found out we were both having girls about three weeks apart, and that made the deal even sweeter.

The scary thing that no one dared to talk about was that almost the same situation had happened with my mom and Erica's mom, Rachel. They were both pregnant at the same time, but when Rachel was about six months along, her baby boy, Jared, was born. He was underdeveloped and lived only three days. The whole family held their breaths as Erica and I went through our pregnancies. It was especially tough after Febe and Carlos lost their baby.

All that to say, this Thanksgiving Day was truly a thankful one. We all drove up to the Denver area, where Mom's mom and two sisters lived. We laughed, hung around the house, watched football, and played with babies. I felt as if Erica and I were playing house and bringing our dolls to play with. It was fun to talk about babies the whole time. Hugo entertained Mattias most of the day. We also went to Aunt Ronda's house to visit her and her husband, Mark. It was an awesome day because Mattias got to ride a horse and drive a tractor. Hugo got into the scoop of the tractor to record it on video, while Mark helped Mattias drive around the big yard. Good memories.

In December, Hugo and I decided to take the kids on a trip to Shelby, North Carolina. Our friends, Tim and Steve, lived there (they were the pastors who had purchased the new motorcycle for Pastor Aby). They had invited us to come, and we took them up on the offer. We flew with both the kids to Charlotte, and Tim picked us up and took us to a nice hotel. The room we got was amazing. It was like a honeymoon suite. It had a king-sized bed, a pull-out couch, a fake fireplace with a TV built into the wall over it, and a Jacuzzi tub in the main room. The Jacuzzi in the bathroom had a waterfall instead of a faucet.

Mattias said, "Wow! Mommy, look at this place."

"I know, Mattias." I said.

"Wow is right," Hugo said.

Mattias went right for the Jacuzzi, and I immediately stripped off his clothes and started the waterfall to fill up the tub. After he was done playing, I filled up a hot bath for myself and marveled at how nice it was to be in a Jacuzzi and watch TV with Hugo on the bed at the same time. I could get used to this.

Sunday at Bethel Baptist Church was awesome. We gave our testimonies and talked about what we did with SCORE in the Dominican Republic. Hugo and I wore our matching blue SCORE shirts. And Pastor Sims, like a good Southerner, knew how to preach!

Hugo leaned over to me and said, "Is there any way we can move here, just to go to church?"

I whispered back, "I know. Good, huh?"

On Monday, Pastor Steve took us to tour the Billy Graham Library. Reminiscent of Billy Graham's upbringing on a dairy farm on the outskirts of Charlotte, the library building was styled after a dairy barn, and his boyhood home had been restored a short walk from the main library building. It was really neat, more so than we expected, and Mattias loved the talking cow at the beginning of the tour.

That night, some of the teens from the mission trip that summer came for a reunion dinner and meeting. A lot of the kids had school functions and could not make it, but some of them skipped their regular activities so that they could be there. Hugo and I decided that I would give my testimony this time. So Hugo helped me prepare a PowerPoint presentation that even had a short interview with my parents at the end, talking about what it was like to trust God for that first mission trip I went on.

The presentation went really well. After I was done, Hugo preached a little about Caleb from the book of Numbers and how he stood alone for one night declaring that the Israelites could conquer the land God had given to them. The following morning Joshua also declared the truth that God would give them the land.

Pastor Steve also had us share some of the things we sacrificed to be on the mission field.

I gave some funny examples such as, "Lucky Charms are too expensive to buy and, most times there is no good internet service." But I also shared some serious ones including "missing holidays with my family."

Then Pastor Steve said something that struck a chord deep within me. He asked the teens, "What would you give up? What would you give up to rub shoulders closer with your Jesus?"

After our return to Kansas, lots of activities kept life busy, yet fun. Remember I said that when I was 29 this man, Hugo, changed my life's direction again? Within the next week, my life would change dramatically.

On Wednesday of the week, Hugo got his first job. Now that he had his residency and Social Security number, he could finally work. He interpreted for one of my mom's co-workers and a Latina woman who needed some help with her son. The meeting was about two hours long.

On Thursday, December 17th, Hugo said, "Let's buy our tickets back home to the DR today!"

"Okay," I said, and we spent most of the day looking for tickets. It was an exciting day for us. We could not wait to get back on the mission field

On Friday, Hugo and I took Layla to practice for the living nativity that would be performed with a reading on Christmas Eve at our church. Hugo and I were going to be Joseph and Mary, and Layla would be baby Jesus. After practice, the North Oak church youth group had its white elephant gift exchange.

Hugo was his normal crazy self, trying to make the night interesting for everyone. Someone opened a fuzzy black monkey that squeaked. Hugo immediately put all his efforts into trying to steal the monkey and end up with it at the end of the game.

Somehow he managed to secure his treasure, and, to be sure that no one would steal it back, he unzipped his coat and stuffed the monkey in.

All the teens complained, "Hugo's cheating!" But they laughed, and the game was the funniest it had ever been because of Hugo and his obsession for this black monkey. We all had a blast, and Hugo got to take his monkey home.

On Saturday, Hugo and I were inspired to go on a date. The church had blessed us with a $25 gift certificate to a local restaurant, and one of mom's friend's had given us movie passes at a baby shower gift back in October.

We were itching to get back to "us," especially after so much traveling, raising support, time apart, and having Layla. We needed to reconnect. The problem was that Dad and Mom had a Christmas party to go to and our normal babysitter, Jackie, had a birthday party that night. Our other option, Katherine, lived out of town, and it was kind of a last-minute plan. But we really wanted to go out, so we tried her anyway.

She said, "I have to work, but I'll try to get off so I can babysit. I love your kids."

I thought for a moment and said, "Well, that is up to you, but you don't need to do that. We can just go on Monday."

Katherine responded, "I'll call you right back and let you know."

We hung up, and five minutes later she called back. "I can't do it. The girl who would cover for me can't do it tonight. But my mom and I were talking, and my mom said that she wouldn't mind driving into Hays to babysit for you guys."

Katherine's mom, Anita, was a good friend of my mom, but it seemed really weird to ask her to drive so far to be with the kids, especially when Hugo and I could just wait until Monday and have Dad and Mom watch the kids. I looked over at Hugo, and it was obvious that he wanted to go out this night so badly.

I said, "Yes. Tell your mom thank you, and we'll see her soon."

Anita showed up a couple hours later, and Hugo and I were dressed up and ready for a special night out. We drove to the restaurant. We were already a little behind schedule because we had given so many directions to Anita, so we needed to eat quickly to make it to the movie. We were going to see "The Twilight Saga: New Moon." Hugo had a thing for vampires, so he wanted to see lots of action scenes between the vampires and werewolves.

One step into restaurant, and we knew we were in trouble. It was packed with people. But we wanted to use our gift card, and our taste buds were already set on dining at that restaurant.

I asked the host, "What is the wait time? Do you think we have enough time to be seated, get our food, and make it to the 7:30 p.m. movie?"

"Well, it will be tight, but if you sit at the bar, you can be seated and order right away."

Hugo and I looked at each other. The thought had never occurred to us. This was a family restaurant, and we always had kids with us when we were there, so we'd never really noticed the bar. The thought seemed freeing and attractive.

Hugo and I came to the same decision without even talking. "Great!" we said together. We sat next to each other at the bar, and the waiter behind the bar took our food order. I looked over at the TV screen close to us on the right. It was basketball, our favorite sport. I looked at the score. "Hey, Hugo, your team is playing."

"Yeah, go Memphis!" This was a joke that Hugo had kept up since March Madness years before. Once Kansas was out of the NCAA tournament, Hugo decided that Memphis was his team. Not because he knew anything about them, but because he liked to say the word "Memphis!" He still cheered for Memphis when the team was on TV. The game was really close, and it was fun to watch while we ate good food and chatted.

Sitting at the bar provided an intimate shoulder-to-shoulder closeness. Our bodies touched, and our heads leaned together as we reconnected. It was a different sort of date than we'd ever had. We went to the movie and were just in time.

"Twilight" was much more romantic than Hugo thought it was going to be. As we walked hand-in-hand to the car, Hugo said, "Well, the book was better." This was always our big joke after a movie, because we both knew that Hugo hardly read books, but it was something other people were always saying. We both laughed. He also complained, "I think I need to go watch "Gladiator," or do something manly." It was a great night, and only cost us $5 for a tip at restaurant, so we were excited about that, too.

Sunday we left early in Dad's new truck. We were all going to Butterfield Baptist Church in Coldwater, Kansas, for our last church visit. The pastor and his wife were long-time friends of my parents. We wanted to share with them about SCORE in hopes that the church would get involved more in missions.

It was a long three-hour drive, especially because Mom's hip started hurting, and my back was not reacting well to sitting in the middle in the front. With two car seats in the back of the cab, it was a snug ride. During the service, Hugo and I both shared, and then Hugo preached. He did a great job. I was so proud of him. We spent some time after the service with people who were interested in missions. It was such a nice country church. The church and the parsonage were the only buildings around.

On the ride home, we decided that Hugo would sit in the front in the middle, because neither Mom nor I could handle sitting on the bump any longer. So, Hugo and Dad ended up next to each other, and I sat next to Hugo in the front. Like a little kid, Hugo had to touch all the buttons on the new truck.

It was kind of annoying me, and I halfheartedly complained, "Stop pushing all the buttons."

Then he found out you could talk to the truck. He pulled the vehicle instructions out of the glove compartment and handed them to me.

"Tell me how I talk to it." He did not read instructions, but he knew I was good at figuring out things with directions in hand. I humored him and found the page about voice-activated commands. I read through it aloud.

Hugo pushed a button and said, "Radio."

The female voice in the truck asked, "Did you say, 'Line in?'"

"No," Hugo responded. Hugo and the female voice in the truck went around and around, getting nowhere. Hugo did not give up on electronic problems very easily, and he persisted in trying to figure out how to use this cool tool. I was getting more and more upset and annoyed. When someone does the same thing over and over, it drives me crazy.

But in the end, the truck won. Frustrated, Hugo started speaking Spanish really fast. When he stopped his Spanish ranting, he leaned back into his seat, dejected.

A few moments passed, and then the female voice in the truck said, "Did you say 'line in?'" We all laughed.

Monday, December 21ˢᵗ, was Mom's first day off work for winter break, so she went out shopping. Hugo got up with the kids so I could sleep late. They seemed to be doing well, because I did not hear any cries coming from upstairs. I went up at about 8:45 a.m. and Hugo was sitting in the pink rocker.

I kneeled on the floor and nuzzled my nose into his warm neck. "I love you, Teddy."

"I love you, too, Koala," he said, kissing me on the eyebrow.

"I have a physical therapy appointment for my back this morning, and I'll be back about eleven."

"Okay, great. That will be perfect, because I'm playing basketball at noon," he said.

"Yeah, but you have to work hard on the prayer cards while I'm gone, so that we can get them printed soon and have them ready for when we go back in January."

"I'm on it," he said, and soon I left for physical therapy.

When I returned, he sat me down at the computer and showed me all the progress he had made with different designs and ideas for the prayer cards. Plus, he had a phone number for a church we had a connection with that could possibly print them more cheaply.

"You just have to call them and ask for information on how much it would cost. I wanted you to do the calling because your English is better, and you will understand all the details."

"Okay, I'll call them right now." He had gotten a lot done, and I wanted to keep up the pace. I really wanted to get this done today.

He charged downstairs to change into his basketball clothes. He liked to be there early, so he could be in the first group of guys to play. He wasn't part of an organized team; he just liked to play pick-up ball with friends. He had only been able to go once or twice since he got back from the Dominican Republic.

As he ran downstairs, I dialed the phone number. Layla was napping and Mattias was walking around in a diaper, trying to keep up with Hugo. We were so close to making some decisions on these prayer cards, and we were running out of time. I thought, "I really should ask him to stay home from basketball, because we've got to finish this." But I knew he was so excited to get out, and I just didn't have the heart to ask him to stay.

I was now talking to a guy on the phone about the cards. I heard Hugo double step up the stairs, grab his coat, and yell, "Bye!"

I put my hand over the phone and shouted, "Bye!"

The office door slammed shut at the same time. Mattias came running to me, crying because Daddy had left. His little diaper sagged as he ran.

"It's okay, Matti. Daddy will be right back. He went to play basketball," I said, trying to console him and talk on the phone. Layla was starting to stir; she'd be hungry soon.

Family picture in front of new slide and play fort (Hays, KS 2009).
L-R; Dad, Mom, Mattias, Sarah, Hugo, Anne, & Mark

Daddy Hugo totally in love with his beautiful baby girl, Layla Elizabeth, born October 16, 2009

Sarah and Hugo take Layla, when she is 3 days old,
to the pumpkin patch for a new family picture.

Grandpa Breeden's family. He is in the middle. Grandpa's youngest daughter,
Karen, is front left. In back, by couples, are Carolyn and her husband, Ron;
Mark and Anne; David and Debbie; Hugo holding Mattias and
Sarah holding Layla.

Christmas family portrait taken on November 29, 2009 at Mt. Pleasant Church near Quinter, Kansas. Hugo and Sarah had just shared about their ministry with SCORE International. L-R are Sarah, Layla, Mattias, and Hugo

Last family picture taken to create new prayer cards to include Layla's addition to the family. December 17, 2009.

Please visit my website, www.my-onceuponatime.com/, to see more pictures and videos from each chapter.

Chapter Fourteen

And They Lived Happily
Ever After? – The Twist
December 2009

Kansas

The phone rings just as I finish nursing Layla, so I tell Mattias, "Get the phone and give it to me, please." Being the good helper that he is, he happily runs and gets the phone for me. By the time he brings it to me, the phone has rung three times, and now I am standing, Layla still in my arms.

I hear Mom enter through the office and yell her usual, "Hi, I'm home!" just as I click the "on" button.

"Hi, this is Sarah."

"Hello, this is Mark, your mom's boss. I play basketball here downtown with Hugo."

I glance at the clock. It is just now noon; they couldn't be playing yet. Hugo forgot the cell phone, and I wonder what he needs.

"Okay," I say.

"Hugo just had a seizure, and you need to come down to the basketball court."

I drop to my knees. I still have Layla in my arms. I look to see if I have dropped her, but I have not. She has already fallen asleep.

My mind is already reeling. First I think, this is horrible. Then, it is just a seizure; people survive those all the time. Then, our flight to the DR is already booked, and we'll have to postpone our trip, because Hugo is going to have medical check-ups. Annoying but, God, we can do this; just one step at a time.

I feel like what is happening is surreal, but I am aware that Mark is still talking, and I try to listen to figure out my first step. Tears have started to fall, but I bat them away and swallow the fear in my throat. Now is no time to panic; my husband needs me. I have to focus. I listen intently.

"Just be careful and drive to the basketball court. We've already called the ambulance."

"Okay, I'm coming."

Mom already knows something was wrong by the time she gets to me. I click the phone off and say, "Hugo's at basketball, and he had a seizure." My voice cracks and I start to cry again. "I have to go now."

"Okay. He is going to be okay. Give me Layla."

I hand her Layla and focus my mind again. Stay calm, I tell myself. He's going to be okay. It's just a seizure.

I grab my winter coat and sprint downstairs to get Hugo's wallet. I know we'll need his ID and insurance card at the hospital. I know he left it in his jeans when he changed to go to the court. I unclip the chain from his jeans and stuff it in my pocket. I take two steps at a time and take the only car available, Mom's.

I force myself not to think about anything on the drive there. I know Hugo will be okay. But the five-minute drive feels like an eternity, so my mind wanders. This is bad timing, with Christmas around the corner, and we're leaving for the Dominican Republic soon, but these things can't be helped. Poor Hugo; he is going to feel so bad that this messes up our plans for going back.

I stop at a stop sign, and the car in front of me wants to turn left. He has not left space for me to turn right. I am so close to the basketball court, and starting to get really anxious. Hurry, hurry, hurry! Oh my gosh, turn already! I think about honking, but try to be patient. There is no need to hurry; Hugo is going to be fine. The car in front of me finally turns, and I quickly turn right. I speed as much as I dare on 13th Street, and cross Main, Fort, and Ash Streets, barely stopping at the stop signs at Fort and Ash. I whip into a parking spot behind my Dad's truck, so I know Mom must have gotten hold of Dad. His office is only blocks away.

I jog quickly into the 12th Street Hays Recreation Center gym. As I cross the court, in my peripheral vision, I see a dozen other basketball players standing to the right of the gym watching, but my eyes are only for Hugo. The EMT's already have him on the gurney.

"She's his wife," I hear Dad say behind me, as I put my head close to Hugo's and start to talk to him. I had not seen Dad, but I am glad he is here.

"Hey, Hugo. I'm here. Mattias and Layla are with Grandma. I'm here with you. You're going to be okay. I love you, honey," I say to him. I want to help him relax and know that I am taking care of him. I look up at the two EMT's. They know I want answers.

"We are breathing for him right now. He stopped breathing for a short time. Now he is taking breaths on his own, but his breaths are irregular, so we are going to help him out. He has not regained consciousness yet, but he is stable enough to transport him to the hospital. Would you like to go with us?"

"Yes, of course." I kneel down and talk to Hugo again.

"Okay, babe. We are going to the hospital. I'm going to ride with you. Everything is going to be okay. Just relax. I love you."

They wheel him out. I turn and hand my car keys to Dad. Someone else hands him Hugo's jacket, street shoes, and car keys. I look at Dad.

"I'll meet you there," he says.

Jeff, a friend of Hugo's from basketball, gives me a big hug. "Let me know how it goes. We'll be praying."

"Thank you," is all I can manage, and I walk out to the ambulance.

I have to sit up front, but I look back at Hugo as much as I can. I look at his orange basketball shoes and think that he must have just changed into them. One of his arms comes free from the gurney restraints, and it flops powerless to the floor. Seeing his body without any control switches something in me, and I feel fear creeping up.

The EMT at the back of the ambulance with Hugo keeps shouting, "Hugo! Hugo, can you hear me? Open your eyes for me."

"God help him to be okay," I pray silently. Hugo would hate to be disabled from this. He is so active and strong.

The ambulance parks near the emergency room. I get out quickly, but I can only stand by helplessly while the EMT's pull Hugo out of the back. I talk to him so he knows what is going on.

"We're at the hospital. They are going to check you out and see what is wrong. You're going to be fine. Everything is okay."

A nurse tells me, "I need to get your information while they check him over. Just follow me to the waiting room."

"Okay." I watch them wheel Hugo into the emergency room. I pull the wallet from my coat and give the nurse Hugo's license and insurance card.

The nurse continues to ask me questions and then finally says, "I'm going to make a copy of this card. So please wait for the ER doctor here in the waiting room."

He opens the door to a deserted waiting room. I start to pace and think. Focus. What needs to be done? I need Mom. She is great with medical questions and words. She has to be here now! I whip out my cell phone and call her.

"Mom, you have to call Jackie to come baby sit the kids now. I need you here!"

"Okay. Dad's here. I'll leave the kids with him until Jackie comes." Even though Dad said he would meet me at the hospital, he knew I really needed Mom's help and support, and he would have to give her the truck and take the kids until someone else could come and watch them.

"Fine, just get here now."

"I'm on my way."

We hang up, and I keep pacing. What next? What do I have to do? Call Hugo's mom. How? Hugo calls her through Skype, and I can receive Skype phone calls on my cell because they are forwarded from the computer to my cell phone, but how can I call them? Think, Sarah, think. There is a way to let Hugo's family know; you just have to think of it. What is taking them so long? I want to see Hugo.

The nurse that took the insurance card returns. He hands me the card. I ask, "What are they doing? Why is it taking so long? Can I be with Hugo?"

"The doctor will be in soon to talk with you. It takes time to evaluate him and prep him for what needs to be done. If he is not breathing on his own, they have to intubate him, and they also need to put in a catheter." He gives me a sympathetic look and leaves.

I am alone again. "God, please," I pray, "please let Hugo be okay." Right now, I don't believe his life is in danger. I'm considering the possible effects of this incident on his quality of life. "Please, God. Please."

I am watching out the window for my mom. I want her to know where I am. I see Ken Ediger, the senior pastor from our church, and I'm impressed that he got here so quickly. But then I think, if it is so serious that Pastor Ken had to leave work, it must be more serious than I think.

Mom arrives moments later. "Hi, honey." She gives me a big hug. I start to cry. I am getting frustrated with waiting. There is no one around to answer my questions.

"I've been waiting for so long and I don't know what is going on. They're prepping him, I guess, like cutting his clothes off. Stuff they didn't want me to see, but they are taking a long time."

"It's going to be fine. Hugo's going to be fine. People have seizures all the time and are okay. Just relax." We sit and wait together.

Finally, a doctor comes in with another nurse. "Well, it looks like Hugo's had a seizure of some sort, but we are still not really sure what is going on. Can you tell me what happened?"

I start telling him what I overheard from the basketball men.

"He was sitting on the floor against a wall, and then he just slumped over and started to have a seizure. He had not even started stretching or running yet. The ambulance came a few minutes later. He was not breathing normally by then."

The doctor thinks for a moment, then asks, "Did he hit his head at all?"

"Not that I know of. He was sitting down and just slumped over." I'm feeling confused. Why don't they know what's going on? It was just a simple seizure; just do some test and give him medicine.

"We are going to have to run some tests. We just don't know what caused this. We are breathing for him, and we had to put him on a drug to relax him so he won't fight the tube in his throat. But you can be with him while we do the tests."

Mom and I follow the doctor and nurse back into Hugo's room. He now has an IV with several bags, a catheter, and breathing tubes. It's the first time mom has seen him, so her first impression shows her denial. I can see it on her face: Why does he have breathing tubes? He does not need breathing tubes. What are they doing?

I instinctively reach for Hugo's hand and start to talk to him again.

"Hey, honey. I'm back. You're doing great! Everything is going to be okay. Just relax. They just have to run some tests and figure out what's wrong. I love you so much, and the kids love you so much. We need you, so you have to fight and be strong."

I lean close to his face as I speak to him, and caress his check. His whiskers are scruffy because he has been growing them out so he can play Joseph for the church service. I hope he'll be okay in time for the New Year's Eve service. I snuggle my head next to his on the pillow.

"I love you, Hugito." I kiss his nose and the corner of his mouth. The tubes do not permit me to kiss his lips. I look at his closed eyes, and I can see tears. I feel like he can hear me, and I know that he is afraid. Afraid of what is going on and why he cannot move or communicate. Afraid of not being able to take care of me and the kids properly.

"It's okay, Hugo. God is with us. He will take care of you. Just relax."

The nurse comes back in. He is busy doing lots of things around us. He starts to talk to the heart technician that has been called to do the angiogram of Hugo's heart.

"Should we do the heart sonogram first, or the CAT scan of his brain?" the nurse asks the technician.

"Well, I could wait, if you need me to."

"How long will it take you?"

"About twenty minutes," the technician says.

"I guess you're already here."

"But I can wait. It is your call."

"No. You go ahead. Do the heart sonogram first and then we'll take him to do the CAT scan."

The technician starts his process, and twenty minutes later he tells us, "His heart is only pumping at 35 percent, and it needs to be up around 60 percent."

The doctor thinks out loud. "He must have suffered some sort of heart attack or a stroke. Either could have caused his heart to not work properly." He looks at Mom and me. "We need to send him to Wichita by Life Flight. A specialist will have to look at him, since he is so young. He is going to need a lot of special care."

I don't know what the doctor means by, "He is going to need a lot of special care," but I don't understand much of anything that's happening right now. Everything seems to be a whirlwind of activity. I think about the Life Flight to Wichita. I feel sad because Hugo probably won't remember the flight, and it will be such a unique experience. Neither of us has ever ridden in a helicopter. He will be so mad when he finds out we flew in a helicopter, and we both missed it completely, him for lack of consciousness, and me because of all my worry.

The nurses tell me that if I'm going with him, I have fifteen minutes to go home and pack. I do not want to leave, but Mom and I start to plan. I dictate to her, and she takes notes on a scrap of paper. I tell her the clothes and necessities that I need and then say, "You'll have to bring Layla with you, because I have to be able to nurse her."

"Okay. I talked to Jeff and Jessica, and they said they could watch Mattias."

"Yes, that's fine. Go home and start packing. I'll wait here and go with Hugo."

"Pastor Jeff is going to stay with you until you leave."

"Okay, love you. See you soon. Drive safe." Mom and Dad leave to pack.

Jeff and I stand in the doorway as the EagleMed team comes in and starts to prep Hugo for the Life Flight to Wichita. It will be a 45-minute flight in a small airplane.

In the ambulance on the way to the airport, I take the time to make a few phone calls. I call the SCORE International office and tell them that Hugo has collapsed from a possible heart attack, and needs lots of prayer. I call my best friend, Danielle, and tell her to contact all our friends to have them praying, too. While doing this, I am still wracking my brain to figure out how I could can Hugo's family in El Salvador. They have to know what is going on. I take a deep breath and try to think. Hugo always accuses me of being a detective, and I am trying to use those skills to solve my problem.

"Roberto," I say to myself.

Jeff overhears me and says, "What?"

"To contact Hugo's family, I can call Roberto in Houston, and he can call his brother Carlos and tell him to call me on my Skype phone, which will forward to my cell phone. I can't call them, but they can call me."

"Right. Okay. Do you have Roberto's phone number?"

"Yes, it's right here." I scroll through the R's and click on his name.

I explain the situation with Hugo to him, and he promises me, "I will call Carlos and Febe. Don't worry about us. I will have Carlos call you in an hour or so."

"Thank you, Roberto, for your help."

"No problem. Don't worry. We'll be praying."

The EagleMed flight team has Hugo ready to go, and I follow them to the ambulance. I call my brother on the way to the airport. He already knows because Dad had called him, but I need to hear his voice.

"Hi, Sis," he says. "How's he doing?"

"They say it is his heart. We are flying to Wichita now."

"Really? I haven't told Anne yet because she's at work, but I think I'll just go get her and we'll come to Wichita."

"Just talk to Dad and Mom and decide. Whatever you think is best. I'll call you when we know more."

"Okay, we're praying for you. Love you."

"Love you too, Mark." I hang up and quietly cry for the last few minutes before we get to the airport.

This is the first moment I've been able to sit and breathe since everything started. "God," I pray, "please heal Hugo's body and let him not have any permanent effects from this." The thought of him not surviving has not entered my mind yet, but at this point my mind briefly touches on the thought. However, I quickly dismiss it, knowing that I'm getting ahead of myself. "God, help him to be okay," is all that I can say.

We arrive at the Hays Municipal Airport, drive onto the tarmac, and park next to a small plane. The pilot gets in first, and then emergency workers push the specialized gurney up to the right side of the plane. The pilot comes back to help and pulls at the front end of the gurney, which slides into place. Stairs are brought out so I can board, followed by the EagleMed workers. The three of us sit next to each other on a bench that runs the length of the small plane.

Hugo is directly across from me. Our knees touch his gurney. His head is close enough that I can touch his face and talk to him. The pilot is to my left, and I watch closely as he works the controls and looks at the gauges. I want to remember every detail of this flight, so I can tell it all to Hugo later.

I look at him. His head slid off the pillow during takeoff, so once we level off I lean over and carefully push his head back into a comfortable position. I try to talk to him in his ear again, but I know he can't hear me over the noise of the plane. I hold the side of his face, so he can be comfortable. I trace his eyebrows gently with my finger. They are so soft.

The flight is fast, and soon we land. We take another ambulance to a Wichita hospital. I get nervous as I see a huge line of cars. There has been an accident in a construction zone, and traffic is backed up. The ambulance driver pulls up to the first policeman that is directing traffic and tells him, "We have a code blue. We need to get through."

The police officer nods, waves us on, and starts to radio other police officers directing traffic in front of us. I'm grateful to know that the traffic jam won't slow us down too much, but I'm also confused and worried. What the heck does "code blue" mean? Then the woman in the back starts to ask the driver where the spare oxygen is. Why did he not check the oxygen and make sure it was full? I'm still trusting that this isn't a big deal, but it sounds like a big deal.

When we get to the hospital, the ambulance driver looks at me and says, "Well, I got us here. It wasn't my best run, but we're here."

I mumble something about, "I didn't notice," but I'm thinking, "Are you insane? My husband is in bad shape, and I'm scared, nervous, and worried. Do you think I really care about your driving, or want to talk to you at all?" But I know that although this is one of the worst days of my life, it's just another day at work for him.

We go to the cardiac unit on the third floor. Again, they make me wait in the waiting room while they move him from bed to bed and get all the tubes and IV's hooked up again. I'm all alone. There's another man in the waiting room, but my family, my kids, and my friends are not here yet.

In these moments, deep meaningful prayers are hard to form, so all I can pray is, "God, heal Hugo. Please protect him. Give the doctors wisdom and heal him." I repeat variations of this prayer for twenty minutes. I have to go to the bathroom, but I don't want to miss the nurse coming to find me.

I ask the other guy in the room, "If they come looking for me, could you tell them I'm in the bathroom?"

"Sure, what's your name?"

"Sarah."

In the bathroom, I look in the mirror. I still have on my exercise clothes from physical therapy, with my hair in a ponytail and puffy eyes. I look horrible. Well, Dad and Mom will be here soon with my stuff. I'll be able to shower and look nice for when Hugo wakes up.

I go back to the waiting room, nod a "thanks" to the guy, and try to be patient. Finally, a nurse comes to take me back to Hugo's room. Hugo's whole body is shaking a lot, and when he breathes the shaking gets worse. I ask the nurse, "Is he cold or what's wrong? Why is he breathing like that?"

"The relaxant drug is wearing off, and he is fighting the breathing machine and tubes. It's good that he is trying to take breaths on his own, but he still needs help. I'm waiting for the doctor to sign off on another dose of relaxant."

I know my husband, and I know him well. I know what he's thinking or feeling in each situation. I remember Hugo's strong gag reflex. Knowing that and reading his body language, I can tell he's afraid of choking on the tubes. I put my right arm across his chest, lean over, and snuggle my head next to his as best as I can.

"Hi. I'm back. You're doing really good, babe. I'm so proud of you. Just try to relax. Don't fight the tubes. Just relax. They will give you more drugs soon to help you, but you need to calm down." I massage his arm and his shoulder jerks. I hold his hand.

"Honey, can you squeeze my hand?" I want to know he can hear me. I wait.

Nothing.

"Can you open your eyes? Can you wake up?" I watch his eyelids intently, trying to see if his eyes are moving under his eyelids.

Nothing.

"It's okay, Hugo," I say, as I lean over to talk in his ear. "You're doing a great job. Just fight really hard, okay? Mattias and Layla and I need you. We love you so much. Layla is coming here soon, and Mattias is going to stay overnight with Pastor Jeff. They love you and I love you. You're going to be okay."

I study his face. I want to remember every detail. I see tiny tears pooling again in the corners of his eyes. I know he heard me, but I think he felt helpless to respond. His head moves toward me. I pray it's because he heard my voice.

"I'm still here," I say. "Hugo, I see your tears. I know you can hear me. I love you too, and we are going to get through this together. Don't be afraid. Just relax and fight."

Soon Normadine, a friend from church, shows up. She was at the hospital in Wichita visiting other family. My pastors knew about her trip and called her right away to come over and be with me. Normadine prays over Hugo and me, and I feel better now that she's there.

She also introduces me to our associate pastor's son-in-law. "Sarah, this is Levi, Pastor John's son-in-law."

"Hi, it's nice to meet you." I'm a little confused why they've sent a stranger to hang out with me. Or why he even wants to be here. I do not want to meet more people right now.

But Levi explains, "I met Hugo at the men's retreat in September and got to know him. I was impressed with how he led worship and his passion for life and having fun. When I heard, I knew that I had to be here. I will serve you in any way you need. I know Hugo would do the same for me. Have you had lunch?"

"No, I have not eaten today."

"Well, it's about 3 p.m., so you need to eat. I'll go get you a sandwich."

"Okay," I say. And with that, Levi is off.

Normadine and I talk, pray together, and pray over Hugo. We claim God's healing and God uses her to comfort my heart. I truly believe that Hugo will be fine.

The doctor comes in and finally approves the drugs Hugo needs to be calm again and not fight the breathing tubes and machine. I am grateful that Hugo seems more relaxed, and his body is not shaking as much. I massage his legs and feet. Hugo loves it when I massage his feet.

The cardiologist explains, "Hugo's heart is not pumping blood correctly, and we might have to put a pacemaker into him. It would sit right under the skin, and if this happened again, it would shock his heart and save his life. He would have to wear it for about six months and then we'd re-examine him and take it out. Right now, we need him to be sleeping, but maybe tomorrow we can wake him up."

I nod as the doctor leaves and I'm left to my thoughts again. My first thought is "Whew, they are making him sleep. He is going to be awake tomorrow." Then I think, "God this really messes up our plans to go back to the DR. We are going to be in the States for a while, and then if we do go, we'll probably have to come back a lot for tests and check-ups. God, I don't see how this is a good plan for our family, but together we can do this. Everything is going to work out fine. I know I need to relax and take this one step at a time. What do I need to do next? Layla. I need to ask the nurses where I can breastfeed Layla, or pump, or something. This is going to be an extra stress, but she needs to eat."

I observe the nurse checking Hugo's vitals. She looks Latina. She looks at me and I say, "You can talk to him in Spanish. He's from El Salvador." She smiles at me and softly tells him in Spanish everything she's doing.

When she is done I say, "My baby girl is going to be here soon, and I need a place to nurse her. Can you help me?"

"You cannot nurse her on this floor because of swine flu and other diseases that are more of a risk on this floor. You can do it in the pediatric ward, though. I will call down there and ask if they have a quiet room available for you and if you can borrow a pump. I will ask the maternity ward to get the sterile kit that works with the pump. That way, you can pump and someone else can feed your baby in a safer location."

"Thank you. That sounds like a good plan."

Levi has come back with my sandwich, and I try desperately to eat. I know I will need my energy today. Every bite is so hard to swallow. My throat feels tight and dry, despite the bottled water Levi brought. I slowly choke down half the sandwich and promise myself I will finish the other half soon. I look at Hugo. I can't believe this is happening. I stand and cross the room again to be next to him. I kiss his cheek.

"You're doing great, honey. I love you so much. Dad and Mom are going to be here soon and Layla is coming with them."

I talk to Hugo off and on for two more hours. It feels as if time has stopped. I feel someone watching us, and I look up.

Dad is there. I am so glad to see him. He gives me a big hug. "Mom's here. She has Layla in the waiting room."

I rush to the waiting room. My heart wants to hold Layla so much that my arms ache. When I get there, my mom hands her to me. I wrap my arms under Layla and all around her; I hold her tightly to my chest and tuck her head under my chin. It feels so good to hold her, like when it is stifling hot in a room and someone opens the door to let in a cool breeze. I start to cry.

Layla is only 2 ½ months old, and I know she cannot understand me, but it still hurts me to tell her about her daddy. I whisper in her ear, "Layla, Daddy is very sick, and he is not doing well. His heart is not working right. But, don't worry. Daddy loves you, and he is very strong. Just pray for him, my little baby, pray for Daddy."

Mom speaks. "The nurses told us that Layla is not permitted on this floor at all. It is dangerous to her health. She shouldn't even be in the waiting room as soon as we can figure out a plan. Levi went out to help Mark and Anne park and show them where we are. They will be up here soon."

I nurse Layla and watched her beautiful face. Just holding her helps me to relax and refocus my emotions. Mark and Anne appear in the doorway of the waiting room. I give Layla to Mom and give them both a big hug.

"Thank you for coming," I say. "Let's go and see Hugo."

Layla stays with Levi in the waiting room while the rest of us go to see Hugo and make a plan about spending the night. We need to decide on where and how I should feed the baby. I instinctively go to Hugo's side and start to talk to him again.

"I just nursed Layla. She is so beautiful. Just like you said on the day she was born, but she gets more beautiful every day. Mark and Anne are here now. We are trying to make a plan. You're doing great. I love you so much, and Mattias loves you and Layla loves you."

I look up at my family. Mom is the organizer, so she starts the brainstorming. The problem is, we all want to be up with Hugo, but someone has to watch Layla outside of the hospital.

Mom says, "Levi said he could take Layla to his house. He and his wife have an 8-month-old. He would come and get the bottles you pump, and then go back to his house and take care of her."

"No," I say, "we can do this."

In the end, we decide to get two rooms at the hotel across the street. Mom and Anne will take care of Layla for the most part, but the guys will help out too. I will go and pump first, and then they'll go settle in.

I ask at the nurses' station how to get to the pediatric section of the hospital. The nurse is very nice and starts to explain, "Actually, you need to go to the NICU. It is the ICU for babies. That is the best place, and they are expecting you. You go down this long hallway, then turn right and then left, then down the other long hallway, and then use the elevators to the right. Go up one floor and get off to the…it's really complicated. Maybe I should take you the first time."

My face must have indicated my confusion. With everything that is going on, my ability to think and navigate is low. She notifies the head nurse and walks with me.

She says, "So, you are a Christian?"

"Yes," I say, but I'm not sure what to add.

"I can tell. Your faith is really strong, and it is a testimony to the other people around, even if you don't know it."

"Good. I really trust God to heal Hugo. I have faith that he will be fine."

"I leave my shift soon, but I will keep praying for you."

"Thank you. I need it."

She rings a doorbell at the entrance for the NICU. A woman comes out with a professional breast pump. She leads me to a quiet room and helps me hook up the sterilized tubing and attachments. Again, my patience for complicated tasks is minimal, and I am grateful to have her help. She leaves me to have some privacy. I finish, and the first nurse walks me back. On the walk back, Carlos calls me.

"Hola, habla Carlos."

Whether or not I feel capable of deep thinking, I am going to have to force myself to understand and speak Spanish with Hugo's family. I bet they feel so helpless, and after just losing Tito, it is a scary time for them. I need to reassure them that everything is going to be okay.

I tell Carlos in Spanish, "The doctor told me Hugo had some sort of heart problem and they will have to monitor it for awhile. He has to sleep today, but hopefully tomorrow they can wake him up."

"We will keep praying. I am not going to tell Mom and Cesia in Argentina yet, because Cesia is still fragile from losing Tito. I will call back in a couple of hours to check up on the situation."

"Okay. I'm sorry I can't call you. There is no internet here that they will let me use to call you on Skype. You have to call me."

"It's okay. Don't worry about us. You take care of Hugo."

"Okay, talk to you soon."

The nurse takes the small bottles from me, labels them with Hugo's name and room number, and puts them in the refrigerator. Dad and Mom leave to get Layla settled in the hotel. Mom will feed her and get her to sleep, and then Dad will take over just watching her sleep in her travel box.

Shortly after they leave, a neurosurgeon arrives. He asks what happened, and I tell as much as I know. He pinches Hugo's right shoulder, and Hugo's hands curl into fists, and his arms draw up close to his body. The doctor pinches the other shoulder, and again Hugo shows signs of pain. The surgeon opens Hugo's eyelid and flashes a light into his eye. His pupil is dilated. No response. He then uses a sterile gauze pad to poke Hugo's eyeball. The eyelid twitches, indicating pain. He leans close to Hugo and says loudly, "Hugo, can you wake up? Can you hear me? Open your eyes for me."

I'm confused and I say, "I thought they drugged him to keep him asleep."

"No, I looked at his chart. He should be responding. He is on a very low dose of that drug. He should still be able to wake up. Let's go ahead and do the CAT scan."

He says it in such a casual way that Mark, Anne, and I think it must be a routine procedure, rather than a necessary one due to what the doctor found.

Soon a nurse comes in. "I'm here to take Hugo down to the CAT scan room."

"When we get back, could you check his temperature? His skin looks redder than usual." I put my hand on his forehead. "He seems warm to me."

"Sure. Do you three want to go with him to the exam?"

Mark, Anne, and I all follow Hugo's bed as the nurse wheels it down to the CAT scan room. We have to stay in a waiting room until he is finished, so Mark and Anne talk, and I call Mom to check on Layla. I feel that I just need to keep a level head and go through all the motions, and in the end it will be fine. I'll just keep praying and trusting God, and He'll provide the outcome He has planned. I don't pray specifically for the CAT scan. It's just routine, because they skipped it in Hays after the echo showed that his heart was bad. The problem is with his heart, so I don't think anything about this other test.

Once back in Hugo's room, Mark, Anne, and I are standing around Hugo, as if we're hanging out with our best friend, sometimes even laughing. I ask Mark if he's found a new job.

"Yeah, I think we are going to move to Tulsa, (Oklahoma), soon. I got a job in Tulsa, and they want me to start next Monday."

"Great! Hugo was so mad at your boss for firing you two weeks before Christmas. What a heartless jerk."

The mood is still lighthearted when a nurse comes in and hands me a portable phone from the nurses' station.

"Hello, this is Sarah."

"Yes, this is the neurosurgeon. I am looking at Hugo's CAT scan right now …"

"Okay," I say, not knowing where he is going.

"Well, it does not look good …"

Fear and panic strike my heart, but I do not want to jump to conclusions. "What does that mean?" I say calmly, but sternly. Mark comes over to stand close to me.

He says it again, "It does not look good …"

I raise my voice and cry into the phone, "What does that mean?"

"It means your husband has had a major brain aneurysm, and there is only a 20 percent chance that he will survive. If he does survive, he will be a vegetable."

"Oh, no … no, no …" All my strength leaves me, and I start to fall. I don't know what happens to the phone, or if the doctor is still talking. Mark catches me in his arms and starts to cry, too.

"What? What did he say?"

"He said Hugo is probably not going to make it."

I cry and cry. I weep harder than I ever have in my life. Mark just holds me until the nurse moves a chair close to us so I can sit down.

Anne rushes to call my parents and she tells them, "It is worse than we thought. You have to get back up here right away." Layla is having trouble falling asleep, so Mom just scoops her up and they run over.

As I sit in the chair weeping, my mind cannot think, not even to pray. For the first time, I let my brain entertain the thought that I might lose my husband. The thought is crushing. In my agony and complete brokenness, a thought comes to my mind.

"God, this, losing Hugo; we cannot do this. I cannot do this. Not even a little bit. I love Hugo too much. You will have to do it all. I'm done. It's simply too much."

Dad and Mom rush into the hospital room, Layla awake in her Grandma's arms. I tell Mom what the doctor said, and she comes to me. Anne instinctively takes Layla, and Mom passes her off without even realizing it. She holds me, and we cry loudly together. The pain in my heart is excruciating. I can barely breathe.

I am not aware of other activities around me. Nor am I aware of time passing. Apparently, Mark walked into the hallway and talked with a nurse. He is mad that the doctor gave me the information about Hugo's CAT scan over the phone, and wants to know if anyone could come and talk with us personally. They assure us another neurosurgeon was called by the first doctor in order to get a consultation, and that neurosurgeon will be down to explain more to us soon. They also stress to us that Layla is not safe on this floor and we need to make some plans for her.

"Call Levi," I tell my mom. "I need you here. Layla will just have to stay with Levi and his wife tonight. We can't handle her and Hugo at the same time. I will keep pumping milk. He can come get it from the fridge and then give her formula if she needs more."

"Okay, I'll call him. Don't worry. We'll take care of this."

We sit and wait some more. Waiting is a constant companion in the hospital. The waiting is mixed with a horrible panic, a longing for this experience to be over, and a fear that I'm too much in shock to be experiencing it at all. I try to relax, to ease the pain, but also take in my surroundings and absorb what is happening.

The consulting neurosurgeon finally arrives. This man is very considerate and gentle in his explanation. He looks directly at me and talks softly.

"This is very, very serious. I just looked at the CAT scan, and your husband has suffered a major brain aneurysm. Normally we can tell where the aneurysm came from but, in your husband's scan, there is so much blood we can't even tell where it originated. It was a main artery, and the blood circles the entire lower part of his brain. Because it is in an area low in his brain, the brain stem is damaged. The brain stem controls basic life functions. This is why his heart is not working well and his breathing is so sporadic."

"Can you operate on him?

"No, there's no surgery that can repair this. There is nothing we can do. Even if he had been in the hospital and had dropped right in front of me, the damage was done in the first instant. We will still put a PICC line into his arm and send strong medicines straight into his brain. You will have to wait overnight to see if his reactions get better or worse."

He explains again what he saw in the CAT scan and where Hugo's brain is damaged. He says again, "This is very, very serious."

"Is there any hope at all?" I ask, looking at Hugo.

"This is a very serious aneurysm. We will do some tests in the morning to see if there is any brain activity." He starts to explain everything again.

I look away. Mom can tell it is too painful for me. I cannot hear the explanation of my husband's impending death one more time.

Mom takes the doctor out into the hallway. She is feeling guilty that she did not push for a CAT scan in Hays to find the aneurysm sooner. She asks him, "Would it have made a difference?"

"No, ma'am. The damage was done in the first instant. Even if he had been on the operating table when it happened, there is nothing that anyone could have done."

Hugo is going to die. Or live, but as a person I won't recognize. I will never see my husband as I knew him again.

I hear these words in my head, but my heart still clings to hope. I know doctors are wrong sometimes, and God can still give me a miracle. I leave Hugo's side and open the hospital room door. I look at Mom and say, "You tell them to bring Mattias." I am almost yelling, because it's either that or cry my eyes out.

"Okay, I'll call Pastor Jeff and tell him to bring Mattias in the morning."

I have to go pump milk again. Mom goes with me this time. The same lady helps me arrange the machine again. I break down crying.

"Honey, just take a deep breath," Mom comforts me. "Just focus on this."

"I don't want this milk."

Mom holds me, rubbing my back. She tries to let me explain in my own time. I do not want to tell her.

The woman helping us decides to be more firm with me. "Why not, dear?"

"Because it has to be bad. I will always know that this was the milk I had when I found out that her daddy was going to die!" I am sobbing by now. Controlling any emotions is getting harder and harder.

"Oh, honey," the nurse says. "That is just not true. The milk is not bad. You and your husband want the best for your baby girl, and that milk is what is best for her. If she does lose her daddy, she is going to need this connection with you. Your husband would not want you to lose that."

"You're right." I am still crying, but she is right, and I know that I have to go ahead and nurse Layla. This is what is best for her, and Hugo would want me to keep nursing her. It takes quite a while, but I finally calm my crying enough to pump milk. Tears still stream down my face, but God has given me the strength to be calm.

When I return to Hugo's room, I sit in a chair near the door. Mark, Anne, Dad, and Mom join me in the room. We are all crying and quiet. The door opens, and the hospital's chaplain comes in. At first I am upset, because I do not want this stranger to interrupt us and bother me.

Luckily, Dad steps in and takes the lead. "Hi, my name is David Breeden. She is my daughter, Sarah. Her husband is Hugo and he's from El Salvador. This is my son and his wife, and my wife, Debbie."

None of us really acknowledges the chaplain's presence. Adding small talk to our situation might actually kill me, too. The chaplain picks up on this and does the right thing. He prays. Only prayer and Bible verses ease my pain at all. When he has finished, he decides to try a conversational question with my dad.

"Breeden, huh? Do you have any connections to Quinter?"

I burst out laughing. It's a strange reaction, but at this point, I do not care what people think of me. Everyone gives me funny looks, but they don't seem to know whether I'm laughing or crying, so Dad just answers him like nothing is wrong.

Mark is annoyed by the small talk, too, and says, "Dad," motioning for them to go chat in the hall.

My brief moment of hilarity came about because Hugo and I had this joke about how the world revolves around Quinter, Kansas. My dad can meet almost anyone, and somehow they are related to someone or something in Quinter. It is really bizarre, and Hugo and I joked about it a lot. So for this one chaplain to say he was from Quinter felt as if God was allowing me to have a painless moment of relief.

I know this will not be the last, so I decide to collect them and call them moments of "Hugo Humor." Only a creative, merciful, and loving God can work humor into the hardest moment of your life and make it look tactful.

Carlos calls again, and it is back to reality and pain. I try to think back to when I talked to him last, and how much he and Febe know. I feel like throwing up as I realize that they do not know how serious this has become. Last they knew, Hugo's heart was bad, but it has gone far beyond that. I explain it all in Spanish as best I can, because I know almost no medical words. All I can manage is, "Hugo's brain is dying. They will do tests in the morning to see how much activity is left, if any."

"Okay, I will call in the morning. We have the whole church in the sanctuary and they will be praying all night."

"Thank you, Carlos. Have you called Irma and Cesia?" I ask.

"Yes. Cesia is not doing well. Irma has to stay strong for her, so she is doing okay. But don't worry about us. You take care of yourself, Hugo, and the kids."

"Okay. Adios."

It is about 10 p.m., and I am so tired from everything. I just want to go home and forget that any of this is happening, but Mom and I talk and try to come up with a realistic plan. We decide that I should go take a shower at the hotel, put on some clean clothes, and then come back to spend the night with Hugo.

After my shower, I put on the new lotion that Hugo liked, the one from the spa I went to the day I had Layla. The same one I used the night he came back from the November baseball clinics. I know how much he loves the smell on me.

When I get back, I tell Mark and Anne, "Just go and sleep now. Dad, you too. I will need you all tomorrow, so go and sleep now."

They all agree, and Mom stays in the hallway to talk with Dad a little more. I go into Hugo's room. I look at him. I still can't believe this is happening. I put my arm under his nose.

"You smell that, honey?" I say softly, stroking his hair with my nails. He loved it when I did that. "Do you remember that night when you came home from the DR? I love you so much Hugo. I need you. I don't want you to die. Please God, save my husband."

I go to the other side of the bed and sit in an uncomfortable reclining chair. I have on my big winter coat, but I'm still shivering with cold and nerves. Mom wraps a warm blanket around me and helps me snuggle up to Hugo's arm as closely as possible.

"Mom, you should go to sleep, too. I'll be fine for a couple hours. Come back before five."

"Are you sure?"

"Yes, we are fine. There is nothing you can do now and I need you tomorrow to ask questions and help me."

"Call me if you need me."

I curl up in the chair and lay my head on his arm. I look at the multitude of hospital bracelets on his arm, and wonder why he needs so many. I notice a black band underneath the hospital bands and dig it out. It's Hugo's rubber wristband that he wore all the time. I used to tease him about the bands. I told him they were faddish and silly. He started with the original one from Lance Armstrong, Live Strong, and wore that one for a long time. Within the last couple of years, he traded bands every six months or so. I look at this new one, which I haven't noticed before, and read it slowly: "I AM SECOND."

"I am second?" I think to myself. "What does that mean?" But I know what it means. Christ is first, and I am second. I know Hugo was excited about the "I am second" movement. He showed me the website and the testimonies on it from professional athletes, celebrities, and everyday people too, all standing up and saying, "I am second, Christ is first in my life." But, what does it mean today? For Hugo, for me, in this moment, I am second … I am second … I am too tired to come to any conclusions. I feel Hugo's shoulder twitch as I fall asleep holding his hand, with my head nestled in his palm.

I wake a couple hours later, at 2 a.m. I feel hungry. I look at Hugo. He looks more peaceful than he did at any point the day before. I figure that even if you have a brain aneurysm, you still get tired and need to sleep, so he is probably sleeping. I decide I can go down to the cafeteria and get a quick snack.

Hugo's wallet is still in the pocket of my winter coat, and I start crying as I dig it out to pay for my food.

The older lady at the cash register just looks at me and says, "It'll be okay, sweetie. Things will get better."

I just want to scream at her that my husband was dying and it is not going to get better, but I know she is just trying to be nice. She probably gets customers having emotional breakdowns every day.

I take the food to Hugo's room and eat as much as I can, which is a yogurt cup. I know I have to keep eating for Layla, or I will not have milk for her.

I reach for Hugo's Bible that my parents brought. I want to find comfort in the right place, but where? Where should I start reading? All I can think about is the verse in James that says, "The fervent prayers of a righteous man avail much." So I decide to read James. I read all of chapter one, but the highlights that seem to burn a hole within me are:

"Count it all joy, my brothers, when you meet trials of various kinds, for you know that the testing of your faith produces steadfastness. And let steadfastness have its full effect, that you may be perfect and complete, lacking in nothing … Blessed is the man who remains steadfast under trial, for when he has stood the test he will receive the crown of life, which God has promised to those who love him … Every good gift and every perfect gift is from above, coming down from the Father of lights with whom there is no variation or shadow due to change … But be doers of the word, and not hearers only, deceiving yourselves … Religion that is pure and undefiled before God the Father, is this: to visit orphans and widows in their affliction, and to keep oneself unstained from the world."

I haven't gotten to the verse about fervent prayer, but it's all the way over in chapter five, and I just can't read on. I realize that I am probably going to be one of those widows the Bible is talking about.

As crushing as this is, the rest of the verse encourages me. I have to live what I have read and believed all my life. I almost smile as I think of some "Hugo Humor," the phrase I used to say to him in Argentina when we were studying: "It's do or die time." I pray for God to give me the strength to live His will through the pain. My heart clings to Hugo, and I do not want to let him go. I cannot accept the fact that God's best will, first of all for Hugo, but also for me and my children, is to allow Hugo to die.

I hang my head in defeat. I do not want to give Hugo to God, but God's will has to be done. I look at Hugo's hand. I want to memorize every inch of it, in case I never see it again. He has a scar in the middle of the cuticle on his thumb.

Why don't I remember how he got that scar? I know he told me, but now I can't remember, and I'll never get a chance to ask him again. I rub his first finger, feeling the long callus from years of playing bar chords. Another stabbing pain: I'll never hear him play his guitar again.

I notice the spinner friendship ring that I gave him is gone. I look at his other hand. His wedding ring is still there. Having seen his pre-game rituals many times over our years together, it suddenly occurs to me what he was doing when he originally collapsed. Once he removes his street shoes and laces up his basketball shoes, he removes his rings and slips them into the toes of his street shoes. He once jammed his ring finger with his wedding band on and it was almost impossible to get it off. I imagine he had just taken off his friendship ring and was about to take off his wedding ring when he suffered the aneurysm.

My thoughts are cut short as I notice his black wristband again. "I am second … I am second … I am second." I am meditating on this concept when I hear Hugo in my head. I have heard God's voice many times before, but this is the first time I've heard Hugo's.

He tells me, "Sarah, if God needs my life, if He needs my death, then it's okay. Because this life is not about me, it's about Christ and Him being glorified. I am second."

If that is not profound enough, he continues, "And Sarah, if God needs your suffering, if He needs the kids to grow up without a daddy, then that's okay, because it is not about you. It is about Christ and Him being glorified in this life. You are second. And the kids are second, too."

I am stunned. It's like a wave has knocked me off my feet. I am still staring at the bracelet. Something breaks in me. I look at Hugo's sleeping face.

"God, may Your will be done. If You need to take Hugo for You to be glorified, then I trust You with that."

This is the first time I've allowed myself to pray not just for Hugo's earthly healing, but for God's perfect will to be done, even if that means losing my love, my husband, my best friend, and the father of my precious children. God gives me a verse, and I repeat it over and over in my mind: "For I consider that the sufferings of this present time are not worth comparing with the glory that is to be revealed to us." (Rom. 8:18)

I cannot cling to Hugo's earthly body any longer, so I cling to that verse. I know that this pain will be nothing someday compared to the glory revealed in us in heaven. I fall asleep again with these thoughts in my mind. Even though this is a moment of light, there will be more dark times to come.

Mom comes back to check on me a couple hours later. She sits with me beside Hugo's bed. At 5 a.m., the nurses start to rush in and out and around our chairs. They are quiet, and trying not to raise any panic, but then one of the nurses says, "His blood pressure just dropped dramatically."

I hold on to both of Mom's arms and stomp my feet on the ground. I feel my skin crawling everywhere, and I have to get the nervous tension out. I half-cry and half-yell at Mom, "What does that mean? What does that mean?"

"It's okay, honey. It's okay. They are just giving him some meds to keep his heart pumping. It seems to be working, so it's okay." Her voice is so calm, and it helps me calm myself again.

Later that morning, the nice neurosurgeon comes in to check on us. He checks Hugo's reactions again. He pinches Hugo's shoulder. Nothing. His arm. Nothing. He opens his eyelids, and the pupils are still dilated. He asks the nurse for a gauze pad again. He touches Hugo's eye with the corner. Nothing. All of the reactions we saw last night are gone.

The doctor looks at me. "We have to do three separate tests to confirm, but he is brain dead."

"Okay." Somehow this information is not as crushing as it was when he explained it yesterday. I might have known that Hugo would die then, but I could not bring myself to pray for anything other than Hugo's complete healing until the wristband experience brought me to pray for God's will.

I tell my mom to ask the nurses about organ donation. Soon, a representative from Midwest Organ Donation comes to the room. She is so nice and sensitive. She explains to me that she can't proceed until Hugo is officially pronounced dead by the doctor.

"I understand, but I have lots of questions." I look at Hugo's face, and I feel an unnatural strength. I should not be strong enough to talk about donating my husband's organs while he is still living and lying next to me, but I know what I have to do. "I know Hugo wanted to be an organ donor, because he told me that he was jealous of the little heart that I have on my driver's license, and he was going to get one on his when he renewed his license in March."

"Let me just give you general information about the process, so you can think about it during the day. There are still a few tests that will have to be done, as they are hospital procedure, and then the neurosurgeon can pronounce the death. Then I can walk you through the forms. But you have to know that Hugo must be left on the machines. The machines have to keep him breathing and his heart pumping to get blood and oxygen to the organs."

I just look at her. That never occurred to me. I sit down. The lady leaves so I can talk with Mom.

I think for a while and then confess to Mom, "I really want to donate his organs, but I don't think I can do that. I can't just leave him when he looks like he is sleeping. I can't do that."

"I know. I don't think I could do that either. Let's just not think about it right now and focus on what needs to be done next. Mattias is on the way and will be here soon."

My phone rings in my coat pocket. I looked at the caller ID, and it is my Skype phone forwarding.

"It's Carlos." I stand and walk to the window. I take a deep breath and say, "Hola."

"Hola." I am surprised to hear Cesia on the phone line.

I don't want to tell her first, of all the people in their family, but she asks me in Spanish, "Sarah, is Hugo going to live?"

I can't stop myself from answering. I want to tell her gently, but I can't find the words. All I say was, "No, Cesia. No, his brain died."

I hear the phone drop, and I will never forget Cesia's painful screams. "Noooo … nooo." Tito had died only a month and three days ago.

Irma picks up the phone. "Sarah, what happened?"

"Hugo's brain died. They have to do a few tests to confirm, but he is gone."

"Okay, I will call again. But I have to help Cesia."

I hang up and cry. It is even more painful for me to imagine what they must be feeling, losing Hugo and being so far away. I look out the window for a while. How can the world still be normal when time has stopped for us?

I'm startled by the phone ringing again in my hand. I think it must be Irma calling back, but then I hear Carlos's voice on the other end. Irma and Cesia must have called Carlos and Febe and told them, because he asks me.

"Sarah, is it true? Is Hugo dead?"

"They have a few more tests to run to confirm that he has no brain activity." It is difficult for me to state to someone else the finality of what I know in my heart. But I know they need the absolute truth.

He asks me, "But, Sarah, is there any hope?"

"No, Carlos. The tests are just to confirm what we already know. He is dead. He is already with his Savior."

"Okay. Don't worry about us; we will get Irma to Kansas."

"Carlos, do you think it is okay if I donate Hugo's organs? Hugo always wanted that, but I just want to be sure."

"Sarah, you are his wife. You know what he wanted. Don't worry about us. You do what you know in your heart is right."

"Thank you." We hang up. I am grateful that Hugo's family is being so supportive.

Mom enters to let me know that Mattias is here. I ask God to give me super-natural strength to endure this moment. Even the thought of taking my beautiful boy into his daddy's room to say goodbye brings me to tears.

From the moment I meet Mattias in the waiting room, God gives me the grace I need to lead my son though this. Despite the seriousness of the situation, Mattias is still a little boy. I look around and notice many friends that have come to support me and my family. Ken and Mary Ann give me a big hug. A pastor friend of our family and his wife are here. Jeff and Michelle are also here, along with the couple Hugo and I stayed with while Hugo had his eye surgery. I want to talk to people, but I can't.

Mattias comes in. "Mommy!" He runs to me and gives me a big hug. He drags me over to the window and says, "Look, trees!"

We talk about everything that we see out the window, and I take time to hug him and caress his cheek with my knuckles, a sign of affection that I show him mostly at meal times. We'll be sitting next to each other, and I'll stroke his cheek with the back of my knuckles. Then he'll do the same to my arm, or he'll insist that I lean over so he can touch his sticky knuckles to my cheek.

I look at him and say, "Mattias, Daddy is very sick. He is here in the hospital and we are going to see him."

"Okay, Mommy."

"Daddy has tubes in his mouth, but they aren't hurting him. It looks funny, but it's normal."

"Okay, Mommy." He seems to understand everything I'm telling him, so I carry him down the hall and into Hugo's room. Mattias clings to me tightly, not because he is scared, but because there are other people watching, and he is being shy. He looks around the room, points at a bag of fluid hanging behind Hugo, and says, "Mommy! Daddy drinking!"

"That's right, Mattias! Daddy's drinking water!" I try to be excited with him to encourage him to relax and be more confident. "Do you want to lie down next to Daddy?"

"Yes," Mattias says, and I lay him on the bed. He snuggles into Hugo's side for a moment, but then looks up at Hugo's face. He reaches out. I almost take his hand away, thinking he's going to grab the tubes, but I stop when I see him turn his hand and gently rub his knuckles on Hugo's cheek. Then he reaches out for me again.

I pick him up. "Mommy, look, buttons!" He points to all the buttons on Hugo's hospital bed.

"Yes, those buttons move Daddy's bed, so we don't want to touch them." We stay a moment more, and Mattias snuggles with Hugo again. He is getting tired, so he wants me to hold him.

I pick him up and tell him, "Say bye to Daddy."

"Goodbye Daddy." He waves his little hand at Hugo.

"Say, 'I love you, Daddy.'"

"Love you, Daddy." He kisses the palm of his hand and blows it at Hugo. I walk him out of the room. It is done. I will always be able to tell Mattias that he said goodbye to his daddy, and he might even remember it.

I take him back to the waiting room, and Ken and Mary Ann promise to get him some lunch and a nap. I hug Pastor Ken and Pastor Jeff. They were the ones that brought Mattias to the hospital.

"Thank you," I tell them.

"Let us know how else we can help," Pastor Ken says.

My pastor friend, Jerry, catches me as I'm going back to Hugo's room. He tells me, "Isaiah says, 'Behold, God is doing a new thing.'"

His words strike something deep within me. I'm not sure what all they mean for me, but I know he is right.

Soon after that, Hugo is officially pronounced dead by the neurosurgeon. Just twenty hours have passed since he first collapsed on the basketball court.

I asked the organ donor representative to stay close by, and she is faithfully waiting in the hallway. I nod to Mom, and Mom goes to get her.

We all stand around Hugo again and I say, "I've been praying about this, because it is going to be really hard to leave Hugo here. But our cousin, Justin, is a kidney recipient, and Hugo and I talked about how thankful we are to the person who helped Justin so that he can live a much more active life. I know Hugo would love to help someone in that way. Also, Hugo was a giver in life. Of course he would want to be a giver in death."

The woman listens intently to every word I have to say. She is very patient and understanding. "If that is your decision, then we will go into one of the private waiting rooms. It will take about an hour to go though the paperwork with me."

"Okay." I say. My cell phone rings again. It's Irma. I turn away from the crowd near the bed and walk to the window again.

Irma's voice falters and cracks. She is a strong woman with a huge faith in God, but being separated from her baby boy as he lies dead in another country is too much.

She asks me, "Sarah, is there any way to keep Hugo on the machines until I get there?"

I start crying at the thought of enduring this hospital room torture for more days. I don't even want to ask if that was possible.

"No, Irma. I can't. I'm sorry." I cry because I feel I've failed her by not having the strength even to entertain that possibility.

"Then will you tell my son goodbye for me, and that I love him, and that I will see him at the gate of heaven soon? Give him a kiss from me."

"Yes, Irma I will tell him and give him a kiss from you."

"Thank you. Cesia wants to talk to you, too."

I am surprised at how calm Cesia's voice sounds. "Sarah, when Tito died, Hugo told me that God has a perfect plan for my life. And I want to tell that to you, too. God has a perfect plan for your life."

"Thank you, Cesia."

"Sarah, do you remember the e-mail that Hugo and I were arguing about recently?"

"Yes, Cesia. But that is the past. Hugo told you that he forgave you. He had no bitter feeling towards you. He loved you."

"Okay. Please tell my little brother that I love him and I will miss him."

"I will." I am crying hard by now. The thought of having to tell Hugo goodbye from his mom and sister is crushing. It's unfair that they can't say goodbye to him in person, but it's also unfair that I have to try to do it for them. No one should have to say goodbye to a son from his mother. But there is no other option. I am the only one who can do this for them.

When I hang up, I put my forehead on the bed next to Hugo's ear and say, "Hugo, your mom says she loves you. She says goodbye for now, but she will be looking for you at the gate of heaven. She sends you a kiss." I kiss his cheek gently.

"Hugo, I also talked with Cesia. She says goodbye. She will miss you on this earth. She loves you. She sends a kiss." I kiss his cheek again. "And I know Febe, Carlos, Daniela, and your dad all say goodbye too." I kiss his cheek five more times.

I leave the room. I need some air. I also want to get the rest over with, because there's a snowstorm coming and I'm ready to get home. I do not want to be stuck in this horrid hospital a moment longer than I have to be. I decide to wade through the paperwork with the lady from the transplant network. She takes me to a private waiting room. For an hour, she asks me questions about Hugo's background.

Halfway through, she has to wait patiently as I take another phone call from Carlos.

"Hugo's dad wants to know if he can see Hugo's body."

"No. I am having his body cremated. Hugo always wanted that; we talked about it."

"Okay. He wanted to know, so I told him I would ask."

"How is Hugo Sr. doing?"

"He is driving from Santa Ana to be with us in our house for a while. He shouldn't be alone. He is not taking it well."

We finally finish the paperwork, and I have given permission for them to take everything they want. I was not aware of all the parts they could use. Not just the major organs, but even skin, arteries, and bones. I cringe at this, but I tell myself that it's an earthly frame Hugo is no longer using. I know Hugo will kick me when I get to heaven if I don't just give it away. He loved to give everything away. That was his life, and I have to honor that spiritual gift in his death. Except for his eyes; I said yes to using his corneas, but no to medical testing on his eyes. It won't help anyone directly, so I told her, "His eyes were too beautiful for that. I need to know that the eyes I fell in love with are with him. He had beautiful brown eyes."

"We are going to transfer Hugo to a different floor that is equipped to deal with transplants. There will be a lady from the transplant team with Hugo all night, but you are welcome to stay until all of the surgeries are completed. He will be in and out of surgery all night and most of tomorrow. But honestly, dear, I think it would be best to go and be with your kids. Once you have decided in your heart that Hugo is not there anymore, just say goodbye and go home to be with your family."

I think for a moment. I pray for wisdom. I do not want to abandon Hugo here, but I know Hugo was too practical for that. We both know he is not here, and I need to take care of the children and myself first. His body is just a body now. He won't feel abandoned. And I know that seeing Hugo's body after surgeries is not another image I need to add to this pain.

I decide. "When you transfer Hugo to the other floor, I will not go with you. That way, it will be like him leaving me, instead of me leaving him."

"Okay, you will have to wait until the shifts change. That is when they will transfer him. That will be in a couple hours."

"Fine." I know that will be the time we all need to say goodbye.

"Also, there is one last test that we will be doing that is standard before we start a transplant. We will measure his oxygen level while he is still on the breathing machine, and then we will turn it off for ten minutes. The most basic function for the brain is to take a breath when it is needed. We will see if his brain takes a breath, and then measure the oxygen levels again after ten minutes. I will call you if his brain reacts and takes a breath, but I have to know either way. Do you want me to call you if he does not take a breath?"

"No, you don't need to call."

I go back to Mom and Dad and tell them to invite everyone from the waiting room into Hugo's room to pray, sing, and say goodbye.

Soon, there is a small circle of friends gathered shoulder to shoulder around Hugo's bed. I sit in the chair I spent the night in. Dad brings in Mattias, and he snuggles into my arms. I'm glad Mattias is getting another chance to be close to Hugo.

It's too hard for us to talk, so we sing a little instead. Mattias catches on to our singing and said, "Bah bah?"

I translate for everyone else, "Mattias wants to sing 'The B-I-B-L-E.'" We all smile and sing the requested song.

When we finished, Mattias says, "Deep and Deep."

"Mattias wants to sing 'Deep and Wide.'" We continue our singing, grateful that someone has ideas about what to do in this difficult moment.

The last song Mattias wants to sing is "Jesus Loves Me." I tear up as I sing, remembering all the times Hugo and I sang that song to Mattias, from the time he was in the womb to every night at bedtime before we turned out his lights.

A few others share verses. Then everyone leaves to go back to the waiting room. They know the time has come for us to say goodbye to Hugo. Mattias says goodbye again and leaves with Ken and Mary Ann.

Dad, Mom, Mark, Anne, and I are left. Jennifer, the woman from the transplant network who will watch over Hugo while he goes in and out of surgery all night, comes in to stand with us.

Mark looks at her and asks, "Can you play music for him tonight while you are watching over him? He loves music."

"Sure," she says. "I'll see what I can do."

Mark laughs, "Just watch out – he'll probably steal your ipod. Never trust a Latino!"

We all laugh at some more "Hugo Humor" and then grow quiet again. Jennifer slips out the door without a sound, and we all stand around Hugo's bed crying, as we know our goodbyes are close at hand. I look at Hugo and finally look up at Mark and Anne. I haven't bothered to really look at them during all of this, and I realize that they are suffering, too. I can see it in their tear-streaked faces, crying desperately beside me, sharing in my nightmarish pain.

They have only been married for two years. I cringe at how fearful they must feel that this could happen to them. It is not a reality any of us believe could ever happen to us. But now that they have seen it up close, will they be able to love as deeply, knowing that life is so fragile and can be snatched away without notice? I am still so grateful to have them here. I will need them in the time to come.

I look down at the black "I AM SECOND" bracelet. I slip it off Hugo's wrist and put it on my own. I walk to the other side of the bed. I work at getting Hugo's wedding ring off. I don't want it to get lost. Hugo always had to lick his finger to get it off. The nurse brings some soap, and my mom reaches out to help me.

"No," I say softly, "I put it on him; I will be the one to take it off him."

The nurse applies the soap and the ring slips off. I put it on my thumb. I am trying to wait for the shift change so they can take Hugo away from me, and I won't have to leave him. But I look into his face, and I know in my heart that he is gone. If I don't leave now, this divine courage might pass.

I kiss him on the lips, so warm and soft. He looks as if he is sleeping. I put my hand on his chest. It still rises and falls, though more shallowly than before. I put my lips on his one last time, never wanting to forget the love we had for each other.

"Goodbye, Hugo. I love you." I feel a surge of courage turn me around and move my body down the hallway. The transplant team is there. I did not warn my family, so I leave them with Hugo to say their own goodbyes. When I turn the corner, I see in my peripheral vision that the team is wheeling Hugo to the other floor. My family is following close behind me. I find Mattias in the waiting room. Everything is already packed, and we are just waiting for Levi to bring Layla and arrange the car seats.

When it's all ready, we leave the waiting room and push the button for the elevator. Mattias is in my arms. He looks at me and asks, "Mommy, Daddy?"

He knows that Hugo is not with us, "No, Mattias, Daddy is not going with us."

"Me see Daddy?"

I look at Mom, heartbroken. She heard it too.

"No, Mattias. We cannot see Daddy anymore." I dig my head into Mattias and weep. Even a two-and-a-half year-old can see this is not right. Hugo is gone.

It is dark, about 7 p.m., and the snow and ice are already falling. Pastor Jeff and Pastor Ken drive us home. Mom, Layla, and I go with Pastor Jeff, while Pastor Ken drives Dad and Mattias. I make constant phone calls to keep my mind occupied. One of the first calls is to Ron Bishop, the founder and co-president of SCORE. I tell him the news of Hugo's passing.

"Oh, Sarah. I'm so sorry. I'm so sorry. Hugo was a great servant of God. I don't want you to worry about a thing. SCORE will take care of you as long as you need. You take the time you need to be with your family."

"Ron, I don't know how, and I don't know when, but I will return to the Dominican Republic. God called me to the foreign mission field when I was fourteen years old. That call on my life does not change now that Hugo is gone."

"Praise the Lord. Just do what your kids need and what you need. Your SCORE family will be here for you. Let me know what you need. And please call me every day, just to check in with me for a minute and let me know how things are going."

"Okay, I will."

I hang up and think about the transplant woman, Nancy. She said she would call if Hugo took a breath during the oxygen test. I cling to the phone, but I knew she will never call, and she doesn't. I cry again as my mind repeats, "My husband is dead." I keep trying to accept it, but every time the thought occurs to me, it is as if it's the first time.

I call Tom and Fae in Florida. They were our great friends who helped us survive Bible school in Argentina. They both answer the phone, thinking it is Hugo and me wishing them a Merry Christmas. They immediately know something is wrong, and they cry with me bitterly as I explain Hugo's unexpected death.

Layla cries and cries on the way home. We finally have to stop to feed her. I am so dehydrated from crying that I don't have enough milk for her. Thankfully, Levi sent a bottle of formula mixed with my breast milk. It helps Layla calm down enough to get most of the way home, though a couple blocks from our house I finally give up and take her out of her car seat.

We park, and I quickly carry Layla through the falling snow and into the house. The house feels harsh and cold. Everything I see tears at my heart. I slowly walk through the house as everyone else unloads the cars.

Tears stream down my face. I see Hugo's presence all over the house. We were just here together yesterday. It feels as if he's still here, but my mind has to keep reminding my heart over and over that this is not a dream. He is really gone. His flip flops are under the coffee table. They were abandoned so casually that it's obvious he planned to come back for them. How can they be lying there? They don't look like flip flops belonging to someone who is dead. My heart almost feels hope looking at them. Then the fresh realization comes again. He is gone. My mind will not accept his absence from this earth.

Mom puts the kids to bed in her room and tucks me into the guest bedroom. We will deal with Hugo's and my room downstairs tomorrow.

She tells me, "Sarah, you just have to turn your mind off. You have to sleep."

"Okay." I am so broken in that moment I do not have the will to think about anything. I sleep.

Early in the morning, I wake up. The fresh realization hits me again. "He's gone." I cry. I cry hard. My throat hurts each time I cry. It feels raw. My face muscles are in pain, too. But it's my heart that burns the worst.

Mom comes in and sits with me as I cry. She cries with me, "Lord Jesus, please. It's too much. We can't do this. Lord Jesus, please help us."

Please visit my website, www.my-onceuponatime.com/, to see pictures and videos from each chapter.

355

Chapter Fifteen

The Princess Runs to Her First Love
2010

Kansas, Dominican Republic

Hugo died on Tuesday, December 22nd, 2009. My whole spirit, soul, and body screamed in horrible, unbearable pain during the next two days. I couldn't pray. All I could do was groan. I wasn't mad or asking why. I just wanted Hugo back, and knowing that wasn't possible was a searing pain burning a hole in the middle of me.

The crying kept my throat raw, despite the antibiotics my mom had gotten for me. I could eat only soup. Nothing more would fit down my tight throat. Besides, food just didn't matter; hunger never crossed my mind.

I did go downstairs to our room on the 23rd. I was seeking some way to be closer to Hugo. I found his friendship ring in his street shoes, just as I knew I would. I slipped it into my pocket. I found the SCORE shirt he had worn to church the day before he went to basketball. It still smelled like him. I curled up on our bed and cried. Mom came and sat with me. She rubbed my back and prayed for me. She told me to take a shower, and I'd feel better. We could hear the kids crying, and I knew that Dad needed her help.

Mindlessly, I went through the motions of getting in the shower. There, I felt Hugo's presence. Maybe my mind was experiencing what it was craving, but maybe God lets Christians say goodbye in a tangible way. I know that God will show me the truth when I get to heaven. Whatever the case, I could almost see Hugo in the corner of the shower. My eyes did not see anything, but instinctively I reached out to touch his face. The only words I felt him say were, "Patience, Sarah, patience." Then he was gone.

I let the words roll around in my soul and prayed to the Holy Spirit. Patience … what does that mean? The Holy Spirit spoke to my heart, "Patience is the key to everything, but you need to have patience for two things in particular right now. In your grieving you need patience. It will get better. And also in your longing to see

Hugo again. You will see him again in heaven. Life on earth is short; you just need patience."

Later, my friends Danielle and Julie came and sat with me. They let me talk and retell the whole story. I was so grateful to have them with me. Even though I had not asked for them, they knew they needed to be there. My whole being felt so raw, like a finger with the fingernail ripped off. Every movement caused pain in the deepest parts of me. But as much as I just wanted to lie in my bed and cry with my friends, I could not. Like a cruel joke, there are a million things to do the first day after losing a loved one.

I had to go with my parents to meet Pastor Ken at the funeral home. Some arrangements had to be made that day, especially with Christmas only two days away. Driving up and parking in the front felt so surreal. I numbly got out of the car. Dad opened the door to the funeral home, and I mindlessly followed him and Mom in.

Suddenly, I snapped back to the reality of what was happening. My mind reminded me what I was actually doing: "You are at a funeral home making arrangements for your husband's funeral and burial." It was the nightmarish moment I'd always feared, and here I was experiencing it at only 29.

I looked at Mom in a panic. "Mom, I don't want to be here, I don't want to do this."

She looked at me with tears in her eyes and understood. She felt the same. "I know, honey, I don't want to do this either, but one step at a time. We'll do this together."

She held my arm and led me to a sitting room. Pastor Ken was already there. He gave me a hug and introduced me to the funeral home director, Rick. My panic worsened, but I dutifully sat, or perhaps fell and landed, in my chair. My mom was aware that this situation was going from bad to worse, and politely asked Rick to bring us some water. We needed a moment to collect ourselves before we could calm our emotions and think clearly.

Rick disappeared, and I closed my eyes and tried to pray, asking God for help in this dreadful moment. Rick reappeared, carefully balancing water in two Dixie cups, one in each hand. Mom and I looked at him at the same time, then looked at each other and instantly burst out laughing.

Rick was instantly embarrassed and said, "This was all I could find in the other room, but I will look in the back for bigger cups." He set down the Dixie cups and hurried away to bring bigger drinks.

"Wait, Rick, this is fine," Mom tried to explain, but Rick was already out of the room. Mom and I continued to laugh, and it was so nice to have tears in my eyes from a good laugh rather than from a heart-wrenching cry.

When Rick returned, Mom explained, "We weren't laughing because you brought us small cups. The drinks were perfect. It's an inside family joke. Once Hugo, Sarah, David, and I took a drive to New Jersey to visit Hugo's dad. We left Denver late one night after visiting my family and drove 24 hours straight through to New York to stay with some old friends of ours. On the long trip we laughed about a lot of stupid stuff. One of the biggest jokes came after I asked a gas station attendant for a complimentary cup that I could use to get water. The man handed me a small Dixie cup and, though I was disgusted at the size of the 'compliment' I proudly filled it and took it to the car. 'Look everyone, this is my complimentary cup.'

"They all laughed, but Hugo took the joke a step further, and at every gas station after that he'd ask me, 'Debbie do you have your cup? Don't forget to fill it up. You might get thirsty.'

"I'd always get it and fill it up at every stop we made. I kept the cup the whole ride there and the whole ride home. Ever since then, whenever we saw small cups, Hugo would joke, 'Hey, it's Debbie's complimentary cup.' So, when you came around the corner with our two cups, we knew God had sent us some 'Hugo Humor.'"

God had once again used "Hugo Humor" as He had in the hospital to give grace in an excruciating situation. The mood changed 180 degrees as I felt the Lord strengthen me for the upcoming meeting.

We discussed possible dates for the memorial service. In the end my dad's idea was best: "We should have it on Monday, because people will be traveling home from Christmas through the weekend."

We talked about some of the things that we'd like for the service. We decided that Hugo's youth group worship team would do a great job with the music, but would need a lead guitarist and worship leader. I knew instantly whom Hugo would choose, but I wasn't sure if he'd be willing. "What if Mark played lead guitar? Musically he is the strongest guitar player I know and closest to Hugo's worship style. Plus, Mark and Hugo recently played at North Oak together, so it seems fitting. I'll ask him though; I don't know if he'll be able to do it emotionally."

After we made a few other plans for the memorial service, Rick had other details to discuss. "Sarah, I talked with the transplant team. They will have Hugo for one more day, and then they will be calling me to ask for final details. What do you want done with the body?"

It felt weird knowing that Hugo's body was still around on this earth, still doing something—going through surgeries, breathing on machines, even just lying in a bed. In one sense he still felt alive to me, because someone on earth was looking at him, touching him, caring for him. I had to quickly remind myself that though his body was in Wichita, it was just his earthly tent and not him. He was in heaven, very much alive.

I asked, "Is it possible to have him brought to Hays, so I can see his body one more time, and then have it cremated here?"

"If you want to see his body one more time, we can arrange that. The issue is that there is no place to cremate his body here in Hays; we'd have to send him to Salina to be cremated. But if that is what you want to do, we can do that."

I thought carefully. Being practical, and also knowing Hugo's wish not to have an expensive funeral, I asked, "But it will be more expensive to do it that way?"

"Yes," Rick said quietly. I thought some more. Part of me wanted to see Hugo one more time, without all the machines. When I left him in Wichita, he looked like he was sleeping. He did not look dead as my grandpa had looked in his casket. But the other part of me thought it would be better to remember Hugo as he looked when he was still alive. I knew what Hugo would want me to do.

"Just have him cremated there in Wichita after the transplant team is done."

"Okay. I have a mortician friend in Wichita, and I will have the hospital release Hugo's body to him. He will take care of the cremation, and I will have him send the cremains to me here. I'll let you know when they get here, and we can plan what you want to do with them."

He spoke to and looked at me with such compassion and gentleness. I knew that this was Rick's job, but it felt as if this was so much more for him. It was his calling and ministry to hurting people. He confirmed this thought in my heart when he told me, "Sarah, I know you and Hugo didn't have any life insurance, so I would like to provide my services as my memorial gift to you."

Pastor Ken, Dad, Mom, and I cried when he said this. This was his job, his livelihood. If he had compassion on everyone who came through his door, he would never make a living. Why me? Here was God at work, using Rick as one of the many people who blessed me during this difficult time in real, practical ways.

I went home, and Danielle was there again. My friend Kristy and her husband Michael were also there. I was thankful to have their help, because one of the things I had to do right then was pick out a picture to put in the newspaper for Hugo's obituary. I needed to e-mail Rick as soon as possible with some details of Hugo's life, another task that did not coincide with my human desire to hide in my blankets for a couple of weeks.

Once again, God used my friends to bolster me and help me get through this next project. I sat down at the computer, my friends behind me. I wondered how in the world I would find the right picture for the newspaper. I clicked on iphoto. I looked at the viewing options, contemplating how I should start; by date, event or just look at all the pictures? I noticed an option called "faces."

Excitedly, I clicked on the option and said, "Hey guys, look! Hugo just installed this new update last week to our iphoto. It's an application that helps your computer recognize a particular face, and then iphoto pulls up all the pictures that have that person in them. Hugo already has it programmed to recognize all of the family's faces."

I clicked on Hugo's face icon and the computer instantly loaded thousands of pictures. Hugo's face was beaming across my screen two dozen times. There was an icon to show the picture in its entirety, and another icon to see the picture in a cropped version with just that person's head in a thumbnail. I was in the headshot view, and I quickly filtered through hundreds of pictures of Hugo's smiling face.

Kristy said, "Sarah, I don't know how you can do this without crying."

I kept scanning the pictures and said, "I don't know either. God has given me a unique strength to get the necessary tasks completed. In some ways I have to disconnect to get anything done. But, with this … it gives me comfort to see Hugo's smiling face." I stopped scrolling. "There it is."

It was a handsome picture of Hugo in a tie. It was perfect. I wondered where it was taken and clicked to view the whole picture. It was a family picture with Hugo holding Mattias, me, Hugo Sr., Irma, Cesia, Febe, Carlos, and Daniela. We had taken the picture in April, when Hugo, Mattias, and I had visited El Salvador. I felt a pang in my heart imagining what his family must be going though. I pushed the thought out of my mind. My own grief was enough without taking on the grief of others. I quickly e-mailed the picture to Rick along with the details of Hugo's life and family.

I started thinking more about Hugo's family. I already knew that Irma and Cesia were not able to come for the memorial service. Carlos had said that he and Febe would be able to come, but then we had tentatively decided that they would not come for the service, because it would be a crazy time for me. They preferred to come all together, with Irma, in January, and spend some quality time with the kids and me. But the more I thought about it, the more I could not imagine having a memorial service without any of Hugo's family. I knew it would be a huge financial burden for them. They had just been to Argentina for a vacation, and then Irma and Febe went again to be with Cesia. Irma was still there, so for Carlos and Febe to fly to Kansas was a huge sacrifice. I wasn't sure I could ask them to do it.

That night I talked with Carlos. Finally he said, "Sarah, don't worry about the money. God will provide. You make the decision. You tell me, and I will make it happen. We want to do what is best for you. Are we going to make everything harder, or do you need us there?"

I started to cry and, through my tears, I said, "I need you here."

Carlos's voice wavered as he repeated, "Okay, don't worry. I will arrange everything, Febe and I will be there." Later, I found out that, in order to pay for the plane tickets, he planned to sell their old Mini-Cooper, Carlos's dream car that he was fixing up. He did not know that God would provide more than abundantly through friends in my church so he could keep his car.

Around 6 that evening, Danielle and my parents went with me to the church. The youth group was gathering together to share in each other's tears and heartache. They too were all hurting from losing Hugo. I knew Hugo would be very concerned about them and how they would handle his death. I felt he would want me to go and say something to them. Also, more than anything, I felt the urgent need to make Hugo's life and death count the most in glory. Hugo was always in awe of martyr stories and, though he was not an official martyr, his story could impact the world just the same if I were faithful to share it when God asked me to. I wanted Hugo's death to count most for eternity in the group that he cared about most.

When I entered the youth room, about thirty people were sitting in a circle of chairs. Hugo's close friend, Pastor Jeff, was speaking, but as soon as I walked in, he stopped. Everyone looked at me.

"Hi guys," was all I could say before everyone stood and started giving me hugs. When I hugged Spencer, a young man whom Hugo had taught guitar and spent time with, I held him at arm's length and spoke directly to him. I don't recall what I said, so that makes me think that it was a message from God that Spencer needed to hear at that moment. Tears were in my eyes and on my face, but I did not lose control of my tears, which I had feared would happen. Instead, I could feel an amazing peace and strength that God had given me.

Once everyone sat down, I read the passage from James that I had read the night I was with Hugo, and I shared a few thoughts. I challenged them to make Hugo's life count, to know that their time was short, and to realize that they'd better get right with God and get going.

December 24th was the day Hugo and I were supposed to be Joseph and Mary for the Christmas Eve service. I had been so excited to have Layla play the part of baby Jesus. This was yet another reminder of events we had planned that were no longer a part of life. Our family usually let Hugo open one gift on the 24th, because in El Salvador they open all their gifts on Christmas Eve. This year, his gifts sat unopened under the tree.

Irma called to tell me, "I left my U.S. visa in El Salvador when I went to Argentina to be with Cesia. I can't fly straight to the U.S. There are no flights to El Salvador until January. Cesia is not capable of flying now, nor is she able to be on her own yet. In addition to emotional insecurity, her elbow is still so bad that I have to help her get dressed and do her hair in the morning. I will not be able to fly to Kansas for the funeral."

"It's okay. We will figure out something else to do later." I hung up and went to cuddle with Mattias. Being with my kids was the only thing I could do. Though Mom was taking care of their needs, I still snuggled with them. Mattias felt hot. "Oh great," I thought, just what I need, a sick kiddo. I put him to bed in Mom's room.

We had already decided not to open gifts on Christmas morning. The excuse was that we had to wait for Mark and Anne to arrive from Oklahoma City. But we all knew that we had to do the whole day differently in order to get through it at all. As soon as I woke up, I started crying again. Hugo had wanted Christmas to be really special that year. I'm sure that this was not what he had in mind. I tried to cry quietly, but soon I could not help it, and I cried so loudly that Mom came in again. She stayed as long as she could, but Mattias was sick and hot with fever and needed her.

I was done. I was at the end of myself. I didn't know what to do. Nothing was helping. There was nowhere to hide from the pain. I would have to face it. I reached for my Bible on the nightstand. I opened it to Psalms, the only place I knew where I could find something quick to sustain me. I read:

"Answer me quickly, O LORD! My spirit fails! Hide not Your face from me, lest I be like those who go down to the pit. Let me hear in the morning of Your steadfast love, for in You I trust. Make me know the way I should go, for to You I lift up my soul." (Psalm 143:7-8)

"I cry to you, O LORD; I say, 'You are my refuge, my portion in the land of the living.' Attend to my cry for I am brought very low!" (Ps. 142: 5-6a)

"With my voice I cry out to the LORD; with my voice I plead for mercy to the LORD."

After I read these verses, I did plead to the Lord in prayer. I begged the Lord, "God, please. This pain is too much. Please have mercy on me. My spirit fails, and I don't know which way to go. I am very low, and You have to answer quickly. Please have mercy on my soul!"

That was all I could pray, but it was enough. This act of reaching out to God in my brokenness was a turning point for me. I allowed God to touch my devastation instead of keeping it to myself. I lay there on the bed, but my heart did not feel as stricken. I felt a tiny lightness in it. God had mercy on my heart and took enough of my pain that I knew I would not die enduring it.

Looking back on this experience, I think of Heb. 4:12: "For the word of God is living and active. Sharper than any double-edged sword, it penetrates even to dividing soul and spirit, joints and marrow; it judges the thoughts and attitudes of the heart." The living Word of God had penetrated and divided pain from my heart and soul in the form of God's sufficient mercy.

I soon found that the living and active Word of God was the only place where I could find comfort and solace. I wrote verse after verse in my journal. Words of comfort that God gave me in my own times of pouring out my heart or through other people who wanted to encourage me.

Mattias was sick for Christmas. He had been running a fever for a couple of days, and now I was getting worried. "God, why does everything have to happen at once?" I thought.

I didn't want to take him to the emergency room, because he did not have any symptoms that pointed to such drastic measures, but I still considered it. The pediatrician's office would be closed for the next several days for Christmas and the weekend. The memorial service for Hugo was Monday. I prayed for my nerves to stay calm and the wisdom to know what to do. Finally, Mom and I decided that we should call Dr. Martin. He and his family went to our church, and he was an oral surgeon. He could at least tell us whether we needed to be more concerned. I felt as if all my ability to think, reason, and make decisions was gone. I needed help making the simplest choices.

Mom called Dr. Martin, and they had already opened gifts. He said he would soon be over to help us. He wheeled in a blood pressure monitor and used a clipboard to do a full evaluation of Mattias. I think he knew I needed some peace of mind. The end result was okay, but he said Mattias probably had some sort of infection that would need antibiotics. He suggested keeping an eye on Mattias to see if his system would work it out on its own, since Mattias had no other symptoms besides the fever. We may not have gotten much of a diagnosis, but at least we knew to keep the ibuprofen going, and our nerves were a little calmer.

I kept forgetting that it was Christmas. It did not feel like the special, memorable Christmas Hugo had wanted. Though my mind was slow and seemed to be in a fog, God did reveal something special to me that Christmas. I was more thankful that year than any other that God had sent His son Jesus as a baby to the earth to save us from our sins. If it weren't for the baby Jesus, Hugo would have died and been lost. It would have been a useless, senseless death.

BUT GOD so loved the world that He sent His one and only son. And because of that, Hugo was now face to face with that baby from Bethlehem. The King of Kings, the Prince of Peace, Hugo's Savior, Jesus Christ. In all my overwhelming earthly heartache, I celebrated the true heavenly meaning of Christmas more that year than any other year of my life.

That evening, Mark and Anne arrived from Oklahoma. We soon began our earthly celebration and opened some presents. I left the family room periodically to gather my thoughts and tears. But for the most part, I kept my mind focused on helping the kids have a great time. I still wanted them to have a good Christmas. It was Layla's first Christmas, and I wanted her to have all the right pictures to put into her baby book someday. Happy pictures of her family, helping her open her first Christmas gifts. There were a few tearful moments for all of us though.

Mom left to get the Christmas present Hugo had bought for me. He'd told me that he had not bought me a gift yet, but Mom brought out three gifts and told me the story. "Hugo bought this back in October for your birthday but, when he bought your sunglasses, he decided to save this gift for Christmas. He wrapped it a couple weeks ago and hid it in my closet and told me how he was going to give it to you. It has three parts."

I slowly opened the first part. It was the smallest of the packages. There were four gray circle disks. I opened the next gift. It was a Wii balance board. Now I got it. Hugo had taken the feet off the board and wanted to give them to me first to confuse me. The third gift was a palettes Wii game that I had wanted. It was a very thoughtful gift. I had wanted a Wii Fit Plus for a long time so that I could exercise in the house and watch the kids at the same time.

I put the gift aside and ran downstairs. I had the kids' gifts under our bed where Hugo and I had hid them together. I had never gotten my emotions under control enough to actually wrap them, but I knew I had to get this over with now. As I reached under the bed, my mind thought back to when Hugo and I had picked out the gifts.

We had gotten a track for Mattias and Hugo to put together and race cars on. We had gotten a variety of baby items for Layla, a new rattle that was soft and looked like a flower, and a few other baby toys. We had what we needed for Christmas, and

I had gone to grab a few diapers before we left. Hugo had walked into another baby aisle to look while he waited for me.

I'll never forget his face as I rounded the aisle to find him. He had a plush giraffe up next to his face and a cute little look on his face. He had looked down at the giraffe. "I'm going to buy this for Layla too." Even though we had spent enough, I knew I wouldn't be able to talk him out of this giraffe. And it was so cute.

But now the awaited moment was here, and Hugo was not. How could I do this? "Lord, help me," I prayed in a deep sigh, and walked up the stairs. I gave Mattias his gift, and he was excited to get it open and start putting it together. "Wait," I said, "Layla has to open her gifts first."

I gave Layla her other little toys first, let her play with them for a bit, and then moved them aside. She was lying in the middle of the family room, the Christmas tree brilliantly lit in the corner. I lay on my stomach next to her. The room was quiet, but for me only Layla and I existed in that moment.

I spoke softly to her. "Layla." I snuggled the giraffe next to her on the floor. Her wild, out of control hands batted at the new object. "This giraffe is from your daddy. He loves you so much and picked it out especially for you. I'm sorry that he is not here, but he still loves you. I love you too." I laid my head next to her face and my tears dripped on her cheek. I kissed them off. "Happy first Christmas, baby."

All of Hugo's gifts from other family stayed under the tree. It made me sad to think about how excited Hugo would have been. He always got really pumped about gifts, and it was fun to give him surprises. I had secretively bought the gift from Mattias and Layla while Hugo was actually shopping with me. It was a Nalgene bottle that could clip onto Hugo's backpack. I told Hugo that it was a pointless item to buy because he already had a camel pack, and the Nalgene would not hold enough water for his daily needs.

He was totally bummed and said, "Yeah, you're so right. It is not practical. I really like it. But oh well."

As I was shopping around, I decided that Christmas presents don't have to be practical. I circled back and got it when Hugo was not looking, and then at the checkout I told the cashier to double bag it so that Hugo would not see it in the trunk. He never suspected a thing, and it was going to be an awesome surprise. Mattias had even helped me wrap it in an old shoebox and picked out the paper and bow to put on it.

(Nearly a year later, Mattias and I were playing house with that shoebox and Mattias said, "Daddy ... water ... Daddy ... water.")

(For a while I did not know what he was talking about, until finally I asked, "Mattias, do you remember wrapping Daddy's water bottle in this box?")

("Yes, Mommy, yes." I had not remembered the box until Mattias reminded me.)

My gift to Hugo was practical, but it was something that he had been wanting, and we needed it in the DR. It was a cordless power drill, and I was even more excited about it because I had woken up at four in the morning on Black Friday to get a great deal on it. I had been looking forward to telling Hugo the whole story about Dad's and my adventures at the store that morning.

There was also a blue New York Yankees hat that Grandpa had given him money to buy. We had actually purchased it back in November when we were in Denver. Hugo had begged me to let him wear it for Thanksgiving weekend, saying that afterward he would wrap it up for Christmas and not use it.

I was being stubborn. "It is a Christmas gift; you have to wait."

"Fine!" Hugo had said after we argued back and forth about it for a while.

I could see he was really hurt and wanted to wear it. Finally I had given in. "Honey, if it's that important to you, it's okay. It is really not a big deal, and if you want to wear it that badly, it's okay. We can wrap it up later."

He wore it proudly all weekend. When I finally did open the hat we had wrapped up, how glad I was that God had broken my stubbornness and softened my heart to let Hugo wear it for that weekend. I hung his hat on the coat rack in the kitchen, and it has not been removed since then.

The day after Christmas I was praying to God about why he did not help Hugo and me get our life insurance. SCORE requires it, but we were not able to get it the year before because Hugo did not have a Social Security number. We had asked in Hays, but they said we needed to ask the U.S. Embassy in the Dominican Republic. When we asked them, they said they could only help American citizens get their Social Security numbers, so we'd have to ask in Kansas again. Frustrated, we went back to the office in Hays as soon as we got settled into life in Kansas. He finally got his number.

Then we got busy having Layla, and I had just e-mailed a SCORE friend about getting paperwork started for our life insurance. I got an e-mail back from him two days before Hugo died. Life insurance was my December project, and now it was too late. No life insurance money. "Now what God?"

I was also thinking about whether to return to my home in the Dominican Republic. Hugo and I had wanted to live there long-term because we had moved around so much. Part of my crying and pain was just grieving the life that we had dreamed of, which had been stripped away from me. Would I also lose the mission field I had so desperately wanted? I had waited 13 years to finally be where I thought God wanted me. Would that also die with Hugo?

These were the thoughts on my mind when I read Jer. 29:11-14: "'For I know the plans I have for you,' declares the LORD, 'plans for welfare and not for evil, to give you a future and a hope. Then you will call upon Me and come and pray to Me, and I will hear you. You will seek Me with all your heart. I will be found by you,' declares the LORD, 'and I will restore your fortunes and gather you from all the nations and all the places where I have driven you,' declares the LORD, 'and I will bring you back to the place from which I sent you into exile.'"

I felt this verse was telling me many things, the main one being that God had a hope and a future for me. But I also saw that God would "restore my fortunes," which meant to me that God would provide for my financial needs.

God wanted to provide for me and show His power in provision; He did not need me to have life insurance. "And gather you from all the nations and places where I have driven you" stirred in me the thought that God had sent me to so many countries, all stepping stones to the mission field, and now He was going to bring me back to that place. I felt in my heart where that place was, but what would people say? I'd have to pray and be sure.

At that time, however, I had more menial decisions to make that were higher on the priority list. I had tried to have someone go and buy me something to wear to Hugo's service, but did not like the choices I had been given. I knew I'd only be happy if I picked out the outfit myself. I wanted to throw up at the thought of doing something like shopping at a time like this, but it had to be done.

Mom was deep into receiving, refrigerating, and freezing food items that friends from the church were bringing. She was also keeping up with Mattias and Layla. I couldn't imagine what she was going through, having to watch me go through this pain, being strong for me, taking care of my kids, answering phone calls, and handling a host of details that I didn't need to be bothered with. She had no time to grieve on her own, but I couldn't think about her, so I chose not to. I was totally consumed by my own heartache and grief.

My Aunt Caroline went with me to shop for an outfit. When we entered the store, I felt panic strike my heart. My house had become a sanctuary for me, and being out of it took me back to the "finger without a nail" feeling. The bandage had been carelessly ripped off, and every heartbeat made the wound throb and sting. My eyes darted back and forth at the racks, and I could barely focus. How in the world would I be able to pick out something to wear for my husband's memorial service?

A friend from church who worked at the store spotted me and came right over. Her warm Southern hug and understanding smile warmed me. She knew why I was there and immediately started helping me. I was able to focus, and soon Aunt Caroline, Cynthia, and I had options for me to try in the dressing room.

I decided on a knee-length black skirt, a black tank top, and a silky red button-up top. I wanted to wear something happy, but classy. This outfit was exactly what I had prayed for, and I knew I would have one less thing to worry about the day of the memorial service. I know myself, and if I don't like my clothes for an important event, there are normally tears while I'm getting ready. I was so thankful to have this shopping over with, and to be able to get back to the safety of the house.

On Sunday, I was encouraged again by more verses. I could not face confronting everyone at church and then have to do it all over again at the memorial service the following day, but I was still deep in the Word and in prayer. Every breath I took was sustained by the verses I read in Scripture.

"And my God will supply every need of yours according to His riches in glory in Christ Jesus" (Phil. 4:19).

"It is my eager expectation that with full courage, now as always, Christ will be honored in my body, whether by life or by death. For to me to live is Christ, and to die is gain" (Phil. 1:20-21).

"Rejoice in the Lord always; again I will say, Rejoice. Let your reasonableness be known to everyone. The Lord is at hand; do not be anxious about anything, but in everything by prayer and supplication with thanksgiving let your requests be made known to God. And the peace of God, which surpasses all understanding, will guard your hearts and your minds in Christ Jesus" (Phil. 4:5-7).

I woke up. "Monday," I thought to myself. "The memorial service for my husband is today. Horrible. I do not want to do today."

It was early, but Mom came into my room carrying Mattias. "Mattias still has a high temperature. We need to get him into the doctor today."

This problem I did not need, a sick child the day of my husband's funeral. I was a little upset with God, but Mattias needed me, so I threw some clothes on and called Dr. Pope. I wasn't sure how to explain my predicament to the receptionist. "I have to get in right away, because my husband's funeral is at three."

She was taken aback and said, "Oh, I'm so sorry. I can get you in with a nurse at nine."

"Fine, whatever, I just need someone to see him."

Mom and I took Mattias to the hospital. I cringed when I saw the big garage door where the ambulance had parked to take Hugo into the emergency room. That felt like a completely different life. So much time seemed to have passed, but in painful slow motion. Only a week before, I been standing right here, certain that God was going to save Hugo.

I felt a twinge of anger at that girl who had been so wrong to hope, and also at God for not choosing to save Hugo. My human desire to have my best friend back constantly wrestled with my spiritual certainty that God was good and knew what was best for Hugo's life.

I turned my eyes to the task at hand and walked Mattias up to the pediatrician's office. Dr. Pope had found out about Hugo, and she graciously pushed her appointments around to fit me in. I was so thankful to see her, instead of having to explain the whole situation to another new doctor.

She looked him over and said, "Well, let's check for strep throat, and then take him downstairs for an x-ray of his chest. Some kids hide pneumonia, and I can't hear it with a stethoscope."

As annoying as it was to have a sick child on this day, it was really the best way to keep my mind off the impending sadness that I faced later in the day. Not only was it my husband's funeral, but I hate being the center of attention. Everyone would be looking at me and wanting to hug me and talk to me.

We waited in the x-ray waiting room for quite a while. Finally, Mattias's name was called. We went in, and I have to admit he was so cute and so brave. The x-ray technician took off Mattias's T-shirt. I thought he would cry and want me to hold him with all the machines and the uncertainty of what was going on.

"Mattias, they are just going to take a picture of your chest. Nothing is going to hurt."

He trusted me completely. He raised his arms over his head just as the technician had showed him. The light came on and the technician arranged the light square on Mattias's small, bare chest. I smiled at how handsome he looked with his shirt off and arms up, almost like he was showing off his muscles. "Daddy would be so proud of you," I said.

Two clicks later, we were done and on our way back upstairs. Dr. Pope confirmed it, "He has pneumonia. Here is a prescription you should get filled so he can take a least one dose before the service and maybe feel a little better. He's not really contagious, so it's no problem if he goes."

By the time we got home, there were people arriving from out of town. All of Mom's family was there. Dad's family was still around after Christmas. Uncle Ron was Layla's savior; he was the only one who could really get her to relax and sleep. He said, "The trick is to relax and let her melt into you."

I was still nursing Layla at this point, but other people were taking care of everything else she needed. Mattias was starting to unravel between being physically sick, having so many people in the house telling him what to do and where to go, and not understanding why his daddy was gone and his mom was crying all the time. He was an emotional mess and wanted me to hold him most of the time.

Some of my friends from SCORE had arrived as well. Ron Bishop wanted to be there, but had just had hip surgery and could not travel yet. John Zeller came in his place, but also as a friend who cared. Our Dominican Republic directors, Tim and Ginny, came, as well as Ryan and Megan. Even if they hadn't been our leaders, they were still our friends, and I knew they would have made the long trip just to support me and remember Hugo.

I visited with my friends and family for a while, but then Mom said I needed to get ready. I wrote out what I planned to say at the funeral. Dad came over and handed me three verse cards. The one that caught my attention was from I Cor. 15:58: "Therefore, my dear brothers, stand firm. Let nothing move you. Always give yourselves fully to the work of the Lord, because you know that your labor in the Lord is not in vain."

I knew Layla was hungry, but I wanted her to nurse right before I put on the nice bra I needed to wear with my new outfit. Once I put on the bra and my new silky shirt, it would be really hard to nurse Layla without unbuttoning and wrinkling all my clothes. She would have to breastfeed the minute I got out of the shower, right before I put on my nice clothes. I told Mom the plan so she would know when to bring Layla in. But I had waited so long to nurse her that the warm shower caused letdown.

I quickly got out and grabbed a towel to stop the flow of milk before Layla got there. I tried using the other end of the towel to dry off. But I had put the towel down to get my underwear on. At that point I was literally spraying milk, and I quickly snapped two tissues out of the box and held them up to my chest. I couldn't put on my bra yet and save myself with bra pads, because I needed to nurse Layla first. I was still waiting for her.

Holding my tissues with one arm, I tried to comb my hair and put on deodorant. My Aunt Ronda brought Layla in then. I was kind of embarrassed that I was only wearing underwear, but I grabbed her and lay on the bed to feed her. Right when I got started, Mattias walked in crying. Thankfully he shut the door, but he crawled on the bed with me and told me that he wanted me. "Me carry you, Mommy. Me carry you," which meant, "You carry me."

He is normally very rational when I explain things so I tried to tell him, "I am nursing Layla right now. I can't hold you."

"But me carry you Mommy." Mattias was bawling now. Being tired and sick had pushed him over the edge, and he couldn't function at all. But what could I do? Layla was also crying, because I was moving around too much and she couldn't eat properly. I was getting milk all over the bed, and the tissue on my other side was about maxed out with milk, too.

My aunt heard the noise from upstairs and came to check on me. I'm sure I looked a fright, as I was lying on my bed, in only my underwear, with two crying kids. My look of exasperation must have told her what I needed and she asked, "Do you want me to get your mom?"

"Yes, Please."

This whole milk disaster was not what I needed on the day of my husband's funeral, but I tried to laugh about it. Some more "Hugo Humor" to help me make it through.

Mom was doing a million things upstairs, but she came down to rescue me. She took Mattias upstairs so I could finish with Layla and get ready. We needed to leave soon. I was finally able to get ready without further incident. I went upstairs and passed Layla off to Uncle Ron, the official baby soother at this point.

I found Mattias with his favorite bunny-bear on the couch. I knew if I could mentally prep him for what was coming, he'd know what to expect and what was expected of him, and he'd do better overall.

"Mattias, we are going to church, and there are going to be lots of people there. You can stay with Mommy, but I cannot carry you. I have on my pretty clothes, and I don't want them to get wrinkly until later. You are going to hold my hand and walk with Mommy to the front of the church. We will watch Uncle Mark play guitar. We're going to see lots of pictures of Daddy, and some friends are going to talk about Daddy. You can sit with Mommy the whole time, but you have to sit; it's not playtime. At the end, Mommy is going to go up front to talk. You will stay and sit with Grandma and Grandpa. Okay?"

"Okay, Mommy."

I repeated the same instructions a couple of times before we got to the church, and he seemed to understand. We waited until we were supposed to walk in all together. Mattias was holding my hand, and I was so concerned about him doing well that I temporarily lost track of Layla. We were about to walk into the sanctuary, and Layla was not in Mom's arms as she was supposed to be. I had decided she should stay with us as long as she did not cry. If she did get fussy, Danielle would to take her to the nursery, and the lady there would take care of her for the rest of the service.

Just then, Ronda rushed up with Layla; she had left to change Layla's diaper. We walked in, Mattias holding my hand all the way to the front even with everyone watching him. When we were sitting in the front row, Mattias pointed and said excitedly, "Candy!"

There was a candy bar plant on the front table, from the kids to Hugo, and Mattias obviously liked the selection. There were sunflowers on the table from me, to remind me of all the sunflowers that Hugo had given me throughout our marriage, but also for Hugo to know his "Kansan Girl" was saying goodbye.

Word of Life in Argentina had sent a big spray of flowers. One of the presidents of the school, Andres Fernandez Paz, had called and left a message on my cell phone, too. I was very touched by both of these gestures. Both SCORE and North Oak had sent arrangements. SCORE had helped me set up a memorial fund, and we had asked people to give to the fund instead of send flowers. The flowers we had were plenty. Hugo always used to remind me of what his mom liked to say: "Why do people give flowers in death? They should give flowers in life. The person will enjoy them much more."

As much as I dreaded being at this service, I actually enjoyed it so much. It was so glorifying to God and honoring to Hugo. I know Hugo would have been proud of how everything turned out, especially the music. My brother led the youth team and did an amazing job. I just had to lift up my hands and praise God! One of the songs we sang was the one that Hugo had just sung and cried to a little over a month earlier when Tito had died, "Blessed be Your Name." I raised my hands and sang to God,

"You give and take away
My heart will choose to say
Lord, blessed be Your name"[1]

I really did and do believe that with my whole heart. When it was my turn to share at the very end of the service, I tried to explain that to the people attending, but also add some humor, as Hugo would have wanted. When Pastor Ken called me to the podium, I took a second to arrange my notes and collect my thoughts. When I looked up, I was overwhelmed. I had not looked behind me the whole service. The sanctuary was full, with people sitting in chairs out in the foyer as well.

I was totally taken aback, and I said, "Wow, there's a lot of people here …" I almost lost it before I even began. I was so humbled, and I knew Hugo would have felt so honored and would have cried too.

I swallowed and continued with what I had prepared, "First of all, I just want to assure everyone that I know God is in control. I trust God's heart, His perfect plan for me and my kids. Isaiah 55:8 says, 'For My thoughts are not your thoughts, neither are your ways My ways,' declares the LORD. 'As the heavens are higher than the earth, so are My ways higher than your ways and My thoughts higher than your thoughts.'"

I kept my points as short as possible and let the Holy Spirit help people come to the conclusion that God had already brought me to. My next thought was simply, "Hugo always talked in wonderment about lives that God used to glorify himself. I know Hugo would have been honored, and I count it an honor, for God to think us strong enough to endure this tragedy."

Next, I wanted to be true to Hugo's funny side, but also share the hope I had that I would be okay and laugh again. I said, "I want to share a few of Hugo's philosophies about life, as deep as they are."

There was scattered laughter in the audience from those who knew Hugo well.

"Never listen to a whole song, because there are a lot of songs and not enough time. Eat all the food you want, because you never know when Christ is coming, and we don't want to leave it for the Antichrist."

But the point of sharing the funny stuff that was classic Hugo was to make the main point about another thing that was Hugo's.

"And the other thing I want to share is Hugo's fetish for wristbands. In almost all the pictures you can see here, you'll see his phases of wristbands. It started out with the original Lance Armstrong one, Live Strong. Then he had a white one. I don't remember what that was for. Then he had the wordless book one. He even wore a green one about organ donors for a while, because my cousin Justin is a recipient. But his newest fling was a special black one.

"Last Monday, I stared at this black wristband all night. It says, 'I AM SECOND.' Hugo was in the bed, and I was holding onto his hand, which had this wristband on it. I just kept staring at it.

"I kept hearing Hugo in my mind, saying time and time again, 'Honey, it's not about us. We're second. It's about Christ. It's about God being glorified in our lives, whether in life or death. It's not about us. It's not about us. It's about God. It's about God.' And I just heard it over and over again. Hugo knew his life was second, and that Christ was first. I know that I am second, and that Christ is first. The verse that echoes in my mind is Romans 8:18, which says, 'The sufferings of this present time are not worthy to be compared with the glory that shall be revealed in us.' I know that glory will be revealed in Hugo's life and death. I know that glory will be revealed in my life and in my children."

The last thing I said before leaving the stage was, "And I'm so thankful for …" I got choked up and had to stop for a second. I started again, "I'm just so proud of Hugo for the life that he lived, and that I can hold my head high and tell my children about his life. He was an awesome man, a great husband, and a great daddy. Thank you."

I returned to my seat and immediately started crying. People were clapping, but I wasn't really paying attention. Then I noticed they kept clapping. And now they were standing. I cried harder. I prayed they only saw Christ in me and were clapping for His strength and comfort in my life, because alone I was so weak and frail.

At the end of the service, the pianist played "I Can Only Imagine,"[2] by Mercy Me. Hugo had loved that song and had played it a lot on guitar. He loved it so much that he entered the sanctuary on our wedding day to that song, played by the same pianist that was playing it today. Only God knew that between those two songs would be fewer than six years of marriage. But it was worth it, and God was glorified in us and in our marriage.

During the whole service, Mattias either watched, slept, or stood next to his chair and put his head on Grandma's leg. He didn't say a word, except when the slide show started and he said, "Daddy!" When the picture of Hugo with his colored baseball glove came on the screen, the same picture that we had printed to put at the front of the church, Mattias said, "Look, Mommy, Same." Nothing gets by him.

Only after the service did Mattias go crazy again on me. He walked out with me, but then went to play with another boy. He quickly got lost in the sea of legs that were coming out from the sanctuary. I was unaware of anything that was going on with him. A girl brought him to me, and he was upset and crying. I tried to greet people, listen, and give hugs with Mattias attached to my hip, but my back was quickly giving out. I looked at Mom in pain and she understood. Mattias once again went kicking and screaming bloody murder. There was nothing I could do; so many people wanted to give me condolences.

I was surprised at some of the people who came. I was so touched at how much everyone truly cared for Hugo. He was not from Hays. He was Latino. But I could see the impact that he had had on us all. He was a missionary to Hays and had brought us all closer to God. All of my mom's work friends came, including her boss, Mark, who was with Hugo when he first collapsed on the basketball court. Also, several of the basketball guys who he played with in the past were there that day.

A van full of friends from Kansas City Baptist Temple had driven the five hours to be there for the two-hour event, and then driven the five hours back. Katie, a friend from Tabor College, whom I had not seen in ten years, was there. There was even a family friend who lost her son on the mission field to appendicitis. She had found out about the funeral that morning and had gotten in the car and driven three hours from her house to attend. She wanted to support me; her son was about the same age as Hugo when he died.

It was nice that it was Christmas, because a lot of people who wouldn't normally be in Hays were in town visiting family. A young man that Hugo once tutored in guitar, CJ, was there. He was a Marine by now, and Hugo and I had not seen him for several years. I saw him standing with his family in the foyer. I did not get a chance to visit with him. Looking at the guestbook later, there were so many people with whom I would have loved to stand and talk more, such as Anne's parents. But it was hard to find the time to connect with everyone.

In an overdramatic moment, I complained to my brother, Mark, that I was mad because Hugo had ruined Christmas forever.

Mark wisely said, "Just think about this. You will always be with friends and family on the day that Hugo died."

I was so happy to be with friends and family. And so grateful that Carlos and Febe had made the trip. I spent a couple of moments with them, just sitting in the living room away from other people and catching up in Spanish. We made some plans for when Irma could come. Also, Carlos was very interested in making sure I was taken care of financially and did not have any needs.

I explained to him how God was providing in this area. We visited quietly about Hugo, too, and reviewed exactly how it all happened. There were a lot of details that I hadn't told them over the phone. We had a lot of catching up to do, and I was sad because I knew there was not enough time to share with them all I needed to share.

I also wished Irma was there so I could comfort her with all the stories of God's grace and care during this time. We also talked about Cesia, because losing Tito was still fresh in our hearts. I feared that God had given Cesia too much when He took her husband and brother so close together. I tried to trust God's plan for Cesia, but I couldn't imagine surviving the loss of Hugo and my brother like that. I hoped she'd remember what Hugo had told her: "God still has a perfect plan for your life."

Carlos showed me a picture of the mutilated truck on his cell phone.

"So how is Cesia handling all of this?" I asked.

Febe had been with her for several weeks after Tito's death and had insight, "She is handling it better than I would have thought. She is seeking God so much more. Her friends don't understand how she can be doing so well. Some of Tito's family members are on relaxants or sleeping pills, and some have completely lost it. But Cesia is really turning to God for help in her time of tragedy and change."

"Do you think she will stay in Argentina?"

"We are not sure, and I don't think she is sure yet either. Everything in her life is changing right now. Tito held the family together, and without him the family has no idea how to function or get along. She is feeling a little bit like an outsider."

"Well, I feel so blessed to have a family that loves and cares for me and makes me feel welcome, even without Hugo. I just feel so horribly for Cesia. Not only does she have the pain of losing her husband, she also has to struggle through the trauma of the car accident itself.

"There are so many 'what ifs' in that scenario. I feel blessed that there are no 'what ifs' in my mind. There was no car accident, no medical mistake, no one was at fault. God wanted Hugo for His good purpose, and He took him from the earth. If there is such a thing as a merciful death, then God gave that to Hugo. And He gave me mercy. It could have happened during that half hour that we were together talking about the prayer cards. Then I would have the memory of seeing Hugo have a seizure, and Mattias would have seen it too. God spared us from that. The aneurysm could have happened while Hugo was driving to basketball, and he could have hurt someone else. That would have been even more horrible. God chose the perfect timing for this to happen to Hugo."

Carlos looked directly at me and said, "It is good to thank God for His provision, even in Hugo's death. It helps to see how God was in control of the situation, even though it feels as if He wasn't. And Sarah, you always have a home in El Salvador. We would find a place for you to live close to us, and I could get you a good job. You'd have ministry too. Just let me know, and I can arrange everything for you."

He almost convinced me to just move to El Salvador, but deep down I knew God had other plans for me. "Thank you Carlos."

Carlos and Febe left the day after the memorial service. I couldn't have done it without them. Carlos had given a message in Spanish on behalf of Hugo's church and family, which really made the service special and honored Hugo's heritage. My extended family stayed and hung out with me for another day. The little baby girls had fun wriggling together on the floor.

Letters continued to pour in, and I found it comforting to sit and read the Bible verses that people would send to me each day. It was so amazing to see how God had used Hugo and me to touch so many lives. And it was humbling to receive such generous memorial gifts and encouraging cards from friends, family, SCORE teams, acquaintances, people in the community, and people who had never met us.

I even heard from the Billy Graham Library we had visited, as well as author and artist Joni Erickson-Tada. God used many letters to encourage me, and they stayed by my bedside as I read them over and over in my darkest times. Cards from other widows who knew what I was going through helped the most.

Despite the deep pain of losing Hugo, in my soul I also felt a unique passion and urgency to point others to Christ. With the reality of mortality fresh on my mind, the usual inhibitions that normally go with talking to people about their eternal state seemed to almost disappear. There were several people I felt God giving me clear direction to speak to openly.

On Wednesday, I called a couple pastor friends and Ron Bishop and asked them to pray because I was going to go to the basketball court to talk with the basketball players who were with Hugo when he first collapsed. Dad, Mom, Mattias, and Layla went with me. Dad walked around with Mattias, and Mom held Layla. Pastor Jeff had gotten my message to pray and soon showed up to give moral support.

Because it was Christmas break, there were only about six guys there, including Mom's boss, and a friend of Hugo's named Jeff. I bravely stepped forward and asked if I could say something.

They stopped warming up and stood around me on the court, respectfully listening. They were so nice; they even looked at me and made eye contact. I talked about life being short, and how we need to know where we are going to spend eternity when we die, and how we can know for sure. It was about ten minutes long, but I felt a little justified in taking up their time. God had truly emboldened me to speak truth.

I noticed that people spent more time listening to me than they had before. I guess people feel like they are obligated to listen to widows more than regular people. I was definitely going to use that advantage to further the kingdom of God. Maybe people listened more because they felt sorry for me, but I also think it was because they could see an active faith, and they knew that it is real.

I remember a couple months before Hugo died, there was a quote from Beth Moore that I really wrestled with. Beth asked, "Do you really have faith, or are you just spoiled?"[3]

On the drive back from Bible study, I thought, "Do I really have the strong faith that I think I do, or has nothing bad ever happened to me?" Through losing Hugo, God showed me that my own faith was real. It wasn't just lip service or a feel-good relationship. My faith in God and His character had not wavered. Instead, I felt empowered to take the platform that God had given me and use it to glorify His name even more than I ever had with Hugo by my side.

I thought back to Pastor Steve's challenge to the youth group the week before Hugo's death. "What would you give up to rub shoulders closer with Jesus?" I now understood that I could hold onto Hugo in many ways. My heart could hold onto him, even though his body was no longer on this earth. I could idolize him in my heart. I could reject this as God's good plan, and become bitter and angry. I could pull the covers over my head and not make a difference for eternity, saying, "God took away my husband, so now I can mope around and be sad for the rest of my life."

Or, I could give up the human response to death, grieve how God wanted me to grieve, while cultivating my deep relationship with Jesus, and then share what God had taught me at every opportunity.

I also felt that losing Hugo validated my ministry in the Dominican Republic. I felt that now, when I stood before Dominican ladies who have suffered much through life, they could no longer say, "But you are just an American. You have never gone though anything bad in your life." I had gone through tragedy, and could personally say that God is faithful, and He is worthy to be praised when He gives AND when He takes away.

One the most important ways that I wanted to use my platform to have someone hear the saving power of the gospel was with Jerry. Jerry was the man talking with Hugo the moment he collapsed. He was the last one to see Hugo's smile, hear him laugh, hear Hugo say his wife's and kids' names and that he loved them. Jerry wrote to me after the memorial service,

Dear Sarah and Family,

My name is Jerry, and it now appears that I was the last person to talk with Hugo before he died. In addition to expressing my most profound sadness at your loss, my desire is that this letter will provide some consolation to you and to all who knew and loved him.

I had known Hugo since he first started coming to noontime basketball. He was a good man and a happy man. He was well-liked and respected by all the players. He could be a fierce competitor, but he always displayed positive sportsmanship, poise, and self-control.

On that Monday noontime I shook his hand, welcomed him back and inquired about his family. He had a beautiful smile on his face as he spoke about his wife and, with justifiable pride, his small children. His expression that I will always remember could only be described as one of great love, tenderness and joy.

As I looked away and looked back, I realized something was terribly wrong. He was unconscious. He experienced no pain that I could see and never to my knowledge regained consciousness.

I was honored to have known your husband and to have called him my friend. I was moved to write these words in the hope that they would be of some small comfort in your loss. Again, my condolences to you and your family. God bless Hugo, and may he rest in peace.

Sincerely,
Jerry

I felt God wanted me to invite Jerry and his wife, Christine, to have coffee at my parents' house and visit. I had to know if he was as sure of his salvation as Hugo had been. Ten minutes before he arrived, I felt so sick. Mom was there and we prayed. Mom said, "Maybe Satan does not want you to witness to Jerry, and this is spiritual warfare going on."

I ran to the bathroom just as they arrived. I felt horrible, but this was really important to me. Everyone was already sitting down at the dining room table as I joined them. I got a drink from the fridge first, to try and collect my stomach. The cold water seemed to help little, but as soon as I started talking with Jerry and Christine, I felt much better. We talked about Hugo, and Jerry recounted for me again Hugo's last moments in the gym. Jerry works as a psychotherapist, and he said, "I have seen many seizures before, so when I saw Hugo's seizure, I knew it was bad. It was different from others I have seen."

He was very honest about the details, but very kind and careful in his wording of what he had experienced. I shared with him some of the comfort that God had given me during these first few days.

He said, "Well, it has been very good for me to sit and visit with you and see that your faith is helping you to do well. It helps me to see that."

We were wrapping up our conversation, so he and Christine stood to leave. I had Layla in my arms, but I stood too. I felt in my heart that I had to complete the task God had given me to do, "Jerry, I want to ask you something, and I hope that you are not offended."

"Okay, I will listen to anything you have to say," he said gently.

"If it was you that day, and not Hugo, do you know for sure where you would pass eternity?"

"Sarah …" he searched for the right words, "I cannot speak definitively about something I do not understand."

"I just want you to know that you can know for sure. A person is born with sin, and because of that he is separated from God, and there is nothing humanly possible he can do to get into heaven. When we realize that we are sinners, ask God for forgiveness, and thank Jesus for dying on the cross for us, we become true children of God. This is the only way that God allows people to enter into His heaven when they die. Once we ask Jesus to cleanse our hearts from sin, then we can be 100 percent sure that we will be face to face with Jesus when we die."

"I see. Thank you. I will think about this."

"Would you read something if I send it to you?" I asked.

"I will read anything that you send to me," he responded politely

"Okay, I will send you a book. Also, Jerry, I want you to know that I am thankful that it was Hugo, because he was 100 percent sure of his salvation and could speak definitively about it." There was much passion in my voice and my words hung in the air as they seemed to sting at all of our hearts as the meaning of what I had just said settle in on us. But, I had said the truth according to the view of someone looking at the eternal perspective.

I did send Jerry that book I had promised him and pray for him faithfully. God is working great things in his life. Months later he shared with me in an e-mail:

> "With over 25 years in the mental health field I have come to understand and truly believe that healing and recovery come from a Higher Power, and if grace occasionally flows through this, my calling, it indeed gives me the beginning of an understanding of humility. In an attempt to simplify and clarify as well as I can His purpose for me, I can best reference Micah 6:8 . . . 'do justice, love mercy and walk humbly with your God.'
>
> "I offer you my support, encouragement and prayers for your ministry. I appreciate your thoughts and prayers for me.

> "In His light and love, Jerry"

The next matter I set my energy into praying about was what God wanted me to do next and where? I looked back on the verse card that Dad had given me the day of the memorial service, I Cor. 15:58: "Therefore, my dear brothers, stand firm. Let nothing move you. Always give yourselves fully to the work of the Lord, because you know that your labor in the Lord is not in vain."

I really felt that I just wanted to go home. My heart still felt at home in the DR. All my material stuff was there, our car, my awesome pillows and comfortable bed that I missed. I just wanted to go home. Had I lived in Colorado when my husband died, I wouldn't have moved back in with my parents, so it didn't make sense to do that just because I lived in another country.

Eventually I had to go home and try to establish a new normal. The Dominican Republic was like another state, just a tiny bit further away. I could decide to go back now and, if life did not work out the way I imagined, I could come back.

Besides, if I stayed in Hays, my parents and friends would be working during the day. I'd still be alone and living a normal life, but not even in my own house. It didn't make sense to stay in Kansas.

In the DR, I live in my community of missionary friends. Maybe if Hugo and I were out in the boonies of Africa or another place where we had been secluded from other missionaries or security, going back would have been a concern, but we had not been in that situation. God had ordained us to work with this mission group, and live at SCORE with 24/7 security guards. This was the perfect scenario for a widow and her two children to return to the mission field. I'd have help with the kids too, as Bethany would soon be coming to the DR to start her ministry to the missionaries by watching children.

Most of all, we were a family in the DR. Everyone would chip in and help, oftentimes at a moment's notice, whereas here in the States play dates are usually planned in advance. And in the DR I would have awesome spiritual friends to uplift me and help me though any hard moments. It seemed to be the best option, but I wondered if I was just crazy.

I asked Mom, and she saw the wisdom in my going back. She wanted someone to check her thought process, so we also asked Dad, my boss Tim, and Ron Bishop. They all agreed that this was the best decision. We would try it, and, if it did not work out, then I could fly back to Kansas.

But I was confident that I would stay, because I knew that in Hays I would be sitting around, and I wanted to be doing the work of the Lord that would never be in vain. Hugo finished the work that God had for him to do. He did that work well, and I'm confident he heard, "Well done, my good and faithful servant" from the lips of his Savior upon entering glory.

But my work here on this earth was not done. I could be the next 29-year-old to drop on the basketball court. I wanted to make this life mean something for the next.

The decision was made; I'd be going back to my beloved mission field. Going home! I felt part of my sadness fall away. I hadn't realized how much the stress and fear of an uncertain future had been wearing me down. I was not looking forward to calling the airline to explain to them about Hugo's death, file paperwork, and try to get the plane tickets pushed back from January 15th to the 22nd.

I would not be ready by the 15th, because I was trying to get a life insurance policy for myself, get my taxes done, and wait on the death certificate. Most importantly, I wanted to have half of Hugo's ashes buried in the Hays cemetery before I left; the other half would travel to El Salvador and be sprinkled or buried. I wanted to be done with the hard part. There was a lot still to do.

I called the airline. They looked up my reservation. "Ma'am, those tickets were never purchased, because the credit card did not go through. I will cancel these reservations, and you go ahead and buy whatever tickets you want."

I breathed a sigh of relief that it only took a five-minute phone call. I wondered what had gone wrong, though. My memory was very limited, and I had forgotten many details of the days before Hugo had died. I thought for a long time, and I finally remembered our conversation. I had told him, "Use the new bank credit card."

"Did you activate it yet?" Hugo had asked me.

"I think so, just try it and see," I encouraged, thinking the airline would reject the card right away if it wasn't going to work.

"Well, it looks like it worked. I'll check our reservation later to confirm," Hugo had told me. We were so busy over the next couple of days with our date, the youth group activity, and speaking in Coldwater, that he never checked the e-mails in our account. We had never actually purchased tickets back to the DR.

It was funny that I was so excited about something that, under normal circumstances, would have been really annoying, and Hugo probably would have been upset about it, too.

I made another call. It was to a friend of Hugo's from our church in Hays. "Dustin, I am making plans to go back to the Dominican Republic in January. But, I really want to have the emotional stress of burying Hugo's ashes done before I go. Would you please make a box for me to put Hugo's ashes in?"

"Sarah, I don't know what to say. I've never done anything like that before, but I will figure it out. I'd be honored to make this for you."

"Thanks. I actually need two, one to bury here in Hays, and one to carry half of Hugo's ashes to El Salvador."

"No problem. Just let me know what you want engraved in the top. I'll be over in a couple days to show you a sketch."

The list of things on my to-do list got longer. But I took time out to celebrate New Year's. I did not want to be around too many people, so we drove to Ellis, a small town about 15 minutes west of Hays, and hung out with Bill and Anita. Anita was the woman who had watched the kids when Hugo and I went on our last date. We talked about what a God thing that was.

We left Ellis early, and I camped out with the kids under the Christmas tree. Hugo and I had been waiting to do that, but we never got the chance. I really wanted to do something special with the kids, though, and I love sleeping under the lights of the tree, so that's what we did New Years Eve.

At church, I mentioned to a friend's father that I was praying about whether I should do a monument. It seemed right, so I wanted to talk to him about it. This man, Ron, owned a monument shop by the cemetery. Hugo had accompanied him several times, especially in the spring when the ground was soft, to place monuments on graves. Ron agreed to help and called me a few days later. I made an appointment to see him at his office with my parents.

In the meantime, I called City Hall to see how much it would cost to buy a plot at the cemetery. It was a lot cheaper than I thought it would be: $150, plus a $50 opening and closing fee. My parents, Ron, and I met the caretaker at the cemetery on a cold, snowy day to see if I liked the plot's location before I bought it.

The caretaker scuffed some snow off a ground marker with his boot while looking at a map. "Well, this is it."

It was too cold to take a lot of time to decide. Did it really matter anyway? My eyes darted in the direction of the heart tombstone where Hugo had hidden the last clue to my birthday scavenger hunt. "I bet he did not think the 'death do us part' would come so soon," I thought. The plot was close to the cemetery road, which was good. I couldn't think of any other criteria that should influence my decision. "It's fine," I said over the wind.

"Okay. You can call City Hall to buy it. They will contact me about the details of when to open and close."

I cried a few tears when I got the paperwork and receipt in the mail saying that I had bought a grave plot.

I met Dad and Mom at Ron's office to talk about memorial stones. Ron met us at the door and showed us to a table to sit and talk. "Would you like any coffee or water?" he offered.

Mom and I both asked for coffee. I'm not much of a coffee drinker, but I felt really cold and needed something. I prepared it the way I drink it and took a couple sips. It did not warm any of the coldness within me. This was one of those surreal moments that I wished I didn't have to experience. Ron was so caring and gentle, however, that he made it okay, almost natural, to be talking about tombstones.

He showed us a couple of thick picture books of different possibilities. I hadn't realized the number of options available for a memorial stone. Not only did I have to decide on the stone, I had to pick a shape and a texture. Then I needed to decide not only what it should say, but how. Did I want the name with the middle initial or without? And what typeface did I want for the lettering? This was something that would take more than one meeting to decide.

I started to understand that this meeting was not for final decision-making, but to explain to me all that I needed to think about, so I could go home and pray about it. I did just that but, before we left, Mom asked Ron, "What is the price range that we are talking about for a memorial stone?"

"I don't want Sarah to worry about the price. Please choose what you want, and the other details will work out." It was another way that God provided for me through the body of Christ. Ron continued, "Just take the books home and design Hugo's memorial the way you want. But may I suggest that you put your name on the stone as well? Your plot can legally hold two sets of ashes. You can be buried there one day if you choose to be cremated. Even if you choose not to be buried there, you can have your dates listed next to Hugo's either way. It's important for your children to visually see the love and connection their biological parents had. Pray about it and let me know when you have a draft of what you want."

I pored over the books for hours and prayed for God to give me wisdom to put just the right words on the stone. Two days later I called Ron back and said, "I have a draft."

"Okay, bring it in and we'll talk it over," he said.

Mom met me at his office during her lunch hour, and we finalized the details of the headstone. The stone would be brought from overseas, made during the winter, and placed in the spring or summer. I felt peace sweep over me at having made another huge decision and satisfaction that I had done the right thing. I knew Hugo would have loved how I designed it. Hopefully he has a chance to see it from eternity.

I started going though Hugo's clothes and packing. After I took out special items for Mattias, Layla, and other family members, I was going to donate all his winter clothes to Goodwill and take all of his summer clothes back to the DR to give to his Dominican friends.

For some reason, I was more attached to some of his new clothes that he had never even gotten a chance to wear. His new sunglasses that we had bought after his LASIK surgery were really special to me, as were his guitar, his leather watch, his wallet, his new tennis shoes, and the SCORE shirt that he wore that Sunday in Coldwater (I still slept with that shirt). These were the items that were most special to me.

When I was going through a stack of papers that needed to be dealt with, I found the long birthday card that he had written to me. I put the stack of papers aside so I could really read and appreciate the last love letter he had ever written to me. He wrote in Spanish:

Hey Sarah:

Before anything, I just want to remind you that you are the best after God in my life. Thanks to you, I can know that there is a God for sure, because only He knew what I needed in my life, and that was you. I love you. I love you today much more than before. It is so beautiful to know that when I love you I can adore God at the same time. Again, thank you for being a part of my life and of my future here on earth.

Like I have told you before, heaven has to be incredible if we are not going to need to be together because God is there. In reality I can't imagine that now, but I trust that God knows this for our future.

I give thanks to God for giving me the privilege to know you first as my friend; well, first as a missionary serving on the ship and working for God in El Salvador. I remember when I saw you for the first time. WOW! Later, to know you as my friend and even today as my best friend is a great blessing. To have someone like you at my side in good times and in hard times – thank you. To know you as my girlfriend and fiancée, and now as my wife. Thank you because, even if you don't believe it, you help me to see God more in my life with how you trust in me for everything, as the one who can protect you and help you to grow in God. And now to know you as a mother. Sarah, I don't know if I tell you enough, but you're incredible!!

Your strength, your love . . . how can I tell you . . . you are my hero! Thank you for loving Mattias and now Layla and me. I have peace in trusting that I have you at my side in our future as a family. You are very important for me and never doubt it! I love you.

Now that you turn 29 years old, I give thanks to God for allowing me to be part of the last 5 years and almost 9 months together in your life, and in truth I am excited to see what God has in the next 105 years in the future, because I am sure they will be a blessing and an anticipation of what heaven will be like.

I love you, and with the help of God it will be like that for as long as He permits it. (Or in other words, until death do us part)

With all my love and admiration,

Hugo

I just sat there on the floor and did not know what to think. He had literally said goodbye to me in my birthday card. When I first read this card on October 29th

I thought, "Aw, that is so nice." And I had said to Hugo, "Thank you for the love letter and for loving me so much."

In light of Hugo's death, the card's impact and message were very different. He had mentioned heaven three times and had signed it "until death do us part." I was just dumbfounded. I translated the card and read it to Mom. She was as shocked as I was. We knew that it was a gift, another way that God had been gracious to help me see that He was in control from the beginning until the end, even now as I entered a new season.

An early journal entry marks other new beginnings for me.

1/9/10

I finally washed the sheets that Hugo and I last slept on together. I cried taking them off the bed, and cried even harder when I found Hugo's boxers crammed into the foot of the bed.

Mattias was with me and he asked me, "Mommy, what happened?" He came and sat on my lap while I cried. He did not cry with me as he usually does, but just hugged me and sucked his thumb. I told him, "It's okay, Mommy just misses Daddy."

I told Mom today that if I ever do remarry, I wouldn't want to change the kids' last name. Also, I think it would be a miracle to find another husband in the DR, but if God did it once (a boy from El Salvador and a girl from Kansas), He can do it again! I just hate being in the single world again! It is so frustrating to have to decipher motives and moves from guys. But, as Hugo always said, "Just run towards God, and if you see someone keeping pace and running in the same direction, then join teams and run together."

Hugo was my one and only; my only boyfriend, ex-boyfriend, boyfriend again, fiancé, husband and best friend. My Teddy. I love and miss you Hugo. I hear him telling me, "Patience." Second Corinthians 4:16-18 says, "Therefore we do not lose heart. Though outwardly we are wasting away, yet inwardly we are being renewed day by day. For our light and momentary troubles are achieving for us an eternal glory that far outweighs them all. So we fix our eyes not on what is seen, but on what is unseen. For what is seen is temporary, but what is unseen is eternal." Wow!

This verse helped me feel confident that the unseen eternal glory would "far outweigh" Hugo's death and my suffering now. My suffering did not feel light and momentary, but I chose to fix my eyes on an eternal view.

The next day, God gave me a quote that spoke to me about my return to the DR. I knew I was supposed to go back, but I didn't know into which ministry I'd fit. I would not be able to host teams and keep up with my kids too; the job was too demanding. So what would I do? Teach English? I wasn't sure my passion was in that area.

The quote was from Dawson Trotman, founder of the Navigators: "If you can't see very far ahead, go ahead and go as far as you can see." I knew then that I just had to be obedient to return to the DR, and God would show me the very next step that I needed to take.

Another journal entry:

1-11-10

Two days ago, God gave me 2 Corinthians 4:16-18 to comfort me. Today I woke up, and I knew it was going to be a hard day. I called Mom, and she got an emergency babysitter for Mattias. I'd been watching movies, but finally decided to check e-mail. Kara had sent me Elisabeth Elliot's newsletter.

It didn't fix my day, but it reminded me how God has an orchestrated plan. Elisabeth writes in her May/June 2003 "The Elisabeth Elliot Newsletter"[4]: "I know the proportion of that pain, and there is no minimizing it here and now. I also know the truth of 2 Corinthians 4:17, 'These little troubles (which are really so transitory) are winning for us a permanent, glorious and solid reward out of all proportion to our pain.' The bigger the pain now, the bigger that 'weight of glory' will be. It's mysterious, it's unimaginable, but it's going to be, and for that we give thanks."

(Elisabeth Elliot is a Christian author and speaker. Her first husband, Jim Elliot, was killed in 1956 while attempting to make missionary contact with the Auca (now known as Huaorani) of eastern Ecuador. She later spent two years as a missionary to the tribe members who killed her husband.)

The day after I received the newsletter a massive earthquake struck Haiti.

1/12/10

Haiti had a huge earthquake today. I feel many things. Sadly, right now, I feel more pain for one man's death when I am certain of his salvation, than I do for thousands of people who likely went to hell. I am excited, though, because my parents, the kids, and I bought our plane tickets this morning before the earthquake. That's good if the prices go up now, but I am excited because I will be closer to Haiti, and maybe somehow I will be able to help in relief efforts. Maybe we can get water filters to Haiti.

Many things were happening all at once. It was hard to keep my head above water. I got a call from Nancy from the Midwest Transplant Network . She informed me, "Hugo's liver saved a 24-year-old girl's life. A 64-year-old woman got a kidney. She was two years on the transplant list. His other kidney and pancreas saved a 42-year-old woman who was on the list for two years and seven months. She had been doing daily dialysis.

"Also, they had a place for his heart in Minneapolis, but because of the weather the team couldn't get there. His heart was not even taken out of his body. They also were not able to use any of the other parts that you had agreed to donate. Hugo had lived in the Dominican Republic for a year, and it is considered an 'at-risk' country, because of its proximity to Haiti among other issues."

Though on the one hand I was sad that Hugo was not able to give more in his death, on the other hand I was grateful to know that his body ended up more "normal" than torn apart. I was glad his heart stayed with him.

I asked her, "Did the girl that stayed with Hugo play any music for him?"

"Yes, she told me she played John Mayer and the Beatles the night that he was in and out of surgery to remove organs."

I smiled. John Mayer was a new favorite of Hugo's, and the Beatles were an old favorite. So perfect. "Thank you Nancy, for being so helpful and understanding."

"You have my number. You call me if you need anything."

I did my best to help Mattias process what had happened. We talked about Daddy often. I'd ask him, "Where is Daddy?"

He'd always reply, "In heaven with Jesus Manger." Because it was Christmastime and we had talked about Jesus being born in a manger so much, I think that Mattias thought that Jesus's last name was "Manger."

After Mattias and I would establish that Daddy was in heaven, Mattias would pat his little chest and ask me, "Me heaven too? Me go heaven?"

He just wanted to see his Daddy, but I'd try to explain, "No, heaven is a place we go when we die. But hopefully you will be Grandpa Great's age or older when that happens."

This also led to many conversations about Jesus and the cross. I'd explain, "Mattias, you know that the only people who can go to heaven are those who believe that Jesus Christ died on the cross for their sins. Do you believe that Jesus died on the cross for you?"

At first he told me, "No." But then he laid very still and thought for a moment and said, "Yes die ... yes die." There are so many things that I never thought he'd understand, but God has shown me that he does.

My church was helping me in so many different areas. I never realized how far people would go to help. They did extraordinary things, almost always without me asking. And if I did ask, they were there in a second.

One huge blessing was a meeting I had with a woman from the church. She told me, "I am a widow and I just feel the Lord wants me to visit with you."

I knew her husband, so I was surprised when she told me she was a widow.

When Debbie arrived, we sat in the front room and she told me that her husband was 25 years old when he died of a heart attack. Their daughter was two. She gave me a book called *To Live Again* by Catherine Marshall[5] and said, "This book really helped me when my husband first died. Maybe it can give you some encouragement too. Also, I came to tell you that I am going to commit to pray for you every day for this first hard year."

I looked down at my hands. "Thank you, Debbie. I know I am going to need it."

"Also, here are some verses that helped me a lot." She handed me two note cards. The first had Jer. 29:11-12 written out. God had already revealed that Scripture to me, but confirmed it again in my heart through Debbie. The second card had Ps. 27:13-14: "I know that I will live to see the Lord's goodness in this present life. Trust in the Lord. Have faith, do not despair. Trust in the Lord."

I exhaled slowly, letting the verse sink in like the first whiff of homemade bread. Then I breathed in slowly, almost as if I were taking my time to eat that bread I had smelled, and make it a part of who I was. The words were true, active and powerful. God would be faithful to this promise, and I looked forward to experiencing "the Lord's goodness in this present life."

1/15/10

Last night I had a dream about Hugo. He was playing guitar at a basketball court off to my left, and I could hear that he was playing my love song. I was trying to cross a wooden plank to get to him, but I was too slow, and the song ended before I could cross. It was such a weird dream, but it was nice to hear him play guitar again.

Later I decided that Hugo was probably still playing guitar, but he was playing for Jesus in His courts instead of for me. One of the things that was hard to do early on was remember where Hugo was. Sometimes I just thought of him as gone, like non-existent. I had to work on reminding myself that he is still alive, just not here. He is still smiling, still laughing, still Hugo; he is just doing it in heaven instead of here on earth. Reminding myself of this truth in dark times really helped me to find the hope in Christ that I needed.

This was especially meaningful as I prepared myself for some important milestones before I returned to the DR. I had asked Pastor John to prepare a baby dedication for Layla. She was supposed to be dedicated the week after Hugo died, but we pushed it back until the last Sunday we could. But I really wanted to do it. It was important for me to try to keep her childhood as "normal" as possible, although it never would be. There were certain events that I wanted to follow through with, even though they were harder without Hugo.

Pastor John did a great job dedicating Layla to Christ, meaning that my parents, the church, and I committed ourselves to raise Layla to be a disciple of Christ. I believe, and was told by others too, that there were more tears that morning than during Hugo's uplifting memorial service. Pastor John even had to ask Pastor Ken to finish the dedication in prayer. The elders also came to lay hands on my shoulders and commission me to the mission field again, something the church always did before Hugo and I returned to the field. I felt incredibly alone in that moment. I had fought tears during Layla's dedication and had lost. Now I was losing the battle again.

The tears continued into the afternoon, as today was the day we would bury half of Hugo's ashes. Mattias and Layla did not go with us, because I did not want Mattias to think that Daddy was there in the ground. After our conversations about heaven, I felt he understood, but I didn't want to confuse him. So, Mattias and Layla stayed with a babysitter that chilly afternoon, as friends and family gathered to put Hugo's ashes into the ground.

It was a small group. That was how I wanted it. At the gravesite were the church's three pastors, their wives, my grandma, my grandpa, my parents, my friend Danielle, and Danielle's husband, Steve. The funeral home director, Rick, stood close by for any assistance we needed. At the last minute, I remembered that I should record this, so Hugo's family could see it. I called my friend Brandon and his wife Sarah to videotape and take pictures.

Dustin and his wife Sheila were also there. Dustin had made the box to hold Hugo's ashes, and he started our time at the cemetery by telling about the meaning of the box. "When Sarah called me, at first I did not want to do it. It took me a while to get into it. I went to the shop, and cherry wood was the best wood they had, so that's what I used. After that, I wanted everything about it to be the best that I was capable of. It may have imperfections and flaws because I have never done this before. I made it by hand; that was what I was supposed to do.

"It has 28 dovetails on it; that's as close as I could get to his age. I went to the garage and got it all cut out. It took a couple of days to get motivated. I tried to get in the right mindset, so I just turned on the worship music. At the last minute, I decided there was something missing. The black is ebony, and it represents sin in our lives, before Hugo came to Christ. Then it changes to the white hickory, and that's when he finds Christ – when he came into the light. Then it leads to the white cross. I did not want the sin to wrap around completely to the other side. It was rewarding to build it, and I consider it a privilege."

The burial was the last big thing on my to-do list before the kids and I flew to the Dominican Republic. My parents went with us. It was an eventful trip; on the second flight I ended up in first class with both kids, which was funny and frustrating at the same time. It was funny because Hugo and I always complained that we never got seat upgrades in all of our travels, and the first time I flew without him I rode in first class.

But it was frustrating because I needed help with both kids, and my parents were stuck all the way in the back by the toilets. At one point I had to walk all the way to the back and pass off Layla to Mom, so I could help Mattias eat his lunch. I felt bad because the cabin didn't get lunch, and adding Layla to the already cramped space seemed cruel, but I didn't think I could juggle both kids without being thrown out of first class.

Once we landed in the DR, my stomach started to knot up. So many emotions were rushing through me. I was excited to be home, but I also felt as if something were amiss without Hugo. It was as if I had forgotten to pack something important, like my arm, or rather, half my heart. There was also a part of me that kept thinking that he was there waiting for me. That he hadn't come back from the November baseball camps he had gone to with Mark and was just waiting for me. It felt as if he should be there.

I entered my apartment at SCORE, but no, he was not there. It was like the moment I had returned from the hospital and seen his flip flops under the coffee table. His presence was in every room, but his physical body was not. I sat on our bed and cried. Not about any one thing, I just needed to cry. I missed Hugo so much.

Layla was my saving grace for that day. So many people wanted to meet her and see her. I enjoyed taking her around to all the other missionaries. The cooks, the maids, and other Dominican friends at SCORE loved meeting her too. Mattias was already down at Mali's house picking up where they left off, playing on the swings on the back porch. Some things had not changed, and this was a huge comfort to me in my changing world.

We held another memorial service on January 30th. Pastor Ken, his wife, and two other couples from my church came down to attend the service. Ron Bishop gave the gospel, and Pastor Tim from Shelby, North Carolina, also spoke. Later that day, I thanked Pastor Tim again for the amazing hotel room his church had blessed our family with. It was our one and only family trip together, and it was a great one.

We sang "Days of Elijah"[6] in Spanish at the memorial service. It was special because we had sung it in English at the Kansas memorial service. We also sang "Levanta Tu Casa,"[7] which was one of the church plant's favorite songs that they'd learned from Hugo. Shelly, a youth volunteer from North Oak in Hays, sang and did the motions, as Hugo had taught this song in Spanish to our youth group. Mattias even did the motions, and he looked at me excitedly as he recognized the song that Daddy sang with him a lot.

My parents left the next day, but I would see them again in a month or so. Another memorial service for Hugo was scheduled in El Salvador for March 14th. I had to make it through our sixth wedding anniversary on February 14th, then Hugo's birthday on March 4th.

I knew it would be hard, but I was relieved to get all the hard days out of the way early, and not have to dread them all year long. My grandma, who had lost her husband almost ten years ago, had advised me to celebrate both and make plans beforehand. She had learned that just letting the day pass without plans always seemed to be worse than planning to do something special.

On our anniversary, I ordered a cake from an amazing bakery in the capital called La Cuchara de Madera, or "The Wooden Spoon." The cake was chocolate and vanilla checkerboard, with chocolate frosting. Hugo and I had tasted this cake once at a friend's birthday and loved it. It was the perfect way to celebrate. I invited anyone who wanted to, to come and eat cake at my apartment that night. Many friends showed up to support me on this important day. It was the best way to celebrate what could have been a very sad occasion.

There were still tears, but mostly out of joy for the years I had spent with Hugo. There were also "I miss you" tears, and some "how can I do this without you?" tears, and even some "poor me" tears—all of which I thought were okay.

Stages of grief, right? Sometimes the stages flow together quickly. I had to focus on anchoring my center in Jesus, so that as I grieved at each stage, I would continually come back and be face to face with Christ. As First Thes. 4:13 says, "Brothers, we do not want you to be ignorant about those who fall asleep, or to grieve like the rest of men, who have no hope."

Yes, I grieved. Hard. But I did so in hope. Jesus Christ was my hope, and I anchored my soul firmly to His steady hand. It was only through this steady hand that I was able to "celebrate" our anniversary without Hugo.

I received many e-mails from people on that day to remind me that they were praying for me. But one that encouraged me the most was from Pastor Jeff's wife, Jessica. She wrote, "We are thinking of you and praying for you today. Well, we do every day, but especially today. Dare I say … Happy anniversary!"

She was bold enough to say what no one else thought was appropriate, but it was what I really wanted. I want my wedding day to always be a happy reminder of God's unique plan for my life.

Another e-mail from my friend Michelle also helped remind me of this unique plan. She wrote: "I wanted to send you a note since I know today is your anniversary, and I'm sure that that is really hard. I have been thinking a lot about your wedding this week and how beautiful it was. I will never forget our summer on the Island and how much you were struggling with whether to marry Hugo and what your family thought and all these different things.

"It was amazing to see how the Lord ultimately brought you together, and there wasn't a question in anyone's mind whether it was right. I remember all the time I got to spend with Hugo's family and how awesome it was to see your families loving each other even when they didn't speak the same language. It was an incredible picture of the way the gospel brings cultures together. The really cool thing is that your families are united forever because of Mattias and Layla. None of this brings Hugo back or changes the pain in your heart, but it's encouraging to me that so much was done through your lives even though your marriage was cut short."

I celebrated Hugo's birthday on March 4th in much the same way. This time I ordered a strawberry cheesecake from La Cuchara de Madera, and I asked Pastor Aby to cook an Argentine *asado* (Argentina's gourmet version of a barbeque) and serve it to me and some friends. It was a low-key, relaxing meal out on the patio by the small pool. It was touching to see several of Hugo's Dominican friends stand before the meal and give tributes to him.

After the birthday party, I began preparing for my two-week trip to El Salvador. I was stressing about it, to say the least. I'd be traveling alone with the kids for the first time. Plus, all eyes and ears would be on me. I hate being the center of attention, and Hugo's family, friends, and church would all be looking to me for answers and comfort. But they would also want to comfort me.

Without Hugo to smooth over everything, to speak Spanish for me when I was shy, and to work out all the personal relations in his family, this was going to be a stretching trip for me. I knew that I needed to help Hugo's family find some closure and some of the peace and comfort that I had found. Plus, there were so many stories that I hadn't shared with Hugo's family over the phone. There were so many things that I needed to tell them, so they could see the hand of God in all of this.

As soon as I walked out of the airport, I was greeted by Irma, Hugo Sr., and Carlos. As happy as their smiles were when they saw me, their eyes betrayed their sadness, too.

Irma later told me that she half-expected Hugo to walk out of the airport with me, and it was so hard for her to see me and the kids walk out without him. She said, "Because I wasn't there for the funeral, my mind just thinks that he is in the States or the DR. I forget that he is gone. I know that in my mind, but seeing you actually come here without him, my heart is finally starting to understand the reality of Hugo's death. It just doesn't seem real."

I gave her a big hug. This was why I had come, and it was already starting. I spent almost every night visiting with Irma, and sometimes the rest of the family, too. I told them many stories of how God was carrying me through. There were my hospital experiences, the chaplain from Quinter, the Dixie cups, and the Hugo Humor.

I shared about the birthday card, and on and on. Every night I'd wrack my brain for more details to share. Sometimes Irma and I would pass the afternoon together talking, or I'd play the video from the memorial service in Hays or in the Dominican Republic, and I'd translate it for her. We also watched the video from when we buried the ashes. We cried together.

One of the most important conversations we had was when I told her, "Irma, I did as you asked. I never told you this before, but I think that it is important for you to know. I did say goodbye to Hugo from you. I told him in his ear, 'Hugo, your mom says, "I love you very much my son. Goodbye, and I will see you at heaven's gate."'"

She said, "Thank you. I never knew if you had a chance to tell him for me, but I'm glad you did."

My parents arrived a couple days before the memorial service. We were a little worried about transporting human remains, but had acquired all the necessary papers. Mom said it was quite a reverent scene passing through airport security.

She spoke softly to the agent on duty, "We are transporting cremains to El Salvador in this box."

The officer nodded his understanding of the delicate circumstances and indicated to her the proper procedure. "You need to remove the box containing the ashes, place it in its own container to pass through the X-ray machine, and place a coin under the box."

"Okay," Mom said, and started unzipping her suitcase. Then she asked, "What is the coin for?"

"It is just to confirm to the X-ray technician that he can see through the whole box."

The officer left and explained the upcoming scan to the man looking at the X-rays. Several other officials standing nearby heard him and started watching. Other people in line caught on to what was happening, and Mom told me later, "Everyone was quiet. You could have heard a pin drop. They all watched Hugo's box of ashes pass through the X-ray machine. There was a respectful hush evident in the room. It was so amazing. I put the box back in my carry-on and wheeled it away. It was so touching. Hugo would have cried, like he did when he saw the commercial where everyone in the airport starts clapping for the soldiers coming home."

The memorial service was held at Hugo's church. We sang "Days of Elijah"[6] again, the uniting theme of all three memorial services. Some of Hugo's old worship team members came together to help with the worship. This revealed the new hole of Hugo's absence as well as the continuing hole created when Jose Carlos died. He had been in heaven for two years by this time.

One of the elders spoke during Hugo's service: "For some reason God has chosen to take two of the good ones from our church family. Both Jose Carlos and Hugo had gone to Bible school and dedicated their lives to full-time ministry. It doesn't make sense to us as humans, but we'll just have to trust in God's unique plan. But He must have been crazy to bring those two boys together in heaven. One by himself was funny, but put those two boys together and you're just asking for trouble."

It was funny, but so true. Hugo was always a people-pleaser by himself, but with Jose Carlos in the room too, they were out of control.

I retold the story of the "I am Second" bracelets that I had shared at the other two services. Many of Hugo's friends and family were there, including some friends that Hugo and I did not even get to see the year before.

This memorial service was the hardest and most tearful for me. It had been several months now, and the protective bubble that I had lived in at first had worn off. I had done enough grieving to know that if I did cry, I would not totally lose it and make a scene, so I was more comfortable with crying now.

But I think it was sadder because of whom I was with. This was Hugo's family. As much as people in Kansas loved him, they only really knew one part of Hugo, and had only known him for maybe six years. SCORE friends loved him dearly too, but had only known Hugo for two years at the most. Even though in the end, as his wife, I knew him the best, I still only knew Hugo for the last ten years of his life. His church and his family had known him for all 29 years of his life. The grief that I felt in this church, sitting with his family, was much deeper than I had felt elsewhere.

Cesia had chosen not to watch the slide show of all of Hugo's pictures before the service, but during the service, when we started the video and pictures of Hugo started to flash across the wall in front of us, I moved from my seat with my parents and sat with Cesia. We sat arm in arm and cried and cried. We also laughed at some of the pictures on the screen. It was sad, but healing in some way.

Cesia and I passed a lot of time talking about Tito and Hugo. We felt connected to each other in such a deeper way because we totally understood what the other one was facing. Somehow we made it through the memorial service together as a family.

The next afternoon, Irma stood in the doorway of the living room. I sat on a lounge chair next to the door. We talked about how beautiful the service was.

Then she was quiet for a moment, and I saw tears forming in her eyes. She said, "I feel like I buried my son yesterday."

We both cried. It was hard to hear her say that, but I knew in my heart that my purpose for coming to El Salvador—closure— had been fulfilled. It was slowly happening for Hugo's mom, three months after his death.

We had planned to go to a nice resort the next day and sprinkle Hugo's ashes in the ocean. But we were all so exhausted from the memorial service that we couldn't bring ourselves to leave the house. Also, Cesia was feeling sick, so we would have to wait until Friday when Carlos had the day off from his pastor duties.

We had decided to go to a beautiful resort called DeCameron. Hugo and I always had joked that it should be put into a will that one's ashes should be sprinkled in Hawaii or Fiji or some nice place, so that the family has to go on a nice vacation to comply with the deceased's wishes. That was partly my thinking, but I also wanted to scatter his ashes in a place that I might visit again, especially with the kids, so I could explain to them the significance of that place.

Carlos, Febe, Daniela, Cesia, Irma, Hugo Sr., Dad, Mom, Mattias, Layla, and I stayed one night at the resort. We spent the first day in the pools, eating and drinking all we could hold. We laughed and played in the sun. We ate a nice dinner together and went to a children's show. Then we made plans for the next day.

We all awoke early and met on the beach right after the sun came up. We knew we wouldn't be able to sprinkle ashes on the resort beach, but we crossed over the rope that was the boundary to the resort and held our service on the public beach.

I set up my video camera on a small tripod in the sand behind us, because I knew it would be important for the kids to watch this someday. We all sat on the bigger rocks that were in the sand, facing the water. I placed my beach bag in front of us and pulled away the sides to reveal the beautiful wooden box that Dustin had made. It was similar to the one that was buried in Kansas, only this box had the phrase engraved on the top in Spanish. Dustin had added three small red lines on the cross, one for me, one for Mattias, and one for Layla.

Hugo Sr. had brought his guitar, and we started to sing a hymn. Hugo Sr. made what was likely his first ever musical mistake, and we ended up singing the wrong words to the wrong music. I didn't even realize we had done that until I watched the video later, but I think it shows the true heart of Hugo Sr. in that moment. Though he never says much, he was so preoccupied with the events that were happening that he could not even do what he does best, music.

Carlos gave a short message. Mattias and his cousin, Daniela, played in the sand quietly. Layla lay between my legs, enjoying the feel of the sand on her toes.

Then we stood and pulled the bottom off the box. I had unscrewed the bottom piece off the night before to make this part go more smoothly. Carlos untied the twisty tie and handed the bag of white ashes to Irma.

As soon as the ashes hit the water, the gentle waves started to take them along the shore. They billowed out into a big white cloud. A stronger wave washed over Irma's feet. I felt like Hugo was kissing her and saying, "Bye bye, Mama. I love you."

We all watched the beautiful cloud for a long time. I noticed that some of the ashes had sunk directly to the rock and stayed in a little pile. I knelt down and waved my hand in the water. I felt the ashes bump into my hand as they danced away in the current. I looked again at the white cloud dissipating before me. "Goodbye, Hugo. I love you. Patiently I wait to see you again soon."

The big events were over; maybe now I could start to heal a little more.

Two wooden urns were made by a friend of Hugo—one in English to be buried in the cemetery in Hays, Kansas, and the other to hold the cremains that were sprinkled in El Salvador. "Matt. 25:21 Well done, good & faithful servant… Husband, Daddy, Son, Brother, Friend."

Mattias and Layla loved to go see, "Daddy's Rock," as Mattias calls Hugo's memorial stone, and then they have to walk around the "rock park."

The new Liborio family. Adults L-R; Sarah, Cesia, Irma,
Febe and her husband Carlos. Kids L-R; Mattias, Layla, Daniela

Sarah and the kids on Easter 2011 at their church in Juan Dolio, Dominican Republic

Mattias and Layla are the blessing and joy of Sarah's life.
Taken in 2011, Mattias is 4 years old and Layla is 1 ½ years old

Please visit my website, www.my-onceuponatime.com/, to see more pictures and videos from each chapter.

Epilogue

Healing and Ripples

Only a *true* "happily ever after" story can happen when we are all united in heaven and worshipping our Savior together with all our loved ones. That is the day I look forward to and desire more than anything—to be in my heavenly home. And not just to see Hugo, I know seeing him will be icing on the cake. But, Ps. 73:25 says, "Whom have I in heaven but you? And earth has nothing I desire besides you." I want Christ. He is my first love, although I have realized since Hugo's passing something profound.

Hugo made me feel more "at home" here on earth than I had ever felt before. Now, without him, I feel more distinctly the fact that I do not belong here. I am a social misfit who does not fit into "couple life" any more and struggles with the "single life scene." All of this just tells my heart further, "I do not belong on this earth. My home is in heaven."

Yet, I know that my work here on this earth is not finished. So I seek to do His will until He chooses to bring me to my true home. I understand Hugo did the work God had prepared for him to do. He's already heard, "Well done my good and faithful servant . . ."

I, however, keep my focus on the "bema seat," knowing that when God judges my works (not my salvation), I want to have done everything He has prepared for me to do. "God prepares good works before the foundations of the world." I have to keep my head up and remember my work is not finished. That is why I returned to the mission field. First Cor. 15:58 says, "Therefore, my dear brothers and sisters, stand firm. Let nothing move you. Always give yourselves fully to the work of the Lord, because you know that your labor in the Lord is not in vain."

A friend of mine told me, "You're like a modern day Elisabeth Elliot, because she returned to the mission field after Jim Elliot was killed." While I humbly admit there are some similarities to our stories, and I pray God could use my story to reach as many people as Elisabeth has reached in her life, that thought got me thinking: "I should write to her."

I looked for information online, and her website, www.elisabethelliot.org/, said that a handwritten letter must be sent to her now-husband Lars. Her health is poor, and she is not able to keep up with all the correspondence, so Lars has stepped in for her. He soon wrote back to me:

> Dear Sarah,
>
> Thank you very much for your kind letter, and for letting Elisabeth know how *Quest for Love*[1] and *Passion and Purity*[2] had influenced you as a high school girl. It is terribly sad to read of the ending of one phase of missionary life with the death of your husband after waiting so long to be on the mission field. I'm sure that it was a joyful time for you. You have the unusual character of "stick-to-it-iveness" (if that's a word) in being able to return one month after Hugo's passing. It reminds me very much of Elisabeth, who lost Jim when Valerie was less than a year old. People expected her to take the baby and return to the States. Her reply was something to the effect of, "I was a missionary as a single woman and also with Jim, and, until the Lord gives me further guidance, I will remain so."
>
> We do hope that if the project continues and is published that it will be a blessing to those who have encountered such losses as you have; and also that it may spur others to the mission field. May God bless you and your two little ones.
>
> Lovingly,
> Lars and Elisabeth "Gren"

So, my life presently, returning to the mission field alone with my kids, might not be the "ever after" that happens in fairy tales. But perhaps the best "ever after" that I can offer this side of glory is a verse from Psalms 27, which says, "I am still confident of this: I will see the goodness of the LORD in the land of the living." That sounds like a "happy ever after" to me.

I know God is not done with me yet because he says in Phil. 1:16, "For I am confident of this very thing, that He who began a good work in you will perfect it until the day of Christ Jesus."

Until my true "happily ever after" is written in heaven, I know that God has a foretaste of heaven here on earth for me. I am confident of this because He promises it in John 10:10, "I come to give you life and give it abundantly." Also the Bible says, "You turned my wailing into dancing; you removed my sackcloth and clothed me with joy..." (Ps. 30:11)

I have seen already God's goodness in many ways, but to name a few:

After the memorial service in El Salvador, before Cesia traveled back to Argentina, she went forward in the church and recommitted her life to the Lord and announced she would now be seeking Christ and walking closely with Him. And, when she returned to live in El Salvador, she would like to be a part of the church.

I cried sweet tears of joy when Cesia told me this. Hugo and had been praying for this moment for many years.

Another earthly joy is that Febe and Carlos became parents again, with a little girl. They named her Sara after me. I cried tears of love and humility, as Febe told me that their family loved me so much and wanted to have a reminder of me close to them, and that they also pray that their little girl can love and serve God the way I have in my life.

I write this Epilogue exactly one year since I lost Hugo. I look back on the last year and feel the time went so quickly, and it was just yesterday that Hugo and I were on this road of life together.

Yet, in another way, I feel as if a lifetime has past over this year, and my life with Hugo was just a great dream I had once. The greatest thing I can say about this year is I now know "the fellowship of His sufferings" (Phil. 3:10) and how curiously wonderful that relationship with Christ can be.

I was compelled to write this Epilogue because of that unique relationship with Jesus over these first tender 12 months. I want to help others in grief to see or feel what it might look like to open their hearts to the fellowship of His sufferings. Yes, there is pain—but with a sweetness—and Christ draws nearer to you than you have ever felt Him in your entire life.

Second Corinthians 1:3-5 says, "Praise be to the God and Father of our Lord Jesus Christ, the Father of compassion and the God of all comfort, who comforts us in all our troubles, so that we can comfort those in any trouble with the comfort we ourselves have received from God. For just as the sufferings of Christ flow over into our lives, so also through Christ our comfort overflows."

First of all, I want this chapter to give praise to Lord Jesus for being the Father of compassion, and I pray it will be a testament to His tender care for his loved ones. But may it also comfort those in any trouble. As you have read about my sufferings, I want even more for you to read about my comfort that overflows from Christ.

I had to choose to open my heart to the Holy Spirit. No one could tell me exactly how to heal. I had never lost a husband before, and I kept telling my mom, "I don't know how to do this."

The Holy Spirit knew this, and, more importantly, He knew me. He led me in my healing. It was painful. I had heard the grief process is like childbirth. I had recently had Layla, so the following quote interested me. I don't remember where I heard it, but it said, "If you resist the pain, it will take longer and hurt more, but if you accept the pain and 'just let it hurt,' it will go better with you."

From that moment on, I tried to face the pain and not be afraid to hurt. Temporary pain could not kill me, but grieving forever might. What God did in my life over this last year, and what He continues to do, is worth the past and present pain.

One of the first elements God taught me was to learn to say "yes." After I read any verse in the Bible, I would say, "Yes." A few of the verses the encouraged me many times were:

Job 23- When He has tested me, I will come forth as gold. Yes!
Psalms 73- God is the strength of my heart and my portion forever. Yes!
Isaiah 43- When you pass through the waters, I will be with you. Yes!

I believe God is big enough for our questions and outcries of rage, if need be. But how refreshing it is to just say "yes" and claim His powerful promises from His word as our own. His promises are true and alive.

I relish a child-like faith, because it is so simple to just say, "Yes, Jesus, I believe your word" and even curl up in his lap and sleep in his arms if I need to.

I also said "yes" to books. I accepted any book that anyone gave to me, or sought out ones people suggested. It was another walkway in which I felt at least I had a starting point for the Holy Spirit to guide me.

I would be reading along, and something would jump off the page. Most of the time I'd set the book down and meditate on what I had read for a couple of days. Sometimes, it would be a thought, but God would help me develop that thought into a form of change in my heart. I would like to share a few of my grandest realizations:

One of the first books I read was, *To Live Again,* by Catherine Marshall.[3] She says, "After comfort, the next need of the bereaved is for the ability to distinguish between body and spirit."

In her book she shares that while waking up one morning it seemed that her late husband, Peter Marshall, spoke to her and said, "Don't think of me as dead."

There was a lot to this concept, and I started thinking on it a lot. The thought was there, but I had to meditate and pray about the idea before it could take on a concrete form that could help heal my heart. Finally some solid ideas formed, chiefly being, Hugo is still alive.

Death is only an earthly term to signify that person is no longer on this earth, but "death" is not a heavenly term. Hugo was still alive—just not with me.

How something so basic could give so much joy! I would imagine Hugo still smiling his toothy grin, still laughing, but now he was probably laughing at something Jesus said.

It calmed me to think Hugo was still playing guitar, but now he was doing it before his Savior. How selfish of me to think Hugo could only play for me, when the Lord wanted to hear the gift He had given Hugo in a live concert. Just confirming in my heart that Hugo was not dead now, nor would he ever be, gave me such peace and comfort in my grief.

Another thought I had about Hugo in heaven actually gave me chills. As anyone who knew Hugo well could attest, Hugo was notorious for many things. The best of these was that he constantly talked about how much he loved me and his children.

I started to imagine Hugo walking with Christ in a garden, and they are discussing a lot of the questions Hugo always told me he was going to ask Christ when he got to heaven.

Then, out of the blue, Hugo starts talking about me and the kids and how much he loves us and is so proud of everything we are doing. And knowing more about me and the kids than Hugo does, Jesus joins in on this topic too. Here's where I get goose bumps: Jesus just said *my* name. He's talking about *me.*

I know from the Bible that Jesus knows my name, but there is something different about knowing someone that is actually in the presence of my Lord. And I know my husband enough to know that he has told all of heaven about me.

To know with certainty that my name is being spoken in heaven, in the throne room, before my Savior and the King of all Kings, is a thought that brings me to tears in humility and wonder.

Another deep thought that took me several days to contemplate was simply a Bible verse I had read in *The Misery of Job and The Mercy of God,* by John Piper.[4] It is a beautiful book of the book of Job told in poetry form, with beautiful photographs on each page.

The last section of the book opens with the verse from Job 42:5, "My ears had heard of you, but now my eyes have seen you."

I felt a rush of emotions hit my heart. Instinctively I closed the book and my eyes at the same time. I realized I had stopped breathing, and I purposefully breathed in slowly. I thought about how I have heard about God all my life, loved Him, served Him; I thought I "knew" something about God. I have come to realize how little my knowledge was.

He is much greater and majestic than any box I could put him in. In many ways, I feel I have truly *seen* God for the first time in my life. I recently said at a women's conference concerning the above verse in Job, "I have loved Him. I have always loved Him, but now I can say that I've seen Him. Be jealous of me and my sufferings."

I added, "I am somewhere between never wishing this [losing a loved one] on my worst enemies and loving the sufferings I have had in Christ." My heart has been so torn because I love seeing God in a way that I have never experienced him, but I don't love living this life without Hugo.

One quote that carried me far in my healing came from a book called Let *me Grieve but not Forever*[5] by Verdell Davis. It exactly pinpointed my heart's tug of war. Davis quoted James Means' book, *A Tearful Celebration:* [6]

"The very fire that blackens my horizons warms my soul. The darkness that oppresses my mind sharpens my vision. The flood that overwhelms my heart quenches my thirst. The thorns that penetrate my flesh strengthen my spirit. The grave that buries my desires deepens my devotion. Man's failure to comprehend this intention of God is one of life's true calamities" (Davis, p. 15)

I had felt these ideas inside of me, but could not put them into words until I read them on the page. It was a profound revelation that, because God is God, He is powerful enough to take the worst event in my life and work it for my good. Romans 8:28 comes to mind, "And we know that in all things God works for the good of those who love him, who have been called according to his purpose."

Davis encouraged me yet again when I read, "Even Christ struggled with the suffering that lay ahead . . . (p. 35)." Davis also quoted C.S. Lewis saying, "Suffering is not good in itself. What is good in any painful experience is, for the sufferer, his submission to the will of God (p. 35)."

We know that in the end Christ did pray, "Yet not my will, but yours be done." (Luke 22:42) Knowing that even Christ had struggled to come to the point where he could accept God's perfect will for His life gave me great assurance of where I was in my grief journey with losing Hugo. I felt even more permission to grieve how it came to me: to hurt, feel pain, struggle, and fight for a new hope to hold onto on the bad days.

I followed Christ's example and struggled deeply, but I also followed His words and continually said to God, "Not my will, but yours."

A topic that some people are careful never to bring up, and others, lacking in sensitivity but not curiosity, invariably bring up is: "Do you think you will remarry?"

This is the inevitable question for any widow, but especially young ones. Even within the first weeks of losing Hugo, I felt that I needed to ponder such things.

In those first days, I recoiled in horror at ever changing my last name or having my children call another man "Daddy." I questioned a widowed friend who had remarried the month before, after three years of raising her three kids alone.

She told me, "It seems impossible now, but when God prepares you for another man, He will give you the grace to accept such changes, and you will be ready to let go of that resistance for change for fear of losing his memory."

She also wisely counseled me, "Loving another man is like having your second child. Your love for the first does not diminish when you have your second. Divinely, God gives you a new capacity to love the second with the same strength as the first, and also appreciate the differences they might have."

I had always told Hugo that I would probably not remarry if he died, solely because of the time investment it takes to start and carry a relationship to marriage. But, as I prayed about everything more, I realized at least four factors:

First, I believe it is Biblical for young widows to get remarried, if it is the Lord's will. First Tim. 5:14 states, "Therefore, I want younger widows to get married, bear children, keep house, and give the enemy no occasion for reproach."

Second, after knowing the delight of companionship, it is a terrible thing to be alone. I know Hugo would not want me to be alone. He was too practical for me to think that he would be jealous. I also realized that now his love is perfected in Christ and is exactly what it should be from I Cor. 13, "Love is not jealous . . ." Hugo does not have the capacity to be jealous of any man that God might bring into my life. Hugo would only want the best for me.

Thirdly, I know Hugo would want someone to be a daddy to his beautiful children, to play with them, teach them about life, and show how to be passionate about spiritual things. Hugo loved being a daddy to Mattias and Layla, and whatever Hugo loved he always wanted to share with someone else. I'm certain Hugo would want another man to experience the joy of raising two amazing kids.

Lastly, I have found it is almost nearly impossible to do life and ministry without a partner. Only through the grace of God can it be attempted at all. I have felt that grace of God during this last year while living in the Dominican Republic. But, it is definitely not ideal.

Ecclesiastes 4:9-10 states, "Two are better than one, because they have a good return for their work: if one falls down, his friend can help him up. But pity the man who falls and has no one to help him up!" Life in general is rocky, single parenting is a huge challenge, and ministry can also be discouraging if there is not that second person to balance the ups and downs of life.

These still are my convictions about remarriage. When God brings them to light, they are good, honest thoughts about remarriage, and there is nothing wrong with that.

Then God shot a few holes in my hidden intentions. Sometimes I do not even know what I am holding in my heart until the Holy Spirit reveals it to me and shows me how to fix it or tells me I need to let it go.

The important thing is for me to always be open to the Holy Spirit's guidance in areas of my heart.

I was reading a book titled, *When God Interrupts,*[7] by M. Craig Barnes, and in four sentences in one paragraph the Holy Spirit ripped to the roots of hidden intentions that I did not realize were there.

The story was about the man by the pool of Bethesda, and Jesus passed by and asked him, "Do you want to be made well?" The man started to tell Jesus how the world around him worked and was already hinting at the plan he had formed about needing someone to help him into the pool when the angel stirred the water.

Then Barnes says, "Notice that *Jesus didn't help the man with his plan* to get into the pool." Barnes continues and specifically hit the nail on the head with me: "He didn't get him *married* or divorced. He didn't get him a new job that paid better. He didn't set him up with friends. *He didn't do anything that would distract the man from his brokenness. What Jesus did was heal.* (Barnes, p. 89)." *(Italics mine)*

Through this one paragraph, God revealed to me that though my justifications for desiring remarriage were good and true, my heart was in the wrong place. He showed me my heart was hurting—badly. Somehow I thought if I could just get remarried, the pain would go away. Loving another would fix the pain. Jesus does not want to distract me from my brokenness by helping me with my plan to be remarried. Jesus wants to heal me because He is the healer of hearts.

God used His Word and many other books to unearth parts of my heart and soul I had dared not look at yet, and he also used people. God chose my friends and fellow SCORE missionaries to encourage and support my ministry work this past year. They are key to my life and ministry in the DR.

I also was strengthened by the many widows whom God brought to me through the short-term mission groups visiting SCORE. Many of them sat in my living room and retold their stories and let me retell mine. We shared many tears, and God used these times to bolster and encourage me. I even met a woman who at one time had had a brain aneurysm. She shared with me her experience of hearing her husband's voice and trying to respond and not being able to move.

She remembered being in a helicopter, when they transported her to another hospital; she just didn't know why she was there. She could feel her husband's touch and tried desperately to open her eyes and squeeze his hand, but to no avail. Her body would not respond to her mental promptings.

Hearing about her experiences comforted me because I was more confident that Hugo had heard me before he died. He heard me tell him I loved him and the kids loved him. I was more certain the tears I had seen were a result of Hugo's emotions and not his body's reaction to something. It was important to me that I had connected with my husband one last time on this earth, and through this woman God gave me that extra assurance.

These widows taught me steps they had taken that had helped them. One suggestion was to make a list of things I need to let go of and then take my time letting them go.

I wrote things such as, "Not sleeping with Hugo's T-shirt. Give away Hugo's dress suits. Change voicemail message on our answering machine."

I took my time and only let go of those things when it felt right to do so. Another suggestion was to list what I had lost. Not solely my husband, but what else did he complete in me that I now did not have? I wrote at least a thirty-item list to start with and still occasionally add to it.

On it I have listed such things as, "My computer and electronics guru, my safeguard for fun adventures, an extra set of hands with the kids, someone to eat my hash browns when I get a McDonald's breakfast meal, someone to remind me to do things, my driver in the car, tickler and energy expender for the kids," and the list goes on and on.

I may not grieve much for the loss of Hugo; I trust God so much with His perfect will in taking Hugo. I do grieve everyday in having to live life and continue on without Hugo.

The lists help me to feel like I am doing something concrete to help me heal. They were great learning tools. I did everything anyone suggested to me, anything to stay open to the Holy Spirit's work in my life.

I wanted to do my part in healing, so that when God was done using my brokenness in my life I would be ready to move on and He would not have to wait for me.

I'm sure my greatest downfall is not being patient with a process that takes time. Constantly God reminds me to "Wait, and He will renew my strength," or "Be still, and know that I am God."

As much as I prefer to do something, God has brought me to his green pastures (or maybe it was a desert) time and again to learn how to be what He wants me to be.

Another way God has helped me heal is through unique circumstances. They may seem random to some, but I know they are divinely planned. To share a few:

On Thursday, April 22nd, four month after Hugo's passing I wrote an entry on my blog. Some of the story will be familiar to you after reading the full story in my book, but I still think it is important to share. I wrote:

"Today has been 4 months since Hugo got the best upgrade ever! Into heaven! Hugo and I always joked about how we never got so lucky to get an upgrade into 1st class!

"Funny how when I came back to the DR one month after Hugo died, the first time I flew without him, the kids and I got an upgrade into 1st class! I could hear Hugo laughing!

"I wish I could tell you there have not been tears today. There have. I miss him a lot. But, I noticed last night that I don't miss him like when he'd be gone for a trip. I still miss him, but the advantage now is that I can talk to him whenever I want.

I'm not in the huge practice of it, but when something special happens, or I really want Hugo to know that I miss him, I just pray, 'Jesus, could you give Hugo a message for me? Just lean over and whisper in his ear that Sarah misses him right now, and Mattias just pooped on the porch!' (It is so awesome to know the Lord is listening to that great laugh Hugo has!)

"I believe relationships are important to God and maybe he doesn't pass along messages, but I know that Hugo would think heaven is not perfect without me and the kids, so maybe it does work this way.

"So, I shed tears for the following story:

"When Hugo came back in November to the DR, he found out our printer was not working. He also brought our computer back to Kansas to get the DVD player fixed. Since I have been back, I have not been able to get a proper replacement printer. I tried a few options and finally took the old one in to see if, by a huge miracle, they could fix it, and it would not cost me an arm and a leg.

"I left it at a place before I left for El Salvador and now, after much stopping by and asking, a month later they finally have it done. I picked it up this morning, paid $25, and about 6 tonight I got a chance to plug it in.

"Immediately it started printing what Hugo had tried to print back in November. It was several worship song lists. He wanted to have on paper which songs were on each worship DVD, for the SCORE baseball clinics. (In the evenings the men had worship times, and Hugo and Mark had to think on their feet and be flexible with the leader.)

"After eight pages of that, I canceled the repeated attempts to print. (All the while I'm imagining Hugo's frustration and confusion on why the printer was not working.)

"The next thing that started to print was in Spanish. I read the title, which I see first as it is being printed. It reads, "Aveces vamos a estar solo" (Sometimes we are going to be alone).

"It was sermon notes on Caleb from the book of Numbers that Hugo had prepared for a youth group in North Carolina. I started crying. Good tears, though, knowing that even after four months my Hugo is still with me in ways, still speaking to me through his life he has left for me to find.

"Here is a statement that might take a while to sink in, but is true. 'When you have lived a one-flesh marriage, as God depicts in the Bible, even death does not strip it from you quickly.'

"I remember in the hospital, after Hugo was declared brain dead, and we were getting ready to leave, I removed his I am Second bracelet that I had stared at all night. Then, I went to his left hand and tried to remove his wedding band. It was tight, and I was having problems getting it off. Someone asked if they could help me. I stopped them and calmly said, 'I put it on him, I will take it off him.'

When Hugo and I were first married and living in Argentina, when something would happen that would signify a deeper bond as a married couple we would yell, 'Integration!'

"For example, while organizing our closet I started to hang some of my long dresses on his side of the closet, and some of his shorter shirts on my side. After realizing what we did, we looked at each other and yelled, 'Integration!' Or, the first time I accidentally used his toothbrush . . . 'Integration!'

All that time of one-flesh marriage that *integrates* a couple together takes a long time to . . .to . . . to something, but I am not sure what, because it is never going to "unstick." Maybe it will change into a different form of integration, like a nice dream burned into your memory that you will always remember and smile.

Just yesterday I was deep cleaning and found a small stash of Hugo's whisker shavings, I smiled. I think God lets him send messages to me too. This one said, 'I'm still here, Koala. Integration still rules!'

"When I pushed the power button on his phone the other day to find a phone number, the first screen popped up, "T.A.C.T.E.C." (Te Amo Con Todo El Corazón.) This was our fun game that we left in secret places for each other. It means, 'I love you with all my heart.'

"' . . .When I found him whom my soul loveth. I held him, and would not let him go,' Songs of Sol. 3:4.

"Hugo, I will always love you. T.A.C.T.E.C.

-Koala Bala
(con patas frías, que rasca la pancita con un tenedor)

There have been several ways that I have seen how Hugo's life can never be unstuck from mine. I have a container of lotion that still has Hugo's whiskers stuck to it when I once taped it shut to shove it into my luggage. Hugo's continued presence in my life may even be as subtle as the "beep-beep" of Hugo's sport watch as it continues to announce the hour tucked away in a box of Hugo's things that I am keeping for Mattias and Layla.

When I open any of the programs on my computer, they are forever registered in Hugo's name and another footprint of Hugo's presence in my life.

As I mentioned in my blog post above, I don't know if God lets people already in heaven send subtle messages to their loves ones left on earth. But, I don't believe in coincidences, so there is something divine about events such as the printer incident.

I might add also that Hugo's same "Sometimes you might be alone" sermon printed again on exactly the six-month anniversary of Hugo's death. It was very strange, but there is a logical explanation. I turned on the laptop for the first time that day, because the printer had been fixed. Hugo must have tried to print the sermon from the laptop too. Still, the timing of all the events was interesting. I just took it as a message that God still is aware that I am alone. He has not forgotten about me, nor does He overlook the pain of my situation. I also silently hear Hugo cheering me on in the background.

Another such event happened a month or so after the printer episode. My dad had won an ipod Touch. This fact in itself would have sent Hugo laughing, because we joked about how my Dad is the luckiest guy ever and wins everything.

Anyway, Dad was using the microphone app and e-mailing voice messages to Mattias. He'd tell stories or update Mattias what Grandpa and Grandma were up to.

I'd save them all in a file for Mattias, and we'd listen to them when we had time. It was another way for Grandpa and Mattias to stay connected.

It was a great idea, so I wanted to record Mattias's voice and send e-mails back to Dad and to Hugo's family.

I had never used the microphone app before, so Mattias and I sat on the coach together while Layla was napping to figure out what we needed to do. The hardest part was finding where Hugo had stored the earphones that had a microphone on them. The app is pretty simple, so soon we recorded Mattias singing his ABC's, "Deep and Wide," and the "B-I-B-L-E." Basically this is his normal repertoire of songs.

Then in reviewing the files we had created in the app, I ran across four files that were just marked with dates. One was a girl singing at our church. Another was Hugo reminding himself to look up a certain song on itunes and download it because it was a good one. One was part of a sermon he was really into.

When I clicked on the last one, I didn't expect what I heard and I clasped my hand over my mouth in shock. Immediately silent tears started falling down my cheeks. I made myself not cry aloud so I could hear the remainder of the message. It was only 15 seconds long. It was Hugo's happy playful voice saying:

"Hey Sarah, Hey Sarah, Um this is Hugo. I just want to say that I love you, and I miss you. Hello, Mattias! Be nice with Mommy. I'll see you soon. Bye-bye."

A chill ran up my spine. It was as if Hugo was so close. He voice sounded so alive I had to remind myself that I was listening to a recording. I checked the date on the recording again. I was more than a year old, from July 2009. I could faintly hear a few noises in the background and believe he was bored while picking up a SCORE team at the airport and decided to make a recording to pass the time. Mattias was staring at me the whole time, a little confused, and asked me, "Mommy, you sad?"

"Mattias, listen to this." I put the ear bud lightly into his ear and started Hugo's voice again. Mattias was focused, but when he heard Hugo's voice he looked up at me and smiled. When Hugo said, "Hello Mattias!" Mattias instinctively responded, "Hi!" Mattias was so excited to hear his Daddy's voice again. Not only did the recording bring comfort to me, but so did Mattias's reaction to hearing Hugo's voice. Even after six months he had not forgotten his daddy, not even a little bit.

My children have been part of my healing process too. I have to get up and tend to their needs everyday, whether I feel like it or not. I also get to see the best of Hugo in both of my kids. I have a picture of Hugo when he was two years old, Mattias is a spitting image, except Hugo's hair was long then, which looks more like Layla's smooth dark hair. Because Mattias was two and a half, I believe he will remember quite a bit about Hugo. We have many pictures and videos to help him reinforce his memories, plus my family has a history of good memories, and I believe Mattias got that from me.

Another way that Mattias helps me to heal is he doesn't have the inhibitions that others have to talk about Hugo. If Mattias has something to say or ask about Daddy, he just says it. He doesn't think about what is appropriate or what will hurt my feelings. I like that about him. In my case, I like to talk about Hugo. I don't want to forget him, nor do I want other people to forget him. Hugo should be a normal conversation, not one reserved for hush tones or tender eyes.

One of my favorite things that Mattias does is when he plays our Nintendo Wii, he always uses Hugo's Mii person (in Wii one can create a cartoon person that looks like you). I don't even know where the option is on the Mario Kart game to use your Mii, but Mattias has that game all figured out. I usually am cooking or washing dishes while Mattias is playing. He usually finds Hugo's Mii person and then chooses a car that is funny looking and has flowers. I'm sure serious gamers know which car I am referring too.

That's not all. While I'm in the kitchen, I'm keeping up on the progress of Mattias's game. He's almost always last, usually because he found a jump to fly his car off of in the game, and he likes and keeps going back to jump over it. When he does finally cross the finish line, Mattias raises both his arms in victory and jumps off the ground and yells, "Yes! Daddy Win! Daddy Win!" My heart does the same jump and victory shout, knowing the spiritual truth behind what my son is saying.

I have talked to Mattias a lot about Hugo and continue to do so. In one of our first conversations soon after we got back to the DR, I asked, as I had many times, "Do you know where Daddy is?"

"Yes. Heaven with Jesus Manger."

"That's right Daddy's with Jesus." I leaned closer to him resting my elbow on the table to steady me. I looked into his eyes. "Mattias, did Daddy die?"

"Yes, die. Daddy die." He responded to me matter-of-factly. I feel he does understand, but there is still some of that child part of him that occasionally will look at me and ask me, "Daddy here?"

The first time seemed normal because it was the day after Hugo died when I went and talked to the youth group at the church. This was a familiar situation to Mattias, a place where Hugo was regularly. While I was there, Mattias came up to me and asked, "Mommy, Daddy here?"

I'm sure the few people within earshot were just as heartbroken as I was to hear his soft words. I gently explained to him.

A few weeks later I walked into my parent's house and called out the customary, "Hey, I'm home!"

Mattias was at the table and said, "Hi, Mommy!" He looked behind me, "And Daddy?"

I stopped and asked him, "Honey, where is Daddy?"

"I don't know," he told me.

"Remember? Daddy's in heaven?" I said gently.

He laughed and said, "Oh yeah!" It was as if he forgot and thought it was funny that he had forgotten. Mattias's response to Hugo's death has blessed me a lot.

Now ,a year later, Mattias continues to prove to be a huge comfort in certain ways. In small things, such as the time we passed big sprinklers watering a football field, and Mattias got all excited and said, "Mommy! Me . . . Daddy . . . run . . . water!"

I helped him confirm what he was talking about. "You remember running in the sprinkler with Daddy in the baseball fields in the DR?"

"Yes! Mommy, yes!" Mattias was recalling an event that had happened a year and a half before.

Another adoring thing Mattias has is his excitement for Hugo's gravestone. When I went back to Kansas in August 2010 to start on this book, I wanted to see the memorial stone that had been placed on Hugo's grave. I went first by myself and then took the kids. When we got out of the car, I explained to Mattias what I wanted him to know about this place.

"Mattias , this is a big park. It is a special park because in it, as you can see, there are lots of rock. But, these are special rocks because they have names of people we love on them."

We walked over to Hugo's memorial stone. "This rock is one that Mommy put here for us to remember Daddy. See, here is Daddy's name, and that means that he is in heaven, and we love and miss him. And Daddy wanted your name and Layla's name and Mommy's name on it too, because he loves us."

Mattias didn't say much, but was very excited to touch the stone and trace all the letters with his little finger. Layla liked to sit on the edge of the concrete that holds the stone. Mattias climbed on the top of the stone and laid his head down.

He sat up and motioned in wide circles with his arms, "Mommy, lots of rocks!"

Now every time I drive close to the cemetery, Mattias yells excitedly, "Daddy's name! Daddy's Name!"

He always wants to go and see all the rocks. He almost always asks me, "Can we go see Daddy's name?" Sometimes we stop, but the cemetery is on one of the main streets, so I would never get to church or the store if I stopped every time he asked.

Now that his language skills are more developed, he has learned to ask me, "Can we pass by?" That is because once I told him we could not stop, but only drive by. We often do "drive by."

He even asked me to take a picture of him with Daddy's name so he could show his teacher at school. Remember what the monument man, Ron, had told me about my children seeing the love and relationship between Hugo and me in this memorial stone? He was right. Mattias and Layla will treasure this stone for years to come, and I pray that it will mark a good time in their lives. A time when God laid the foundation for His perfect plan for them, a foundation of Christian parents who loved God, loved each other and loved them.

I never want Mattias to feel that he has to fill Hugo's shoes in any way, but God has used my son to fill in a few small gaps that Hugo left in my life.

Remember my list of things that I lost? I laughed when Mattias filled a part of that something missing in my life. One thing on the list was "someone to tell me that I am beautiful and compliment me when I dress up." Now, when I put on new clothes or dress up for church, Mattias has gotten into the habit of telling me, "Mommy, you're so beautiful. That dress my favorite one!"

Another thing on the "things lost list" was someone to have inside jokes with. Recently I have learned that Mattias has developed Hugo's sense of humor. A few months back Mattias randomly started repeating for most of the day the same phrase, "Piece of Paper." But "paper" he would say faster, and it almost sounded like "pepper." It was really catchy, and soon I was saying it too.

The next day we were walking home from school, and I saw trash on the ground. I said, "Hey, Mattias." He looked at me, I smiled and said, "Piece of pep-per!" He laughed, and we walked home.

The next day I send him out to get the newspaper from the porch and when he brought it in to me, he said, "Hey, Mommy." I looked at him, he smiled, and I could barely make out what he was saying before he started laughing, "Piece of pep-per!"

I laughed and tackled him to the floor and tickled him. He is so funny, and I love having a crazy boy that understands doing silly games for the fun of it. Oh yes, and now Mattias eats my hash brown when I get my McDonald's breakfast meal.

The last thing I want to share about Mattias is the most recent discussion Mattias and I have had about Daddy. Now, at age three, he still talks about Hugo whenever a situation reminds him of Hugo. When Mattias got his hair cut recently, on the way home he announced to me, "Me get my hair cut like Daddy."

Hugo used to always convince Mattias to get his hair cut with the clippers because then Mattias could be like Daddy.

Mattias had to get tubes in his ears in December 2010, and except for the thirty minutes directly after the procedure when the anesthesia made him feel really yucky, he did really well. About an hour after the tubes had been inserted, the nurse felt Mattias had recovered enough and was ready to go home. I was putting Mattias's clothes back on him and he asked me, "Mommy, where's Daddy?"

I stopped what I was doing, because I never want to make light of his questions. I looked at him and hoped to help him remember, "Mattias, where is Daddy?"

He looked upset and whined, "I don't know."

I knew he was not in the best mood for this conversation, so I carefully repeated to him the same thing I have told him all year, "Daddy's in heaven?"

Usually he is satisfied with this answer and we go on, but he had something more to say, "Mommy, is this heaven?"

My heart broke. He remembered that we had left Hugo in a hospital and he thought the hospital was heaven. I tried to keep upbeat for him and said lightly, "No Honey, this is the hospital. Heaven is up really high in the sky. Way up past the clouds, past the moon, past the stars."

"Okay," he said, and I busied myself with getting him dressed to keep from crying. Mattias really missed his daddy, and I am confident Mattias will always remember the presence of Hugo, even if details of their adventures together fade over time.

Another part of my healing comes from when God reveals a small part of the eternal ripple effect that Hugo's life and death are having around the world. I know of at least four people who received Christ as a result of God elevating their awareness of their own eternity through Hugo's death.

God has taught me how He looks at all eternity and, though he loves us all individually, His plan is to save the masses, and He desires all to be with him in heaven. God works his plan accordingly— to save the masses of people—and sometimes taking one key individual jump starts a domino effect of eternal good and glory to God (which should be our goal in life as well).

Remember Jerry? He was the man who was with Hugo during Hugo's last moments, and I shared my faith with him at my parents' house. I saw Jerry recently. I was working on this book and had just been writing about him that day when he and his wife walked into the coffee shop where I had been for several hours.

At first we only nodded politely at each other. The sight of each other still stirs great emotions, and, understanding this, we always approach each other cautiously, making sure the other is ready to engage in deeper conversation.

But, that day Jerry and his wife, Christine, pulled up chairs close to mine. We talked about several things, but soon I asked him. "Jerry have you thought more about what I spoke to you about or about the book I sent you?

"Yes. I've been meaning to tell you. Thanks for sending the book and note to me, and I want you to know God is working on me. Thank you for praying." Seeing the hand of God in Jerry's life has brought me great joy, knowing that Hugo's life has rippled over into Jerry's quest for God.

Another one of these ripples God allowed me to witness was in the life of a young man named CJ. Hugo had discipled CJ when CJ was in junior high and high school. Hugo taught CJ guitar, and we even secretly bought CJ a guitar to cultivate his love for worship music.

We kept in touch with CJ over the years, and Hugo always had a special place in his heart for his friend. CJ was at Hugo's memorial service, but I was unable to visit with him because of the many other people I needed to visit with. I felt God wanted me to challenge CJ, though, and to do that I would need to connect with him some time.

A couple of months after I got back to the Dominican Republic I was turning off my computer and noticed that CJ was on Facebook. I sat down for what I thought would be a quick chat to say "Hi and I need to talk to you later," but it ended up being at least an hour-long chat.

In our conversation, I told CJ how much he meant to both Hugo and me. I also told him for the first time that it was Hugo who had bought the guitar for him.

CJ told me Hugo was the person most like Jesus that he had ever met. He also shared that for or the past three years his relationship with God had suffered. His family had changed churches a lot.

"My faith slowly degraded after moving to the Kansas City area," CJ said. "I eventually just completely strayed. Recently, within the past three weeks, things have slowly started to change, and then, since this weekend, have changed drastically."

"What happened this weekend," I asked him. "Or maybe you are already telling me."

CJ replied, "During those three years that I strayed away and until now, I questioned my faith, STRONGLY questioned it, doubted it to the extreme — to the point where for a while I claimed absolutely no religion or faith at all. The ONE thing that always kept me holding on by a thread to my hope that it was all true, to my faith, and everything, was always Hugo. I asked myself, "How can Christianity not be true when someone like Hugo lives the Christian life so passionately?"

By now, I was shaking and crying hard. "You don't know how much Hugo and I have prayed for this light to come in you life. Especially now that you have a wife and baby to be responsible for."

I could never share all the bountiful ways that God has made my burden lighter and given healing to my heart. Still one more big one sticks out in my mind. This book. God first told me to write a book when Hugo and I were in our first year at Bible school in Argentina.

People always wanted to know how we met and our love story, and it was such a long detailed story, one with God's fingerprints all over it. God gave me the idea to write it down. I even remember God confirming this passion to write a book with some scriptures and a message I heard at a women's Bible study.

I didn't know how to write a book or what all to include, so I just started by typing into our laptop computer pages and pages of journal entries I had written while Hugo and I were getting to know each other, dating, and engaged.

I didn't know where to go from there and didn't feel any more direction from God, so I stored the floppy disk and the printed copies of what I had typed up. Every year or so I'd find those journal entries again in a keepsake book and wonder why God had asked me to write a book, confirmed it through several circumstances, and then not show me how to finish it.

Several months after Hugo had died, I had already read about five "widow books," and I vowed I would not ever want to write a book, because it was such a cliché thing to do.

It seemed if you lost your husband, then you were entitled to write a book. I did not want to fit into any typical pattern of widowhood. A couple months later I could feel God tapping on my heart saying, "It is not about you, especially not about your pride to want to be different from other widows. I gave you this story for my glory."

In June 2010 I started to pray about the possibility of writing a book. I wrote it down in my prayer journal. At this same time I was praying about starting a foundation. I have a heart to give to missionaries, especially native missionaries who cannot travel to the United States to raise support. Many of my friends from

Bible school in Argentina are full time missionaries living on nothing or working full-time jobs on top of full-time ministry work. Maybe my book could help fund a foundation and get other people interested.

My parents came to the Dominican Republic in July 2010 to watch the kids while I was hosting a basketball team and helping with SCORE's busy summer months.

One Tuesday afternoon I told my mom, "I'm thinking about writing a book and starting a foundation." I could tell by her body language that she thought I had too many things on my hands already. But she smiled and said, "Well, that sounds like a good idea. If you think that is what God wants you to do."

That same night I gave my testimony for the teams as I had done all year long. The very next day a man came up to me and said, "Sarah, have you thought about writing a book and starting a foundation?"

"Uh . . . um . . . as a matter of fact I have. Who are you?"

"My name is Bill High. I am the president of Servant Christian Community Foundation in Kansas City. Helping people start foundations is what we do, and I have lots of connections to help you write a book. Here's my card."

I numbly took the card from him. I looked at mom. Her face was as shocked as mine was. Bill was there as a leader for his son's soccer team. We kept in contact.

Two weeks later my good friend, Michelle, who is mentioned in this book several times, came to visit me in the DR. We have kept in contact over the years, but not in every detail of our lives. She had been teaching in New York City, but now was going back to school. The first night she was in my house I asked her, "So, what are you going back to school for?"

"I'm getting my Masters in Creative Writing." She said. I looked at Mom again. We both knew. "Really?" I said. "How'd you like to help me write a book?"

"I'd love to. Let's talk." Michelle and I also kept in touch after she left.

This time the guidance to write the book felt much differently than when I had started writing in Argentina. I could literally see God placing the exact people I needed into my life. But, it was up to me to get the story on the page. I started by finding the journal notes I had typed up in Argentina.

I couldn't find any computer to run the old 3.5 floppy disk, so I had to scan the journal notes into my computer. They were so faded, though, that I had to read through them all and correct a lot of the words while I looked at the originals. I read about when Hugo and I first met all the way through to when we decided to get married.

I worked when the kids napped or in the evenings. I would cry and cry; it hurt to remember the beautiful love we had. I had known Hugo loved me, but to see it in words, page after page, was like seeing all his love all at once, and it was terribly hard for me.

After one particularly bad day of correcting pages, I finally broke down so hard I went to my bathroom to get a tissue and ended up on my knees sobbing. I had a journal in my hand and I cried aloud, "God why? Why would you take away a man who loved me so much? His love was so great. No one loves me like that now. I miss being loved."

I let the tears flow; I was totally broken. In brokenness sometimes there is no thought, no ideas, the brain just hurts, along with everything else. My mind was in this state of numbness, and my eyes aimlessly scanned over the pages of professed love for me. Then . . .

"I love you more than this."

God had spoken to me so strongly in my being, I thought I actually heard His voice. It was like lightning, and it shocked me so greatly I instantly stopped crying. I sat up and tried to focus my brain. I needed to understand what God was telling me.

"What?" I asked God, "Tell me again; I don't understand."

Softly, as an echo rumbling again over my heart, "I love you more than this."

I looked down at the journal in my hands, Hugo's professed, deep, passionate, pure love for me dripping from each page. Then it hit me hard, and I understood. I had read about Christ's love, I had known it to be true, but God was revealing to me a fresh deepness of the extent of that love.

I was processing a comparison of love. Hugo had loved me so greatly, and I was starting to see how, as the Bible says, a marriage is an example of how Christ loves the church. But, my thoughts went deeper; Christ's love is not for the church as an institution, but much more. His love is for the people, for me.

I looked down again at my journal. Somehow Hugo's love for me had humanly contained a small part of Christ's uncontainable love. Hugo's love had enabled me to understand a portion of Christ's love for me.

I thought, "To physically experience a human love through Hugo, and then for God to tell me that Christ's love for me is greater than that. Wow!" I burst into tears again. But, this time not as a girl whose heart had lost the love she desired, but one whose heart was full of the only love in any universe that nothing can ever steal, not even death.

Romans 8:38-39 came to mind: "For I am convinced that neither death nor life, neither angels nor demons, neither the present nor the future, nor any powers, neither height nor depth, nor anything else in all creation, will be able to separate us from the love of God that is in Christ Jesus our Lord."

Over the next week I meditated on aspects of this huge concept God had revealed to me. Through many channels God confirmed this message, and I experienced great healing in my heart. I wrote in my journal the place that God had brought me to:

"I have not lost the best thing in my life. The best thing that happened to me is Jesus, not my Prince Charming. My relationship in Christ, his work on the cross, my forgiveness from my sins and the awesomeness of all of this—that is the best thing in my life, and it gives me great peace to know that I can never lose that.

"The Lord gives and takes away, but blessed be the name of The Lord!"

*This is my story, this is my song,
Praising my Savior all the day long;
This is my story, this is my song,
Praising my Savior all the day long.

1. Blessed assurance, Jesus is mine!
Oh, what a foretaste of glory divine!
Heir of salvation, purchase of God,
Born of His Spirit, washed in His blood.
Chorus
2. Perfect submission, perfect delight,
Visions of rapture now burst on my sight:
Angels descending bring from above
Echoes of mercy, whispers of love.
Chorus
3. Perfect submission, all is at rest,
I in my Savior am happy and blest:
Watching and waiting, looking above,
Filled with His goodness, lost in His love.
Chorus
Blessed Assurance by Fanny (Frances) Jane Crosby, 1820-1915

God has given me a story. Maybe it was not the one I would have chosen or even wanted, but it is the one God entrusted to me. I told it because He asked me to tell it, and all for His Glory, I wrote my story.

On the Victory Side,
Sarah Liborio

Please visit my website, www.my-onceuponatime.com/, to see pictures and videos from each chapter.

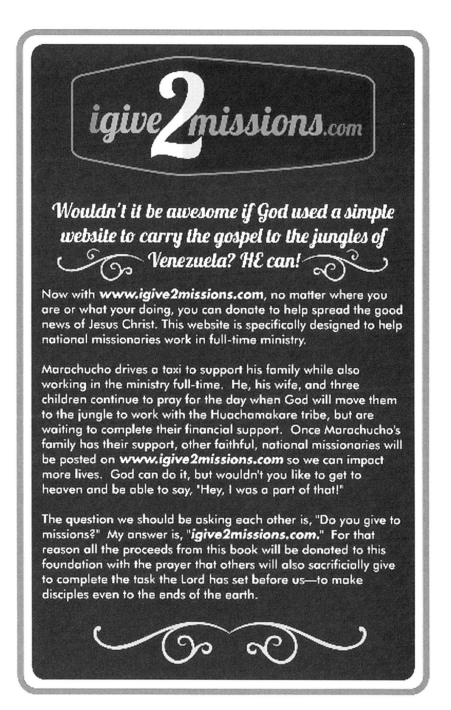

igive2missions.com

Wouldn't it be awesome if God used a simple website to carry the gospel to the jungles of Venezuela? HE can!

Now with **www.igive2missions.com**, no matter where you are or what your doing, you can donate to help spread the good news of Jesus Christ. This website is specifically designed to help national missionaries work in full-time ministry.

Marachucho drives a taxi to support his family while also working in the ministry full-time. He, his wife, and three children continue to pray for the day when God will move them to the jungle to work with the Huachamakare tribe, but are waiting to complete their financial support. Once Marachucho's family has their support, other faithful, national missionaries will be posted on **www.igive2missions.com** so we can impact more lives. God can do it, but wouldn't you like to get to heaven and be able to say, "Hey, I was a part of that!"

The question we should be asking each other is, "Do you give to missions?" My answer is, "**igive2missions.com.**" For that reason all the proceeds from this book will be donated to this foundation with the prayer that others will also sacrificially give to complete the task the Lord has set before us—to make disciples even to the ends of the earth.

T.J. Nix, Graphic Designer, NewSpring Church, 12200 E. 21st St. N.,Wichita, KS 67206 Ph: 316.630.8500

Endnotes

Introduction

1. Moore, Beth. (2008). *Esther: It's Tough Being a Woman*. Nashville, TN: LifeWay Press. pp. 11-14, 81. Reprinted and used with permission.
2. MGM Pictures. (2006). *Miss Potter* (film).

Chapter 1

1. Kelfer, Russell. (1980) *Wait*. Martha Kelfer. Reprinted and used with permission. For more poems and lessons by Russell Kelfer, see www.dtm.org/.
2. Nelson, Greg, and McHugh, Phill. (1984). *People Need The Lord*. River Oaks Music Company & Shepherd's Fold Music.
3. The JESUS Film Project. (1979) *Jesus* (film).

Chapter 6

1. Cunningham, Loren, with Rogers, Janice. (1984) *Is That Really You, God? Hearing the Voice of God*. Seattle, WA: YWAM Publishing.
2. Sanz, Alejandro. (1997). *Amiga Mia*. WEA Latina.
3. Mercy Me. (2001). *I Can Only Imagine*. Almost There (CD). Nashville, TN: INO Records.
4. Byrd, Marc and Hindalong, Steve. (2000). *God of Wonders*. Pyanagrin Music (SESAC).

Chapter 7

1. De Vita, Franco. (1988). *Te Amo*. Al Norte del Sur (CD). Nashville, TN: Sony.
2. Carlton, Vanessa. (2002). *A Thousand Miles*. Be Not Nobody (CD). A&M Records.
3. Oversteet, Paul and Schlitz, Don (1988). *When You Say Nothing At All*. RCA.

4. Jones, Debby and Kendall, Jackie (2002). "Chapter 9, Lady of Conviction." In *Lady in Waiting: Devotional Journal and Study Guide*. Shippensburg, PA: Destiny Image Publishers.
5. McKinney-Hammond, Michelle. (1998). *Secrets of an Irresistible Woman*. Eugene, OR: Harvest House Publishers.

Chapter 9

1. Mercy Me. (2001). *I Can Only Imagine*. Almost There (CD). Nashville, TN: INO Records.
2. Vidal, Marcos. (1997). *Una y Carne*. Mi Regalo (CD). Nashville, TN: Sparrow-Piedra Angular.

Chapter 12

1. Jude, Erica. (2008). *The Vintage Girl*. Erica Jude, judemissions@hotmail.com/.

Chapter 13

1. Redman, Matt. (2005). *Blessed Be Your Name*. Blessed Be Your Name: The Songs of Matt Redman Vol. 1 (CD). Alpharetta, GA: North Point Community Church.

Chapter 15

1. Redman, Matt. (2005). *Blessed Be Your Name*. Blessed Be Your Name: The Songs of Matt Redman Vol. 1 (CD). Alpharetta, GA: North Point Community Church.
2. Mercy Me. (2001). *I Can Only Imagine*. Almost There (CD). Nashville, TN: INO Records.
3. Moore, Beth. (2008). *Esther: It's Tough Being a Woman - Video Sessions* (DVD). Nashville, TN: LifeWay Christian Resources.
4. Elliot, Elisabeth. (2003 May/June). "To a New Widow" from *The Elisabeth Elliot Newsletter*. Used by permission of the author. www.elisabethelliot.org/newsletterarchive.html/.
5. Marshall, Catherine. (1957). *To Live Again*. New York, NY: McGraw-Hill Book Company.
6. Mark, Robin. (1995). *Days of Elijah*. Robin Mark.
7. *Levanta tu Casa*. Author, publisher and copyright unknown.

Epilogue

1. Elliot, Elisabeth. (1996). *Quest for Love*. Grand Rapids, MI.: Fleming H. Revell.
2. Elliot, Elisabeth. (1984). *Passion and Purity*. Grand Rapids, MI.: Fleming H. Revell.
3. Marshall, Catherine. (1957). *To Live Again*. New York, NY: McGraw-Hill Book Company. p. 28.
4. Piper, John. (2002). *The Misery of Job and the Mercy of God*. Wheaton, IL: Crossway Books, p. 63.
5. Davis, Verdell. (1994 repackaged edition 2004). *Let Me Grieve but not Forever*. Nashville, TN: W. Publishing Group, p. 15
6. Means, Dr. James. (2006). *A Tearful Celebration*. Colorado Springs, CO: WaterBrook Multnomah Publishing Group.
7. Barnes, M. Craig. (1996). *When God Interrupts: Finding New Life Through Unwanted Change*. Downers Grove, IL: InterVarsity Press, p. 89.